TOWARDS A CRITICAL VICTIMOLOGY

Also by Ezzat A. Fattah

FROM CRIME POLICY TO VICTIM POLICY: Reorienting the
Justice System

THE PLIGHT OF CRIME VICTIMS IN MODERN SOCIETY

CRIME AND VICTIMIZATION OF THE ELDERLY (*co-author*)

UNDERSTANDING CRIMINAL VICTIMIZATION

Towards a Critical Victimology

Edited by

Ezzat A. Fattah
Professor of Criminology
Simon Fraser University
British Columbia

St. Martin's Press

Selection, editorial matter and Chapter 1 © Ezzat A. Fattah 1992
Chapter 2 © Donald R. Cressey 1992
Chapter 3 © Robert Elias 1992
Chapter 4 © Lynne N. Henderson 1992
Chapter 5 © Leslie Sebba 1992
Chapter 6 © Donald R. Ranish and David Shicor 1992
Chapter 7 © Howard C. Rubel 1992
Chapter 8 © Thomas L. Feher 1992
Chapter 9 © Anthony Walsh 1992
Chapter 10 © Tony Dittenhoffer and Richard V. Ericson 1992
Chapter 11 © Burt Galaway 1992
Chapter 12 © Robert Elias 1992

First published in Great Britain 1992 by
THE MACMILLAN PRESS LTD
Houndmills, Basingstoke, Hampshire RG21 2XS
and London
Companies and representatives
throughout the world

A catalogue record for this book is available
from the British Library

ISBN 0–333–54222–3

Printed in Great Britain by
Billing and Sons Ltd, Worcester

First published in the United States of America 1992 by
Scholarly and Reference Division,
ST. MARTIN'S PRESS, INC.,
175 Fifth Avenue,
New York, N.Y. 10010

ISBN 0–312–07551–0

Library of Congress Cataloging-in-Publication Data
Towards a critical victimology / edited by Ezzat A. Fattah.
p. cm.
Includes index.
ISBN 0–312–07551–0
1. Victims of crimes.
HV6250.25.T68 1992
362.88—dc20 91–45851
CIP

To my dear friends and distinguished colleagues

Denis Szabo
Henri Ellenberger
Hans Joachim Schneider
Koichi Miyazawa

Contents

Acknowledgements

The editor and the publisher wish to thank the following journals and publishers for authorizing the reproduction of previously published copyright material:

Chapter
1 **Ezzat A. Fattah:** 'Victims and Victimology: The Facts and the Rhetoric' originally appeared in the *International Review of Victimology*, Vol. 1, No. 1 (1989), pp. 43–66, and is reprinted by kind permission of AB Academic Publishers, London.
2 **Donald R. Cressey:** 'Research Implications of Conflicting Conceptions of Victimology' originally appeared in 1988 in *Victimology: International Action and Study of Victims*, *Vol. 1, Theoretical Issues (General Part) and Documents* (papers given at the 5th International Symposium on Victimology, 1985, Zagreb, Yugoslavia), and is reprinted by kind permission of the editor of the collection, Professor Paul Zvonimir Separovic.
3 **Robert Elias:** 'Which Victim Movement? The Politics of Victim Policy' originally appeared in A.J. Lurigio, W.G. Skogan and R.C. Davis (eds), *Victims of Crime: Problems, Policies, and Programs* (1990), and is reprinted by kind permission of Sage Publications, Inc.
4 **Lynne N. Henderson:** 'The Wrongs of Victim's Rights' originally appeared in *Stanford Law Review*, Vol. 37, 937 (1985). The material is © 1985 by the Board of Trustees of the Leland Stanford Junior University and is reprinted by kind permission of both the *Stanford Law Review* and Fred. B. Rothman & Co.
5 **Leslie Sebba:** 'The Victim's Role in the Penal Process: A Theoretical Orientation' originally appeared in the *American Journal of Comparative Law*, Vol. 30, No. 2, (1982) pp. 217–40 and is reprinted by kind permission of the Journal.
6 **Donald R. Ranish and David Shichor:** 'The Victim's Role in the Penal Process: Recent Developments in California' originally appeared in *Federal Probation*, Vol. 49, No. 1 (March 1985), pp. 50–7, and is reprinted by kind permission of the Administrative Office of the United States Courts, Washington, DC.
7 **Howard C. Rubel:** 'Victim Participation in Sentencing Proceedings' originally appeared in the *Criminal Law Quarterly*, Vol. 28,

No. 2 (March 1986), pp. 226–50, and is reprinted by kind permission of the author and of Canada Law Book Inc., Ontario.

8 **Thomas L. Feher:** 'The Alleged Molestation Victim, the Rules of Evidence, and the Constitution: Should Children Really Be Seen Not Heard?' originally appeared in the *American Journal of Criminal Law*, Vol. 14 (1988), pp. 227–55, and is reprinted by kind permission of the Journal.

9 **Anthony Walsh:** 'Placebo Justice: Victim Recommendations and Offender Sentences in Sexual Assault Cases' originally appeared in the *Journal of Criminal Law and Criminology*, Vol. 77, No. 4 (1986), pp. 1126–41, and is reprinted by kind permission of Northwestern University, School of Law.

10 **Tony Dittenhoffer and Richard V. Ericson:** 'The Victim/Offender Reconciliation Programme: A Message to Correctional Reformers' originally appeared in the *University of Toronto Law Journal*, Vol. 33 (1983), pp. 315–47, and is reprinted by kind permission of the University of Toronto Press.

11 **Burt Galaway:** 'Restitution as Innovation or Unfilled Promise?' originally appeared in *Federal Probation*, (September 1988), pp. 3–14, and is reprinted by kind permission of the Administrative Office of the United States Courts, Washington, DC.

12 **Robert Elias:** 'Community Control, Criminal Justice and Victim Services' originally appeared in Ezzat A. Fattah (ed.), *From Crime Policy to Victim Policy* (London: Macmillan, 1986).

Preface

One of the most disquieting aspects of recent victim legislation, victims' Bills of Rights, and the new initiatives designed to help crime victims and to 'adjust the balance of justice' is the extreme celerity with which they were introduced, the readiness with which they were accepted with very little or no criticism, and the ease with which they sailed through the legislative bodies in many countries of the western world. The lack of any meaningful challenge or critique is all the more surprising since some of the implemented or proposed 'reforms' do have far-reaching implications and the potential for fundamentally changing the system of criminal justice as we know it today. As Elias points out in Chapter 3, some of the proposed constitutional amendments in the United States seem to be poorly defined and hastily designed, have enormous yet unexamined effects on the legal process, have uncertain means for enforcement, and create rights conflicts with no apparent resolution.

Another disturbing feature of the victim movement in North America is its distinct conservative bias and its unmistakably punitive, retributive bent. Victim advocates have erroneously created a false dichotomy dividing policies and policy-makers into two camps – those who have the interests of the victim at heart and those who favour the offender (R.I. Mawby and M.L. Gill, *Crime Victims: Needs, Services and the Voluntary Sector* London: Tavistock, 1987, p. 116).

One of the purposes of this book is to challenge seriously the law and order perspective on victims' rights and the false contest that is usually created between those rights and the rights of offenders. This popular, though unnecessary, law and order focus is based, as Mawby and Gill (1987) point out, 'on a zero-sum equation alleging that in the interests of offenders' rights the interests of victims have been disregarded' (p. 116).

Another purpose of the book is to shed some light on the way victim initiatives emerged, the timing of those initiatives, their seemingly ulterior motives, and the political interests they are meant to serve. In so doing, the book attempts to separate the facts from the rhetoric and to expose the hollowness of many of the slogans often used in the so-called 'struggle' for victims' rights.

The book also offers a critique of recent developments in the discipline of victimology, particularly the shift from a scholarly stance to a lobbying posture and highlights the dangers of the missionary zeal exhibited by some victimologists in the interest of crime victims.

The book is equally an attempt to demonstrate how unwarranted and misleading is the fanfare that surrounded the introduction of the supposedly innovative measures designed to improve the lot of crime victims. At closer scrutiny most of the measures (victim-impact statements, victim/offender reconciliation programmes, state compensation, offender restitution, and so forth) prove to be unfilled promises at best and political palliatives or judicial placebos at worst.

EZZAT A. FATTAH

Notes on the Contributors

Tony Dittenhoffer is a senior researcher with the Canadian Department of Justice in Ottawa.

Robert Elias is Associate Professor of Politics and Chair of Peace and Justice Studies at the University of San Francisco.

Richard V. Ericson is Professor of Criminology at the Centre of Criminology, University of Toronto, Canada.

Ezzat A. Fattah is Professor of Criminology at the School of Criminology, Simon Fraser University, Canada.

Thomas L. Feher is a practising attorney and associate, Kaufman & Cumberland, in Cleveland, Ohio.

Burt Galaway is Dean of the Faculty of Social Work, University of Manitoba, Winnipeg, Canada.

Lynne N. Henderson is Professor of Law at the School of Law, Indiana University, Bloomington, Indiana.

Donald R. Ranish is Professor of Political Science at Antelope Valley College in Lancaster, California.

Howard C. Rubel is a practising attorney with the firm Heller & Rubel in Toronto, Canada.

David Shichor is Professor of Criminal Justice at California State University in San Bernardino, California.

Leslie Sebba is Professor of Criminology, Faculty of Law, The Hebrew University of Jerusalem, Israel.

Anthony Walsh is Associate Professor of Criminal Justice at Boise State University, Boise, Idaho.

The Late **Professor Donald R. Cressey**, a distinguished American criminologist, taught for many years at the University of California, Santa Barbara.

Inherently, of course, the fundamental basis of the power of the victim's movement lies in public and political acceptance of the view that its clients are good people, done in by those who are bad. This item alone has made its growth irresistible . . . The plight of crime victims is dramatic and determinable. Their relief is feasible. It has strong social, political, and personal appeal. Any of us, at any time, could become a crime victim. And so a movement was born – and grew.

Gilbert Geis (1990)
Crime victims: practices and prospects, In A.J. Lurigio,
W.G. Skogan and R.C. Davis (eds), *Victims of Crime: Problems,
Policies and Programs* (Newbury Park, Calif.: Sage, pp. 259–60).

. . . criminal injuries compensation was supposed to mollify the reactionary victim-vigilante, and reparation was a device to divert offenders from custody. In both instances, victims were the creatures of penal imperatives, invested with the characters needed to get on with the business of reforming prisons. Compensation and reparation did not have much of a foundation in the declared or observed requirements of victims themselves: they were bestowed on victims in order to achieve particular ends.

Paul Rock (1990)
*Helping Victims of Crime: The Home Office and the Rise of
Victim Support In England and Wales*
(Oxford: Clarendon Press, p. 408).

Prologue

The Need for a Critical Victimology

Ezzat A. Fattah

WHAT IS CRITICAL VICTIMOLOGY?

In her penetrating analysis of the emergence of child abuse as a social issue and its rapid placement on the policy agenda, Barbara Nelson (1984) borrowed from electoral research a distinction between 'valence issues' and 'position issues'. A valence issue, she explains, is one that elicits a single, strong, fairly uniform emotional response and does not have an adversarial quality. Position issues, on the other hand, do not elicit a single response but instead engender alternative and sometimes highly conflictual responses. In other words, valence issues are consensual issues whereas position issues are largely conflictual and confrontational ones.

It seems fair to say that until now the issue of victims' rights has been largely a valence issue. The quasi unanimous response to the rhetorical cry of 'justice for victims' has been favourable. The reaction to what has been described as 'redressing the balances of justice' has been overwhelmingly (and rather surprisingly) non-controversial and uncritical and the issue has not generated much negative concern, any serious criticism, or any meaningful confrontation. Victims' rights legislation and programmes to help victims of crime have been greeted with enthusiasm and encountered very little or no opposition. As a result, there has been very little discussion of, or research into, their actual or potential dangers (for example, compromising long-established legal safeguards), their likely negative effects (increasing the use of imprisonment, lengthening the periods of incarceration, delaying conditional release, prolonging the traumatic effects of victimization, and so forth), or the impact they were likely to have on the criminal justice system, and on society in general. In most cases, the legislation have breezed through Parliaments and legislative assemblies with unusual ease and remarkable speed! For a legislative issue to generate so little debate, so little opposition in the highly confrontational, highly partisan world of politics, is extremely unusual. It is, of course, an indisputable fact that victims of crime have long been a

3

disentitled group, a group that has suffered for centuries not only from society's neglect (see Fattah, 1989) but also from the expropriation of their rightful dues (fines) by the state. It is also true that they had their personal conflicts stolen by professionals and by the criminal justice system (Christie, 1977). However, the exceptional speed with which they were rediscovered and their cause adopted by politicians, let alone the political climate that prevailed at the time of their rediscovery, are bound to raise questions about the real interests and motives behind what has been portrayed as a genuinely humanitarian and disinterested cause. Now that the political rhetoric has calmed down and the initial enthusiasm has subsided somewhat, it is time to scrutinize the victim movement and victim legislation carefully and critically in an attempt to shed light on the social forces and the interests that were influential in placing the issue of victims' rights on the political agenda.

British sociologist Paul Rock (1986a, 1986b, 1988, 1990) has done an outstanding job tracing the meteoric rise of the victim movements in Canada and in Britain and highlighting the difference between them. Beside making for fascinating reading, Rock's insightful analysis of how victims of crime became a policy issue and how the issue was placed on the political agenda leaves no doubt as to the vital need for research in this area. It lays the groundwork for a *critical victimology*.

CRIME VICTIMS AS NATURAL TARGETS FOR HUMAN SYMPATHY

Sympathy, empathy, commiseration and compassion for people in distress or suffering great hardship are undoubtedly among the most noble human sentiments. The universality of these feelings has led some to suggest that they are innate and natural. Garofalo (1889), for example, identified what he believed to be the two *basic* altruistic moral sentiments: pity and probity. He defined pity as the revulsion we feel against the deliberate infliction of pain and suffering on others.

The more helpless and defenceless the victim, be it an infant, a child, one of the elderly or even an animal, the stronger is the sense of indignation at the victimizer and the pity we feel for the object of victimization. Absence of compassion for the agony of others is often seen as a sign of pathology: it used to be considered one of the major symptoms of 'moral insanity' and is presently regarded as one of the most revealing indicators of a 'psychopathic personality'.

Victims of any kind have always been the primary targets of the altruistic human sentiments outlined above and victims of crime are no exception. This is because many crimes cause enormous pain and suffering to those who are victimized: death, physical injury, psychological trauma, degradation, humiliation, fear, financial loss and so forth. It is only natural, therefore, that any attempt to alleviate the human suffering and the plight of crime victims will be readily accepted and will be greeted as a manifestation of the deep humanitarian desire to help and care for unfortunate fellow beings. In view of this, the lack of critical scrutiny of recent initiatives, touted as essential to help and assist crime victims, should come as no surprise. After all, who would want (or dare) to oppose or to speak against such a seemingly humanitarian endeavour? As Henderson (Chapter 4), points out, the symbolic strength of the term 'victim's rights' overrides careful scrutiny: who could be anti-victim? An identical view is expressed by Geis (1990) who writes:

> The movement to aid crime victims made both logical and emotional sense. Their case is compelling, and they traditionally have been ignored. Strong overt opposition to programs providing assistance to crime victims is not likely to surface. Who, after all, is willing to go on record as opposed to so preeminently worthy a cause?
>
> (p. 260)

And yet, the timing of this renewed interest in crime victims, the political climate that favoured the emergence of the victim movement, the ease and speed with which questionable changes were accepted and introduced, should give us reason to pause. They dictate that we start searching for the real and ulterior motives of the champions of victim's rights, for the hidden agenda of the so-called victim advocates, and should alert us to some of the real dangers inherent in the current, seemingly unstoppable, trend. The time has come to try to separate the facts from the rhetoric (Fattah, 1990) and to differentiate between genuine concern for crime victims and their use as pawns in the politics of law and order. More so since there are reasons to believe that victims, long abused by a non-caring criminal justice system, are now being used by those on the right of the political spectrum to sell to the legislators and to the general public a much harsher penal philosophy than the one criminologists have been vainly trying for decades to humanize. As Phipps (1988) points out, when right-wing politicians speak of the crime problem and when they invoke outrage and sympathy on behalf of crime victims generally, citing instances of injuries, sufferings and degradations of actual victims, their main purpose is to excite hostility against the offender or to discredit the laxity of the criminal justice system. Phipps adds:

> It is also used to promote support for deterrence and retribution rather than for environmental measures to prevent crime. In this sense, the victim in Conservative thinking is maintained in a role similar to that which he or she occupies in the prosecution process – a means to an end.
>
> (p. 180)

As Henderson (Chapter 4) points out, conservatives realized that victims can be an effective political symbol and thus began rhetorically to paint 'the victim' as a sympathetic figure whose rights and interests could be used to counterbalance the defendant's rights. She explains how the conservatives reinforced the image of the 'victim' as a blameless, pure stereotype with whom all can identify. She relates how the word 'victim' was used almost exclusively to describe those who are preyed upon by strangers, a non-provoking individual hit with the violence of 'street crime' by a stranger. The heart-rending (and rather atypical) cases selected by the President's Task Force on Victims of Crime (US, 1982) for inclusion in their final report leave no doubt as to the validity of Henderson's claims. According to Henderson, the victim's rights movement (which might originally have been viewed as a populist movement) has become increasingly co-opted by the concerns of advocates of the 'crime control' model of criminal justice.

Walker (1985) echoes Henderson's view. He also insists that conservatives have seized the victim's rights issue and made it their own. He reminds us that in California, for example, the advocates of proposition 8 were the traditional prosecution-oriented law-and-order leaders, while civil libertarians were the primary opponents (see also Ranish and Shichor, Chapter 6). Walker also cites the example of the President's Task Force on Victims of Crime which was dominated by traditional conservative spokespersons.

MEDIA PORTRAYAL OF CRIME VICTIMS

The popular stereotype of the victim described by Henderson is continuously reinforced through the portrayal of the victim in the media. In an article in *Time* magazine (22 January 1990, p. 29) under the provocative title 'Turning Victims into Saints', Ellis Cose explains how journalists are unable to resist the temptation to recast crime into a shopworn morality tale. He cites several examples of actual cases where victims (particularly those who are wealthy, virtuous or beautiful) were turned into martyred saints in the epic battle between good and bad. This recurrent moral tale pitting good against evil, argues Cose, is guaranteed to generate tears, confirm stereotypes, and get readers to turn the page. Cose describes the danger of such journalistic portrayal in the following manner:

> Such allegories are generally passed off as a search for deeper meaning or an attempt to humanize the injured party. Yet the images are so shopworn and predictable that they in fact dehumanize. And the ostensible larger meaning is patently obvious: here lies another life that could have contributed much to society had it not been crushed by those who deserved to die instead.
>
> (1990:29)

These journalistic portrayals of victims and victimizers perpetuate the popular, though often inaccurate, mental images of offenders and victims. As I point out in Chapter 1, dichotomizing the victim/ offender populations into good and evil, innocent and guilty, lambs and wolves, predators and prey, Abels and Cains, is not only an oversimplification of a complex phenomenon but also a deliberate attempt to ignore or at least to overlook the striking similarities, affinities and overlap between the two populations. In many respects they are homogeneous and overlap to a large extent. The roles of victim and victimizer are neither static, assigned nor immutable. They are dynamic, revolving and interchangeable. There is a continuous movement between the two roles with the victims of yesterday becoming today's criminals, today's criminals becoming tomorrow's victims, and so forth (see Fattah, 1991). These exceedingly unpopular yet indisputable facts frustrate the public's eternal search for a sympathetic victim to empathize with and a hateful criminal to blame and to despise. They go against people's need to believe that victims and victimizers have nothing in common, are as different as night and day.

TURNING SYMPATHY FOR CRIME VICTIMS INTO A CRY FOR VENGEANCE

As mentioned above, pity, sympathy and empathy are among the most noble and worthy human sentiments. Socially, these altruistic emotions are indispensable for group solidarity, for caring for, and sharing with, those unfortunate members of the group who happen to suffer as a result of some misfortune or mishap. Unfortunately, these noble and altruistic human sentiments can be exploited to achieve utilitarian goals or political ends. Sympathy for crime victims has been increasingly (and successfully) used in recent years to generate a backlash against criminal offenders. The declared objectives of victim groups in North America would bear this out.

In Canada, victim groups have been vociferous in their attempts to bring back the death penalty, to tighten eligibility for parole, to abolish early release resulting from statutory remission, and so forth. They have also been relentless in their demands for tougher sentences and longer prison terms. Sex offenders, most of whom are in desperate need of treatment because of sexual, social or mental inadequacies, are usually singled out for particularly tougher penalties. In a brief presented at Toronto City Hall (23 November 1982) on behalf of 'Victims of Violence', an advocacy group, the then group president, Don Sullivan, made the following statement:

> We firmly believe that the sentences that are being handed down in Ontario are far too lenient for sexual offences. The incarceration of such offenders is far too short. They are getting out far too soon, either on parole or 'by law' on automatic release after only two thirds of their sentences. This has become the norm rather than the exception.

> (Amernic, 1984, p. 190)

The brief then went on to demand mandatory minimum sentences for all first-time sex offenders. It stated:

> We firmly believe that mandatory sentences must be prescribed by law for all rapists and sex offenders. A sentence of at least

five years, and preferably seven years, must be given for all first offenders.

(Ibid., p. 191)

What Canadian victim groups were doing was merely to echo what their counterparts south of the border had been fighting for for many years. The increasing militancy of the so-called victim advocates in the United States has had many consequences including a resurgence of vigilante justice (Karmen, 1990) and the formation of vigilante groups such as the 'Guardian Angels' in New York, a group that served as a model for similar ones in several American and Canadian cities. The group received a great deal of publicity through the case of Bernhard Goetz who shot down four unarmed young men who accosted him on a subway train but was found guilty only of possessing an illegal weapon (Fletcher, 1988; Dershowitz, 1988; Karmen, 1990).

In addition to street vigilance, there is also what may be called 'court vigilance'. Mawby and Gill (1987) report that a California group 'Citizens for Law and Order' operated a 'court watcher' programme and published attacks on judges considered lenient. They also cite other groups attempting to influence court decisions through direct intervention such as having a victim advocate representing the victim in court and demanding harsher penalties than those asked for by the prosecutors.

The 'horror story syndrome' (Walker, 1985) which has been the trade mark of the victim movement in Canada and the United States gained a stamp of approval in the final report of President Reagan's Task Force on Victims of Crime (US, 1982). A brief excerpt from the report will illustrate the tone and the tactics used by Task Force members who, for all practical purposes, served as the spokespersons for the American victim lobby. After claiming that murder, kidnap and rape are commonplace, the Task Force then goes to great length to show that offenders are not being punished enough but are being 'pampered' by the CJS:

The judge sentences your attacker to three years in prison, less than one year for every hour he kept you in pain and terror. That seems very lenient to you. Only later do you discover that he will probably serve less than half of his actual sentence in prison because of good-time and work-time credits that are given to him immediately. The man who broke into your home, threatened to slit your throat with a knife, and raped, beat, and robbed you will be out of custody in less than 18 months . . .

The defendant's every right has been protected, and now he serves his time in a public facility, receiving education at public expense. In a few months his sentence will have run. Victims receive sentences too; their sentences may be life long.

(p. 11)

THE IDEOLOGICAL TRANSFORMATION OF VICTIMOLOGY

Elsewhere (Fattah, 1979; 1990) I tried to outline the fundamental changes that occurred in the discipline of victimology in the last twenty years or so. I highlighted the shift from a victimology of the act to a victimology of action, the move from a scholarly stance to a lobbying posture, the switch from a theoretical discipline focused on the study of crime victims, their characteristics, attitudes and behaviour, their relationships and interactions with their victimizers, to an activist movement campaigning on behalf of, and for the victims. The search for theory, characteristic of the early days of victimology, gave way to an obsessive preoccupation with policy. Gradually, rhetoric overshadowed research findings and disinterested, unbiased scholarship was in danger of becoming eclipsed by political ideology. In the first chapter, as well as in the epilogue, an attempt is made to separate facts from rhetoric and to show that the seemingly humanistic discourse often masks the real punitive intentions underlying most of the changes demanded by the victim lobby and advocated by the conservative commissions and task forces set up to study crime victims. Many of the statements made, such as those by California's former Attorney General George Deukmejian on Proposition 8 (see Epilogue), reveal not a genuine concern for victims and their plight, but the hidden (or not so hidden) agenda of right-wing politicians. I try to show that even programmes (such as victim assistance programmes) that may at first glance appear to be motivated by a caring attitude towards victims, prove, upon closer scrutiny, to be no more than mere ploys aimed at improving police–community relations, enhancing victims' cooperation with law enforcement agents, and providing the police with much needed information about the movements and whereabouts of future witnesses. The same could be said of many of the new victim initiatives. Victim fine surcharge is a blatant attempt to reduce government funding and to place the financial burden of victim compensation squarely on the shoulders of offenders regardless of whether their crimes are with or without victims (see Epilogue). The right of allocution, victim impact statements, as well as victim's involvement in parole hearings are designed, as Ranish and Shichor (Chapter 6) point out, to intimidate judges and parole board members and to influence them in one policy direction – toward harsher punishment or denial of parole. The punitive intentions are even more evident in the restrictions on release on bail, the elimination of the exclusionary rule, the abolition of parole, and so forth. The primary objective of all these measures is not to help, assist or ensure justice for crime victims but simply to reverse the humanitarian trend of the 1950s and the 1960s. And it could hardly have been a coincidence that the 'rediscovery of crime victims' happened exactly at the time when those of the new political right were in the process of implementing their law and order agenda and their punitive criminal justice policy. One need not be a sophisticated political analyst to realize that the publicity, attention and support given to the cause of crime victims and the legislative changes introduced in the last ten or fifteen years were part of an orchestrated effort designed to take the criminal justice system back to where it was half a century ago. The following list of some of the developments that took place simultaneously with the rediscovery of crime victims and the calls for victims' rights would bear this out:

- A return to the death penalty and the resumption of executions in several American states after more than a decade of *de facto* suspension resulting from the US Supreme Court decision in the Furman case.
- The rise of the neoclassical penal philosophy with its retributive model of 'just deserts'.
- A return to fixed, determinate sentences, the introduction of minimum mandatory sentences for several offences under the guise of reducing sentencing disparity, and the abolition of parole in many American states.
- A much greater use of incarceration, much longer prison sentences and a resulting overcrowding of penal institutions.
- The denunciation of the concept of rehabilitation and the insistence that treatment programmes do not work.
- The emergence of incapacitation as a major objective of penal sanctions and as one of the primary functions of the prison system.

- The emergence of fear of crime as a major social issue and an important research topic (see Fattah, 1991b)
- The great publicity given to the victimization of the elderly and to the physical and sexual abuse of young children.

Only when examined in conjunction with these concurrent developments in criminal justice would the emergence of victims' rights as a policy issue and the political interests that promoted this issue and placed it on the agenda be understood.

THE DANGERS OF MISSIONARY ZEAL

In his scholarly critique of the discipline of social gerontology, Smith (1989) warns against the danger of the 'missionary zeal' exhibited by some social gerontologists in the interests of those members of society who are older than others. Smith suggests that this missionary zeal could easily endanger the researcher's 'scholarly stance' and his/her potential contribution to social policy of research on old age. Having outlined the many dangers for gerontologists of over-identifying with older people, Smith goes on to advocate the search for a rigorous way of thinking about the relationship between that identification and scholarly research in social gerontology.

Reading Smith's paper, one cannot fail to see the striking parallels between the situation in social gerontology and recent developments in the field of victimology. The ideological transformation of victimology from the study of the victim into the art of helping victims, the over-identification with crime victims, and the missionary zeal with which the 'interests' of those victims are defended and pursued were quite manifest in victimology conferences held in recent years (Zagreb, 1985; Jerusalem, 1988; Rio de Janeiro, 1991). Those concerned about the lost neutrality and objectivity of the discipline could not be but distressed to witness dispassionate, unbiased and impartial scholarship being replaced by political advocacy and open partisanship.

The missionary zeal exhibited by many victimologists on behalf and in the interest of crime victims is fraught with danger. First, as suggested above, it is jeopardizing the quality of scholarship and the scholarly stance of the discipline of victimology. As a result, victimology is increasingly being regarded as a humanitarian and ideological movement rather than a scientific discipline (see Cressey, Chapter 2).

Secondly, missionary zeal and partisan stance are moving criminal law and the criminal justice system into a punitive, retributive direction. There is also a third danger. Since the victim lobby has chosen to focus on traditional crimes rather than white-collar crime or acts of abuse of power, there has been a distinct shift of focus in research to the former type at the expense of the latter. Victims of white-collar crime, corporate crime and abuse of power have once again been relegated to the shadow.

More serious still is yet another danger. In the diligent quest for victims' rights there seems to be a manifest or latent willingness to sacrifice offenders' rights. A false contest is created between the rights of both groups. Karmen (1990) cites those who assert that victims' rights ought to be gained at the expense of offenders' rights, and their claim that too much concern has been shown for the 'rights of criminals' and not enough for the plight of the innocent people they harm. Karmen gives the following summary of the demands of victims' advocates:

> To restore some semblance of balance to the scales of justice, which have been tipped in favor of criminals, some of the 'anti-victim' opportunities and privileges offenders have accumulated must be stripped away. According to this analysis, victims need rights to counterbalance, match, or even 'trump' the rights of criminals. In this context, reform means reversing previous court decisions and legal trends, shifting the balance of power away from wrongdoers and toward injured parties.
>
> (Karmen, 1990, p. 331)

Certainly the report of the President's Task Force in the United States (1982) and its recommendations can be read as a damning indictment of many of the legal safeguards that the American criminal justice system has established over the years to protect against the conviction of the innocent and to uphold the rights and freedoms so deeply cherished in a democracy.

It should be pointed out, however, that the emphasis on victims' rights and the insistence on creating a contest between the rights of victims and offenders has been much more pronounced in North America than in the United Kingdom and many other countries. In tracing the development of the victim movement in both Britain and the United States, Mawby and Gill (1987) concluded that while the British movement gained major impetus from those on the right of

the political spectrum, the focus still remained on victims' needs and
how best to meet those needs. In contrast, the victim movement in
North America has been more directly concerned with rights. Having
explained how simplistic it is to suggest that victims gain far less from
the criminal justice system than do offenders, Mawby and Gill opt for
a carefully balanced stance. They make it clear that while victims'
rights should be acknowledged, this has to be done without caricatur-
ing the state of law and order or the so-called 'privileges' accredited
to defendants or offenders.

MISSIONARY ZEAL: THE CASE OF CHILD ABUSE

Nowhere is the missionary zeal more evident than in the highly
sensitive and emotional area of child abuse. No other type of victimization seems to inflame emotions or to bring about stronger demands for punishment than the victimization of young, helpless,
defenceless children, particularly when the perpetrators are those
responsible for the care and protection of those children. Strong
sympathy for the victims and strong indignation at the perpetrators of
child abuse probably explain the willingness, even the eagerness, to
accept the most overblown estimates of its incidence despite the lack
of reliable figures (see Wexler, 1985). It might also explain why in the
absence of any independently verified credible evidence many are
still willing to believe in the existence of a vast international network
of satanic cults practising the ritual abuse and sacrifice of children
(see Putnam, 1991).

The repulsion we feel at the victimization of children explains best
the phenomenal speed with which broad and far-reaching child abuse
legislation was passed in all fifty American states. The incredible
celerity of legislative action is a clear indication of the religious
fervour animating the pursuit of the 'new monsters': the child abus-
ers. The sheer number of legislative bills introduced is staggering. It
is reported, for example, that the State of New York considered no
less than 43 bills while California looked at 100 (Wexler, 1985). The
sweeping provisions and the low standards of proof required under
the new bills are largely responsible for what has been described by
one commentator as 'an invasion of latter day child savers who
sometimes destroy children in order to save them' (ibid., p. 20).

Not surprisingly, the religious fervour with which the issue of child
abuse was pursued stopped short of outlawing corporal punishment

of children. Thus, with the exception of few countries, such as Sweden (where corporal punishment of children became a criminal offence in 1979) and Finland (where it was criminalized in 1984, see Korpilahti, 1989) most still provide parents (and teachers) with a legal licence to use physical violence against children. Section 43 of the Canadian Criminal Code, for example, stipulates that:

> Every schoolteacher, parent or person standing in the place of a parent is justified in using force by way of correction toward a pupil or child, as the case may be, who is under his care, if the force does not exceed what is reasonable under the circumstances.

Obviously, law and order advocates were not too anxious to champion a reform that might erode the traditional authority of parents over their offspring or undermine the power of those parents to discipline them even by means of physical violence.

That children, since the beginning of time, have been subjected to every conceivable kind of abuse is beyond question. Bakan (1971) reminds us that:

> Children have been whipped, beaten, starved, drowned, smashed against walls and floors, held in ice water baths, exposed to extremes of outdoor temperatures, burned with hot irons and steam pipes. Children have been tied and kept in upright positions for long periods. They have been systematically exposed to electric shock; forced to swallow pepper, soil, feces, urine, vinegar, alcohol, and other odious materials; buried alive; had scalding water poured over their genitals; had their limbs held in open fire; placed in roadways where automobiles would run over them; placed on roofs and fire escapes in such manner as to fall off; bitten, knifed, and shot; had their eyes gouged out.
>
> (p. 4)

It is therefore undeniable that the problem is both old and real. It is also undeniable that recent child abuse legislation is, for the most part, well intentioned. Equally indisputable is the fact that the best of intentions can and do backfire. Many interventionist policies can lead to very serious and quite often irreparable harm. Unfortunately, once we are willing to admit the failure of these policies and their disastrous consequences it is more often than not too late to repair the harm that has been done. The examples of well intentioned policies

that caused more harm than good abound. It was, after all, the noble
intention of 'humanizing and civilizing the savages and saving their
souls' that led to the virtual disappearance of the native culture, the
near destruction of the first nation in Canada and the United States
and the quasi annihilation of the Aborigines in Australia.

Responding to social problems by means of criminal legislation and
by mobilizing the criminal justice system is not a new phenomenon.
In fact, the punishment solution seems to be the most popular way of
solving all kinds of social problems from substance abuse to prostitution. What is difficult to defend (though not too difficult to comprehend) is the insistence upon, and the persistence in, using such
approach despite its manifest failure and despite its serious negative
consequences. Not infrequently, the urge for punishment prevails
over and supersedes other considerations, particularly the need for
policies of social prevention. The religious fervour with which perpetrators of sexual abuse have been (and are being) pursued and prosecuted (sometimes for offences committed twenty or even thirty years
earlier) appears to reflect more the unrelenting demands for punishment than a genuine concern for prevention. By focusing almost
obsessively on the need to have the 'bastards' pay for the crimes they
committed, attention is detracted and resources are diverted from
what *should* have been done and *could* be done to prevent this type of
insidious abuse from recurring. So while endless police investigations
are conducted followed by a steady flow of criminal charges, little
research has been done into the contexts, situations and patterns of
abuse, or to find effective means of prevention other than punishment. There also seems to be little concern for the potential trauma
victims can suffer as a result of reliving events that had taken place in
their early childhood.

At the investigation into allegations of sexual abuse at the Mount
Cashel Orphanage in Newfoundland, abuse that took place more
than fifteen years earlier, one of the victims lamented: 'It was part of
my life I wanted to put in the past. I thought it was all behind me'
(Canadian Press, *Vancouver Sun*, 11 June 1991, p. A6). And at a
recent conference on child abuse (Toronto, June 1991), British
pediatrician Dr Roy Meadow was quoted as saying:

> There's more and more evidence that the consequences of disclo-
> sure influence outcome [for the child] far more than the type of
> abuse . . . We're in danger of intervening in ways that may be
> more harmful than the original abuse.
>
> (*Globe and Mail*, 7 June 1991, p. A5)

This is confirmed by Wilson (1981) who insists that the removal of the child from his/her family home can be more devastating than the actual sexual act that occurred. Wilson also makes reference to the findings of several researchers who maintain that far more damage is caused by the confrontations the child has with the parents or the legal authorities than by the act itself (p. 108).

DANGERS OF CHILD ABUSE LEGISLATION

Although it is still too early to assess the long-term social impact of child abuse legislation, it is possible to point out some of the visible and hidden dangers these new laws represent for the victims, the caregivers and for society.

Wexler (1985) warns that the broad and vague reporting laws requiring professionals to report any suspicion of child maltreatment could easily lead to intentional and unintentional abuses. He further adds that since all those who report are guaranteed anonymity, the reporting laws can be a potent tool of harassment. Furthermore, the enormous power and the broad discretion invested in social workers lend themselves quite easily to all kinds of abuse:

> A social worker, acting solely on personal discretion, can usually list a family in a state's central register for life. There is no hearing beforehand; the family must fight its way out afterward. If the case is considered serious enough, the worker can take the family to court, where a judge can order a child removed from the home. In so-called emergencies, the worker can do this temporarily without a court order.
>
> (Wexler, 1985, p. 20)

Reporting laws also have the potential of preventing parents and other caretakers from seeking treatment for children who suffer accidental injuries for fear of being accused of child abuse and being separated from their children. This fear is reinforced by actual cases of parents whose children are susceptible to injury because of brittle bones or a bone disease, OI (osteogenesis imperfecta), who have been suspected of, and charged with, child abuse.

One real danger of the new laws is the removal of the child from his/her natural family environment when such removal is not absolutely necessary. Overzealous child workers may see separation not as a last but as a first resort despite the nefarious consequences such separation could have on the child's development, particularly when the child is quite young. Even in cases of sexual abuse where the father is almost invariably the abuser, the child may be separated from the mother as well. It is reported, for example, that in Cleveland, England, *most* of the 121 children who in 1987 were diagnosed by Drs Higgs and Wyatt (who reported on a new technique for diagnosing child sexual abuse) were separated from their parents and their home, approximately 70 per cent by place of safety orders (Walklate, 1989, p. 66).

Another serious danger of the current hype about sexual abuse of children is the deprivation of young children of physical contact and the physical expression of affection. Elshtain (1985) reports on how those working in child-care programmes abstain from any physical contact with the children in their care for fear of being falsely accused of sexual abuse. Since psychologists have always maintained that good child care requires physical contact, these new attitudes and practices could be detrimental to a healthy emotional development. Pointing to the danger, Elshtain (1985) writes:

> One result of the current uproar is that toddlers, some of whom are in day care from 7 a.m. to 5.30 p.m., may find themselves deprived of normal human contact by day-care workers who have been frightened away from hugging or holding their wards.
>
> (p. 26)

Elshtain also relates how many divorced or separated fathers express fears of holding or hugging their children, or even changing their soiled diapers, for fear that a vindictive former spouse may conjure up a tale of sexual abuse. She further explains how 'awareness' programmes aimed at alerting children to sexual abuse (programmes that are becoming more popular and widespread every day) can foster mistrust of adults in general and family members in particular. She writes:

> Whether such programs achieve their desired results remains to be seen, but they surely enhance the fears of children and perhaps even inject a premature sexual context into their relations with adults.
>
> (p. 24)

A similar view was expressed by Dr Roland Summit of the Harbor

UCLA Medical Center at the aforementioned Toronto Conference (*Vancouver Sun*, 8 June 1991, p. B11) when he stated that 'the fear is that if we teach kids to be suspicious of anyone trying to touch them, that they may become afraid of touching altogether.'

One of the most frightening aspects of child protection laws is that they apply not only to actual abuse but also to '*neglect*'. Patrick T. Murphy, former head of the Juvenile Litigation Office of the Legal Aid Society of Chicago (quoted by Wexler, 1985, p. 20), likens the neglect statute to a fisherman's net that catches every fish swimming through and allows the fisherman to pick what he wants to keep and which to throw back. Other professionals quoted by Wexler declare that the laws severely injure thousands of children who have never been harmed by their parents because they confer on child-protective investigators the power to disrupt children's lives. And as Wexler (1985) correctly points out, child-neglect laws blur the distinction between poverty and neglect since the vast majority of the so-called neglect cases are in reality poverty cases. He adds that what these vague and low standards of proof laws do is to make it easy to pull children away from their parents and throw them into the nation's chaotic system of foster care.

Another commentator, Elshtain (1985), deplores the fact that sloppy notions of 'child neglect' are often used to condemn families – particularly single-parent households headed by women – simply because they are poor. In so doing the accusation of neglect is often hurled against those who have themselves fallen victim to societal neglect!

Another disquieting feature of the new laws is that they have for all practical purposes reversed the fundamental presumption of innocence. Once there is the slightest suspicion of abuse (physical or sexual) it becomes incumbent upon the person suspected to prove his/her innocence. The laws have also opened the gates to a flood of false accusations that have ruined lives and reputations. For obvious reasons there are no reliable statistics or even rough estimates of the number of those who were falsely accused. Some well-publicized cases served to highlight the severe traumatic effects not only for those who are accused but also for the children who are repeatedly subjected to interrogations by inadequately trained investigators and lawyers who relentlessly bombard them with repetitive and pointed questions.

In the Jordan, Minnesota, case (see Feher, Chapter 8), one child was interviewed nine times before the joint investigation began;

another child endured at least thirty interviews in the course of the original investigation. The Attorney General Report on the investigation, cited by Feher, gave examples of separating children, who steadfastly refused to admit that any abuse took place, from their parents for several months. These children were repeatedly interrogated by their foster parents about the alleged abuse. Feher cites other examples where the children were told that their reunion with their parents would be fostered by 'admission' of their parents' abuse.

One highly publicized case is that known as the 'McMartin Pre-School molestation case'. The case reportedly cost the state of California over 15 million dollars. The two main defendants, Peggy McMartin Buckey, 60, and her son Raymond Buckey, 28, spent a long time in prison. A jury composed of eight men and four women heard testimony for two and half years and finally acquitted the two accused of 52 counts of child molestation.

Many of the false allegations of child sexual abuse are made during custody and access disputes between parents. One such case is that of Lawrence Spiegel whose life was completely shattered as a result of being falsely accused of sexually abusing his 2½-year-old daughter following a bitter divorce and custody fight. Spiegel decided to relate his harrowing experience in a book (*A Question of Innocence*, 1987). In an interview with *Time Magazine* (11 May 1987, p. 51) Spiegel maintained that the increased determination of authorities to uncover child sex abuse has had a less wholesome consequence: a raft of false charges that devastate the lives of those accused. The same *Time* article reported on the nationwide growth of a group called VOCAL (Victims of Child Abuse Laws), a lobbying and referral group which was started in Minneapolis in 1984. The forming of the group followed a case in the small city of Jordan, Minnesota, in which 24 adults were charged with sexually abusing children. Only one was convicted. Two were acquitted and charges against the remaining 21 were dropped (see Feher, Chapter 8).

It is not only men who are the targets for false accusations. A recent British Columbia case reported by Mia Stainsby (*Vancouver Sun*, 15 March 1991, p. D7) is of a falsely accused mother. The daughter, aged three, was taken away from her mother and placed in a foster home where she stayed for five months because it was alleged that the mother 'sexually abused her daughter by french kissing her'! The charges were made, according to Stainsby, by a spurned ex-boyfriend and a private day-care operator, a friend of the ex-boyfriend.

Another case is that of a Saskatchewan woman, age 34, who was convicted (possibly for the first time in Canada) of incest on the basis of her son's uncorroborated testimony and sentenced to two years less a day. About three weeks after the sentence, the alleged victim confessed to a retired Crown prosecutor that he had lied about his mother having sex with him. In December 1990, the Saskatchewan Court of Appeal quashed the conviction and it was left to the Crown to decide whether to lay charges against the son for lying under oath (Canadian Press, reported in the *Vancouver Sun*, 4 December 1990).

Even young children do not seem to be immune from allegations of sexual abuse. Another well publicized case, this time in the state of Washington, is of a 10-year-old boy who was charged of two counts of rape of another child in the first degree (a felony that can result in 20 years to life imprisonment for adult offenders). The boy allegedly placed rocks up the other boy's anus and his mouth on the victim's penis. According to the report, there was no physical evidence, medical evidence or witnesses. The alleged victim initially blamed his 13-year-old brother for the assault but changed his version after talking to his parents and accused the 10-year-old defendant instead. The 10-year-old boy was found guilty but was later acquitted on a technicality since Washington state law requires that when a rape victim is less than 12 years old, the offender must be at least 24 months older for a crime to have occurred (Doug Ward, *Vancouver Sun*, 22 November, 27 November and 19 December 1990).

The tragic lot of those wrongly accused of sexual abuse is well described by Feher (Chapter 8) who notes that the passion surrounding this issue makes the lot of the accused a particularly undesirable one. Unfortunately, at least until now, the tendency has been to ignore or to dismiss the negative consequences in favour of the rhetoric of the 'noble cause' and to insist that the end result 'the protection of children against sexual abuse' amply justifies the cost to the innocent who suffer.

It is too early to tell what the impact will be of the recent removal of some of the traditional safeguards in rape cases. Rules of evidence used to require that the testimony of alleged rape victims be corroborated to protect against false accusations. Almost all American states have already relieved the prosecution of the burden of providing corroboration of the rape accusations (Feher, Chapter 8). Noting that child sexual abuse is a crime that will often leave no physical evidence even when it actually has occurred, Feher draws attention to the inherent danger. He writes:

In the context of an *actual* occurrence of abuse, the repeal of this rule [corroboration] would appear beneficial. But in the context of a man on trial for accusations which are the product of the interviewing process, the result is that one more procedural safeguard to incorrect convictions has been removed.

In addition to eliminating the corroboration requirement, some jurisdictions have introduced new rules that severely inhibit the defendant's ability to cross-examine the child witness. Other changes include permitting a videotaped statement or live testimony through closed-circuit television instead of the normal under-oath deposition followed by cross-examination.

To protect victims of rape against secondary victimization and unnecessary intrusion into their private affairs, many jurisdictions have introduced the so-called rape-shield laws. One such law is the Texas Criminal Rule of Evidence 412 which went into effect on 1 September 1986. The law prohibits the use of either reputation or opinion evidence of an alleged rape victim's past sexual behaviour (Anonymous, 1988). What rape-shield statutes do is limit the introduction of evidence of the victim's prior sexual conduct and restrict the circumstances in which and the extent to which the defendant in a rape case may present this type of evidence to the jury.

Herman (1976/77) offers an excellent analysis of the threats that rape-shield laws present to the principle of fair trial within an adversary system, the bedrock goal of which is to avoid erroneous convictions. Herman notes that some of the new provisions (or proposals) unreasonably interfere with the defendant's constitutional right to confront and cross-examine the complainant. He adds that 'were it the rule that a cross-examiner could not inquire into embarassing matters, the right to cross examine would be reduced to a hollow shell' (p. 72). Herman makes it clear that the solution to the problem of unjustified acquittals is not to declare relevant evidence inadmissible. To do this 'is to bluntly disadvantage the defendant who ought to be acquitted merely because defendants in other cases have not been convicted' (p. 72). In his conclusion, Herman expressed doubts about the constitutionality of rape-shield laws. However, his implicit wish that they be declared unconstitutional was not fulfilled. In May 1991, in a 7–2 ruling, the Supreme Court of the United States upheld the Michigan law. Justice Sandra Day O'Connor, writing for the majority, stated that the Michigan statute (which contains one of the most stringent standards for admitting sexual history evidence; see Davis,

1984, p. 289) is 'a valid legislative determination that rape victims deserve hightened protection against surprise, harassment and unnecessary invasions of privacy' (*Globe and Mail*, 21 May 1991, p. A9).

Three months later, (August, 1991) the Supreme Court of Canada ruled in the opposite direction. In a 7–2 ruling, the court declared the rape-shield provision of the criminal code to be unconstitutional because it could lead to the conviction of innocent defendants. One of the Court's female justices, Justice Beverly McLachlin, stated that the law went too far. She wrote:

> In achieving its purpose, the abolition of the outmoded, sexist-based use of sexual conduct evidence, it overshoots the mark and renders inadmissible evidence which may be essential to the presentation of legitimate defence and hence to a fair trial.

WHERE TO GO FROM HERE?

This relatively brief review of recent developments in victimology, victim legislation and victim initiatives is meant to draw attention to the actual and potential dangers of current trends and to highlight the need for a critical victimology. The rhetoric of the advocates of law and order who championed the victim's cause has gone unchallenged for too long. Now is the time to critically examine the so-called 'reforms' to assess their impact on victims and offenders, on the criminal justice system and on the larger society. In other words, there is an urgent and pressing need to transform the victims' rights problem from a valence issue to a position issue and to question the uncritical acceptance of many of the changes that have been portrayed as being in the best interest of crime victims, as absolutely essential to alleviate their plight and improve their lot. Because as Elias (Chapter 3) points out, although victims are the ones who were supposed to benefit the most, they have received far less than promised. The picture Elias paints of the achievements of the victim movement is gloomy and the questions he asks are vital:

> Yet for all the new initiatives, victims have gotten far less than promised. Rights have often been unenforced or unenforceable, participation sporadic or ill-advised, services precarious and under-funded, victim needs unsatisfied if not further jeopardized, and victimization increased, if not in court, then certainly in the streets.

Given the outpouring of victim attention in recent years, how could this happen, and who benefits instead?

A great deal of research is needed to find satisfactory answers to these burning questions.

And what about the future direction of the discipline of victimology itself? Where should it be heading?

At least two of the directions Malcolm Johnson (1978) suggested for a sound development of the discipline of social gerontology do apply as well to victimology. We only need to replace his reference to old people with a reference to victims of crime. Following Johnson's advice we can thus say that if the discipline is to mature, victimology will have to address at least two fundamental issues. First, it is absolutely necessary to develop sound theory in order to bring 'real understanding' through the organization and interpretation of the vast amount of data about victims of crime that is rapidly becoming available. Second, a redefinition of the discipline's core problem will have to occur, with less attention paid to the needs and problems of victims of crime and more attention paid to the process of victimization. Understanding criminal victimization will have to become once again the major focus of research and theory: such understanding is indispensable for guiding social policy on victims of crime.

REFERENCES

Amernic, J. (1984) *Victims: The Orphans of Justice*. Toronto: McClelland and Stewart–Bantam Limited.

Anonymous (1988) The Texas Rape-Shield Law: Texas Rule of Criminal Evidence 412. *American Journal of Criminal Law*, Vol. 14, pp. 281–306.

Christie, N. (1977) Conflicts as property. *British Journal of Criminology*, Vol. 17, No. 1, pp. 1–15.

Cook, F.L. and Skogan, W.G. (1990) Agenda setting and the rise and fall of policy issues: the case of criminal victimization of the elderly. *Environment and Planning C: Government and Policy*, Vol. 8, pp. 395–415.

Cose, E. (1990) Turning victims into saints – journalists cannot resist recasting crime into a shopworn morality tale. *Time Magazine*, 22 January, p. 29.

Davis, E.M. (1984) Rape shield statutes: legislative responses to probative dangers. *Journal of Urban and Contemporary Law*, Vol. 27, pp. 271–94.

Dershowitz, A. (1988) *Taking Liberties: A Decade of Hard Cases, Bad Laws, and Bum Raps*. Chicago: Contemporary Books.

Dolliver, J.M. (1987) Victims' rights constitutional amendment: a bad idea whose time should not come. *The Wayne Law Review*, Vol. 34, pp. 87–93.

Elshtain, J.B. (1985) Invasion of the child savers: how we succumb to hype and hysteria. *The Progressive* (September), pp. 23–6.

Fattah, E.A. (1979) Some recent theoretical developments in victimology. *Victimology*, Vol. 4, No. 2, pp. 198–213.

Fattah, E.A. (1986) *From Crime Policy to Victim Policy – Reorienting the Justice System*. London: Macmillan.

Fattah, E.A. (1989) *The Plight of Crime Victims in Modern Society*. London: Macmillan

Fattah, E.A. (1990) Victims and victimology – the facts and the rhetoric. *International Review of Victimology*, Vol. 1, No. 1, pp. 43–66.

Fattah, E.A. (1991) *Understanding Criminal Victimization*. Scarborough, Ontario: Prentice Hall.

Fattah, E.A. (1991b) *Research on Fear of Crime: A Methodological Critique*. Paper presented at a workshop on Victimization and Fear of Crime. Hannover, Germany, April 1991.

Feher, T.L. (1988) The alleged molestation victim, the rules of evidence, and the constitution: should children really be seen and not heard? *American Journal of Criminal Law*, Vol. 14, pp. 227–55.

Fletcher, G. (1988) *Bernhard Goetz and the Law on Trial*. New York: Free Press.

Garofalo, R. (1988) *Criminologie*. Paris: Felix Alcan.

Geis, G. (1990) Crime victims – practices and prospects. In Lurigio, A.J., Skogan, W.G. and Davis, R.C. (eds), *Victims of Crime – Problems, Policies, and Programs*. Newbury Park: Sage.

Herman, L. (1976/77) What's wrong with the rape reform laws? *The Civil Liberties Review* (December/January), pp. 60–73.

Johnson, M.L. (1978) That was your life: a biographical approach to later life. In Carver, V. and Liddiard, P. (eds), *An Aging Population*. Hodder and Stoughton in association with the Open University Press.

Karmen, A. (1990) *Crime Victims: An Introduction to Victimology*. Pacific Grove, Calif.: Brooks/Cole.

Korpilahti, M. (1989) Child abuse and the courts: Finnish and Swedish experiences. In Fattah, E.A. (ed.), *The Plight of Crime Victims in Modern Society*. London: Macmillan.

Maguire, M. and Pointing, J. (1988) *Victims of Crime – A New Deal?* Milton Keynes: Open University Press.

Mawby, R.I. and Gill, M.L. (1987) *Crime Victims: Needs, Services and the Voluntary Sector*. London: Tavistock.

Mawby, R.I. (1988) Victims' needs or victims' rights: alternative approaches to policy-making. In Maguire, M. and Pointing, J. (eds) *Victims of Crime – A New Deal*. Milton Keynes: Open University Press.

Nelson, B. (1984) *Making an Issue of Child Abuse – Political Agenda Setting for Social Problems*. Chicago: University of Chicago Press.

Phipps, A. (1988) Ideologies, political parties, and victims of crime. In Maguire, M. and Pointing, J. (eds), *Victims of Crime – A New Deal*. Milton Keynes: Open University Press.

Putnam, F.W. (1991) The Satanic ritual abuse controversy. *Child Abuse & Neglect*, Vol. 15, pp. 175–79.

Rock, P. (1986a) *A View from the Shadows*. Oxford University Press.

Rock, P. (1986b) Victims and policy in Canada: the emergence of the justice for victims of crime initiative. In Fattah, E.A. (ed.), *From Crime Policy to Victim Policy*. London: Macmillan.

Rock, P. (1988) Governments, victims and policies in two countries. *British Journal of Criminology*, Vol. 28, No. 1, pp. 44–60.

Rock, P. (1990) *Helping Victims of Crime: The Home Office and the Rise of Victim Support in England and Wales*. Oxford: Clarendon Press.

Smith, G. (1989) Missionary zeal and the scholarly stance: policy and commitment in research on old age. *Ageing and Society*, Vol. 9, pp. 105–21.

Smith, S.R. and Freinkel, S. (1988) *Adjusting the Balance – Federal Policy and Victim Services*. New York: Greenwood Press.

Spiegel, L. (1987) *A Question of Innocence*. Morris Plains, NJ: Unicorn.

United States (1982) *Final report*. President's Task Force on Victims of Crime. Washington, DC: Government Printing Office.

Walker, S. (1985) *Sense and Nonsense About Crime – A Policy Guide*. Monterey, Calif.: Brooks/Cole.

Walklate, S. (1989) *Victimology: The Victim and the Criminal Justice Process*. London: Unwin Hyman.

Wexler, R. (1985) Invasion of the child savers – no one is safe in the war against abuse. *The Progressive* (September), pp. 19–22.

Wilson, P. (1981) *The Man They Called a Monster*. Sydney: Cassell.

Part One
Critical Views on Victimology and Victim Policy

1 Victims and Victimology: The Facts and the Rhetoric

Ezzat A. Fattah

Not only does considerable overlap exist between populations of victims and offenders as demonstrated by the substantial proportion of violators having also been victims, but considerable evidence exists that the experience of being victimized increases the propensity for offending and that populations of victims and offenders have homogenous characteristics . . . Clearly any theory that assumes no overlap exists between populations of victims and offenders or that they are distinct types of persons distorts the empirical research.

Albert J. Reiss, Jr (1981)

VICTIMOLOGY: A BRIEF HISTORY[1]

Early victimological notions were developed not by criminologists or sociologists but by poets, writers and novelists. These include Thomas De Quincey, Khalil Gibran, Aldous Huxley, Marquis de Sade, Franz Werfel among others. The first systematic treatment of victims of crime appeared in 1948 in Hans von Hentig's book *The Criminal and his Victim*.[1] In the fourth part of the book, under the provocative title 'The Victim's Contribution to the Genesis of the Crime', von Hentig offered a new dynamic approach as a substitute for the static, unidimensional study of the offender which had dominated the discipline of criminology. Von Hentig had earlier treated the topic in a paper published in the *Journal of Criminal Law and Criminology* in 1940. In it von Hentig noted that:

It is true, there are many criminal deeds with little or no contribution on the part of the injured individual . . . On the other hand we can frequently observe a real mutuality in the connexion of perpetrator and victim, killer and killed, duper and dupe. Although this

29

reciprocal operation is one of the most curious phenomena of criminal life it has escaped the attention of socio-pathology.

In his book, von Hentig is critical of the legal distinction between offenders and victims and the criteria used by the criminal law to make such attributions.

Most crimes are directed against a specific individual, his life or property, his sexual self-determination. For practical reasons, the final open manifestation of human motor force which precedes a socially undesirable result is designated as the criminal act, and the actor as the responsible criminal. The various degrees and levels of stimulation or response, the intricate play of interacting forces, is scarcely taken into consideration in our legal distinctions, which must be simple and workable.

Elsewhere in the book von Hentig points out that:

The law considers certain results and the final moves which lead to them. Here it makes a clear-cut distinction between the one who does and the one who suffers. Looking into the genesis of the situation, in a considerable number of cases, we meet a victim who consents tacitly, co-operates, conspires or provokes. The victim is one of the causative elements . . .

Von Hentig insisted that many crime victims contribute to their own victimization be it by inciting or provoking the criminal or by creating or fostering a situation likely to lead to the commission of the crime. Other pioneers in victimology, who firmly believed that victims may consciously or unconsciously play a causal role, outlined many of the forms this contribution can take: negligence, carelessness, recklessness, imprudence and so forth. They pointed out that the victim's role could be a motivational one (attracting, arousing, inducing, inciting . . .) or a functional one (provoking, precipitating, triggering, facilitating, participating . . .).[2]

Prior to the publication of von Hentig's book, criminological explanations of delinquent and criminal behaviour were focused upon the socio/economic/cultural attributes, the biogenetic abnormalities and/or the psychological peculiarities of offenders. Most of the theories, whether attempting to define causation or association, offered only static explanations. The traits approach either completely ignored or deliberately minimized the importance of situational factors in triggering or actualizing criminal behaviour. The study of the victim, his characteristics, attitude and behaviour, his relationship to, and interactions with, the victimizer, held the promise for transforming aetiological criminology from the static, one-sided study of the distinctive attributes of the offender, into a dynamic, situational approach which viewed criminal behaviour not as a unilateral action but as the outcome of dynamic processes of interaction. Through victimology, it seemed possible to develop a new model of crime encompassing the perpetrator's motives and the sufferer's attitude, the criminal's initiative and the victim's response, one party's action and the other party's reaction.[3]

Von Hentig's book was followed by a number of theoretical studies written by various criminologists, that dealt with victim types, victim–offender relationships and the role victims play in certain kinds of crime. The book also provided an impetus for several empirical studies which devoted special attention to the victims of specific offences.[4]

The term 'victimology' was coined in 1949 by an American psychiatrist, Frederick Wertham, who used it for the first time in his book *The Show of Violence*. Wertham wrote:

The murder victim is the forgotten man. With sensational discussions on the abnormal psychology of the murderer, we have failed to emphasize the unprotectedness of the victim and the complacency of the authorities. One cannot understand the psychology of the murderer if one does not understand the sociology of the victim. What we need is a science of victimology.

FROM MICRO-VICTIMOLOGY TO MACRO-VICTIMOLOGY

In the 1970s individual studies of the victims of specific crimes were overshadowed by victimization surveys, the first of which was conducted in the USA in 1965 for the President's Commission on Law Enforcement and Administration of Justice. Victimization surveys transformed the micro approach, characteristic of the early studies in victimology, into a macro approach aimed mainly at determining the volume of victimization, identifying the victim population and establishing the socio-demographic characteristics of that population. While this new macro approach is essential for studying the trends and patterns of victimization, the social and spatial distribution of some kinds of crime, it tells us very little about the social and personal settings in which those crimes take place. It is of limited value in understanding the psycho- and sociodynamics of criminal behaviour, the process of selecting the victim, victim–offender interactions and the victim's contribution to the genesis of the crime. And although data from victimization surveys can be useful in understanding the correlates of fear of crime, they shed no light on the psychological and behavioural reactions to fear or on the social and personal consequences of criminal victimization for the victims.[5] Despite their limitations and methodological shortcomings, victimization surveys have greatly enhanced our knowledge of the victim population and have confirmed what many victimologists knew for a long time through mere intuition. They showed, among other things, that the risks of becoming a victim of crime are not evenly spread and that victims of violence, in particular, do not constitute an unbiased cross-section of the general population. This reality is constantly ignored in current debates on victims which continue to stress, and thus help perpetuate, the 'bad luck' and 'predator–prey' notions of criminal victimization. By so doing, these debates divert attention from the fact that certain individuals or groups of individuals run, because of certain personal factors (such as lifestyle) or environmental variables (such as area of residence), a higher risk of victimization, and are more frequently victimized than others. Victimization surveys provided empirical support for the belief that criminality is clustered within certain groups and certain areas and that there is a much greater affinity between offenders and victims than we want to admit. As Singer (1981a) points out:

The idea that victims and offenders are part of the same homogeneous population runs contrary to the public's popular impression that criminals are distinct from their innocent victims.

In the current rhetoric of victim movements, victims and offenders are portrayed as two totally distinct and radically different populations. Such portrayal is difficult to reconcile with the knowledge gained from victimization research which reveals striking similarities between the two groups. In the words of Anttila (1974), 'Both victims and criminals, particularly in violent crime, appear to be odd people, inclined to unlawfulness, provocative and easily provoked. The same individuals may alternatingly or even simultaneously turn up as offenders and victims, while the majority of society's ordinary citizens are safely outside.' This is not to say, of course, that *all* victims of crime share the same attributes of their assailants. It is simply to emphasize that the two populations have several common characteristics. It is also meant to show how erroneous it is to portray victims as a herd of weak, helpless, defenceless and unsuspecting lambs who fall prey to a bunch of hungry, savage wolves.

THE STRIKING SIMILARITIES BETWEEN THE VICTIM AND OFFENDER POPULATIONS

The *Canadian Urban Victimization Survey Bulletin* (Canada, 1985) reports that the profile of the victim of crime against the person is similar to that of the offender:

> When we examine the categories of people most likely to be victimized, many popular myths are exploded. Using the victimization data we can draw a profile of the victim of crime against the person: young unmarried male, living alone, probably looking for work, or a student, and with an active life outside the home – not very different from the profile we might draw of the offender.

Criminological studies in Europe, the USA, Canada and Australia show that offenders involved in the types of crime covered by victimization surveys are disproportionately male, young, urban residents, of lower socio-economic status, unemployed (and not in school), unmarried, and in the United States, black. Victimization surveys reveal that victims disproportionately share these characteristics and that the demographic profiles of crime victims and of convicted criminals are strikingly similar.[6]

Analysing crimes of violence in Finland, Aromaa (1974) reported that the victims had much in common with the offenders and they were often – especially where the gravest crimes of violence are concerned – closely related to each other. Reporting on the first national victimization survey conducted in Australia, Braithwaite and Biles (1984) declared that the findings provide strong support for the proposition that victims and offenders share many characteristics.

In the USA, the similarities between victims and offenders were stressed by Hindelang *et al.* (1978):

To summarize, offenders involved in the types of crimes of interest here are disproportionately male, young, urban residents, black, or lower socio-economic status, unemployed (and not in school), and unmarried. In our brief review of victim characteristics above, and in earlier chapters, it was seen that victims disproportionately share these characteristics.

Hindelang *et al.*'s conclusion is the same as that reached by Singer (1981a) who found that in crimes of assault victims and offenders were related in their demographic characteristics and in terms of certain shared responses to perceived situations of physical or psychological threat. Their social interaction suggested certain normative constraints where a violent outcome is dependent in part on the victim's reactions. Singer points out that:

A key question then in explaining personal victimization as a consequence of the victim's exposure to an offender is the extent to which violence reflects a lifestyle that leads victims to alternate as offenders in the same social environment. If victims and offenders share certain understandings and misunderstandings supporting their use of physical force, then both populations are not distinct, but rotate in a web of subcultural relationships.

It is understandable that the frequency with which some individuals become involved in violence – prone situations will affect both their chances of using violence and of being recipients of violence, of attacking and being attacked, of injuring and being injured, of killing and being killed. Who will end up being the victim and who will be legally qualified as the offender depends quite often on chance factors rather than deliberate action, planning or intent. Thus victim/ offender roles are not necessarily antagonistic but are frequently complementary and interchangeable. This is particularly true of brawls, quarrels, disputes and altercations. In many instances, dangerousness and vulnerability may be regarded as the two sides of the same coin. They often coexist since many of the factors that contribute to dangerousness may create or enhance a state of vulner- ability. One such factor is alcohol consumption which may act simul- taneously as a criminogenic and as a victimogenic factor enhancing the potentiality of violent behaviour in one party and of violent victimization in the other.[7]

Similarities between the victim and offender populations exemplified

The homogeneity of the victim and offender populations can be easily seen by looking at some of the general socio-demographic characteristics of the two populations.

Age
When young children, who according to the law cannot commit crime, are excluded, it becomes clear that delinquency and victimization rates for the different age groups follow an identical pattern. Younger age groups who commit the largest portion of delinquency and crime are the ones most victimized, while elderly groups who commit the least crime are also the ones least victimized. Intermediate age groups have intermediate rates of both crime and victimization.

Like other victimization surveys conducted elsewhere. The *Canadian Urban Victimization Survey* (1983) revealed that the risk of victimization is closely tied to age. Contrary to popular belief, elderly people were relatively unlikely to be victimized by crime. Those under 25 had the highest rate of victimization in all categories of personal offences and these high rates declined rapidly with increasing age after this point. The actual sample counts of sexual assault and robbery incidents for those over 60 were so low that estimated numbers and rates are unreliable.

The Canadian findings are consistent with those from other countries. American data show that people over 65 years of age (that is the least criminal of all age groups) are the least likely to become crime victims, while young people aged 12 to 24 have the highest victimization rates for personal crimes of violence and theft (US Dept. of Justice, 1978). Australian data reported by Wilson and Brown (1973), Congalton and Najman (1974), Braithwaite and Biles (1984), indicate that the 20–24-year-olds have the highest rates on the majority of offences and the over-60s the lowest.

Gender
Males commit more crimes and are criminally victimized more frequently than females. This is also a consistent pattern observable in official crime statistics and in the findings of victimization surveys.[8] Sexual offences are the most glaring exception since they are predominantly committed against women. Regarding property offences,

purse-snatching and some other forms of theft of personal property are more often committed against women than against men.

The *Canadian Urban Victimization Survey* (1983) shows that women are about seven times more likely than men to be victims of sexual assault (including rape, attempted rape, sexual molesting and attempted sexual molesting). They are also more likely than men to have their personal property stolen (theft of personal property). Men, on the other hand, are almost twice as likely as women to be victims of robbery or assault.

In the United States (US Dept. of Justice, 1981), it was found that, of the personal crimes measured by the survey, men are more often victimized than women for every crime except rape. In 1979, men were victims of violent crime at the rate of about 45 per 1,000. Women were victimized at the rate of about 25 per 1,000. The rates for personal crimes of theft were 99 per 1,000 for men vs. 85 per 1,000 for women.

In Australia (Braithwaite and Biles, 1984), the survey was designed in such a way that only women were eligible for rape, peeping and indecent exposure victimization. Apart from these three, the only offence on which women reported a higher level of victimization was nuisance calls. Men had higher victimization rates for breaking and entering (largely because men were more likely to be nominated as heads of the household), vehicle theft, theft, fraud, forgery, false pretences and assault. Other Australian surveys conducted locally by Wilson and Brown (1973) and Congalton and Najman (1974) both confirm that in aggregate men are more likely than women to be victims of crime.

Marital status
Married people commit less crime and are less victimized than single and divorced individuals. These differences are due, among other things, to variations in age and in lifestyle associated with the marital status.[9]

The *Canadian Urban Victimization Survey* (1984) showed that those who are unmarried (single, separated and divorced) are at higher risk of personal victimization than those who are married, living as man and wife at common law or widowed.

National victimization surveys in the United States reveal a similar pattern and show that persons who are divorced or have never been married are more likely to be victims of personal crime than the married or widowed. In 1979, for example, victimization rates for personal crimes of violence per 1,000 were as follows: divorced 75, never married 62, married 18, and widowed 9. For crimes of personal theft, the rates were: never married 142, divorced 123, married 69, and widowed 33.

Australian data (Braithwaite and Biles, 1984) confirm that widowed persons, because of their average age, have the lowest victimization rates in most crime categories. Once they are excluded from the unmarried category and once this category is restricted to those who have never married plus those who are separated or divorced, the findings are consistent with the Canadian and American ones.

Race and ethnicity
Because crimes of violence are, to a large extent, intraracial (see below), races and ethnic groups with high violent crime and delinquency rates (such as the blacks and hispanics in the USA) also have high violent victimization rates. The American white population, on the other hand, registers lower rates on both counts.

In the United States, the 1979 victimization survey (Dept. of Justice, 1981) shows that blacks were victimized by violent crime at the rate of 42 per 1,000 versus 35 per 1,000 for whites. They were also burgled at a higher rate (114 per 1,000 households versus 80 per 1,000 household for whites). For crimes of theft, however, rates for blacks are generally the same or lower than those for whites. In 1979, rates for household larceny for both blacks and whites were 133 per 1,000. Personal larceny rates were 93 for whites versus 87 for blacks. The same survey also indicates that hispanics generally have higher rates than non-hispanics for household crimes and for most crimes of violence.

Unemployment
Unemployed persons are overrepresented among convicted offenders and among victims. Age and lifestyle are probably responsible, at least partly, for this pattern.

The Canadian Survey (1984) shows the highest victimization rates to occur among students and those looking for work – much higher than the rates of those who were retired or those who were employed for most of the year in question.

Braithwaite and Biles (1984) report that the unemployed in Australia have clearly higher rates of victimization for theft, breaking and entering, peeping and assault. Most striking is the difference with respect to assault, where the unemployed were more than twice as

38   *Critical Views on Victimology and Victim Policy*

likely to report victimization than those in full-time jobs and six times as likely to have been assaulted than respondents not in the work-force or in part-time jobs.

Income
The relationship between income and victimization is not as clear-cut as the relationship between income and crime. Low income categor-ies are greatly overrepresented among convicted offenders. Concern-ing victimization, the situation is far more complex. The *Canadian Urban Victimization Survey* (1983) found, as one might expect, that the higher the family income of urban residents the more likely it is that they will experience some form of household victimization of personal theft. Needless to say the differences among income groups in their levels of tolerance for, and awareness of, some types of incidents are likely to affect the level of reporting to the interviewers. The *Survey* found, however, that lower income individuals are as likely or more likely than others to suffer a personal violent victimiza-tion – sexual assault, robbery or assault.

The picture that emerges from American surveys regarding violent victimization by crime is a clear one. According to the *Bureau of Justice Statistics* (1985), for both whites and blacks there was a direct relationship between family income and the likelihood of violent victimization in 1982: the lower the income the greater the victimiza-tion. While the pattern was consistent for both races and the differences between the lowest and highest income categories were statistically significant, not all differences between adjacent income categories were statistically significant.

In Australia, both Wilson and Brown (1973) and Congalton and Najman (1974) in their local surveys failed to confirm a negative relationship between socio-economic status and aggregate victimiza-tion rate. Cross-tabulations of *National Crime Survey* victimization rates by education, occupation, income of respondents and house-hold income carried out by Braithwaite and Biles (1984) reveal a mixed picture. In some respects, higher socio-economic status re-spondents have higher victimization rates. Tertiary-educated respon-dents are more likely to be victims of non-violent property crimes but less likely to be victims of assault. They found, however, a consistent positive correlation between gross weekly income of household and vehicle theft victimization (possibly because wealthy households own more automobiles).

Involvement in delinquency

Committing a crime increases the chances of further involvement in delinquency. For example, if someone commits an armed robbery, a burglary or an act of shoplifting, the chances that the same person will commit a second offence are much higher than for the rest of the population. The same is true for the risks of victimization. Thus victimization in one event increases the risk of a second victimization and so on.

There is evidence suggesting that criminals are more frequently victimized than non-criminals and that victims of violent crime themselves have considerable criminal involvements.[10] In the follow-up survey to *Delinquency in a Birth Cohort*, a study of self-reported victimization, Singer (1981b) examined the extent to which victims are also guilty of serious assault. He reports that cohort members who were shot or stabbed were most often non-white, high-school dropouts, unemployed and single when surveyed. They were also involved more frequently in official and self-reported criminal activity. Victims of serious assault had the highest probability of having a friend arrested, belonging to a gang, using a weapon, committing a serious assault, and having an official arrest. Singer concluded that his findings, along with those of other studies examining the victim–offender interaction, indicate support for the homogeneity of victim–offender populations involved in serious assaultive conduct.

Johnson *et al.* (1973) followed up all victims of gunshot and stab wounds admitted to the City of Austin Hospital in Texas during 1968 and 1969. They found that 75 per cent of the male victims had a criminal record, and 54 per cent had a jail record. Savitz *et al.* (1977), studying a Philadelphia cohort, also observed an association between official records of having committed assault and assault victimization. And in their London (England) survey, Sparks *et al.* (1977) found victims of violent crime to be significantly more likely than non-victims to self-report committing violent crimes.

Singer's findings are in line with another reality which has been observed for a long time, namely that marginal groups are more involved in crime and more often victimized than non-marginal groups. Typical examples of those prone to victimization are persons implicated in illicit activities or those who have opted for a deviant lifestyle: drug-pushers, drug-addicts, prostitutes, persons involved in illegal gambling, loan-sharking and so forth.

The interpersonal nature of violent crime

The affinity between the victim and criminal populations should come as no surprise. Crimes of violence, particularly those not motivated by financial gain, are known to be interpersonal crimes or crimes of relationship. Because the motives for violence do not develop in a vacuum, it is understandable that these crimes are largely committed between people who know each other and those who are bound together by family, friendship or business ties. The typical contexts in which criminal homicide, attempted murder or assault occur are those of a domestic fight, a quarrel between non-strangers, a family dispute, or other altercations where insult, abuse or jealousy are present. The interpersonal character of crimes of violence, particularly criminal homicide, is well documented in several studies undertaken in different cultures.[11]

A ten-year study of murder in Canada, covering the period 1961 to 1970, and published by *Statistics Canada*, shows that 41.7 per cent of the victims were related to their assailants by some kind of family relationship. Female victims were much more likely to be killed by a member of their family than their male counterparts. Out of a total of 2,674 victims, 417 (15.6 per cent) were killed by their male or female spouse. An updating of the study, covering a fifteen-year period: 1961–1975, revealed that out of 2,046 female victims, one-third (673) were killed by their legal or common-law husbands.

In another study, *Statistics Canada* revealed that most of the 47 children listed in Canadian murder statistics of 1974 were slain by their fathers, usually men who also shot their wives then committed suicide.

Criminal homicides, sexual and non-sexual assaults seem to be predominantly intraracial as well. Studies conducted in the USA where there are two major groups, racially distinct, namely blacks and whites, clearly show that assaultive violence (criminal homicide, aggravated assault and forcible rape) is predominantly intraracial.[12] The majority of these violent crimes involve blacks killing, assaulting or raping black victims while most of the rest involve whites victimizing other whites. Robbery, on the other hand, has a high interracial component mainly composed of younger black males robbing older white males.

And judging by the studies undertaken for the US National Commission On the Causes and Prevention of Violence, it would also seem that criminal homicides and aggravated assaults are predominantly intragender although the intrasex pattern is much less pronounced than the intraracial one.

The geographial proximity of offenders to their targets
Another factor that explains the observed similarities between the victim and offender population has to do with space. There is a well established distance decay pattern in human spatial behaviour. Brantingham and Brantingham (1984) point out that people interact more with people and things that are close to their home location than with people or things that are far away. Interactions decrease as distance increases (distance decay). Some of this decrease in activity as distance increases is the result of the 'costs' of overcoming distance. They further note that the bias of greater density of interaction close to home is also the result of biased spatial knowledge. People have more experience of and are more aware of what exists around them:

> Searching behaviour starts from home and first covers likely areas that are 'known'. Criminals probably follow a similar searching pattern. Although specific studies have not been done on the spatial searching patterns of criminals, the results of other studies show strong traces of such patterns. Crimes generally occur close to the home of the criminal. The operational definition of *close* varies by offense, but the distance-decay gradient is evident in all offenses . . . Generally, violent offenses have a high concentration close to home, with many assaults and murders actually occurring in the home. The search pattern is a little broader for property offenses, but these are still clustered close to home.
>
> (Brantingham and Brantingham, 1984)

CRIME AS A SOCIAL RISK

Stressing the causal role that some victims play in the genesis of the crime is not meant to hold the victim responsible for his victimization nor to blame crime on those who suffer its consequences. Social and behavioural scientists are interested in explanation not justification, in understanding the behaviour not rationalizing it, in aetiology not in guilt or innocence, in the interpersonal dynamics that led to the crime not in legal excuses or extenuating circumstances.[13]

Pointing out the similarities between the victim and offender populations is not meant to depreciate, denigrate or cast aspersions on the victims of crime, nor to belittle the material and psychological consequences they suffer as a result of their victimization. No one, and above all no criminologist nor victimologist, could remain insensitive to the agony, pain and suffering many victims and their families go through, nor to the fear and anxiety generated by crime in the minds of certain groups such as the elderly, unprotected women, widowed females and so forth. However, for obvious reasons, spokespeople for victim movements and other victim advocates are interested in painting a grim picture of the crime situation, in amplifying the volume, extent and nature of criminality, in magnifying the psychological and financial impact of criminal victimization, and in capitalizing on the concern and fear generated or heightened by crime news. Inadvertently, they help reinforce the distorted picture of crime transmitted by the news media and are leading people to perceive the state of crime as being much worse than it really is. No wonder that the Canadian public largely overestimates the volume of violent crime in the country and the chances of falling victim to a killer, rapist, mugger or robber.

In February 1982, for example, more than two thousand adult Canadians were asked a series of questions about the extent of violent crime, sentencing and conditional release practices in Canada. The results indicated that, generally, Canadians vastly overestimate the proportion of crime which involves violence, believe murders have increased since Parliament abolished the death penalty in 1976 (when they have in fact declined) and think people released on parole are far more likely to commit violent crimes soon after release than in fact they are. In short, the image Canadians have of crime is a violent one – far more violent than statistics indicate is the case.[14]

As Clarke (1981) rightly points out:

> There are, of course, many brutal rapes and vicious unprovoked assaults on defenceless people, as well as robberies involving hundreds of thousands of pounds. But these incidents, which are naturally enough given prominence by the media, tend to distort people's views about the crime problem and must be set against the infinite numbers of opportunities for crime – only very few of which are taken up . . .

The sensationalized reporting of atypical criminal incidents by the mass media is not likely to allow members of the public, who are constantly bombarded with visual depictions and written accounts of gruesome acts of violence, to make an accurate, realistic assessment of their chances of becoming victims of crime. And strangely enough, the concept of '*social risk*' is conspicuously absent in the current debates on the crime situation and the rights of victims. Luckily, there are certain estimates of the social risk of crime coming from some European countries whose crime situation is neither much better nor much worse than that of Canada. In his previously cited paper, Ron Clarke (1981), formerly Head of the British Home Office Research Unit, provides some estimates of the risks in Great Britain. He writes:

> For example, it has been calculated that at present levels of risk the average householder in this country can expect to be burgled once every thirty years (much longer than the average tenancy) and that the average car owner will have his car taken only once every fifty years (longer than he is likely to be motoring). The risks of a person falling victim to homicide in any one year (one in 100,000) are a small fraction of the risks of being killed on the road or dying of cancer. And only one in 175,000 passenger journeys on the London Underground results in theft, while one in 8.4 million results in robbery.

Clarke notes that the risks of victimization are not evenly spread and that the chances of falling victim to crime are highly correlated with the chances of being an offender. Thus the highest risks of victimization in the UK (like in other countries) were found to be concentrated among the young (not the elderly) and among those living in cities and in disadvantaged areas. Crime, it was also found, tends to be concentrated in particular locations. For example, assaults were more likely in the environs of pubs and places of entertainment, though there were wide variations in risk between even these places. Houses in some parts of cities or sited in particular spots were at much greater risk of being burgled (and indeed of being repeatedly burgled) than others. Clarke notes further that the average burglary in Britain is committed by a youth under the age of 17 years, who takes less than fifty pounds worth of property while the occupants are away from the house. The great majority of stolen cars are recovered within a short time of being taken. About half the murders cleared up are committed not between strangers but between immediate family members or other close associates and, similarly, most assaults take place between people who know each other and who have been drinking.

What is often ignored in current debates on victims of crime is the fact that modern life is a hazardous life, that the risk of criminal victimization is but one of the many risks to which people are daily and constantly exposed. Yet, while many of the other social risks are covered in the welfare state by some form of insurance, public or private, the risk of becoming a victim of crime is not adequately covered. The recent publicity given to the cause of crime victims does not seem to have sensitized many politicians to the plight of this neglected group. This can be easily seen in politicians' manifest unwillingness even to entertain the idea of a social insurance scheme for crime victims similar to health insurance, unemployment insurance, car or labour accident insurance and so forth. Thus, while many politicians may, for political gain, pay lip-service to the cause of crime victims, nothing significant is being done to alleviate their sufferings, to compensate their losses, or to redress the harm done to them. *Justice for Victims*, the title the Canadian Federal/Provincial Task Force chose for its report, remains a hollow political slogan. Because of stringent conditions of eligibility, lack of funds, or both, less than one per cent of crime victims receive compensation from state funded programmes and for the few who do get it, it is always too little and too late. Still, slogans such as 'Justice for victims' remain popular with politicians not only because they are unlikely to raise objections from the opposition, but also because they can be attractive in electoral campaigns. After all, what could appeal more to ordinary voters than to show sympathy and compassion for the unfortunate victims of crime? The fact that very little money is actually spent to help and compensate victims, both in actual dollars and in proportion to what is spent on punishing criminals, is not likely to be known except to the extremely knowledgeable and alert voter. Even more distressing is that funds initially committed to these state-funded programmes are usually frozen, cut down or totally discontinued at the first sign of economic crisis or recession. It is very telling that one of the first programmes that had their budget reduced when the British Columbia Government brought in its so-called 'restraint' budget in 1983/84 was the victim compensation programme, a programme which by the best of assessments cannot be seen as fulfilling anything but a mere symbolic function. Nor should it be forgotten that these state programmes do nothing to prevent criminal victimization, do not tackle the roots of criminal behaviour, nor the social conditions and injustices that breed crime and create victims. It is not surprising, therefore, that victim compensation programmes have been called, and rightly so, 'political placebos' (Chappell, 1973). They are simply a political manoeuvre aimed at creating the false impression that we live in a helping, caring society, a society that comes to the rescue of its unfortunate members.

THE EMERGENCE OF THE VICTIM'S CAUSE AS A POLITICAL ISSUE

Crime victims are not the first group whose cause is exploited by unpopular governments seeking a higher rating in opinion polls, by opportunist politicians seeking electoral votes, or by incompetent public officials trying to detract attention from their failure to control crime or to reduce its incidence. Showing concern for crime victims acts as a cover-up to the inefficiency of the system, and its inability to prevent victimization. Demanding that something be done to help and to alleviate the plight of victims masks society's unwillingness to deal squarely with the problem of crime. In times of growing concern about crime, showing sympathy for the victim and committing a handful of dollars to victim programmes and services relieves the pressure on politicians to confront social injustices, ethnic conflict, inequalities in wealth and power, and the frustrations of seeing too much and having too little.

The result of the above is that the 1970s and 1980s witnessed the politicization of the victims' cause. And as with many other worthy causes there are always those who are ready to jump on the bandwagon. Some see in it an opportunity for political or financial gain, others may be looking for professional benefits or recognition. A third group may be searching for a good cause to adopt, while others may be craving for publicity and a spot in the limelight. The latter are bound to emerge as victims' advocates. They are, however, self-appointed defenders and spokespeople. Because they do not represent the larger victim population they may convey the wrong message or create a false impression that they are speaking on behalf of all crime victims. Their own personal views and demands may be construed as those of the victim population when at best they represent only a tiny minority of crime victims and at worst they speak for nobody but themselves. Nothing could be further from reality than to speak of, and treat, victims of crime as a homogeneous entity having the same needs or sharing the same interests. And yet this is the message that is always heard from the so-called victim representatives. Their constant talk about victims' rights creates the impression that victimization generates new, hitherto non-existing rights and that the rights of victims are in conflict or incompatible with the rights of offenders. At a meeting held in Toronto in 1985 it was repeatedly asserted that crime victims want recognition to be part of, and served by, the justice system, to be treated with frankness and sensitivity by justice authorities and to be compensated for injuries both mental and physical that they sustained as a result of crime.[15] These are reasonable and legitimate demands but none of the rights asked for is specific to crime victims. They are rights to which every citizen is entitled whether offender or victim, whether party to a criminal or civil conflict, whether injured by intention, negligence, malpractice or accident. The right to compensation, for example, is not exclusive to crime victims, it is a recognized right for a wide variety of groups who suffer as a result of one or more of the injustices, conflicts and hazards that prevail in modern society, regardless of whether they become victims as a result of criminal act, accident or natural disaster. Such rhetorical demands serve only to isolate crime victims from the rest of society, to portray them as society's orphans, and to stigmatize them as helpless weaklings in need of special and specific care and assistance.

Those working in the criminal justice system must be sensitive to all users of the system whether as complainants, victims, witnesses or offenders. All need to be, and should be, treated fairly with sensitivity, humanity, sympathy and compassion. To give preferential treatment to some but not to others, to treat some humanely and others inhumanely would be an affront to justice and to the principle of equality before the law.

Victimization by crime is not qualitatively different from other victimization and loss incurred from crime is not different from other losses. Injury is injury whether caused by accident, negligence or an intentional criminal act. Society has an obligation to care for those who need care, to assist those who need help and to compensate those who suffer non-self-inflicted loss or injury regardless of the origin of their victimization. To differentiate between those who are criminally victimized and those victimized by other causes would create two classes of victims: the deserving and non-deserving victims, the good and the bad victims, the worthy and unworthy victims.

Political definitions rather than actual need would then determine who is to be helped, served or compensated. If government obligation to victims is rooted in the principle of social solidarity, the origin of victimization becomes irrelevant. It also becomes clear that there is no logic in singling out crime victims or in treating them better or worse than others who need government help, care or compensation.

Surprisingly, victim advocates and victim 'representatives' have advanced no valid reasons and no convincing argument as to why victim services should be distinct and separate from other social services, why they should be part of the criminal justice system rather than being based within the community, why they should be 'professional' instead of self-help group programmes. And the way victim services are developing should be cause for concern. Most victim programmes which surfaced in recent years are housed either within police departments or within prosecutors offices. And although some of them rely heavily on volunteers, they are gradually becoming part of an impersonal and overburdened justice system. The preference given to police-based or court-based services when funding decisions are made is not difficult to explain. From an official point of view such programmes have a distinct advantage over community-based ones. Many of them make the cooperation of the victim with the police or the prosecutor a formal or an informal requirement for the provision of service. Like diversion and community service programmes, victim/witness assistance programmes tend to widen the net of social control and to intensify the mechanism of such control. Elias' (1986) evaluation of victim services in the USA led him to conclude that most seemed orientated more to either narrowly controlling victims or broadly controlling discontent, than to controlling crime or meeting victim needs. Victim/witness programmes, in particular, tended to control victims in the criminal justice process, to channel them into the process for official needs and perspectives, instead of providing a cooperative spirit, greater citizen participation, and effective crime control. Rock (1986) reports that very few of the organizations supposedly set up for helping victims were in fact established in a world figured by a politics of victims. They were founded to accomplish distinct sets of purposes which touched only obliquely on victims. This is echoed by Shapland (1986) who found that the major projects aimed at fulfilling victims' needs have been set up without regard to, or even investigation into, victims' expressed needs. The same holds true for Canada. While victim compensation programmes are suffering from an acute shortage of funds, money is being made available to fund various types of services to crime victims. For example, in its last months in office, the former Canadian Liberal Government allocated $4.8 million to victim-related initiatives through the Department of Justice and Health and Welfare, and the Ministry of the Solicitor General.[16]

THE CURRENT CRISIS IN VICTIMOLOGY

At the First National Conference of Victims of Crime (Toronto, 1985) the victim movement was called the growth industry of the decade.[17] In the United Kingdom it is considered the fastest-developing voluntary movement.[18] Victim groups and associations are mushrooming all over North America and Europe. Inevitably, this fantastic growth has had a significant impact on victimology. Victimology meetings are no longer scholarly meetings where the findings of scientific research on victims are presented and discussed, they have become a forum for political and ideological rhetoric. They mirror the transformation of victimology from an academic discipline into a humanistic movement, the shift from scholarly research to political activism. The best that could be said of present day victimology is that it is an applied discipline and a helping profession not very much different from other helping professions such as nursing or social work. At the *Fifth International Symposium on Victimology* (Zagreb, August, 1985) Cressey openly declared that victimology is neither a scientific discipline nor an academic field (like criminology or ecology). He called it instead a non-academic programme under which a hodgepodge of ideas, interests, ideologies, and research methods have been rather arbitrarily grouped. Cressey pointed out the current conflict in victimology between the humanists and the scientists. He said:

> More specifically, victimology is characterized by a clash between two equally desirable orientations to human suffering – the humanistic and the scientific . . . The humanists' work tends to be deprecated because it is considered propagandistic rather than scientific, and the scientists' work tends to be deprecated because it is not sufficiently oriented to social action.

Cressey notes that in the US, at least, a goodly proportion of all victimologists are political activists and social workers whose primary

interest in victimology is in obtaining justice for persons who have
been directly injured – physically, economically or psychologically –
by street criminals. Helping direct victims of crime is more social
work than science. Cressey points out that no empirical research is
needed to support the humanitarian custom of giving aid to the
injured, including the direct victims of crime. He believes that many
of the 'law and order' victimologists who want to get tough on crime
in order to reduce the level of crime victimization in society are
ideologists rather than scientists.

Active campaigning or lobbying on behalf of crime victims, even
when motivated by the most noble humanitarian concerns for the
welfare of the victims, has nothing to do with science. Victimological
research conduced by victim lobbyists is as objective as research
carried out by the gun lobby in the US on the issue of gun control.
Pressure groups, by nature and by choice, lack the neutrality and
impartiality necessary for sound, objective scholarship. Political
activism and disinterested scholarship do not go hand in hand. This is
not a plea for ivory tower idealism or for academic passivity. It is a
call for separating science from politics, for differentiating the role of
the scholar from that of the lobbyist.

As Cressey (Chapter 2) points out, 'humanistic victimologists are
interested in establishing a condition as a social problem rather than
in studying that condition scientifically'. Willingly or unwillingly,
consciously or unconsciously, victim lobbyists are playing into the
hands of the neo-conservatives and the neoclassicists and are helping
propagate the ideas and philosophy of right-wing criminology. In
such a climate, scientific inquiry into victim-offender interactions and
the victim's contribution to the genesis of crime is likely to be sum-
marily dismissed as an attempt to blame the victim.

The recent transformation of victimology has not been without
serious negative consequences.[19] One of the consequences has been
to refocus the notion of criminality on traditional crimes which have a
direct, immediate and tangible victim. White-collar crime, corporate
actions causing grievous social harms, whether they are legally defined as crimes or not, have once again been relegated to the background. Victim activists have focused their attention on, and directed
their action to, the so-called conventional crimes, crimes which have
visible, identifiable victims. This is not always the case with corporate
and business crimes which may victimize millions and millions of
people and still go largely unreported and unprosecuted. Despite the
scope of white-collar crime and although its depredations far exceed

those of traditional street crime, it is totally left out of victim campaigns and so are other socially harmful actions such as the pollution of the environment, the production of hazardous substances, the disposal of dangerous materials or chemicals, the manufacture of unsafe products, the violations of health and safety codes, to mention nothing of the victims of abuse of political and economic power nor of the victims of state terrorism. Whether for ideological, political or practical reasons, victim movements have been largely selective, even discriminating, in their focus, emphasis and action, in the victim groups they adopt as well as in the types of crime they choose to fight against. As a result, the vast majority of crime victims have been left unprotected, unassisted and unheard.

Genuine interest in alleviating human suffering requires that research and action be geared to the understanding, reduction and prevention of victimization whether physical, sexual, mental or economical; whether by intention, accident or negligence; whether in the home, in the street or in the workplace; whether by individuals, organizations, corporations, governments or by the larger society.

Despite its noble objective, humanistic victimology is for the most part unscientific, dominated by ideology, action-not-research-oriented and plagued by the bandwagon phenomenon. It opens the door for politics to enter and dominate a field that previously was trying hard, through scientific inquiry, to advance our knowledge and enhance our understanding of the dynamics of crime. Victimization studies aside, the new victimology has added little to existing criminological knowledge. While victimization research has led to some interesting theoretical formulations such as the lifestyle model,[20] the new 'applied' trend has hindered, delayed and slowed down the progress of victimological theory. This is because ideological postulates have replaced scholarly notions and hypotheses, because attempts to shed light on the dynamics of victimization are being challenged not on scientific but on ideological and philosophical grounds.

As an emerging, young discipline, 'old' victimology had, no question, its deficiencies and its shortcomings but its aim was to provide the scientific foundations for a dynamic criminological theory and an effective victim-based prevention policy. The 'new' victimology is calling instead for more of the same ineffective remedies and worn-out solutions. Advocating a return to the noose, longer prison sentences, restrictions on release on bail or parole, is not likely to make a dent in crime. These measures have not been effective in the past and are not going to be effective in the future. They simply detract

attention and funds from what could and should be done to change
the socio-economic conditions that breed crime and that transform
certain individuals into ruthless, merciless victimizers. Yet, these are
the policy demands made by victim advocates and by the official
committees and task forces that were asked to make recommendations to improve the lot of crime victims. President Reagan's Task
Force on Victims of Crime, for example, recommended abolition of
the 'exclusionary rule' which renders inadmissible in criminal trials
any evidence gathered illegally. It recommends longer prison sentences, the abolition of parole, and the development of a generally
'get tough' policy toward street criminals.

Slogans such as 'Justice for victims' are invariably interpreted by
the general public as meaning more punishment for offenders. A
social climate is thus created in which the ideal of humane, fair and
non-retributive justice is bound to be lost or abandoned, a climate in
which the old notions of punishment and retribution are revived, gain
momentum, take on a new significance and are actively and readily
pursued. This is what has been happening these past few years.
Though research is lacking, there are reasons to believe that the
belligerent posture taken by victim groups has been largely or partially responsible for the unmistakable trend towards more severe sanctions, a wider use of imprisonment, and lengthier terms of incarceration. The irony is that few victims are helped by sending more
offenders to prison for ever-increasing periods of time. Money which
could be positively spent on compensating victims is thus being
wasted on unproductive incarceration. And restitution by the offender, which is the only hope for redress available to uninsured victims
of property crime, is hampered not enhanced by imprisonment.

WHERE IS VICTIMOLOGY HEADING?

Where is victimology heading? Is it heading for a clash between the
humanists and the scientists? Is such a clash inevitable? Could it be
avoided? Would such a clash signal the end of victimology as a scientific discipline? These are all difficult questions to answer. And the
answers at present can only be speculative. Cressey (Chapter 2)
suggests a way for mitigating the possible clash between the humanists and the scholars. He feels that all should be encouraged to
understand that victimology is a scientific research enterprise and that

a society of victimologists is a society of researchers. This, he believes, would leave the humanists out in the cold, but then they could readily find warmth in association with human rights groups, and for those engaged in practice, with social workers:

> Alternatively, victimology could be allowed to fade away. If this course was taken, humanistic victimologists could be encouraged to ally themselves with other champions of human rights and scientific victimologists could be encouraged to ally themselves with the social scientists who call themselves criminologists. Indeed, if the concerns of victimology were restricted to the victims of crime . . . there would be no compelling reason why it would be separated out from criminology.

NOTES

1. For a detailed history of victimology see Fattah (1967).
2. For an overview of these early writings in victimology see Fattah (1971).
3. For a more detailed discussion see Fattah (1979).
4. Among these studies is Wolfgang's classic study of criminal homicide (1958), Amir's study of rape (1967), Normandeau's study of robbery (1972), Curtis' study of crimes of violence (1975a, b), Padowetz's study of marriage swindle (1954) and Verkkunen's study of sexual molestation of children, to name but a few.
5. For a more detailed discussion on the contributions and limitations of victimization studies, see Fattah (1982).
6. See US Department of Justice (1978). See also *Canadian Urban Victimization Survey Bulletin* (1983) and Gottfredson (1984).
7. See Fattah and Raic (1970).
8. One explanation, of course, is that males interact more with members of their own sex than with members of the opposite sex and the same is true of women.
9. Skogan (1981) attributes the high victimization rates of divorced, separated and unmarried women, in contrast to those for married women, to differences in their daily routines, social activity and companions.
10. For example the study of Lind (1970) in Oslo, Norway, reports a strong association between violent victimization and relatively low social status, relatively loose ties to family and work institutions, registered crimes and alcohol problems, in short, many of the factors which are strongly associatied with high delinquency rates.
11. See for example studies by Palmer (1973), Driver (1961), Svalastoga (1956), Wolfgang (1958) among others.

12. See in particular Wolfgang's study (1958), the studies by Curtis (1975a and 1975b) as well as the staff report to the US National Commission on the Causes and Prevention of Violence.
13. See my paper, note 3 above.
14. See *The Criminal Law in Canadian Society*, a Government of Canada publication.
15. See a report on the meeting published in *Liaison* magazine , April 1985.
16. See note 15 above.
17. See note 15 above.
18. See National Association of Victims Support Schemes, Fourth Annual Report 1983–1984.
19. See my paper on the visible and hidden dangers of victim movements (1986).
20. See Garofalo's paper on lifestyles and victimization (1986).

REFERENCES

Amir, M. (1967). Victim-precipitated forcible rape. *Journal of Criminal Law and Criminology* LVIII, No. 4, pp. 493–502.
Anttila, I. (1974). Victimology – a new territory in criminology. In *Scandinavian Studies in Criminology*, 5, pp. 7–10, Universitets Forlaget: Oslo.
Aromaa, K. (1974). Our violence. In *Scandinavian Studies in Criminology*, 5, pp. 35–46, Universitets Forlaget: Oslo.
Aromaa, K. (1974). Victimization to violence: a Gallup survey. *International Journal of Criminology and Penology*, 2.
Biles, D. and Braithwaite, J. (1979). On being unemployed and being a victim of crime. *Australian Journal of Social Issues*, 14, No. 3, 192–200.
Braithwaite, J. and Biles, D. (1984). Victims and offenders: the Australian experience. In *Victimization and Fear of Crime: World Perspectives* (R. Block, ed.), pp. 3–10, US Dept. of Justice (NCJ-93872): Washington, DC.
Brantingham, P.J. and Brantingham, P.L. (1984). *Patterns in Crime*. Macmillan: London.
Canada (1982). *The Criminal Law in Canadian Society*. Canadian Government: Ottowa.
Canada (1983). Victims of crime. *Canadian Urban Victimization Survey Bulletin*, No. 1. Ministry of the Solicitor General: Ottawa.
Canada (1984a). Reported and unreported crime. *Canadian Urban Victimization Survey Bulletin*, No. 2. Ministry of the Solicitor General: Ottawa.
Canada (1984b). Crime prevention: awareness and practice. *Canadian Urban Victimization Survey Bulletin*, No. 3. Ministry of the Solicitor General: Ottawa.
Canada (1985a). Female victims of crime. *Canadian Urban Victimization Survey Bulletin*, No. 4. Ministry of the Solicitor General: Ottawa.
Canada (1985b). Cost of crime to victims. *Canadian Urban Victimization Survey Bulletin*, No. 5. Ministry of the Solicitor General: Ottawa.

54   *Critical Views on Victimology and Victim Policy*

Canada (1985c). Criminal victimization of elderly Canadians. *Canadian Urban Victimization Survey Bulletin*, No. 6. Ministry of the Solicitor General: Ottawa.

Canada (1985d). Justice for all. *Liaison*, 11, pp. 12–18.

Canada, Statistics Canada (1981). *Homicide Statistics* – Catalogue 85–209 Annual. Minister of Supply and Services: Ottawa.

Canadian Federal-Provincial Task Force on Justice for Victims of Crime (1983). *Report*. Ministry of Supply and Services: Ottawa.

Chappell, D. (1973). Evaluating the effectiveness of programs to compensate victims of crime. Paper presented to the 1st International Symposium on Victimology (Jerusalem).

Clarke, R.V. (1981). The prospects of controlling crime. *Home Office Research Unit Research Bulletin*, No. 12. pp. 12–19. HMSO: London.

Congalton, A.A. and Najman, J.M. (1974). *Who are the Victims?* New South Wales Bureau of Crime Statistics and Research: Sydney.

Cressey, R.D. (1985). Research Implications of Conflicting Conceptions of Victimology. In *Victimology: International Action and Study of Victims* (Z.P. Separovic, ed.), pp. 43–54, University of Zagreb: Zagreb.

Curtis, L. (1975a). *Criminal Violence: National patterns and behavior*. D.C. Heath and Co.: Lexington, Mass.

Curtis, L. (1975b). *Violence, race, and culture*. D.C. Heath and Co.: Lexington, Mass.

De Quincey, Th. (1827). *De l'assassinat considéré comme un des beaux-arts*. Gallimard, 1963: Paris.

Driver, E. (1961). Interaction and criminal homicide in India. *Social Forces*, 40, pp. 15e–158.

Elias, R. (1983). *Victims of the system*. Transaction Books: New Brunswick, N.J.

Elias, R. (1986). Community control, criminal justice and victim services. In *From Crime Policy to Victim Policy* (E.A. Fattah, ed.), Macmillan: London.

Fattah, E.A. (1967). La victimologie: Qu'est-elle, et quelle est son avenir? *Revue Internationale de Criminologie et de Police Technique*, XXI, Nos 2 and 3, pp. 113–124, 193–202.

Fattah, E.A. (1971). *La Victime est-elle coupable?* Presses de l'Université de Montréal: Montréal.

Fattah, E.A. (1973). Le rôle de la victime dans le passage à l'acte. *Revue Internationale de Criminologie et de Police Technique*, 26, No. 2, pp. 173–88.

Fattah, E.A. (1976). The use of the victim as an agent of self-legitimization. *Victimology: An International Journal*, 1, pp. 19–53.

Fattah, E.A. (1979). Some recent theoretical developments in victimology. *Victimology*, 4, No. 2, pp. 198–213.

Fattah, E.A. (1981). La victimologie: entre les critques épistemologiques et les attaques idéologiques. *Déviance et Société*, V, No. 1, pp. 71–92.

Fattah, E.A. (1982). Les enquêtes de victimisation: leur contribution et leurs limitations. *Déviance et Sociéte*, V, No. 4, pp. 423–40.

Fattah, E.A. (1986). On some visible and hidden dangers of victim movements. In *From crime policy to victim policy* (E.A. Fattah, ed.). Macmillan: London.

Fattah, E.A. and Raic, A. (1970) L'alcool en tant que facteur victimogène. *Toxicomanies*, **3**, pp. 143–73.

Garofalo, J. (1986). Lifestyles and victimization; an update. In *From crime policy to victim policy* (E.A. Fattah, ed.), Macmillan: London.

Gibran, K. (1921). *Le prophète*. Casterman: Paris.

Gottfredson, M.R. (1984). *Victims of Crime: the dimensions of risk*. Home Office Research Studies Report No. 81, HMSO: London.

Hentig, von H. (1940/41). Remarks on the interaction of perpetrator and victim. *Journal of Criminal Law and Criminology*, **31**, No. 3, 303–09.

Hentig, von H. (1948). *The Criminal and His Victim*. Yale University Press: New Haven, Conn.

Hindelang, M.J., Gottfredson, M.R. and Garofalo, J. (1978). *Victims of Personal Crime: An Empirical Foundation for a Theory of Personal Victimization*. Ballinger: Cambridge, Mass.

Hochstedler, E. (1981). *Crime against the elderly in 26 cities*. US Dept. of Justice, Bureau of Justice Statistics: Washington, DC.

Hough, M. and Mayhew, P. (1985). *Taking Account of Crime: Key Findings from the 1984 British Crime Survey*. Home Office Research and Planning Unit Report No. 85, HMSO: London.

Huxley, A. (1967). *Point Counter Point*. Plon: Paris.

Johnson, J. *et al.* (1973). The recidivist victim: a descriptive study. *Criminal Justice Monographs*, No. 4 (1). Sam Houston State University: Huntsville, Tex.

Lind, B.B. (1970). A Study of injured victims of violence in Oslo, Norway. (Manuscript).

Mayhew, P. *et al.* (1976). *Crime as Opportunity*. Home Office Research Studies, No. 34, HMSO: London.

National Association of Victims Support Schemes (1984). *Fourth Annual Criminologica* V, pp. 11–106.

Normandeau, A. (1972). Violence and Robbery. *Acta Criminologica* V, 11–106.

Padowetz, M. (1954). *Der Heiratsschwindel*. Springer Verlag: Vienna.

Palmer, S. (1973). Characteristics of homicide and suicide victims in 40 non-literate societies. *Sociological Abstracts*, 311.

Reiss, Al. Jr. (1981). Foreword: Towards a revitalization of theory and research on victimization by crime. *The Journal of Criminal Law and Criminology*, **72**, No. 2, Summer, pp. 704–10.

Rock, P. (1986). Society's attitude to the victim. In *From Crime Policy to Victim Policy* (E.A. Fattah, ed.). Macmillan: London.

Sade, de, Marquis (1957). *The Bedroom Philosophers*. Olympia Press: Paris.

Savitz, L, Lalli, M. and Rosen, L. (1977). *City Life and Delinquency – Victimization, Fear of Crime, And Gang Membership*, US Government Printing Office: Washington, DC.

Shapland, J. (1984). The criminal justice system and compensation. *British Journal of Criminology*, **24**, pp. 131–49.

Shapland, J. (1986). Victims and the criminal justice system. In *From Crime Policy to Victim Policy* (E.A. Fattah, ed.), Macmillan: London.

Singer, S.I. (1981a). Homogeneous victim-offender populations: a review and some research implications, *Journal of Criminal Law and Criminology*, **72**, No. 2, pp. 779–88.

Singer, S. (1981b). *Victims in a Subculture of Crime: An Analysis of the Social and Criminal Backgrounds of Surveyed Victims in the Birth Cohort Follow-up*. (Unpublished dissertation, University of Pennsylvania, Dept. of Sociology).

Skogan, W.G. (1981). Assessing the behavioral context of victimization. *Journal of Criminal Law and Criminology*, **72**, No. 2 pp. 727–42.

Sparks, R., Genn, H.G. and Dodd, D.J. (1977). *Surveying Victims*. John Wiley: Toronto.

Svalastoga, K. (1956). Homicide and social contact in Denmark. *American Journal of Sociology*, **62**, pp. 37–41.

US Department of Justice (1978). *A Partnership for Crime Control*. Bureau of Justice Statistics, Government Printing Office: Washington DC.

US Department of Justice (1981). *Victims of Crime*. Bureau of Justice Statistics, Government Printing Office: Washington DC.

US Department of Justice (1985). *The Risk of Violent Crime*. Bureau of Justice Statistics, Government Printing Office: Washington DC.

Walmsley, R. (1986). *Personal Violence*. Home Office Research and Planning Unit Report No. 89, HMSO: London.

Werfel, F. (1920). *Nicht der Mörder, der Ermordete ist Schuldig*. Kurt Wolff Verlag: Munich.

Wertham, F. (1949). *The Show of Violence*. Doubleday: New York.

Wikström, P-O, H. (1985). *Everyday Violence in Contemporary Sweden: Situational and Ecological Aspects*. The National Council for Crime Prevention: Stockholm.

Wilson, P.R. and Brown, J. (1973). *Crime and the Community*. University of Queensland Press: Brisbane.

Wolfgang, M.E. (1958). *Patterns in Criminal Homicide*. University of Pennsylvania Press: Philadelphia.

2 Research Implications of Conflicting Conceptions of Victimology
Donald R. Cressey

The Greek 'o' and 'l-o-g-y' in victimology suggest a special branch of science. In turn, the implied scientific character of victimology suggests a focus on problems that are researchable by empirical methods. It seems timely, at the fifth international gathering of persons concerned about victims of various kinds, to examine this and alternative conceptions of victimology.

Victimology is not a scientific discipline. Neither is it an academic field (like criminology or ecology) to which scholars and scientists trained in various disciplines make theoretical and research contributions. It is, instead, a non-academic programme under which a hodgepodge of ideas, interests, ideologies and research methods have been rather arbitrarily grouped. Indeed, it is possible that the originator of the word 'victimology', Beniamin Mendelsohn, invented the term not because either a scientific discipline or a scientific orientation was present or anticipated, but because 'victimology' was easy to say.* As I have elsewhere noted, the word rolls trippingly off the tongue, even as it obscures conflicting concerns for victims, only some of which are scientific.[1]

More specifically, victimology is characterized by a clash between two equally desirable orientations to human suffering – the humanistic and the scientific. This conflict is unseen by some victimologists and rarely mentioned by others. Nevertheless, it seems to interfere with both the humanitarian and the scientific efforts on behalf of victims. The humanists' work tends to be deprecated because it is considered propagandistic rather than scientific, and the scientists' work tends to be deprecated because it is not sufficiently oriented to social action. Each set of victimologists probably would be better off if it divorced the other and formed alliances outside the shadow of the victimology umbrella.

I shall return to discussion of these two general positions as I take note of several overlapping but nevertheless different kinds of special

interests within victimology. After briefly characterizing each of
them, I will identify vast differences in orientations to empirical
research.

HUMAN DESTRUCTION

One set of generalists in victimology might be called 'indignant
anti-destructionists'. They tend to define and identify as victims all
individuals and groups whose rights as humans have been violated.
Some of these humanists are bent on publicizing the fact that persons
are unjustly and inhumanely victimized by those who officially implement destructive government policies. Thus, persons who have committed no crimes but who are nevertheless punished or otherwise
deprived of life, liberty or the pursuit of happiness by state officials
are victims. Holocaust victims have received the most attention.[2]
War victims and political prisoners resemble them in kind, but not in
degree, of victimization.

Anti-destructionists also try to publicize the plight of persons victimized by people administering unofficial destructive policies of government agencies, including corrupt police officers and members of
military death squads.

Finally, anti-destructionists identify and denounce persons who
control destructive non-governmental machines or organizations. Of
concern here are victims of unsafe working conditions, victims of
environmental pollution, third-world victims of multinational corporations, and even automobile accident victims. As indicated, the
concept of human rights cannot be separated from the anti-destruc-
tionist conception of victimology.

INSTITUTIONAL EXPLOITATION

Humanists also comprise a second but overlapping set of victimologists. Members of this set are interested in identifying and then
reducing the tragedy of persons who suffer from either deliberate or
unplanned injustices by leaders of the five basic social institutions –
economics, politics, education, religion and family. Included are
victims of economic exploitation, of restricted political suffrage, of
educational discrimination, of religious persecution, and of 'family'
crimes such as child or spouse abuse. In all cases, minority-group

members are being victimized by a group which dominates them by manipulation of discourses about 'peoplehood' in such a way that the minority-group members appear to be something less than human. Slaves are dominated in this way by masters; blacks, Jews, women and other minority groups by majority groups; third-world citizens by officials of powerful nations; even the poor by the rich. Not long ago, all children constituted a minority group of this kind. In recent times, girls and women have increasingly been recognized as victims of institutional exploitation and discrimination.

CRUEL AND UNUSUAL PUNISHMENT

Closely related to victimologists' concern for minimizing inhumane destruction and exploitation is their concern for documenting and denouncing punishment, or some kinds of punishment, of convicted criminals. Oddly enough, this concern is rarely mentioned at victimology conferences. Perhaps the pitting of victims' rights against criminals' rights, to be discussed later, has made it easy to neglect the fact that some convicted criminals are victims of governmental destructive policies too. Still, most criminologists who walk in the footsteps of Sellin and Sutherland deplore the victimization of criminals as much as they deplore other kinds of victimization. Some, like Marvin Wolfgang, have helped humanistically inclined lawyers show in court that particularly destructive punishments must be abandoned because they are cruel and unusual. The issue may be illustrated by calling attention to the strange words appearing on a plaque erected in the memory of John Augustus, the father of probation for criminals.

Between 1841 and 1858. Augustus bailed, provided financial assistance and gave personal help to some 2,000 Boston criminals. Then he persuaded Massachusetts officials to take over the system he had invented for mitigating criminals' punishments and, at the same time, for helping the criminals. Probation, as it came to be known, sprang from this Massachusetts programme. Augustus lived in a house which was and is a historical monument because it sheltered colonial rebels during the opening skirmish of the American Revolution in 1775, long before Augustus was born. Today, tourists visiting Lexington Green, near Boston, can read plaques honoring men who fell in the Revolution but, significantly enough for victimologists, they also can read a plaque honoring John Augustus. The plaque attached to the front of the colonial house occupied by Augustus identifies him as 'A friend of the poor victims of the law.'

We can only speculate about what the author of the inscription had in mind. Conceivably, this person saw Augustus as a friend of criminals who were victims of the law because they were officially being subjected to cruel and unusual punishment. Such punishment is forbidden by the Eighth Amendment (1791) to the Constitution of the United States and, thus, is illegal. Over the years, this Constitutional prohibition (and similar prohibitions in the constitutions of all but three of the 50 states) has been the stimulus for assertions that certain punishments are cruel and unusual and that, therefore, any criminal receiving one of them – including excessive fines and excessive terms of deprivation of liberty – is a victim of the government imposing them.[3] The memorial to Augustus makes sense in this context.

ENSLAVEMENT OF CRIMINALS

The memorial to Augustus is also understandable in another context, one that is equally relevant to the concerns and interests of victimologists. Ownership of slaves was still legal during Augustus' active years, and humanitarians then, as now, viewed slaves as victims of their masters. The Thirteenth Amendment became part of the United States Constitution in 1865. This Amendment is widely presumed to have freed American slaves, but it did not do so. It reads as follows: 'Neither slavery nor involuntary servitude, *except as a punishment for crime whereof the party shall have been duly convicted*, shall exist within the United States, or any place subject to their jurisdiction.' (Italics added.) I do not know whether the memorial to Augustus was written before or after the Thirteenth Amendment was proposed, debated and adopted. It really does not matter, for in either case it is conceivable that the person who wrote that Augustus was 'A friend of the poor victims of the law' knew that enslaving criminals makes victims of them all. Certainly this enslavement is of deep concern to many contemporary victimologists.

FEAR OF CRIME AND CRIMINALS

In the United States, at least, a goodly proportion of all victimologists are political activists and social workers whose primary interest in victimology is in obtaining justice for persons who have been directly injured – physically, economically or psychologically – by street criminals. We shall see that special sympathy is extended to people maimed by robbers, to people whose loved ones have been murdered, and to the victims of rapists.

A related, but different, concern of the political activists among American victimologists is for *indirect victims* of street crime and street criminals. These are the thousands of ordinary citizens who every day are injured psychologically and politically by their fear that they will be injured physically by street criminals. This concern is immensely popular among political conservatives. It grew out of indignation regarding what is widely perceived as a tendency of criminal justice administrators to protect criminals' rights while ignoring those of non-criminal citizens. The rise of such indignation in my own country probably indexes a rise of this brand of victimology in other nations.

Relevant to victimology was the fact that ordinary citizens were increasingly perceived as victims of high rates of street crime even if they were not personally attacked, robbed or otherwise damaged. Widespread fear of crime was thus taken to be evidence of widespread victimization.[4] Soon, proponents of this perception made crime victims of us all and then offered us policies for our protection. For example, on the questionable ground that non-criminals' rights are protected as criminals' rights to due process are infringed, President Reagan's Task Force on Victims of Crime recommended abolition of the 'exclusionary rule', a judicial instrument which renders inadmissible in criminal trials any evidence gathered illegally. Further, on the questionable ground that the numbers of both indirect and direct victims of crime will decrease if punishment of criminals is increased, the Task Force recommended that prison terms be lengthened, that parole be abolished, that judicial discretion in sentencing be severely limited, and that, generally, a 'get tough' policy toward street criminals be developed.[5]

Earlier, other proponents of the law-enforcement model of criminal justice had persuaded state legislators to substitute mandatory sentences for indeterminate ones, to require commitment of more and more persons to overcrowded state prisons and county jails, to require increases in the terms of persons sentenced to these institutions, to require deletion of rehabilitation programmes from prisons, and (in some states) to re-introduce capital punishment.[6] An Assistant Attorney General of the United States has summarized this recent history as follows:

The American criminal justice system was designed to be the fairest in history, but during recent decades it lost the delicate balance that was its hallmark. The system has always depended on the cooperation of victims to report crimes and testify in court; yet it has accorded victims none of the protections or rights guaranteed to defendants.

With the growth of the victim/assistance movement, the administration of justice has begun to move back into balance. During the past ten years, many states have developed innovative and effective legislative measures to prevent victimization, to increase the apprehension of criminals and improve their prosecution, and to provide protection for victims . . . By legislatively providing victims certain basic rights and protection, we guarantee them equitable treatment within the system and increase their willingness to cooperate with it.[7]

In the Unites States, there is no doubt that, for some crimes, victimization by the fear of victimization has for some years exceeded victimization in the form of personal losses.[8] For example, over a decade ago Susan Griffin maintained that all women are crime victims because ' . . . rape and fear of rape are a daily part of every woman's consciousness.'[9] She went on to point out that 'The fear of rape keeps women off the streets at night. Keeps women passive and modest for fear they be thought provocative,'[10] A recent mail survey of Seattle, Washington, residents documented these assertions by showing that fear of rape is high among women of all age groups, ranging from 6.98 for young women to 4.89 for elderly women (0 = not afraid at all; 10 = 'very afraid'). Further, women aged 19–35 fear rape more than any other offence (including assault, robbery and murder), but the fear evoked by rape is due in part to fear of other offences that are associated with rape.[11]

A recent Associated Press dispatch illustrates how fear of murder victimizes citizens as surely as does murder itself.[12]

The ensuing reduction in the crime rate, the argument, continues, will result in a decrease in the fear of crime and, thus, in the amount of victimization. Unstated is the argument that deterrence and incapacitation measures give middle- and upper-class persons protection from 'them' – street criminals of lower-class status.[13]

This argument is much older than victimology. Proposals for increasing the peace of mind of middle- and upper-class persons by punishing working-class criminals so severely that their fellow working-class citizens will be afraid to commit crime go back to Beccaria and Bentham. Such a proposal was the intellectual ground for establishing the first police departments, and for years police officers were in fact working-class guards employed by wealthy people to help deter other working-class persons from crime. It was not until well into the twentieth century, when police were charged with controlling the new middle- and upper-class automobile drivers, that police were viewed as law-enforcement officers. The upshot of this charge was, as I have elsewhere shown, a heretofore unheard of conflict between police on the one hand and middle- and upper-class citizens on the other.[14] Even today, the middle-class automobile driver stopped by a police officer for a traffic violation is likely to view himself as a 'poor victim of the law' and therefore to express a belief that police resources are being wasted on catching errant motorists rather than being wisely deployed in reducing the level of victimization from 'real crime'.

Nowadays, some black residents of America's metropolitan slums claim that they are victims of too many police, hired by white, middle-class and upper-class citizens to repress them, as in the olden days. Still, surveys suggest that poor people fear crime more than do others, and for good reasons. Therefore, other ghetto residents, or the same residents at different times, ask for more police officers, claiming to be three-times victimized – first by the politicians who refuse to give poor neighbourhoods the police they need for protection from victimization by criminals, next by the fear generated by the ensuing high rates of crime in these neighbourhoods, and then by the direct hurt experienced when the crimes actually are committed. They insist that they are short-changed in the area of criminal justice administration just as they are short-changed with reference to quality of schools, fire protection, street cleaning, garbage collection, parks, recreational programmes, and most other public services. A generation ago, the California Supreme Court held that poor people are victims of educational discrimination because schools are financed by local economies which, naturally, are poor in poverty-stricken communities and robust in wealthy communities.[15] It is only a matter of time until a court holds, similarly, that local financing of police departments and other criminal justice agencies also makes victims of the poor.

DIRECT VICTIMS OF CRIME

As noted earlier, many victimologists are trying to obtain help for persons who have been directly injured by street criminals. Recognizing that 'victims of crime often suffer considerable financial harm, including property damage or loss, high medical bills and lost wages', the federal government and most of the state legislatures in America have enacted laws designed to reimburse victims – especially people maimed by robbers, people whose loved ones have been murdered, and women who have been raped – for at least some of their crime-related losses.[16] Also, courts have been authorized to order criminals to make restitution payments to their victims. Victimologists devise and administer such programmes. They also construct and administer privately and publicly funded rape crisis centres and similar refuges for abused wives and children. President Reagan's Task Force on Victims of Crime recommended that more programmes of this kind be instituted, and that existing ones be better financed. So far as I know, there are no compensation programmes for victims of white-collar crime.

It is not clear that victim compensation programmes actually assist the victims they are designed to help, that they make victims more cooperative with the prosecution, as they were designed to do, or that they in other ways increase public support for the criminal justice system, also as they were designed to do.[17] Indeed, Robert Elias' study of victim compensation programmes in New York and New Jersey led him to suggest that such programmes actually alienate victims from the criminal justice system. In these states, as in other American states with compensation programmes, payments are limited to victims of violent crimes. The New Jersey law holds that victims have a right to payment for injuries arising from the state's failure to protect its citizens from criminals; the New York law, on the other hand, treats compensation as a form of welfare, requiring victims to prove poverty before they will be paid. Despite this difference, Elias found that in both states about 60 per cent of all claims for compensation are rejected. Moreover, most victims who receive payment are dissatisfied with the amount as well as with the procedural process – awards regularly take eighteen months to two years in New York and even longer in New Jersey. For these reasons, victims who apply for compensation are more hostile to the state than those who do not.[18]

VICTIM SURVEYS

Until about twenty years ago, most of what was known about differences in the crime rates of various societies was based on police summaries of the numbers of crimes reported and the numbers of arrests made. Knowledge about the distribution of crime (by age, sex, race, social class, and so on) in these societies was based on similar summaries.

These summaries are now obsolete. They were first supplemented by surveys in which samples of various populations, especially populations of juveniles, were asked to recount their own crimes in 'self-report' studies. Then Peter H. Rossi, who at the time was Director of the University of Chicago's National Opinion Research Center and a part-time consultant to the United States President's Commission on Law Enforcement and Administration of Justice, hit on the idea of measuring crime rates by asking people to recall and report instances in which they had been victims of crime. Two limited surveys of this kind were conducted for the Commission by Albert Biderman and Albert Reiss. Then a national sample was surveyed for the Commission by the National Opinion Research Center, under the direction of Philip Ennis.[19] Ennis's report on the national survey became a pattern-setting document. Following its publication in 1967, similar victim surveys were conducted in many nations and in many local communities within nations. Since 1972, the United States Bureau of the Census has conducted an ongoing nationwide survey to measure personal and household victimization. At six-month intervals, interviews are conducted with all occupants aged 12 and older of about 60,000 households (about 128,000 persons). The results of these surveys are published in two forms. One is 'victimization rates', which shows the number of criminal victimizations for various major offences per 1,000 population and per 1,000 households. The other is 'households touched by crime', which indicates the percentage of all households in which a member was victimized by crime at any time during the year.[20]

Most of those who have interpreted and analysed the results of these surveys have focused on criminals, not victims. In other words, crime victims have been viewed as sources of information about crime rates. For this reason, the nationwide surveys in the United States are titled National Crime Surveys, not victimization surveys. They have changed people's perceptions of crime rates by showing, for example, that the number of crime victimizations in the population exceeds by a factor of three to five in some crime categories the number of crimes reported by local police.

DIFFERENTIAL VICTIMIZATION

Despite their emphasis on crime and criminals, victim surveys led inexorably to observations about the characteristics of crime victims. For example, the first National Crime Survey showed that males were more likely than females to be victims of robbery, aggravated assault and personal larceny without direct contact, but that females were more likely than males to be victims of personal larceny involving direct contact.[21] Now, victimologists are more systematically using National Crime Survey data to make observations about differential vulnerability to crime.

So far as theory is concerned, the primary concern is with determining the relative contributions of victims and others to the victims' victimization. This endeavour was long ago initiated by Marvin Wolfgang in his studies of 'victim precipitated homicide'.[22] Victimization studies based on this concern were recently stimulated by Patrick Langan and Christopher Innes, of the Bureau of Justice Statistics, who invented a new statistical measure, the Crime Risk Index.[23] These men reasoned that general data about victims had to be refined if they were to be of significant help to victimologists bent on understanding differential victimization. For example, it is not enough to know that, of the different age groups in the population of the United States, the young are most likely to be victims of violent crime. Victimologists want to know the percentages of various categories of young people and of other people who are victimized each year. The Crime Risk Index makes these calculations possible.

By using their Crime Risk Index, Langan and Innes showed that in the United States in 1982 the risk of violent victimization for each of the three youngest age groups (ages 12–15, 16–19, and 20–24) was greater than that for any of the three oldest age groups (ages 35–49, 50–64, and 65 and older). They found the same thing for each of the four major race and sex divisions of the population – white males, white females, black males, and black females. 'For each of these divisions', they concluded, 'the differences in likelihood of violent crime victimization were particularly great between those 16–19 years old and those 65 and older.'[24]

An additional refinement also is helpful. During the ages when risks are highest (16 to 24), nearly equal percentages of black males and white males were victims of violent crime. Nevertheless, the nature of their victimizations differed. Black males aged 16–24 were more likely than their white male counterparts to be robbed; white males aged 16–24 were more likely than their black male counterparts to be assaulted.[25]

Victimologists have mostly not yet produced a literature on the 'why's' of differential victimization. It has been established that crime rates and, thus, victimization rates are high when lifestyle provides for strangers.[26] Yet no one knows what proportion of, say, white male victims or of black female victims 'precipitate' their victimization in the way Wolfgang's homicide subjects precipitated their own deaths. To sociologists, however, it seems likely that such precipitation, no matter what its extent, is secondary to structural victimization. Values of variables such as education, income, wealth, gender, ethnicity, age, have long been known to be associated with high rates of street crime. It is a worthy hypothesis, at least, that crime victimization also correlates strongly with variations in the same variables, though not necessarily to the same degree. For example, the age of victims of street crime seems to be lower than the age of street criminals. Similarly, the sex ratio in the rates of street crime seems to be lower than the sex ratio in the rates of street crime victimization.

Social, economic and political conditions determine the ecological niches in which people live. They also determine both the crime rates and the crime victimization rates of these niches. Most of the poor people living in America's central cities, for example, do not merely suffer from a *lack* of resources and power. As the Norwegian anthropologist Vigdis Christie has shown, they also are weighed down with an overabundance of unwanted things.[27] Among these are the behaviour patterns which produce high crime rates. The unwanted things also include, concordantly, the high crime rates which produce high rates of crime victimization. From these observations, it must necessarily be concluded that the concerns of criminology and the concerns of crime victimology are inexorably entwined.

Some differences in the theory which can logically be used in these two multi-disciplinary enterprises are apparent, however. I long ago noted the scientific advantage of criminological theory aimed at simultaneously explaining individual criminal conduct and the epidemiology of crime.[28] It makes little sense to focus completely on only one or the other of these, for a high rate of true crime is necessarily but a summary statement about the frequency with which individual crimes were committed. However, it does not seem reasonable to ask researchers to analyse individual victimization processes as well as the epidemiology of victimization. This because the process of becoming an individual victim is very different from the process of becoming an individual criminal.

After almost a century of empirical research, it is now obvious to most criminologists that criminality is not 'in' people's biological or psychological make-ups. The fact is that criminality is owned by groups, not individuals, as pioneers such as Henri Joly demonstrated almost a century ago.[29] But persuading even criminologists, let alone laymen and policy-makers, that this fact is indeed a fact has not come easily. Even today, the futile search for biological and psychic traits believed to be responsible for criminality continues. Moreover, hedonistic psychology continues to underlie both the criminal law and economists' explanations of criminality, despite the fact that it has long been abandoned by psychologists. If this experience is not to be repeated in victimology, questionable psychiatric and biological research seeking particular traits or characters among victims of street crime must be discouraged and empirical social psychological research on interactions between criminals and victims, of the sort identified by Luckenbill, encouraged.[30]

RESEARCH IMPLICATIONS

My list of eight overlapping interests of victimologists is not definitive. I selected and described the eight as a way of dramatizing the fact that victimology is but an umbrella programme for a host of concerns for different aspects of unfair human suffering. Among them, only the last four have an empirical research orientation. The other four interests – in human destruction, in institutional injustice, in cruel and unusual punishment of criminals, and in enslavement of criminals – stress the importance of appreciating the fact that certain categories of people are being victimized, the importance of convincing others of this fact and, finally, the importance of reducing the level of victimization. Because social problems are '*the activities of individuals or groups making assertions of grievances and claims with respect to some putative conditions*',[31] all four of the listed interests in victimology actually are interests in establishing a condition as a social problem rather than with studying that condition scientifically.

For example, the humanists I have called 'indignant anti-destructionists' are trying to get widespread audiences to understand that various categories of people are indeed victims of destructive policies and programmes. Doing this is to claim that a new or an undesirable but heretofore unnoticed state of affairs should be a social problem, complete with government programmes to help eradicate it.[32] Similarly, assertions that some criminals are victims of governments imposing cruel and unusual punishments are designed to obtain public recognition of this fact, thus creating a social problem. Persons who point out that American prisoners, at least, are in fact enslaved are trying to do the same thing, as are persons who identify and publicize instance after instance of institutional injustice. The intellectual work of all four kinds of humanists requires scholarship but not empirical research.

Now consider victimologists representing the other four designated interests in the plight of victims – those concerned with citizens who are victims because they fear crime and criminals, those who would offer more aid to direct victims of crime, those who estimate crime rates by determining rates of victimization, and those intrigued by differential victimization. The very existence of each of these four groups depends, or ought to depend, on the results of empirical research. For example, many of the 'law and order' victimologists who want to get tough on crime in order to reduce the level of crime victimization in a society are ideologists rather than scientists. Nevertheless, in the last analysis the neo-conservatives and others who champion stronger deterrence and incapacitation programmes as means of reducing the fear of crime also champion research designed to determine whether these programmes actually do reduce crime and, in turn, the fear of crime. In other words, deciding just how much official terror the citizenry must suffer if the majority is to be free of its fear of crime is an empirical question.

Helping direct victims of crime is more social work than science. No empirical research is needed to support the humanitarian custom of giving aid to the injured, including the direct victims of crime. In the end, however, specific programmes are justified only if they work, and determining whether a programme works requires empirical data. Indeed, 'evaluation research' is now considered a necessary element in every sound social work programme and, for that matter, in every programme involving expenditure of public funds. Robert Elias' recent research on compensation for crime victims, cited earlier, demonstrates why such empirical research is essential to programmes designed to help crime victims.

Consider, finally, victim surveys and studies of differential victimization. These, by definition, are exercises in empirical research. Victim surveys, as such, actually reflect concern for determining true crime rates rather than for the plight of crime victims. Nevertheless, as we have seen, the data gathered in such research enterprises are the same data used in studies of differential crime victimization and, thus, in studies of the relative contributions of victims and others to the victims' victimization. Researchers concerned with differential vulnerability to crime tend to identify themselves as criminologists rather than as victimologists.

CONCLUSION

Clearly, not all of the conceptions of victimology have a research emphasis. Accordingly, they conflict with the scientific one. Facing this fact will, I am convinced, advance the causes of all who are interested in identifying, or publicizing, or helping, or analysing the condition of one or another of widely differing sets of victims. As I said in an address to the Third International Symposium on Victimology in 1979. 'Our ability to "feel free" in matters of defining victimology will doom us to lack of progress as an academic discipline, as has been true of criminology.'[33] This doomsday view stems from my conviction that the current arrangement inadvertently but nevertheless inexorably pits victimologists against each other because they have competing interests.

One way to mitigate the clash between the humanistic and scientific conceptions of victimology is to encourage one and all to understand that victimology is a scientific research enterprise and that a society of victimologists is a society of researchers. This would leave humanists out in the cold, but they could readily find warmth in association with human rights groups and, for those engaged in practice, with social workers. Most criminal justice reformers do not consider themselves criminologists and are not so defined by persons whose work is included under the rubric 'criminology'. Further, practitioners such as judges, prosecutors, defence attorneys, and criminal justice administrators rarely think of themselves as criminologists and are rarely considered criminologists. The reason is this: criminology is, by and large, an empirical research enterprise, and they are not researchers. There is no logical reason why victimology could not also be such an enterprise.

Alternatively, victimology could be allowed to fade away. If this course were taken, humanistic victimologists could be encouraged to ally themselves with other champions of human rights, and scientific victimologists could be encouraged to ally themselves with the social scientists who call themselves criminologists. Indeed, if the concern of victimology were restricted to the victims of crime, as Mendelsohn recommended and many after him have recommended, there would be no compelling reason why it would be separated out from criminology, as Mendelsohn also recommended.[34]

NOTES AND REFERENCES

* Those who attribute the term 'victimology' to Mendelsohn are usually unaware that its first appearance was in Westham's book *The Show of Violence*, in Chapter 1 [Editor's note].
1. Donald R. Cressey, 'Democracy and the Third International Symposium on Victimology', chapter in Hans Joachim Schneider (ed.), *The Victim in International Perspective*, Berlin: Walter de Gruyer, 1982, pp. 503–4.
2. See the papers published in Schneider, op. cit.
3. See Sol Rubin, *Law of Criminal Correction*, 2nd edn, St. Paul, Minn.: West, 1973, pp. 417–49.
4. Herbert L. Packer, 'Two models of the criminal process', *University of Pennsylvania Law Review*, 118:1–68, 1964. See also idem, *The Limits of the Criminal Sanction*, Stanford, Calif.: Stanford University Press, 1968.
5. President's Task Force on Victims of Crime, *Final Report*, Washington, DC: US Superintendent of Documents, December, 1982.
6. Melossi has shown that such programmes of punishment become popular during periods of economic depression. He attributes their increased popularity to changes in the political discourses which arise during the early stages of economic depressions. These discourses, in turn, stem from fear of crime and criminals, even though crime rates do not increase significantly during periods of downturn in the business cycle. Dario Melossi, 'Punishment and social action: changing vocabularies of punitive motive with a political business cycle', *Current Perspectives in Sociological Theory*, 6:169–97, 1985 (Scott McNall, ed.).
7. Lois Haight Herrington, 'Foreword' to Paul L. Woodward and John R. Anderson, *Victim Witness Legislation: An Overview*, Washington, DC: US Department of Justice, Bureau of Justice Statistics (NCJ-94365), July, 1984, p. iii. This publication provides an overview of all the American legislation dealing with victims of criminals.
8. Michael J. Hindelang, Michael R. Gottfredson, and James Garofalo, *Victims of Personal Crime: An Empirical Foundation for a Theory of Personal Victimization*, Cambridge, Mass.: Ballinger, 1978; Wesley G.

Skogan and Michael G. Maxfield, *Coping with Crime: Individual and Neighborhood Differences*, Beverly Hills, Calif.: Sage, 1981.
9. Susan Griffin, 'Rape: the all American crime', *Ramparts*, 10: 26–36, at p. 27.
10. Ibid., p. 35.
11. Mark Warr, 'Fear of rape among urban women', *Social Problems*, 32:238–50, February, 1985.
12. *Santa Barbara News-Press*, July 9, 1985.
13. In some of the American states, including California, the 'law and order', 'get tough on crime', legislation I mentioned earlier was packaged in a single bill titled 'The Victims' Bill of Rights'.
14. Donald R. Cressey, 'Law, order and the motorist', chapter in Roger Hood (ed.), *Crime, Criminology and Public Policy: Essays in Honour of Sir Leon Radzinowicz*, London: Heinemann, pp. 213–34, 1974.
15. *Serrano v. Priest*, 5 Cal. 3d 584, 487 P. 2d 124 (1971).
16. Woodward and Anderson, op. cit., p. 5.
17. Daniel Glaser, 'Review of *Victims of the System: Crime Victims and Compensation in American Politics and Criminal Justice*, by Robert Elias', *Contemporary Sociology*, 14:334–5, 1985.
18. Robert Elias, *Victims of the System: Crime Victims and Compensation in American Politics and Criminal Justice*, New Brunswick, NJ: Transaction Books, 1983, p. 151.
19. Wesley G. Skogan, 'Foreword' to Wesley G. Skogan (ed.), *Sample Surveys of the Victims of Crime*, Cambridge, Mass.: Ballinger, 1976, pp. xvii–xviii.
20. Patrick A. Langan and Christopher A. Innes, *The Risk of Violent Crime*, Special Report of the Bureau of Justice Statistics, US Department of Justice, May, 1985, pp. 1–2.
21. Richard W. Dodge, Harold Lentzer, and Frederick Shenk, 'Crime in the United States: A Report on the National Crime Survey', Chapter 1 in Wesley G. Skogan (ed.), op. cit., p. 5.
22. Marvin E. Wolfgang, 'Victim-precipitated criminal homicide', *Journal of Criminal Law and Criminology*, 48:1–11, 1957.
23. Langan and Innes, op. cit., pp. 1–2, 5.
24. Ibid., p. 4.
25. Ibid.
26. See Sarah Ben-David, 'Rapist–victim interaction during rape', chapter in Schneider, op. cit., pp. 237–46; and Michael J. Hindelang, 'Victimization surveying: theory and research', ibid., pp. 151–65.
27. Vigdis Christie, 'Poverty, social contact, and social class', *Acta Sociologica*, 19:375–86, 1976.
28. Donald R. Cressey, 'Epidemiology and individual conduct: a case from criminology', *Pacific Sociological Review*, 3:37–58, Fall, 1960.
29. Henri Joly, *La France Criminelle*, Paris: Serf, 1889, pp. 45–6.
30. David F. Luckenbill, 'Criminal homicide as a situated transaction', *Social Problems*, 25:176–86, 1977; 'Generating compliance: the case of robbery', *Urban Life*, 10:25–46, 1981; and 'Compliance under threat of severe punishment', *Social Forces*, 60:811–25, 1982.
31. Malcolm Spector and John I. Kitsuse, *Constructing Social Problems*,

Menlo Park, Calif.: Cummings, p. 75. The italics are in the original.
32. Steve Woolgar and Dorothy Pawluch, 'Ontological gerrymandering: the anatomy of social problems explanations', *Social Problems*, 32:214–27, February, 1985.
33. Cressey, 'Democracy and The Third International Symposium on Victimology', op. cit.
34. Beniamin Mendelsohn, 'The victimology', *Etudes Internationales de Psycho-Sociologie Criminelle*, July–September, 1969, pp. 25–6. Cited by Stephen Schafer, *Introduction to Criminology*, Reston, Va.: Reston Publishing Co., 1976, p. 144.

3 Which Victim Movement?

The Politics of Victim Policy
Robert Elias

It is time to recognize the larger contours and consequences of developments political scientists have long studied as fragments . . . Laws and official actions that reassure or threaten without much warrant . . . are doubtless conceived . . . as discrete events; but when, taken together, they reach a critical mass of complementary programs, they become an essential part of a new political pattern . . . that converts liberal and radical watchwords of the past into conservative bastions of the future.

Murray Edelman

What would we say about a movement that apparently forgot to invite most of its professed beneficiaries? What if we discovered, for example, in the victims 'movement' that victims were, politically, all dressed up, but had no place to go? What kind of movement would it be? Would it really be any movement at all?

Reviewing recent victim policy makes these questions all too appropriate. The movement to redress the victim's plight has been much bally-hooed, but we must consider more closely what the movement and its resulting policies represent politically and what they actually achieve. Other than discussing relatively trivial legislative 'debates', the victim movement has been presented mostly as if it had no politics at all. Instead, we should examine the movement's political evolution, particularly in the 'Age of Reagan', which has set the context for victim policy. We'll emphasize 'legislative' policy: What changes have occurred, what new directions have emerged, and what's been the effect of the politics of the 1980s and of the victim movement in particular? Indeed, *which* movement has been receiving such great attention, and what political pattern does it reflect?

RECENT LEGISLATIVE POLICY

> If we take the justice out of the criminal justice system we leave
> behind a system that serves only the criminal.
>
> President's Task Force on Victims of Crime (1982)

The victim movement as legislative policy emerged in 1965 in California with the nation's first victim-compensation programme. In the next decade and a half, national and state legislation steadily increased. Yet, the legislative movement for victims was most successful in the 1980s, which saw a tremendous outpouring of initiatives. Mostly, we're concerned here with US state and national laws, but international legislation has also emerged during this period, casting the movement in a different light.

State legislation

Most legislative activity has occurred in the states, providing victim services, changing the criminal process, emphasizing special groups, establishing victim rights, and dealing more harshly with offenders.[1]

Victim services
These programmes emphasize financial aid, logistical support and personal treatment. Every state has laws bolstering the judiciary's common-law power to order restitution in money payments, transferred property or work. Half the states mandate restitution for many crimes unless the judge explains in writing why it is not to be imposed. Most states have authorized witness fees, some have raised their fee levels, and one pays lost wages. Thirty-five states reimburse rape victims for medical exams.

All but six states have compensation programmes. Most impose eligibility rules, and pay for such losses as medical costs, psychological counselling, lost wages/support, funeral costs, and emergency awards, due to violent crime. Some impose a hardship test, allow pain and suffering awards, and provide some property coverage. A few states support local, non-profit victims groups, compensate parents of missing children and dependents of firefighters and police officers, and pay child care or for lost homes.

All but two states have funded domestic violence services (for safe refuge, and educational, training, housing and emergency medical,

76   *Critical Views on Victimology and Victim Policy*

legal and psychological support). Half the states fund sexual assault programmes for psychological and medical needs. Most states stress the victim's role in court: thirty-four have created local victim/witness services to help victims exercise their rights, get timely information, and participate. A few states have special advocates programmes.

Criminal process

All states have laws to help the criminal process better serve victim needs, if not rights. All but two states allow a victim impact statement, an 'objective' account (for the pre-sentence report) of the injuries the offender caused, prepared by a probation officer, a victim advocate, or victims themselves. Thirty-five states allow a victim statement of opinion (oral or written) about the appropriate sentence. Many states have extended victim participation into other stages of the process, such as plea bargaining and parole hearings, and in the discharge, dispositional, mitigation, supervised or early release hearings.

Most states require victims to receive certain kinds of information about services, their court case and their apparent offenders. Laws require police officers, hospital or compensation officials to inform them about compensation programmes, and prosecutors to inform them about witness fees. Other statutes require that victims be given notice of scheduled court proceedings, usually upon request, cancelled hearing dates, pre-trial release, bail, plea agreements, sentencing, final disposition, parole hearings, pardons, work release, prisoner release and escapes.

Fifteen states allow victims in the courtroom (waiving sequestration rules) at the judge's discretion, and one state makes court attendance a victim right. Eighteen states mandate speedy trials, although with no set time limits. Some states ban excessive cross-examination of victims and reduced plea bargaining (or increase victim influence over the outcome).

All but four states protect against intimidation and retaliation, by toughening criminal penalties, specifying kinds of proscribed harassment, and allowing 'protective orders'. Several states have legislated against the long-term confiscation of recovered property, requiring officials to promptly examine its usefulness as evidence, and allowing photographic substitutes. Other laws help victims by explaining to employers the importance of court appearances. Some states even make it a misdemeanour for an employer to discharge an employee who misses work to attend court.

Victims have been given privacy protections, such as for their psychological treatments after victimization. Twenty-two states protect victims' names and addresses, but only for sexual assault victims in some states. Twenty-three states protect child identities. Five have blanket protections for counsellor–client confidentiality. Twenty provide it for sexual assault counselling, and twenty-four have it for domestic violence counselling. Yet some oppose privacy, claiming it impedes press freedom, public records access, maximum information and victim assistance.

Some states have changed statutory wording (such as rape law reforms that reduce victims' burden of proof), broaden the proscribed conduct, use non-gender specific language, and recognize degrees of force. Other laws define new crimes, purportedly to better protect victims, such as against disclosing domestic violence shelter locations. Finally, 17 states require training on victim issues for judges, prosecutors and police officers.

Special victims
Most states have passed laws for special victim groups. Some emphasize child victims. All but nine try to make child testimony less traumatic, permitting a videotaped statement either alone (unsworn interrogatory) or under oath and cross-examination (deposition), or live testimony through closed-circuit television. Forty states have legislation about missing children, often creating clearing houses to help find them. Over half the states have amended child competency or hearsay admissibility rules, required child guardians, or extended the statute of limitations for child offences. Somewhat fewer states require speedy trials or protect child privacy during prosecution.

Twenty-four states allow background checks of child workers, including access to criminal records. Nineteen states require everyone, and all states at least require professionals (such as licensed teachers, medical staff and child-care workers), to report suspected child abuse, backed by civil damages or even criminal penalties. Some states have extended their adult bill of rights to children; 12 have a children's bill of rights, requiring a guardian to tell the court the child's capacities, the trial's likely impact, when to use videotapes, and to help with emotional problems and court proceedings. Children are sometimes given easier access to compensation, and are exempted from testimony corroboration or grand juries.

Similar protections, such as services and shelters, have emerged for battered women. Better record-keeping, like monthly police reports, are required to track abuse patterns. Other laws provide protective orders, assign possession of the residence, get the defendant to pay support, and set custody and visitation rights. Thirty states authorize warrantless arrests for misdemeanour assaults; ten require it upon probable cause.

Sexual assault victims also receive special attention, with laws for services, such as hotlines and counselling, crime prevention and prosecution, and medical attention. At least one state requires sexual assault victims be given information about AIDS. And changes have been made to reduce the victimization caused by traditional rape legislation.

Elderly victims have elicited laws allowing the victim's age to be used in determining sentences, producing tougher penalties and probation denial. Some states criminalize the abuse or neglect of the elderly. Many states require elderly-abuse reporting, especially by professionals, with 25 states protecting all vulnerable adults and 22 protecting older adults over a certain age. Some states mandate ombudsmen, speedy trials, abuser registries, hotlines, food, clothing, shelter, medical care and other social services.

Other special victim groups have been added. Over 400 new laws related to drunk driving victims have emerged in recent years. Thirty-five states cover these victims for compensation, and all but one state has raised its drinking age to 21. 'Dram shop' liability (for those serving intoxicated drivers) has been imposed by statute or case law in 42 states. Also, hate-violence victims have received some attention. Eighteen states criminalize acts infringing civil rights based on race, colour, creed, religion, national origin or sex; only one protects sexual orientation. Thirty states criminalize the desecration of religious property, and 22 ban the disruption of religious gatherings, and inappropriate hoods or masks. Forty-three states ban violence due to racial or religious hatred.

Victim rights

Victim legislation has been increasingly packaged as statutory or constitutional rights. Since 1980, when the first victim Bill of Rights was passed, 44 states have added similar laws, including the right to information, protection, transportation, property return, waiting areas in courtrooms, input, notification, employer and creditor intercession, speedy disposition, and court attendance. Most have passed formal bills of rights, but five states have packaged existing legislation and four have passed legislative resolutions.

As statutory rights with no real remedies for non-enforcement, some wonder whether these bills really provide rights. Some states encourage enforcement through an ombudsman or grievance procedure, yet officials are immunized against monetary damages for non-implementation. A few states have adopted constitutional amendments to reinforce their bill of rights. They elevate statutory rights to constitutional rights; specify rights to dignity, respect, sensitivity, restitution, compensation and to influence sentencing and be informed and present in the criminal process.

Offender rights
By implication, some victim protections affect offender rights. Some initiatives specify that victim rights shall not erode defendant's rights, yet lack specific provisions for doing so. Indirectly, offender rights may be affected by victim participation in plea bargaining, sentencing, and parole decisions.

Directly, offender rights are curbed by 'notoriety for profits' laws, which confiscate profits generated when offenders sell their crime story, and domestic violence laws, which allow warrantless arrests. Restitution is now an enforceable civil judgment, and offenders are often banned from being considered crime victims themselves. Laws have weakened evidence rules for convicting defendants, eliminated the insanity plea (sometimes for 'guilty but mentally ill' laws imposing prison preceded by a mental institution), and toughened (through 'sentencing enhancement') criminal penalties (such as by distinguishing felonies and 'serious' felonies).

Courts have reduced the exclusionary rule's curb on illegally seized evidence, and legislation has done likewise. Many states have challenged the bail system by allowing preventive detention that jails suspects even if they meet normal bail-release standards. Only 'tort reform', which limits corporate liability for victimization, provides laws helping offenders, although obviously not those stressed by standard law enforcement.

Funding
Victim programmes have been funded less and less through general revenues: only 16 states now do so. Some alternative sources are earmarked to fund particular programmes, such as marriage licence fees for domestic violence shelters; other sources are distributed more evenly.

Some resources come from offenders as a fixed or variable assessment for each crime, a criminal fine surcharge, a driver's licence reinstatement fee, literary profits from crime stories, forfeited crime assets, recovered racketeering damages, and wages earned in prison, on work release or while on parole. Other funds come from bail forfeitures or bondsman taxes, and from levies such as marriage, divorce, birth and death surcharges, alcohol taxes, income tax check-offs, and court filing fees. Funding also comes from the national government in block grants and from the Victims of Crime Act.

Pending proposals
Much more legislation awaits enactment, such as proposals to reduce victim cross-examination, eliminate plea bargaining and the exclusionary rule, substitute affidavits for victim testimony, tighten bail requirements, require 'truth in sentencing' standards from judges, and to add constitutional amendments. In areas such as drunk driving, there's a campaign for increasing compensation, revoking driver's licences upon arrest, confiscating licence plates, incarcerating repeat offenders, issuing colour-coded driver's licences, and passing 'open container' laws. Legislation may also begin addressing some neglected groups, such as rural or arson victims and victimized members of deviant groups.

National legislation

National legislation reflects the same concerns found in the states; indeed, it stimulated many state laws. Yet Congress has also passed its own laws that affect victims both directly and indirectly.[2]

Direct legislation
Although not actually law, the heyday of victim policy began in 1981 with the Reagan administration's declaration of the National Victim Rights Week. In 1982, it established the President's Task Force on Victims of Crime, which soon provided a long list of recommendations, many of which have now been enacted or are being actively pursued.

In 1982, Congress passed the Federal Victim & Witness Protection Act (VWPA) to promote victims in the criminal process, address their needs, and provide model legislation for the states. It required victim impact statements, sanctioned (by criminal penalties and protection orders) victim and witness intimidation, mandated restitution (or written justification why not), and tightened bail standards. It required the attorney general to set national guidelines for treating victims fairly in the criminal process, including services, notification, scheduling, consultation, accommodations, property return, employer notification, law-enforcement training, victim assistance and crime-story profits. The guidelines came out in 1983, but carefully noted that they were not enforceable as rights.

In 1984, Congress passed the Victims of Crime Act (VOCA) to provide direct national resources, through the Crime Victims Fund, to help finance state compensation programmes, and public and private victim/witness assistance agencies. The Fund had a cap of $100 million each year, to be gotten entirely from criminal fines, penalty fees, forfeited bail bonds, and literary profits, and not from 'innocent' taxpayers. The first VOCA funds were spent in 1986, with a fund-limit increase to $110 million. In 1988, a new VOCA made a few changes, such as directing states not to exclude drunk driving or domestic violence victims, increasing the fund limit to $125 and then to $150 million and raising minimum-assistance grants per state.

Indirect legislation
Some statutes have affected victims indirectly in omnibus programmes, providing additional funding and easier procedures, or imposing tougher offender treatment. Before the 1980s, some aid came indirectly from agencies like the Law Enforcement Assistance Administration (LEAA), the Department of Health, Education and Welfare (HEW), and the National Institute of Mental Health (NIMH), and from federal crime legislation. The first general, federal aid from indirect sources in the 1980s came in the Justice Assistance Act of 1984, which provided block grants to states for improvements such as victim/witness assistance plans. That same year, Congress passed Acts on Bail and Sentencing Reform, which tightened laws against defendants to help victims, and urged states to do the same. The bail law allowed preventive detention, stiffened standards, and pushed the victim's role in bail decisions. The sentencing law restricted parole, limited judicial discretion and mandated 'truth in sentencing'.

In 1987, Congress passed the Criminal Fines Improvement Act, which was to track down past offenders and upgrade fines collection, partly to increase Crime Victim Fund resources. In 1988, the new Justice Assistance Act made programmes aiding child, spouse and elderly victims eligible for new block-grant funding, provided some anti-drug financing, and authorized funds to drug crime victims to help law enforcement.

Special victims
Since the 1970s, special victim groups have also been stressed on the national level. Child abuse laws began in 1974 with the Child Abuse Prevention & Treatment Act (CAPTA), which created the National Center for Child Abuse & Neglect (NCCAN) and funded public child-protection agencies, private treatment centres, and inter-agency cooperation projects. NCCAN helped stimulate child legislation in almost every state; in 1978, it began its first purported prevention programme. In 1982, Congress passed the Missing Children's Act to address an apparent wave of child abductions. In the early 1980s, NCCAN's funding was slashed, but it was renewed again by 1985. In 1984, the original law was revised, emphasizing state treatment, identification, and prevention programmes. In 1985, Social Services Block Grant Act money went to training child-care service providers against child abuse, and for health and protection for the next two years. In 1986, CAPTA first received VOCA money under the Children's Justice & Assistance Act, but those funds were cut significantly a year later.

Sexual assault laws emerged indirectly in the 1970s. The NIMH created the National Center for the Prevention & Control of Rape (NCPCR) and the Rape Prevention & Control Advisory Committee in 1976 to provide services, information, training, conferences and technical aid, but no money for direct services. The LEAA funded some services but with non-federal resources, and almost never any feminist programmes. LEAA programmes emphasized victim cooperation and crime control, and its Stop Rape Crisis Center focused more on offenders than victims. In 1980, some aid came from the Rape Services Support Bill of the Mental Health Systems Act, but by 1981 that funding was cut, NCPCR was gutted, LEAA was dismantled, and rape centres abandoned the feminist model and dwindled dramatically. From 1981 to 1987, rape centre funding came from the Preventive Health & Health Services Block Grant of the Public Services Health Act, but by 1985 NCPCR had died.

Spouse abuse initiatives began in 1977 with LEAA's Family Violence Program, which helped begin in 1978 the National Coalition Against Domestic Violence, although it was reluctant to accept LEAA money and its abuse model. In 1980, HEW began an Office on Domestic Violence, but it died in 1981, which was also the last year for funding from CETA, ACTION and HUD programmes for battered women's shelters, programmes which the Reagan administration mostly abandoned. In 1984, the Attorney General's Task

Force on Family Violence guidelines were released, and the Family Violence Prevention & Services Act funded prevention and other assistance, augmented later by VOCA funds.

Elderly victim protections began in the 1970s in LEAA and the Administration on Aging, focusing on security and education, not on direct aid. The Safe Streets Act of 1975 and the Community Crime Prevention Program of 1976 required states and then localities to propose new legislation for the elderly. In 1977, the National Elderly Victimization Prevention & Assistance Program emerged. By the mid-1980s, programmes for the elderly still qualified for some general funds, but most had been completely cut several years earlier.

Other special victims have taken their place. Drunk driving victims have been championed in Washington and given prime attention in the 1988 VOCA. Terrorist and torture victims have received some consideration. The Iranian hostage episode produced the Hostage Relief Act of 1980 and tax exclusions for government hostage victims. In 1986, the Omnibus Security & Antiterrorism Act provided monetary and non-monetary aid for terrorist victims. In 1987, the Torture Victim Protection Act provided alien victims judicial relief in US courts for past torture victimization.

Federalism
Federal districts and territories have passed some laws, but far fewer that most states. The Virgin Islands has victim compensation, and Puerto Rico has used some VOCA funding. The District of Columbia has laws for rape examinations, victim compensation, marital rape, hate violence, vulnerable adults, child-abuse reporting, protection orders, restitution, victim privacy and sexual assault finding, and has proposed a victim bill of rights.

Following the new federalism of the 1980s, national policy has emphasized decentralized victim programmes at more local levels. Little has been carried out by national programmes, which have instead provided guidelines, funding and requirements for local practice, such as the priority for such groups as children, the elderly and sexual assault and domestic violence victims. National laws purportedly let the states set their own standards, yet many programmes impose federal requirements anyway. VOCA funding for compensation has forced states to expand their medical coverage, maximum awards and non-resident eligibility and to reduce minimum awards or deductibles and limits on family violence and drunk-driving claimants.

Pending proposals

National initiatives have been numerous. The President's Task Force on Victims of Crime made 69 recommendations alone; others appear in the Attorney General's reports on victim assistance and family violence, in funding legislation, in annual reports to Congress, and piecemeal through other means.

The national proposals now pending include victim access to parole hearings, family violence statutes, privacy provisions, 'dram shop' laws, sentencing, and bail and hearsay evidence reform. Most controversial are calls for preventive detention, more prisons and capital punishment; limiting judicial sentencing discretion; admitting juvenile records in adult trials: an amendment to the US Constitution; and eliminating parole, plea bargaining and the exclusionary rule.

International legislation

National and state laws are not the only ones that may affect US victims. International or regional initiatives have addressed criminal victimization. The United Nations has passed such legislation, partly resembling and partly diverging from US laws. International bodies have legislated even longer for victims more broadly defined.

Crime victim declarations

International and regional laws and standards have emerged since the late 1970s. The 5th UN Congress on the Prevention of Crime & Treatment of Offenders (PCTO) stressed victimization's economic and social effects. In 1980, the 6th UN Congress on PCTO addressed crime victims more directly (Lopez-Ray, 1985). By 1983, the Council of Europe passed a Convention on the Compensation of Victims of Violent Crimes, a regional model (Willis, 1984). Crime victims were included in the model legislation of the UN Institute on the Prevention & Control of Crime, the International Law Association's Committee on International Criminal Law, and the International Association of Penal Law (Schaaf, 1986).

The UN's 6th Congress was just as concerned with victims of the abuse of power, attributing to it far greater physical, psychological and financial harm than common crime, and calling for global action (United Nation's Secretariat, 1980). The 7th Session of the UN Committee on Crime Prevention & Control in 1982 repeated the call. In 1985, at the 7th UN Congress on PCTO, acting on the World

Society of Victimology's draft, the Declaration of Basic Principles of Justice for Victims of Crime & Abuse of Power was formally adopted and then ratified by the UN General Assembly (Lamborn, 1987a).

While a few nations, like the United States, tried to limit the declaration to only victims in existing national criminal laws, almost all nations wanted (and got) broader definitions, encompassing political victimization (such as apartheid and disappearances) and economic victimization (such as by multinational corporations and national policy). The declaration covered both victim groups, but provided more specific standards for crime victims, such as access to justice, fair treatment, restitution, compensation and services. It invoked international law to reinforce its protections, urged strong legislation against abuses of power, and called for global cooperation to prevent both kinds of victimization (Lamborn, 1987a).

Human rights declarations
The declaration and the preceding deliberations did more than consider different groups of victims simultaneously. It acknowledged relationships not widely accepted in the US victim movement, recognizing that far more victimization comes from governments and business institutions than from those defined as criminal under national laws, and that social victimization causes crime. The declaration was predicated on existing international criminal law and human rights covenants. The former includes at least 22 recognized crimes, incorporating international instruments condemning crimes against peace, war crimes, crimes against humanity, genocide, slavery, hijacking, hostage-taking and torture. It encompasses the 'collective victims' of crime and abuses of political and economic power, as reflected in the standards of the International Society of Criminology, the International Society of Social Defense, the UN Economic & Social Council and the International Penal & Penitentiary Foundation (Bassiouni, 1985; Cataldo, 1985).

International human rights, invoked in the declaration, encompass the UN Declaration on Human Rights, the International Covenants on Civil and Political Rights, and Economic, Social and Cultural Rights, and the many specialized UN rights covenants on women, workers, torture victims and others (Danielus, 1986). It also incorporated the human rights protections of the UN's Draft Code on Transnational Corporations (Lamborn, 1987a). It quite likely encompasses regional human rights declarations, such as from Europe and the

Americas, and even non-governmental declarations like the Algiers Universal Declaration of the Rights of Peoples (Falk, 1981) and the International Tribunal on Crimes Against Women (Russell, 1984).

Pending proposals
Passing the 1985 UN Declaration has shifted the context of victimization, at least in international discussions, toward a broader victim definition, beyond criminal victimization; it has set a precedent for incorporating victims into international law and for an expanded concept of victimization, which will likely provoke more international and regional legislation (Geis, Chappell and Agopian, 1985). It's already stimulated implementation proposals for a covenant to bind signatories (Lamborn, 1987a). The declaration may inspire national legislation, like the proposed Canadian & International Charter of Rights for Crime Victims, which calls for protection, reparation, information and treatment, as well as alternatives to the criminal process and the social system producing most injustice, conflict and victimization (Normandeau, 1983).

EVALUATING VICTIM POLICY

> The system's failure is only in the eye of the victim; for those in control, it's a roaring success!
>
> Jeffrey Reiman

We can evaluate recent victim policy through research and political analysis. What does this legislation provide? How well has it been implemented? What have been its tangible and symbolic effects? Has it helped victims? Has it eroded offender rights? What does it reflect about the victim movement? What is its political or ideological direction?

Programme implementation and impact

The legislation reviewed above shows impressive victim activity in the 1980s. No wonder the period is viewed as a boon for victims. Indeed, these laws translate into many programmes and much new financing. For example, between 1984 and 1986, nationwide victim compensation increased from $67 to $115 million (NOVA, 1988). Each year, the National Office of Crime Victims publishes an impressive list of organizations funded by VOCA money (OVC, 1988). Even some programmes cut nationally have been resumed by state and city governments (Smith and Freinkel, 1988). New funding mechanisms have emerged, and rights have expanded. Some states have been especially innovative: California and Wisconsin for their victim bill of rights, and Michigan and Florida for their constitutional amendments. Programmes are providing help, personally and in court, that would not otherwise be there.

Problems
Nevertheless, victim policy also has problems when we look at its implementation and impact. Some advocates acknowledge what's been achieved, but claim much more remains to be accomplished, and it's happening too slowly: there's not enough victim rights legislation and funding, compensation restrictions remain, and victim bill of rights needs enforcement (NOVA, 1988). Others view laws as not the most effective victim policy (since the laws are often not actually implemented), claiming the courts should lead the way (Austern, 1987). Some worry that government may have promised more than it can deliver, ignoring, for example, information costs (Krasno, 1983; Anderson and Woodard, 1985). Others lament the fragmentation promoted by the 'new federalism' (Smith and Freinkel, 1988).

More seriously, some question officials' real concern for victims, wondering why services get such short commitments, why programmes must be diluted to avoid administration vetoes, and why other programmes are abandoned before solving the problem. One comprehensive study of federal victim policies found them highly selective, underfunded, precarious, symptomatic, contradictory and manipulative (Smith and Freinkel, 1988).

The state and local level seems to fare no better. Consider the victim groups given priority in the 1980s: some states have created trust funds, protective programmes and preventive services against child abuse, but they are poorly funded. Sexual assault programmes have increased in major hospitals, but have declined in community health centres; independent centres have dropped drastically (Smith and Freinkel, 1988). Spouse abuse programmes have survived (with diversified funding strategies) and even increased a little, yet very unevenly, with a few states supporting most programmes while the remaining ones eliminate services (Smith and Freinkel, 1988).

Elderly programmes, always limited anyway to crime avoidance, almost completely stopped when federal funding ended; far fewer local services exist than a decade ago, even though neither elderly needs nor crime have been resolved (Smith and Freinkel, 1988). Restitution programmes have been undermined by increased imprisonment and mandatory sentencing. Compensation programmes have made more payments, but serve only a tiny fraction of all victims. Crime-control programmes, enforcement crackdowns, and imprisonment have increased, yet crime has not declined (Elias, 1983a, 1985b).

Administration
Problems with victim programmes may stem from more than poor resources and meagre commitments. Some obstacles may be organizational, caused by internal structural and ideological conflicts. The new federalism may be an impediment. Conflicts have arisen between traditional institutions and alternative centres, and between governmental and non-governmental agencies, as the most appropriate sites for victim assistance.

Sometimes this is a matter of control: other times, it's professional ideology. Clashes emerge over using volunteers versus professionals, over independence versus institutionalization, and over philosophies of paternalism versus self-reliance. Conflicts arise among the law enforcement, mental health, medical, social service and other perspectives found in victim programmes (Smith and Freinkel, 1988). The problems don't end here: victims have some of their worst administrative problems in the courts.

Victims in the criminal process

The victim's role in court has been much emphasized, producing many initiatives to improve treatment and participation. To implement them and help victims generally, dozens of victim/witness programmes have emerged with the services outlined above. In sheer numbers, the initiatives are a success. Victim/witness programmes have been helped, especially, by a federal funding priority given them in recent years. Many more victims now have help negotiating the criminal process and victimization's aftermath.

Misconceptions and official needs
Nevertheless, problems remain. While new initiatives, such as sexual assault laws, have redefined rape and changed evidence rules, some wonder if they've really helped most female victims in court (Beinen,

1981). Like other services, victim/witness programmes serve a relatively few victims, even though they are better funded. Even victims who have been assisted (by transportation, waiting areas and notification), much less those who are not, often get victimized again in court due primarily to apparent misconceptions about what victims need and want, and about how the courts typically work.

Policies assume that victims want to participate, that participating will satisfy their needs; that they fail to do so due to high costs, intimidation, insufficient rights and opportunities; that court personnel want this participation; and that it's necessary for effective criminal punishments. Yet these assumptions, made by victim advocates, policy-makers, victimologists and the influential President's Task Force, may be wrong. Many victims have no big desire to participate and therefore shun opportunities to do so (Forer, 1980). A victim's testifying may not be a useful, cathartic experience, as argued, since the courtroom doesn't provide an appropriate setting (Henderson, 1985). Victims do not fail to cooperate because of high costs and are not needed (or sought) in most prosecutions; indeed, they are largely shunned as outsiders. Victims may not participate partly due to unresponsive officials or because they realize it will not produce the outcomes or influence they want.

More important, victims are irrelevant as to how most cases are resolved: by plea bargaining in routinized courtroom work groups, where victims jeopardize negotiations, slow proceedings and threaten outcomes. Victim/witness programmes may help promote dissatisfaction by treating victims as prosecution witnesses, thus building false hopes (Davis, 1983; Elias, 1986). Attempts have been made to curtail bargaining, but they will fail: officials rely on it for workload efficiency and professional goals. And eliminating pleas to get harsher convictions will not likely help victims since it is not necessarily what they really want or need (Henderson, 1985).

Ignoring victim needs
Despite apparent victim concern, most officials still view crime as victimizing the state or society, not the victim. Some victim protections in court were devised for official needs and may not help victims, especially with their psychological needs. Indeed, they may be destructive and prevent victims from resolving their experience.[3] Victims can participate in sentencing, yet it may satisfy no penal rationale or victim needs.[4] Despite the many initiatives, victim frustration with the courts apparently continues (Note, 1987). Participa-

tion may not be what victims want or need; non-participation or even non-cooperation might be better (Elias, 1985c).

Rights and punishments

Victim policy often assumes defendants have too many rights, despite contrary evidence (Rudovsky, 1988). It emphasizes a contest between victim and offender rights; thus, most of the former have come at the expense of the latter (Karmen, 1984). Yet victims are poorly served by curbing defendant's rights; indeed, we're all losers by eroding even further our minimal procedural protections.

Some rights curbs are less important, such as banning literary profits from crime. Others are more serious: preventive detention, warrantless arrests, capital punishment, weakening evidence rules, and eliminating the exclusionary rule and the insanity defence. Other changes are also disturbing: mandatory and increased imprisonment, longer sentences and eliminating parole. These reforms seem to be a new dose of historically unsuccessful, get-tough policies that probably don't satisfy victim needs, including not being victimized in the first place. Unleashing the state against criminals does not empower victims to pursue their interests (Karmen, 1984). Beyond offender rights, victim policy may also infringe on the rights of child workers, the media and the public generally.

The courts have found some victim policies unacceptable, ruling victim impact statements unconstitutional in capital cases (Sharman, 1988), and the Victim & Witness Protection Act as denying defendants 5th, 7th and 14th Amendment rights. Yet other courts have disagreed, letting victim policies stand (Kahn, 1982). Those policies have helped produce, and have also resulted from, a climate that has pushed courts further toward eroding offender rights, upholding capital punishment, preventive detention and exclusionary rule limitations (Viano, 1987). The US Supreme Court has led the way, adopting a criminal review model that equates rights only with those who are clearly law-abiding, almost presuming guilt and no rights for defendants (O'Neill, 1984).

Constitutional amendments may further affect defendant's rights, providing a presumption for victim rights. They also seem poorly defined and hastily designed, have enormous yet unexamined effects on the US legal process, have uncertain means for enforcement, and create rights conflicts with no apparent resolution (Symposium, 1987; Lamborn, 1987b). They assume an adversarial process that rarely occurs and that may be ill-advised. They promote a 'rights' approach to society, pitting groups against each other in a high-stakes, zero-sum game not likely to benefit victims, even if appropriate to favour them over defendants (Viano, 1987).

Politics of victim policy and the victim movement

What political pattern does this reveal? We're concerned here not with narrow issues of how victim programmes could be better funded or managed, or how they affect particular rights for victims, offenders and others, but rather what the victim movement and policy represent as a macro-political phenomenon. Why have victim initiatives emerged as they have, and whose interests do they serve?

Who gets what?

Presumably, victims should benefit most. Yet for all the new initiatives, victims have gotten far less than promised. Rights have often been unenforced or unenforceable, participation sporadic or ill-advised, services precarious and underfunded, victim needs unsatisfied if not further jeopardized, and victimization increased, if not in court, then certainly in the streets. Given the outpouring of victim attention in recent years, how could this happen, and who benefits instead?

Offenders have gained since victim policy has not reduced crime, but such is not the case when apprehended, since their rights have deteriorated and prison sentences increased. Victim advocates, including many devoted activists, may have gained from the emerging 'victims industry', yet overall they've lost almost as badly as victims. That leaves only those holding political power who have devised contemporary victim policy: they've gained plenty.

It's hard to believe the apparent concern shown by politicians, not just because victim policy has achieved so little, but because it probably could have been predicted to do so. So why pursue such policies? Perhaps because they provide other benefits, both political and ideological.

Ideological gains

Victim initiatives seem to perpetuate biased crime definitions conveyed in legislation, enforcement patterns or the media, which limit our concept of victimization to 'street' crime, usually ignoring the much more harmful 'suite' crime, be it corporate or governmental

(Green and Berry, 1985). They further narrow those victims to whom we'll devote our attention: *not* to lower class minorities, who are among the most victimized, but rather to the elderly and victims of child, female and sexual abuse, who are not.

These victims are often treated paternalistically as helpless and frail and thus robbed of any sense of power and self-reliance (Smith and Freinkel, 1988). They are designated, although not permanently, as the 'innocent' victims we all want to protect; they may also be 'safe' victims, who can help bound the movement: an apparent exercise in social control (Marx, 1983; Elias, 1986). With offenders, it's no different. The President's Task Force narrows itself to a small array of common criminals, not producing the most harm, portraying them and their supposed rights in mythical terms, creating a biased view of crime and its sources (President's Task Force, 1982; Henderson, 1985).

Similar biases emerge in victim programmes. Consider federal victim services and the 'issue definition' process therein. The extremes of victimization are emphasized, where the most horror can be raised but the least victimization occurs. Emphasis is put on protection, services and education, but rarely on prevention; when emphasized, it's defined only in conservative terms, never examining crime's social sources and instead exhorting victims to change their behaviour. Programmes are treated as temporary, requiring annual lobbying for renewal, perhaps to avoid suspicions that the United States has fundamental social problems or needs any deep-seated 'welfare' programmes: indeed, much is made of how offenders pay entirely for VOCA, and not 'innocent' taxpayers.

As for specific programmes, spouse abuse is viewed as part of a 'cycle of family violence' in 'some' families and never as sexism in the broader society. Child 'abuse' is regarded as the problem, even though child 'neglect' is far more prevalent. Sexual abuse is viewed as a problem of lax enforcement and victim indiscretions, never as a problem of male society. The elderly are viewed as victimized mostly by crime, not by the persistent poverty they often live in. Victimization's causes, when considered at all, never include things like class inequality, American cultural violence or the bankrupt family. High-profile victims are shown apparent concern, yet it emerges more rhetorically than substantively. Worse, the few resources made available for victim services come with 'strings' that spread these ideologies far beyond Washington (Smith and Freinkel, 1988).

The elderly were star victims in the 1970s, as were their programmes. Yet by the early 1980s, they were off the victim agenda, with their needs and victimization unabated. Like a passing fad, the victim torch seems to pass to new celebrities, likewise championed without much substance. Victims of drunk drivers and abducted children are the recent focus, even though research finds these victimizations exaggerated and politically exploited, more safe yet dramatic victims whose stars will also soon fade (Ellison, 1982; Walker, 1985; Eliasoph, 1986)?[5] Is this short-term attention simply innocent politics or the management of dissent with token programmes, used manipulatively until the fervour subsides (Piven and Cloward, 1971; Smith and Freinkel, 1988)?

Co-opting and manipulating the movement

No wonder some believe the victim movement has been co-opted (Henderson, 1985; Viano, 1987; Smith and Freinkel, 1988). The victim movement may be conservative and manipulated, it may be no movement at all, and it may be many movements of unequal influence, but it's hardly the politically neutral phenomenon it's been portrayed. The movement we hear most about may not very well satisfy the definition of social movement. The label 'movement', like 'rights', is often misapplied and overused.[6] A movement is a social or political phenomenon seeking fundamental change through mostly unconventional means (Garner, 1980). Yet the victim movement we know hasn't fundamentally challenged US society in the fields of crime control strategies, social policy or otherwise.

Government has never been conceptualized as crime victims' main obstacle – offenders have; thus the frequent alliance between victim advocates and government policy-makers. If ever a movement, it ceased when it became partners with government. This would be all right if government was really committed to helping victims and willing to admit its own contribution to victimization. Since it is not, the movement may be co-opted, an important revelation since the term 'movement' has a powerful symbolic appeal, implying significant change; yet, this change may not be occurring.

Aside from labels, how did the victim 'movement' arise? It's been associated in the 1970s with liberal politics whose crime-control policies failed, thus ceding the field to conservatives who, in their law-and-order crusade, championed the victim's cause. Yet, the liberal policy of rehabilitation failed because it was never seriously pursued; anyway, it's actually a conservative policy, designed not to question the society's performance but rather to help offenders accept it. An exaggeration of liberal/conservative differences often passes as 'politics' in American society, perhaps diverting us from real politics and power. In fact, mainstream victim activity seems to be associated with conservative crime policies, even when liberals have held office.

In the 1980s, a coalition of so-called 'strange' bedfellows of liberals and conservatives has produced, with Reagan administration guidance, current victim policy. Yet this may not be strange, but rather conventional politics,[7] and no real compromise of political perspectives, but instead a reiteration of conservative policies (Henderson, 1985).[8] The 'movement' may have been co-opted by being diffused, but also by being 'used' for reforms that may have little to do with victims. Yet it allows them to be manipulated to enhance political legitimacy, government police powers, and an apparent agenda of further eroding defendants' rights: a symbolic use of politics to convert liberal rhetoric into thin air or conservative ends (Friedrichs, 1983; Edelman, 1988; Smith and Freinkel, 1988).

But it's misleading to view victim concern as a single movement; important strands exist beyond the conservatives and liberals (Elias, 1989). Some of the most useful initiatives have come from the 'feminist' victim movement, but have been undermined in the 'official' victim movement. There's also an 'international' victim movement, described above, pressing for global initiatives, and recognizing the relationships between criminal victimization and abuses of power. But Washington does not embrace that movement's broader definition of victimization[9] nor does it take seriously another victim movement: the 'human rights' movement, which considers more than merely crime victims, and whose perspectives (except for those stressing Soviet abuses) the Reagan administration has roundly condemned in favour of its international terrorism policy.[10]

In 1981, the victim movement got a national spokesman in Ronald Reagan, apparently launching the heyday of victim concern. Yet, whether measured by the victims of political or economic abuses (of human rights) at home and abroad, or the victims of an administration itself committing more crimes than any other, or the victims of government crime policies counterproductive to ending victimization by others, the Reagan years seem highly victim-conducive, if not victim-producing (Dorsen, 1984; Frappier, 1984; Kinoy, 1988). These are the abuses of power (human rights violations) the international victim movement has linked to the neglect, if not to the source, of criminal victimization. Should we trust such a government to be pursuing the best interests of the victims it has defined, or acquiesce to those it has not?

The recent NOVA Newsletter may not have exaggerated when it said that Congress, in renewing VOCA, was deciding which sectors of the victim movement it would be recognizing (Stein, 1988). We can probably predict *which* victim movements will continue to be included and which will not. US administrations, whether liberal or conservative, seem unwilling to examine crime's social sources (which a human rights analysis might reveal) and make fundamental changes to significantly reduce victimization in the first place. Doing so would be the product of a real victim movement.

An alternative politics

The manipulation of victims for political gain may not have resulted from purposeful intrigue; it may have been merely opportune to do so as the movement developed. Nor have victim advocates been ill-intentioned or powerless in helping shape victim policy. We're concerned here not with individual motives, but with institutional constraints. Yet, however we explain it, the adverse results are real enough. Is this the kind of victim movement we want?

Accepting financial aid and philosophical guidance from governments and groups concerned most with conservative crime policies risks co-optation and manipulation. Instead, we could pursue an alternative politics, building an independent domestic movement that's allied with the international movement, and practice a new victimology of human rights (Elias, 1985a).

NOTES

1. The following review of state legislation relies on National Organization of Victim Assistance (NOVA) (1988); Victims of Crime Resource Center or VCRC (1988); Anderson and Woodard (1985); Henderson (1985).
2. The following review of national legislation relies on Smith and Freinkel (1988); Henderson (1985); Office of Victim Services, or OVC (1988); Stein (1988); Trotter (1987); Murray (1987).
3. Preventive detention has been justified to make victims feel safe, yet victim fear may come less from the offender and more from the shock of victimization. Incarcerating the accused has been advocated under the untested assumption that it will satisfy the victim's desire for justice.

Speedy dispositions will resolve trials quickly, but may not resolve the victimization, probably making it worse (Henderson, 1985: 976).

4. Victim involvement will not apparently enhance *deterrence*, and *incapacitation* relies on offender traits, not those of the victim. Victims can't help *rehabilitate*, except perhaps when related to the offender, where maybe the victim should help implement, but not determine, the sentence. Victim participation for *retribution*, which relies on assessing blame, would raise as many questions about victim blameworthiness as of the offender. It also assumes that retaliation best satisfies victim anger, when forgiveness may better promote psychological healing. Plea bargaining and mandatory incarceration render victim preferences for *restitution* irrelevant or futile (Henderson, 1985: 1001–10). No wonder almost no victims use the victim impact statement right (Villmoare and Neto, 1987).

5. The apparent concern for the elderly, women and children comes from an administration that has massively cut social spending that might have spared these people victimization, both criminal and otherwise. And government policy has turned on the elderly in other ways: to shield them from financial victimization in their waning years, it's pushed 'protective' plans that seem to confiscate their resources and place them in custody (Gordon, 1986). Government has gone from viewing the elderly as victims to viewing them as a new criminal class, the same treatment earlier given women, despite contrary evidence (Cullen, Wozniak and Frank, 1985). How easy it is to manipulate groups: the elderly's main advocates promote the government's conservative, law-and-order crime policies. The government has also used ideological screens in women's programmes: Shelters and independent centres are totally out of favour, and have been defunded, at least if they promote feminist goals of self-reliance and social change (Smith and Freinkel, 1988).

6. Here, rights serve as a powerful rhetorical device to exploit public concerns about crime (Henderson, 1985: 952). See also Scheingold (1974).

7. Non-decisions, or what's kept off the agenda, are a major power source in the US system, which may routinely exclude real alternatives from policy consideration (Smith and Freinkel, 1988: 173).

8. Consider that the victim movement relies on an administration that supports (with few liberal objections) those who would force poor women to have unwanted children, to end foetus victimization, yet, once born, subject children to a lifetime of real victimization (Edelman, 1984; Kimmich, 1985); that labels as victims Nazi criminals, Salvadoran death squads and Nicaraguan contra 'freedom fighters'; and that professes a (yet another) 'war on crime', yet dismantled enforcement mechanisms, such as the anti-trust laws, and countenanced (if not welcomed) extensive corporate victimization, both criminal and otherwise (Green and Berry, 1985; Nader, 1986).

9. The United States was almost alone among nations in rejecting at the UN the relation between criminal victimization and the victimization caused by abuses of power. Although it finally voted for a weaker version of the declaration, it's not likely to ratify it, any more than it has most UN covenants (Frappier, 1984).

10. Yet in pursuing torture and terrorism policy, it designates politically
approved victims (convenient for foreign-policy goals), ignoring most of
the rest (Chomsky, 1988).

REFERENCES

Anderson, J.R. and Woodward, P.L. (1985). Victim and witness assistance:
New state laws and the system's response. *Judicature, 68*, 221–44.
Austern, D. (1987). *The Crime Victims Book.* New York: Viking Penguin.
Bassiouni, M.C. (1985). The protection of 'collective victims' in international
law. *New York Law School Human Rights Annual 2* (Spring), 239–57.
Beinen, L. (1981). Rape III: National developments in rape reform legisla-
tion. *Women's Law Reporter, 6*, 170–89.
Chomsky, N. (1988). *The Culture of Terrorism.* Boston: South End Press.
Cullen, F.T., Wozniak, J.F. and Frank, J. (1985). The rise of the elderly
offender. *Crime & Social Justice, 23*, 151–65.
Danielus, H. (1986). The United Nations fund for torture victims. *Human
Rights Quarterly, 8* (May), 294–305.
Davis, R.C. (1983). Victim/witness noncooperation. *Journal of Criminal
Justice, 11*, 287–99.
De Cataldo Neuberger, L. (1985). An appraisal of victimological perspec-
tives in international law. *Victimology, 10*, 700–9.
Dorsen, N. (1984). *Our Endangered Rights.* New York: Pantheon.
Edelman, M. (1988). *Constructing the Political Spectacle.* Chicago: Universi-
ty of Chicago Press.
Edelman, M.R. (1984). *American Children in Poverty.* Washington, DC:
Children's Defense Fund.
Elias, R. (1983a). *Victims of the System.* New Brunswick, NJ: Transaction.
Elias, R. (1983b). The symbolic politics of victim compensation. *Victim-
ology, 8*, 103–12.
Elias, R. (1985a). Transcending our social reality of victimization: toward a
new victimology of human rights. *Victimology, 10*, 6–25.
Elias, R. (1985b). Community control, criminal justice and victim services.
In E. Fattah. (ed.), *From Crime Policy to Victim Policy* (pp. 290–316).
London: Macmillan.
Elias, R. (1985c). Victims and crime prevention: a basis for social change?
Citizen Participation, Summer, 22–8.
Elias, R. (1986). *The Politics of Victimization: Victims, Victimology & Hu-
man Rights.* New York: Oxford University Press.
Elias, R. (1990). The competing politics of victim movements. In Emilio
Viano (ed.) *Victims and Human Rights* (pp. 37–59), London: Taylor &
Francis.
Eliasoph, N. (1986). Drive-in mortality, child abuse, and the media. *Socialist
Review, 16*, 7–31.
Ellison, K. (1982). On the victims' side: a 'bill of rights' or political hype?
National Law Journal, 46 (April), 1.

98   *Critical Views on Victimology and Victim Policy*

Falk, K. (1981). *Human Rights & State Sovereignty*. New York: Holmes & Meier.

Forer, L. (1980). *Criminals and Victims*. New York: Norton.

Frappier, J. (1984). Above the law: violations of international law by the U.S. government. *Crime & Social Justice, 23*, 1–45.

Friedrichs, D. (1983). Victimology: a consideration of the radical critique. *Crime & Delinquency*, April, 283–94.

Garner, R.A. (1980). *Social Movements in America*. Chicago: Rand McNally.

Geis, G., Chappell, D. and Agopian, M.W. (1985). *Toward the alleviation of human suffering*. Rapporteurs' Report, 5th International Symposium on Victimology.

Gordon, R.M. (1986). Financial abuse of the elderly and state 'protective services'. *Crime & Social Justice, 26*, 116–34.

Green, M. and Berry, J. (1985). *The Challenge of Hidden Profits: White Collar Crime as Big Business*. New York: William Morrow.

Henderson, L.N. (1985). The wrongs of victim's rights. *Stanford Law Review, 37* (April), 937–1021.

Kahn, L.A. (1982). Constitutionality of the Victim & Witness Protection Act of 1982. *Federal Probation, 48* (December), 81–2.

Karmen, A. (1984). *Crime Victims*. Belmont, CA: Brooks/Cole.

Kimmich, M.H. (1985). *America's Children: Who Cares? Growing Needs & Declining Assistance in the Reagan Era*. Washington, DC: Urban Institute Press.

Kinoy, A. (1988). The present constitutional crisis. In J. Lobel (ed.), *A Less than Perfect Union* (pp. 32–40). New York: Monthly Review Press.

Krasno, M.R. (1983). The Victim & Witness Protection Act of 1982; does it promise more than the system can deliver? *Judicature, 66* (May), 469–71.

Lamborn, L. (1987a). The United Nations declaration on victims: incorporating 'abuse of powers'. *Rutgers Law Journal, 19*, 59–95.

Lamborn, L. (1987b). Victim participation in the criminal justice process: proposals for a constitutional amendment. *Wayne Law Review, 34* (Fall), 125–220.

Lopez-Rey, M. (1985). *A Guide to United Nations Criminal Policy*. New York: United Nations.

Marx, G.T. (1983). Social control and victimization. *Victimology, 8*, 54–79.

Murray, M.H. (1987). The torture victim protection act. *Columbia Journal of Transnational Law, 25* (Summer), 673–715.

Nader, R. (1986). The corporate drive to restrict their victims' rights. *Gonzaga Law Review, 22* (December), 15–28.

National Organization for Victim Assistance (1988). *Victim Rights & Services: A Legislative Directory*. Washington, DC: Author.

Normandeau, A. (1983). For a Canadian & international charter of rights for crime victims. *Canadian Journal of Criminology, 25* (October), 463–9.

Note (1987). Victim rights laws sometimes bring frustration, survey finds. *Criminal Justice Newsletter, 18* (December), 3–4.

Office for Victims of Crime (1988). *Report to Congress*. Washington, DC: US Government Printing Office.

O'Neill, T.P. (1984). The good, the bad, and the Burger Court: victim's rights and a new model of criminal review. *Journal of Criminal Law & Criminology, 75* (Summer), 363–87.

Piven, F.F. and Cloward, R. (1971). *Regulating the Poor.* New York: Vintage.

President's Task Force on Victims of Crime (1982). *Final Report.* Washington, DC: US Government Printing Office.

Reiman, J. (1984). *The Rich Get Richer & the Poor Get Prison.* New York: Wiley.

Rudovsky, D. (1988). Crime, law enforcement, and constitutional rights. In J. Lobel (ed.), *A Less Than Perfect Union* (pp. 361–76). New York: Monthly Review Press.

Russell, D.E.H. and Van Den Ven, N. (1984). *Crimes Against Women.* East Palo Alto, CA: Frog in the Well Press.

Schaaf, R.W. (1986). New international instruments in crime prevention and criminal justice. *International Journal of Legal Information, 14* (June–August), 176–82.

Scheingold, S. (1974). *Politics of Rights.* New Haven, CT: Yale University Press.

Sharman, J.R. (1988). Constitutional law: victim impact statements and the 8th Amendment. *Harvard Journal of Law & Public Policy, 11* (Spring), 583–93.

Smith, S.R. and Freinkel, S. (1988). *Adjusting the Balance: Federal Policy & Victim Services.* Westport, CT: Greenwood.

Stein, J. (1988). VOCA revisited, reauthorized, and revitalized. *NOVA Newsletter, 12,* 1–5.

Symposium (1987). Perspectives on proposals for a constitutional amendment providing victim participation in the criminal justice system. *Wayne Law Review, 34* (Fall), 1–220.

Trotter, K.A. (1987). Compensating victims of terrorism. *Texas International Law Journal, 22* (Spring–Summer), 383–401.

United Nations Secretariat (1980). Crime & the abuse of power: offenses & offenders beyond the reach of the law. *UN Doc. A/CONF/87/6.*

Viano, E. (1987). Victim's rights and the Constitution. *Crime & Delinquency, 33,* 438–51.

Victims of Crime Resource Center (1988). Statutes of 1988 pertaining to crime victims. Mimeo.

Villmoare, E. and Neto, V.V. (1987). Victim appearances at sentencing under California's victims' bill or rights. *Research in Brief* (August), 1–5.

Walker, S. (1985). *Sense & Nonsense About Crime.* Belmont, CA: Brooks/Cole.

Willis, B.L. (1984). State compensation of victims of violent crimes: The Council of Europe Convention of 1983. *Virginia Journal of International Law, 25* (Fall), 211–47.

4 The Wrongs of Victim's Rights

Lynne N. Henderson*

In the last few years, the issue of 'rights' for victims of crime has become influential in shaping criminal law and procedure. In 1982 alone, California voters approved a 'Victim's Bill of Rights' that made substantial changes in California law,[1] and the President's Task Force on Victims of Crime issued its final report, recommending numerous changes in the criminal justice system.[2] The influence of the victim's rights 'movement' appears to be creating a new era in American criminal law and procedure.

This article examines the impact that current victim's rights proposals and programmes will likely have both on the criminal process and on victims, and explores the rationales offered in support of these proposals. The discussion focuses on whether changes in the criminal law and criminal process are desirable for those who have already been victimized.[3] The article also makes some observations on whether these changes have any salutary effect on the goal of crime prevention. Part I examines the increasingly public structure of the criminal process and presents a brief history of the victim's rights movement. Part II proposes a theory of victimization which emphasizes its highly individual and experiential nature. Part III outlines a composite victim's rights proposal. Part IV looks at the proposed changes in the legal process bearing on the guilt stage of the trial and examines the usefulness of these changes to victims. Part V then explores whether victim participation at sentencing can be justified in terms of traditional rationales for the criminal sanction, on due process-like grounds, or on individually based, existential grounds. Finally, Part V discusses the problems created by the issue of restitution to crime victims.

* The author gives special thanks to Paul Brest and Robert Weisberg for their friendship and assistance with this article. I would also like to thank Barbara Babcock, Donald Ehrman, Larry George, Robert Gordon, and Mark Kelman for their helpful comments on earlier drafts and their suggestions of resource materials and approaches. Any errors of course remain mine. Finally, thanks are due Jim Klindt, Florida State College of Law, Class of 1986, for his research help.

I. THE ORIGINS OF VICTIM'S RIGHTS

A. The historical role of the victim in criminal law

The available historical work in the field of the criminal law reveals a steady evolution away from the 'private', or individual, sphere to the 'public' or societal one. In Europe and England after the collapse of the Roman Empire, the victim and the criminal process were intimately linked. No formal government structure existed; thus, 'criminal justice' largely depended on self-help or the help of kin.[4] The blood feud constituted the major enforcement mechanism, both in England and on the continent:[5] the victim, or his or her kin, exacted vengeance against and repayment from the perpetrator or his kin.[6] At the same time, however, a rudimentary public enforcement mechanism, 'outlawry', existed both on the continent and in England.[7]

As English society became more organized, and feudal lords began to assert dominion over others, the law of the blood feud became more refined and subordinated to 'public' interests. It became unlawful to begin a blood feud unless an effort was made to extract a sum of money from the offender.[8] At the same time that use of the blood feud was declining as the primary vehicle for enforcing criminal law, monetary compensation to victims or their kin ('bot' and 'wer'), and fines payable to the king ('wite'), developed into a complicated system of tariffs that carefully set out the value of every sort of injury imaginable.[9] This system of compensation would appear to be solicitous of a victim's right to restoration from the wrongdoer, but in practice, victims seldom received compensation.[10]

In England, as the kings gained and solidified authority, the concept of 'the king's peace' prevailed, and criminal acts were seen by the legal system as offences against the crown rather than against the individual.[11] Outlawry was transformed from a punishment to a process for compelling the attendance of the accused at trial.[12] Severe punishments, such as the taking of life and limb, were placed solely in the hands of the king and his representatives.[13] Minor crimes were punished chiefly by monetary fines instead of the wite,[14] and damages to victims or their families were determined and assessed by a tribunal rather than a system of tariffs.[15]

As early as the thirteenth century in England, the law of felony appeared to serve the feudal system and the lords far more than it did the victims.[16] The lords' consolidation of power, the greed of kings, and the need for a coherent system of laws transformed criminal law from a mixture of public and private law, to law of an exclusively public nature.[17] A similar shift from a mixed system to an exclusively public system took place on the continent.[18] As English criminal law became more public, victims lost some discretion once they initiated a prosecution,[19] but still retained an important role in the process through the unique English system of 'private' prosecution.[20] Private prosecution initially appears to demonstrate a solicitude towards victims absent in every other system,[21] but in fact, it was not very beneficial to the victim.[22] By the nineteenth century, the British system of private prosecution had little to do with concern for victims of crime.[23] In England today, serious cases are reviewed and sometimes prosecuted by the Director of Public Prosecutions, and police prosecute most of the other cases.[24] Historically then, even in England, the victim has gradually ceased to be a significant actor with a formal role in the criminal process.[25] But the fact that the victim's role in the process steadily lessened over time does not necessarily justify the lack of a formal role for victims today.

The apparent visibility of the criminal process and the unlikelihood that most victims can successfully pursue the offender through tort law[26] may be partially responsible for the current view that the victim should have a greater role in the criminal process. The following section will discuss the rise of this view in American criminal law and procedure.

B. The role of the victim in recent American criminal law

The American system of criminal law and procedure has reflected a tension between social and individual approaches to crime prevention:[27] liberals have focused on isolating and curing perceived *social* causes of crime; conservatives have concentrated on perceived *individual* wickedness as the cause of crime.[28] From the post-World War II period to the mid-1960s, liberal theories were ascendant, with respect to both the social welfare approach to crime prevention and offenders and the classic liberal ideology of protecting the individual from the overreaching power of the state.[29] Liberals emphasized the social origins of crime – poverty, alienation, lack of education, discrimination – and sought to remedy these perceived causes of crime.[30] They advocated rehabilitation, rather than punishment, of convicted criminals.[31] And they sought to protect the constitutional rights of the accused, finding a responsive majority in the United

States Supreme Court.[32] Some of the liberal experiments failed,[33] and some never had a chance of succeeding as the funds and interest that supported programmes disappeared.[34] Nevertheless, some remnants of liberal programmes remain today, including the application to the states of important provisions of the Bill of Rights by the Warren Court.[35]

Concern for victims of violent crime – at least 'innocent' victims of violent crime – was also on the liberal agenda and took the form of advocacy of 'victim's compensation' statutes in the early and mid-1960s.[36] The impulse behind the enactment of victim's compensation statutes was largely humanitarian and 'liberal': a social welfare argument pervades the victim's compensation literature of that era.[37] By the mid-1970s, many states had adopted some form of victim's compensation programme,[38] and law journals published numerous articles on the subject.[39]

Then the liberals began to lose momentum and initiative in dealing with the problem of crime. The disappearance of liberal influence has several possible and related explanations. First, the 'crime rate' kept climbing, seemingly refuting liberal theories of crime prevention.[40] Second, crime, in the American mind, was often associated with race.[41] The liberals' arguments for racial equality created a political paradox that prevented them from confronting the relationship between race and crime[42] and the ever-present national fear of interracial crime.[43] Third, the fact that many 'crime prevention' techniques historically had been used to oppress blacks and other minorities made liberals cautious: the techniques of crime control were also the techniques of oppression.[44] Finally, liberal rhetoric failed to overcome the reality and fear produced by photographs and news reports of riots, burning cities, and vicious and barbaric crimes.[45]

The decline of support for liberal approaches and the inability of liberals to solve the apparent paradoxes created by their beliefs left the crime issue to the conservatives.[46] Conservatives pointed to the failures of liberal programmes and emphasized that crime was a matter of individual choice and wickedness. They adhered to the 'crime control' model of criminal justice[47] that emphasizes 'efficiency' in the criminal process.[48] The model envisions a summary process, much like an assembly line, with reliance placed on administrative rather than judicial decision-making.[49] Central to the ideology of the crime control model are 'the presumption of guilt'[50] and the belief 'that the criminal process is a positive guarantor of social freedom.'[51] The conservatives thus complained that the courts were 'handcuffing' the police[52] and that swift and sure punishment was the only practical solution for the crime problem.[53] They also invoked the part of nineteenth century liberalism – often ignored by the post-World War II liberals – that rested on the premise that the individual is entirely rational and responsible for his or her actions.[54] Today, refusing to acknowledge the possible social causes of crime,[55] or dismissing those causes as insoluble,[56] conservatives place most of the responsibility for crime and crime control on the 'criminal justice system' and particularly on the courts.[57]

According to the conservative argument, deterrence often doesn't work,[58] rehabilitation doesn't work,[59] and retribution[60] and incapacitation[61] are the only tenable justifications for punishment of criminals. Throughout the 1970s, 'tough' sentencing laws passed legislatures with regularity.[62] Yet even with record numbers of persons in prison,[63] and later with the reappearance of the death penalty,[64] the 'crime rate' continued to increase.[65] In part, conservatives attributed this failure to control crime to the courts. Conservatives had never truly accepted the Warren Court's concern for the rights of the accused: The exclusionary rule and *Miranda* requirements particularly irritated them, because they firmly believed that these rules interfered with efficient law enforcement and crime control.[66] In their view, the courts were letting desperate criminals loose on 'legal technicalities' and preventing the police from protecting the innocent public, and therefore were to blame for the high rate of crime. Yet the Bill of Rights speaks of restraints on the state's power to act against the *individual*, and the procedural protections adopted by the Warren Court sought to remedy the imbalance of the power of the state against the individual accused of a crime. The 'discovery' of the crime victim provided an individual to substitute for the state on the side of the scales opposite the accused, thus making it appear that the balance was more 'equal'.[67]

While law enforcement officers and prosecutors have long understood the symbolic value of the victim, the politicization of the symbol is of more recent origin. The complaint of officers and prosecutors that the courts 'never think about the victim' when deciding cases in favour of defendants made 'intuitive' sense: a violent crime involves at least two persons, but the focus seemed to be only on the one least 'deserving' of attention or regard – the offender. Although for quite some time this argument had been only sporadically raised, by the middle of the 1970s different groups began to focus their attention on the victims of particular crimes. For example, the women's movement did much to emphasize the plight of rape victims in the legal process,[68] while the more recently formed group, 'Mothers Against Drunk Driving' (hereinafter referred to as MADD), brought the victims of drunk drivers to public attention.[69] The success of these groups concerned with particular crimes and crime victims served to highlight the general importance of 'victims' as an effective political symbol.[70] Conservatives thus began rhetorically to paint 'the victim' as a sympathetic figure whose rights and interests could be used to counterbalance the defendant's rights, and called for a new balance to be struck by courts and legislatures.[71]

As a result of the convergence of these factors, the subject of 'victim's rights' has received enormous political, media and legal attention.[72] Both Congress[73] and the states[74] have enacted victim's rights legislation, the President's Task Force on Victims of Crime has published its final report,[75] and groups such as MADD and 'Parents of Murdered Children' continue to receive national attention.[76] Victim's rights proponents have succeeded in inducing the adoption of preventive detention laws in at least nine states.[77] Victim's rights advocates have played a role in bringing about other changes in criminal law and procedure.[78] Partly as a result of victim's rights advocacy, the number of laws requiring mandatory restitution to victims by offenders has also increased.[79]

Most of the victim's rights activity has been far from dispassionate, and currently, the victim's rights 'movement' has a decidedly conservative bent.[80] Although 'victim's rights' may be viewed as a populist movement responding to perceived injustices in the criminal process, genuine questions about victims and victimization have become increasingly co-opted by the concerns of advocates of the 'crime control' model of criminal justice.

The phrase 'victim's rights' has been used by the conservatives to invoke two symbols that tend to overwhelm critical analysis of proposals made in the name of victims. In the criminal law context, the word 'victim' has come to mean those who are preyed upon by strangers: 'victim' suggests a non-provoking individual hit with the violence of 'street crime' by a stranger. The image created is that of an elderly person robbed of her life savings, an 'innocent bystander' injured or killed during a holdup, or a brutally ravaged rape victim. 'Victims' are not prostitutes beaten senseless by pimps or 'johns', drug addicts mugged and robbed of their fixes, gang members killed during a feud, or misdemeanants raped by cellmates. Nor does the meaning of 'victim' encompass the computer corporation whose trade secrets are stolen or the discount store that suffers petty pilfering. In short, the image of the 'victim' has become a blameless, pure stereotype, with whom all can indentify.

This image also takes two temporal forms. 'Past victims' are those who have already been victimized and who give concrete meaning to the symbol. It is the past victim who, through lurid newspaper stories, 'crime scene' shots on newscasts, and anguished statements, is drawn upon to provide the popular image of 'victim'. 'Future victims' are those necessarily unidentified persons who have not yet been mugged, robbed, assaulted, raped or burglarized, but who may become victims at some future time. Past victims may be said to represent individual and private interests, while future victims represent the public's fear of crime and its interest in crime control. Proponents of the crime control model confuse the images of past and future victims by exploiting the public's emotional identification with the anguish of past victims simultaneously with its fear of crime and victimization.[81]

'Rights' is also a powerful rhetorical device, particularly in American history and culture.[82] The term suggests both freedom from something and freedom to do something: it suggests a certain vision of independence and autonomy.[83] In the American political context, the word almost automatically raises suspicions of oppression or deprivation and has been called into service by disparate groups seeking power, entitlements, equality or liberty, often with great success. Hence, the terms 'civil rights', 'women's rights', 'gay rights', 'the right to life' and 'the right to work' pervade the current political lexicon. Similar force attaches to the concept of 'victim's rights'. The term has come to mean some undefined, yet irreducible right of crime victims that 'trumps' the rights of criminal defendants.[84] Although the rhetoric of proponents of 'victim's rights' vacillates between notions of 'past victim's rights' and 'future victim's rights' without explanation or clarity, the term's predominant meaning in the political context has become that of 'future victim's rights'.[85]

Unfortunately, the symbolic strength of the term 'victim's rights' overrides careful scrutiny: who could be anti-victim? Thus, liberals find themselves caught in yet another apparent paradox: to be solicitous of a defendant's rights is to be anti-victim.[86] As a result, 'victim's rights' has produced an emerging structure of criminal law and procedure that closely resembles the 'crime control' model so antithetical to liberal thought. Based on a simplified concept of 'victim' and an unarticulated concept of 'rights', the changes in the criminal process proposed or spawned by the victim's rights movement are the same changes that have long been advocated by conservatives.[87] Ironically, these changes may do little to help even the very narrow category of past victims who give meaning to the symbol. Moreover, the symbolic manipulation of the victim successfully avoids a more serious debate about how the criminal justice process should be structured and disguises the truly revolutionary nature of the reforms proposed. Whether the reforms have anything to do with victims, and whether they are desirable, are unanswered questions. Upon examination, many of the reforms appear to fail under either line of inquiry.

II. A THEORY OF THE IMPACT OF CORE CRIME ON VICTIMS

Before exploring what role if any a victim should play in the criminal law process, it is necessary to explore what it means to be a 'victim'. Although a subspecialty of criminology called 'victimology' has existed for approximately 35 years,[88] little information about the *experience* or psychology of crime victims is available.[89] Instead, the study of 'victimology' has focused more on sociological questions – for example, who is likely to be victimized, what is the incidence of victimization, and what are the outcomes of social services for victims. Thus, while we may *assume* many things about crime victims, few of us *know* much about the experience and its effects.

It is difficult to assign any role to victims in our criminal system without some appreciation of the experience of the victim and the psychological consequences of victimization for the individual. This part proposes a unifying theory of the individual experience of victimization as it relates to the individual[90] and discusses the psychological effect of violent crime[91] on victims as a result of the victims' sudden confrontation with the existential issues of mortality, meaning, responsibility and isolation.[92] If this theory is correct, and recent research supports many of its propositions,[93] it indicates that many current victim's rights proposals are problematic at best and may actually be pscyhologically destructive to the victim.

For many years mental health professionals assumed that psychological disturbances experienced by victims of disasters had their source, in part, in the individual's pre-existing emotional pathology.[94] But studies of prisoners of war,[95] survivors of the Holocaust,[96] and victims of 'natural' disasters[97] indicate that this assumption is inaccurate.[98] These studies of victims are particularly relevant because the recent literature on rape indicates a degree of common experience between rape victims and other disaster victims.[99] Anecdotal evidence[100] and other studies[101] also suggest that a similar community of experience exists among victims of other crimes.

A. Psychological issues raised by victimization

Sudden victimization can lead to extreme trauma.[102] Kai Erikson has defined extreme trauma as 'an assault on the person so sudden and so explosive that it smashes through one's defenses and does damage to the sensitive tissues underneath.'[103] What I term the 'core crimes' of homicide, rape, kidnapping, robbery and aggravated assault are the crimes feared most; the effects of these crimes on individuals would appear to fall within the definition of extreme trauma. Core crimes threaten our existence, either literally as in homicide, or indirectly as in assault, and remind us of the fragility of life. The intrusiveness of these crimes threatens and denies a victim's 'personhood', subjecting the victim to devastating psychological consequences. In short, these violent crimes create an 'urgent experience that propel one into a confrontation with one's existential "situation" in the world.'[104] The more extreme the experience, the more likely the resulting psychic damage.[105] The crimes of robbery, rape, kidnapping and attempted murder directly force victims to confront their own mortality, an experience that 'has the power to provide a massive shift in the way one lives in the world.'[106]

The terror of death, however, 'is of such magnitude that a considerable portion of one's life energy is consumed in the denial of death.'[107] Thus, many people engage in 'death denial' – the belief by an individual that while others can die, he or she is immune to death.[108] In the context of criminal victimization, this denial is related to the belief that although violent crime happens to others, it won't happen to oneself. Actual victimization shatters these assumptions, and the lack of control that a victim feels during an assault deprives the victim not only of his or her belief in invulnerability, but also of his or her sense of control and autonomy in the world.[109] In this way, victimization forces individuals to confront their own mortality, but because people cannot sustain the experience of pure death anxiety for long, the anxiety may be displaced, denied or repressed.[110] As a result, fear of revictimization,[111] feelings of helplessness,[112] loss of a sense of control over one's destiny and lack of security[113] become 'typical' reactions to an intrusive confrontation with death. Indeed, survivors of disasters may conclude that life owes them something,[114] or may commit suicide in response to death anxiety.[115] And victims of violent crime respond similarly.[116]

Victimization can also lead to a shift in psychological perspective from believing that one is 'at home in the world' to believing that the world is a frightening or indifferent place. This shift is closely linked to the confrontation with one's own mortality, and ultimate – and inevitable – isolation from others.[117] The experience of being a victim makes all things and all other people seem unfamiliar and frightening. This unfamiliarity creates a sense of 'dread' – and a feeling of nothingness – that is horrifying and objectively indescribable.[118] The support of friends and relatives may help to mitigate a victim's sense of dread and isolation by helping the victim begin to feel secure in the world again. But to feel at home in the world, to dispel dread, the victim may also seek to find meaning in the experience.

The question 'for what?'[119] exemplifies the search for the meaning of existence that in turn allays death anxiety: because 'death anxiety frequently masquerade[s] as meaninglessness',[120] victims will often try to come to terms with their own mortality by attempting to find meaning in their victimization or in life itself.

But non-instrumental violence is terrifying precisely because it has no apparent meaning in the ordinary sense of reason or justification. 'Why?' or 'why me?' are questions associated with meaning that victims frequently ask of themselves and others.[121] Crime victims may seek meaning to their victimization either retrospectively by blaming themselves or others,[122] or prospectively by collapsing into helplessness,[123] feeling a duty to help other victims,[124] devoting themselves to remedying an evil,[125] or seeking to live their lives more constructively.[126] But making assumptions about victims based on their initial attributions of meaning to the event is difficult, because an individual's attribution of meaning to an event may change over time:[127] a meaning that was once adequate to explain the event may be inadequate in the light of new experiences or reflection. Finding some meaning, however, is important in helping an individual understand and accept even the most extreme experiences.[128]

Taking individual responsibility for the experience may help the victim to find meaning, because responsibility, if defined as the choosing or creating of one's experiences,[129] is related to meaning and autonomy in life. Responsibility in this sense means being 'the uncontested author of an event or a thing',[130] and '[t]o be aware of responsibility is to be aware of creating one's own self, destiny, life predicament, feelings, and . . . one's own suffering.'[131] How a person perceives and defines an event, a thing, or another person, ultimately depends on his or her awareness of responsibility or authorship.[132]

Assuming responsibility for a traumatic experience is a process requiring an assertion or reassertion of control in one's life. Responsibility initially requires an individual to accept that the criminal event occurred. But a frequent first reaction to traumatic experience is a denial that the event occurred at all, in part to avoid the death anxiety produced, but also in part to avoid acknowledgment that such a horrible thing could be a part of life.[133] Yet until the victim acknowledges the actual experience as hers or his alone – that *she* was raped, that *he* was mugged – the victim is virtually powerless to be free from the rapist or the mugger,[134] or to take responsibility for, and thereby reassert control over, the event and the direction of her or his life.[135]

Unfortunately for many crime victims, American culture discourages this kind of personal responsibility and instead emphasizes another type of responsibility – 'blame' and fault finding. By blaming others, the victim escapes responsibility. By blaming the victim for his plight,[136] society further discourages the victim from taking responsibility for the event. Accordingly, the societal emphasis on innocence as a prerequisite to being a 'real' victim, taken in combination with the confusion between 'innocence' and 'responsibility',[137] make it very difficult for a victim to avoid displacing the criminal event from his or her experience. Moreover, the inability of other people, even those close to the victim, to accept the crime victim's experience can further isolate the victim from the experience, thereby blocking successful resolution of the crisis.[138]

Victims frequently encounter social isolation and an invalidation of their efforts to come to terms with their experience, while at the same time confronting the existential isolation presented by the reality of death.[139] Experiencing a violent crime – confronting one's own death – powerfully reminds the individual that he or she *is* alone. Although others may commiserate or empathize, they cannot negate the reality of the event.[140] But friends, relatives and others can help a victim to escape the dread of isolation. Simply because victims are isolated at one level does not mean that relationships with others are not fundamentally important for them. Indeed, it may be just the opposite: a sense of relatedness – of belonging to a larger community, of still *being* – may be essential to recovery.[141] As Buber observed, '[a] great relationship breaches the barriers of a lofty solitude, subdues its strict law, and throws a bridge from self-being across the abyss of dread of the universe.'[142] The inability of friends and relatives of victims to confront the issues raised by victimization – either by 'blaming the victim'[143] minimizing the event[144] or withdrawing from the victim's distress[145] – may deprive the victim of the reassurance of relationship to others. Frequently, like Job's comforters, we are not content simply to console or to provide victims with the connection to others that they need. Rather, we tell the victim what the victim should feel or think, or we blame the victim for his or her plight. In part, non-victims tend to blame victims, misunderstand the particular experience of victims, and expect victims to return to their 'old selves' quickly in order to protect themselves from perceived threats to their own sense of invulnerability.[146] Even if members of the victim's family or community are initially responsive and supportive, tolerance for a victim's feelings of loss, anger, fear or meaninglessness is likely to wane long before the victim has time to begin to integrate the experience.[147]

Answers to the questions of death, meaning, responsibility and isolation vary from individual to individual, just as behavioural and psychological manifestations of these existential issues differ from victim to victim.[148] And these questions do not follow each other in the orderly way in which this discussion has presented them. They merge, overlap and differ in saliency at particular times. The issues of victimization seldom manifest themselves clearly as 'death anxiety' or crisis of meaning: anger, fear, frustration, loss, grief, confusion and guilt are feelings that may relate to or mask these issues, and the underlying issues may take years to express or understand.

B. The implications of the theory

Common assumptions about crime victims – that they are all 'outraged' and want revenge and tougher law enforcement – underlie much of the current victim's rights rhetoric.[149] But in the light of the existing psychological evidence, these assumptions fail to address the experience and real needs of past victims. The theoretical outline just presented speaks to the experience of being a past victim; the prospect of becoming a past victim as the concern of society is evidenced by the concern for future victims. In this way, violent crime touches all of us with the reality of the unpredictable, the threat of death, the dilemma of meaning, the responsibility for choice, and the reality of isolation. To the extent that we examine these issues of our own accord – to the extent that resolution comes through more voluntary reflection and experience – the concern for future victims is very different than that for past victims. For future victims, we can seek to prevent the experience, but for past victims, the experience is already a reality. For past victims, we can only seek to avoid interfering with or denying the individual victim's efforts to resolve these questions.

While questions of existence rarely manifest themselves in a pure, abstract form, the issues are nevertheless unavoidably present for all victims at some level. Past victimization catapults individuals beyond what non-victims or future victims can know; the ontological rules change. What is 'good' for future victims – the prevention of harm, the diminution of evil – is no longer applicable to past victims, who, for at least an instant, have seen the abyss. The rape victim who becomes hysterical soon after police arrive provides an illustration of this tension: hysteria may be a necessary release of tension and an affirmation of being for someone who has just seen the prospect of non-being.[150] But in the interests of future victims – apprehension of the culprit before he creates more damage and punishment of the guilty – the police necessarily seek rationality, information and evidence.

A victim's contact with the criminal justice system may hinder him or her from coming to grips with death, meaning, responsibility and isolation in innumerable ways. The criminal justice system provides a ready set of opportunities for blame and denial, proceeds on the basis of mistaken normative assumptions about victims, and emphasizes rationality – or the appearance of it.[151] To be of value to past victims of core crimes, victim's rights proposals ideally ought to assist, rather than interfere with, the victim's resolution of the experience. The remainder of this article examines the meaning of victim's rights proposals in light of both traditional legal thinking and the existential nature of victimization. Of course, the criminal justice system cannot ultimately answer the individual's questions of death, meaning and responsibility because its focus is on the event itself; its concern is with the narrower issues of identifying the offender and determining legal responsibility. But in so far as the isolation of past victims is concerned, the criminal justice system may provide a social context in which some meaningful 'connection' for the victim exists. Whether or not 'victim's rights' provides this connection will be a central part of the remaining inquiry.

III. A COMPOSITE OF VICTIM'S RIGHTS PROPOSALS

One persistent image of the American criminal process is that it 'revictimizes' the victim. The President's Task Force *Final Report*,[152] for example, portrays the ill-treatment of crime victims in a particularly apocryphal story. The *Final Report* describes the insensitive treatment of a widowed 50-year-old rape victim by the police and hospital personnel. It then details the numerous abuses that the criminal justice system inflicted upon the victim, including an indifferent and ineffective attempt at preventing threatening phone calls to the victim by her attacker from jail, an inconvenient scheduling of line-ups, unethical activities by defence counsel, repeated failures by the prosecutor to inform the victim about her role in hearings and the trial and to promptly notify her about postponements, the emotional and financial burden of delays in the process on the victim, the enormous pressure and humiliation of testifying, and the short sentence that was eventually imposed on the rapist.[153]

The scenario presented in the *Final Report* is indeed horrifying. It is also somewhat incredible to anyone acquainted with criminal law practice, and it is insulting to judges, prosecutors, defence attorneys and law enforcement officers. It is a composite of everything that could go wrong in the process rather than a chronicle of an actual case.[154] Yet the scenario presented in the *Final Report*, and other horror stories like it, have led to numerous victim's rights proposals that purport to remedy the situation.[155] These proposals typically contain one or more of the following elements:

(a) that the suspect remain in custody after arrest;[156]
(b) that few, if any, delays exist between arrest and preliminary hearing, and between hearing and trial;[157]
(c) that plea bargaining either be eliminated or be victim-determined;[158]
(d) that there be minimal, if any, cross-examination of victims by defence counsel;[159]
(e) that exclusionary rules be abandoned;[160]
(f) that victims be allowed to participate in sentencing;[161]
(g) that victims receive full restitution.[162]

This composite portrays an 'ideal' criminal process, one that more closely resembles a model produced by crime control ideology than by supporters of a programme designed to spare victims unnecessary trauma.[163] Nevertheless, it may be that these proposals do in fact benefit past victims. The composite victim's rights proposal just presented has two components: one involves the process leading up to conviction, and the other involves the process of imposing sanctions. Part IV addresses the relationship of the pre-conviction component to the psychological effects of crime on victims; Part V makes a similar inquiry with regard to the sentencing component.

IV. PRE-CONVICTION CHANGES AND THEIR RELATIONSHIP TO THE PSYCHOLOGICAL NEEDS OF THE VICTIM

A. Denial of bail and preventive detention statutes

Although the Eighth Amendment's prohibition against excessive bail would seem to preclude pre-trial incarceration of individuals who can pay bail,[164] the Supreme Court has declined to apply the provision to the states or to address the issue of 'preventive detention' of adults.[165] 'Preventive detention' is the imprisonment of a person *before* a formal determination of criminal culpability based on an assumption that the individual is guilty, dangerous, and should be removed from society.[166] Conservatives have supported preventive detention statutes since the Nixon era, and preventive detention can be viewed as part of the conservative support of the crime control model.[167]

Although preventive detention has slowly gained acceptance in the law, first in the area of civil commitment,[168] then by means of a specific statute adopted in the District of Columbia,[169] the rate of its acceptance quickened because of the emergence of 'victim's rights'. By using both 'past victim' and 'future victim' rationales, conservatives have made substantial progress in formally legitimizing preventive detention.[170] Both rationales focus on fear: the fear experienced by the past victim that results from his victimization and the more generalized public fear of being a future victim. In response to both fears, several states have passed preventive detention statutes.[171] Congress, having already approved preventive detention in the District of Columbia, enacted a bill in 1984 that would make the nature of the charge presumptive evidence that a defendant should be detained in all federal criminal proceedings.[172]

1. The use of a 'past victim' rationale
Supporters of preventive detention have emphasized the fact that

some offenders have threatened or harassed their victims to discourage prosecution.[173] Three immediate criticisms of this rationale exist: first, because some defendants threaten victims does not necessarily justify incarcerating all defendants. Second, little reliable data on the incidence of victim harassment presently exist.[174] Finally, incarcerating the accused does nothing to prevent his friends or relatives from harassing the victim.

The most important indictment of the harassment rationale for preventive detention, however, is that it relies on a misapprehension of the fear reaction of victims. Even if the defendant is in jail, the victim may still not feel 'safe'.[175] Fear reactions to violent crime can generalize far beyond what the law can address: the fear reaction, based on existential terror of death, is very real to the victim, who is likely to be acutely sensitive to possible danger and may perceive a threat even where no threat exists. While locking up the accused may eradicate a specific fear, albeit an often rational one, it does not alleviate the larger existential fear reaction to victimization.[176] Although victim harassment cannot be ignored when it exists, it hardly serves as a justification for wholesale use of preventive detention.

The second argument offered in favour of preventive detention that uses past victims is that by permitting defendants to be released on bail, the criminal justice system leaves the victim wondering whether there is 'any justice in the world'.[177] 'Justice' in this context presumably means that the victim should be entitled to have the accused incarcerated without any formal adjudication of guilt. Such an egocentric demand might be a normal reaction for the individual, but personal frustration with the process of condemnation and punishment does not justify punishment before guilt is established: imposition of the criminal sanction is largely a public response to crime, rather than an exclusively private one.[178] Although proponents of pre-trial incarceration do not argue that pre-conviction punishment is a legitimate function of the criminal law, they assert that imprisonment prior to a guilt determination is not 'punishment'.[179] Theoretically this may be true, but practically there is little difference. Indeed, the distinction between preventive detention and punishment has become infinitesimal, because most existing preventive detention statutes authorize detention upon a presumption of guilt or prior determinations of guilt.[180]

2. The use of a 'future victim' rationale

A final rationale in support of pre-trial incarceration is that it is necessary to protect future victims. Under this 'public safety' rationale,[181] past victims are relevant to demonstrate the need for preventive detention *only* if they were victimized by a person who had been released from custody pending trial.[182]

Preventive detention denies free will or choice and rests on a deterministic, wicked person theory of crime.[183] The accused become 'criminals', and as such, they may be removed from society for society's protection. The transformation of human beings into criminals justifies incarcerating them whether or not they have formally been found guilty of an offence.[184] Moreover, if arrest is taken as sufficient evidence of guilt, the question of punishing the innocent never arises under this rationale.[185]

Preventive detention does encourage efficiency and expediency in the criminal justice system, a central goal of the crime control model. In-custody defendants are pressured, directly or indirectly, to plead guilty to the crimes with which they are charged. If they are locked up in an overcrowded, vermin-infested, stuffy, dark and dangerous jail, they may be motivated primarily by a desire for release, and will be much more amenable to a plea or a 'deal'.[186] Moreover, in-custody defendants frequently are at a disadvantage in developing factual defences, and may even be subjected to theoretically impermissible, yet all too real, pressures from law enforcement officials to confess or to provide information.[187] In contrast, a defendant released on bail may not be as eager to proceed to trial or to plead guilty.

No convincing demonstration exists that preventive detention statutes will result in victims being harassed less frequently. Moreover, although proponents of these statutes invoke the symbol of the past victim in their campaigns to get the statutes enacted, the statutes do little to assist past victims in resolving the psychological crisis of victimization. Thus, the proponents of the crime control model have exploited the past victim to further their agenda.

B. Rapid processing

A second major victim's rights proposal gives victims a 'right' to a speedy trial by giving them a right to oppose continuances.[188] Victim's rights advocates frequently blame defence lawyers for obtaining continuances that unduly prolong the agony of the crime victim by rendering it impossible for victims 'to put their experience behind them'.[189] Proponents of the crime control model view so-called stalling tactics of defence attorneys to be an overwhelming block to both efficiency and swift and sure punishment, two hallmarks of this model.

While defence abuse of continuances occurs, the development of both the prosecution and the defence in a serious case can, and does, take time.[190] Investigation, forensic tests, interviews and visits to crime scenes, among other things, are often time-consuming.[191] And in many cases, motions must be researched, prepared and argued. Although many of those accused of a crime turn out to be guilty, investigation and preparation in even the most seemingly impossible cases occasionally do demonstrate that the accused is in fact innocent.[192] Moreover, rushing to a judgment because of a presumption of guilt serves neither the victim nor society, particularly if the real culprit remains at large.[193]

Victims *are* likely to want a psychological 'resolution' of the matter, but this kind of resolution does not ultimately depend on the outcome of the criminal case. It is simplistic to assert that the rituals of condemnation will erase so profound an experience for an individual. Continuances and delays may cause a victim to relive the event, but a victim is likely to relive portions of the event whether or not there is a delay.[194] Issues raised by victimization do not resolve themselves quickly: a reintegration and understanding of such questions as mortality, meaning and responsibility take time. Therefore, delay may be of great benefit to a victim's psychological state,[195] and time is necessary to heal the psychic wounds created by victimization. Only for those victims who completely deny or repress their experience is a delay likely to be traumatizing, because in having to recover the experience, they will be without defences or understanding.[196]

Sometimes a delay enables victims to be better prepared for the evidence that will be introduced at trial. In one case, for example, a prominent athlete was savagely murdered and dumped in an abandoned house. The police found drugs and evidence of a sexual assault at the scene. Many people, including the victim's father, were unaware that the victim had used drugs, had been bisexual, and had frequented very rough homosexual bars. The horror of learning of his son's hidden life, which police believe had a role in the son's gruesome end, was as hard a blow to the father as was the loss of his only son. Many of the victim's friends were also shocked by the information. The police arrested two suspects, but a writ filed by their attorneys caused a substantial delay in the case. Nevertheless, the delay helped the victim's father and friends recover from their shock. During the delay, they had accepted the reality of the victim's flaws as well as his truly great characteristics. If the defence were to pursue 'drug-crazed homosexual panic' as the reason for the homicide, the prosecution and its witnesses would be able to withstand the accusations against the victim, and indeed, anticipate and disarm the potentially prejudicial effect of this information on the jury. It would not be easy for any of the witnesses or for the victim's father, but it would certainly be better for them than if the trial had proceeded rapidly.

Endless delays and confusion can harm victims, but rushing towards a conclusion can be equally harmful. Temporal distance from the event is important to healing, and treating the victim with respect may ultimately benefit the victim more than rapid process.

C. Restrictions on plea bargaining

Plea bargaining serves a number of pragmatic and instrumental purposes.[197] In fact, guilty pleas constitute the major proportion of convictions in the United States.[198] Plea bargaining can have a 'salutary' effect for the prosecution in some instances, as when a minor participant in a crime pleads to lesser charges and testifies against his coparticipants, or has the charges dismissed in exchange for truthful testimony against more culpable defendants.[199] It also permits a degree of flexibility in cases where the application of a rule would produce an unduly harsh result.[200]

Many crime control advocates and others view plea bargaining in its current form as a nefarious practice that routinely places muggers and rapists back on the streets to terrorize society.[201] This view of plea bargaining produced a provision in the California Victim's Bill of Rights which seeks to abolish plea bargaining in cases charging enumerated 'serious felonies' and in felony driving-under-the-influence cases.[202] California law now prohibits plea bargaining in cases that charge these crimes unless the prosecution has 'insufficient evidence', the testimony of a 'material witness cannot be obtained' or 'a reduction or dismissal would not result in a substantial change in sentence'.[203] The California law forecloses any consideration of a victim's willingness or ability to testify at trial as a justification for plea bargaining, unless the language about 'obtaining testimony' is read more broadly than are California's evidentiary provisions regarding unavailability of witnesses.[204]

One commentator supports laws like California's, asserting that because of plea bargaining, 'victims may be deprived of their opportunity to have the cathartic experience of testifying against the defendant.'[205] But is testifying against a defendant really 'cathartic'? If the term is used loosely to mean the release of tension, testifying can be viewed as 'cathartic'.[206] In strict psychoanalytic terms, however, catharsis involves the retrieval of threatening or painful early life experiences and the process of bringing those emotions into consciousness to be expressed.[207] In this term of emotionally purging the experience of victimization, testifying is not necessarily cathartic. Catharsis encompasses articulation and expression of traumatic experiences in appropriate settings. The appropriateness of the setting is essential because the process of emotionally reliving a traumatic event can be extremely painful and frightening.[208] The victim is unlikely to feel that a courtroom is the right place for this kind of emotional experience. Catharsis is also dependent on a number of variables, including an individual's readiness and ability to face the emotions raised. Catharsis is not a phenomenon that can be forced; nor is it the end of the healing process.[209]

Moreover, abolition of plea bargaining does not actually address the psychological needs of the victim. Instead, it places a priority on obtaining convictions for the offences charged, regardless of the victim's psychological state or preference.[210] To solve the problem of victim alienation associated with plea bargaining, prosecutors could simply provide more information to victims. Although the prosecutor represents the state, rather than the individual victim,[211] courtesy and common sense would seem to dictate that prosecutors treat victims with respect and explain the plea bargaining options to the extent possible. A victim who is not notified about a possible plea bargain, particularly in which the defendant pleads to a lesser charge, may view the bargain as an invalidation of his or her experience. Consultation with victims by prosecutors, and explanations of the problems of the case or the consequences of the plea bargain, would undoubtedly help clarify the situation for some victims and lead some to actively support the particular disposition. Other victims will remain unsatisfied no matter what the results.

Ironically, the Task Force's view of the value of testifying is contrary to the 'catharsis' theory suggested in support of restrictions on plea bargaining. This contrary view asserts that testifying is 'too traumatic' for the victim.[212] Victims are unlikely to consider testifying to be an enjoyable prospect. Victims who have had little or no experience with the courts or testifying cannot be expected to comprehend the process. They may be understandably frightened of seeing their assailants. They may experience a version of stage fright at the prospect of having to speak in public. They may view testifying at a public trial as yet another intrusion on their lives and privacy. Testifying need not to be an unmitigated disaster, however. Some, if not all, of the anxieties associated with testifying can be alleviated by prosecutors when they prepare their victim witnesses.[213] Such commonsense lawyering does not require fundamental changes in the criminal law or process. It simply requires an awareness on the part of prosecuting attorneys that although they and their law enforcement witnesses understand the law, the courtroom procedure and the mechanics of testifying, lay witnesses frequently are not familiar with the process.

Accordingly, an absolute restriction on the use of plea bargains eliminates consideration of the emotional needs of the individual victim altogether, and to restrict plea bargains because some victims are dissatisfied with the results seems ill-advised.

D. Abolition of the exclusionary rule

Perhaps the most cynical manipulation of victim's rights is the invocation of these 'rights' by crime control advocates as a justification for abolition of the Fourth Amendment's exclusionary rule.[214] The California 'Victim's Bill of Rights' attempted to circumvent the exclusionary rule in a section titled 'Truth in Evidence',[215] and the President's Task Force recommended abolishing the Fourth Amendment exclusionary rule altogether.[216]

The exclusionary rule as a mechanism for enforcing the Fourth Amendment's prohibition on unreasonable searches and seizures has been the subject of endless debate.[217] Liberals see the exclusionary rule as a sometimes troubling, but necessary, means of preventing Gestapo-like police tactics.[218] Conservatives see it as a counterintuitive, counterproductive rule that allows 'criminals' to go unpunished.[219] Liberals may overstate the case when they argue that the exclusionary rule is the only thing that stands between the populace and a police state and that any diminution of the rule is a step towards fascism. But the knock on the door at night is just as threatening to existence as the night-time burglar.

Whether or not the exclusionary rule is the appropriate solution to the problem of individual security against the state, it has had a salutary effect on police practices and has promoted efficiency in investigations.[220] Nevertheless, the present Supreme Court has steadily moved toward abolishing the rule. Doctrinally, the Court has narrowed the rule from a general protection against governmental intrusions to a tool for specific deterrence of particular police misconduct.[221]

The exclusionary rule has a minimal effect in the vast majority of cases: the rule affects only a very small percentage of prosecutions.[222] But opponents of the rule perceive it as interfering with effective and efficient law enforcement. They have never abandoned their efforts to abolish it and now have recharacterized their opposition to the rule as an issue of 'victim's rights'. Their assertion that 'victim's rights' compel the abolition of state and federal exclusionary rules seems *post hoc*, and the efforts to define a victim's 'right' that outweighs the constitutional right to be protected from unreasonable searches and seizures are strained. For example, the President's Task Force asserts:

> It must be remembered that the exclusionary rule is a remedy only, and not a very good one. It thus rewards the criminal and punishes, not the police, but the innocent victim of the crime and society at large for conduct they may not condone and over which they have little or no control.[223]

After enumerating all the perceived 'costs' to the criminal process – 'handcuffing police', suppression of 'perfectly good' evidence, court delays, and the lack of any danger to the rights of 'law abiding' citizens – the Task Force goes on to state:

> Victims are adversely affected by the rule's operation at every turn. When the police fail to solve the crime because of inaction, the victim suffers. When cases are not charged or are dismissed and the 'criminal goes free because the constable blundered,' *the victim is denied justice*. When the case is continued interminably or must be retried, the victim is hurt time and time again.[224]

The Task Force uses the symbols of both past and future victims as embodied by society's interest in crime prevention to justify abolition of the exclusionary rule in a confusing way; the Task Force decries the costs to society of allowing the guilty to go unpunished and emphasizes the rule's interference with efficiency in the process. Even the Task Force's claims that are more applicable to past victims are grossly exaggerated, reflecting a hostility to the rule itself, rather than any particular solicitude for past victims. For example, the statement that the exclusionary rule causes police inaction simply does not make sense.[225] The suggestion that the exclusionary rule is the major source of continuances, delays and retrials is not supported by available statistical evidence.[226] In the vast majority of cases involving core crime, the exclusionary rule makes no difference to the result. Indeed, it has become almost a truism in defence circles that, while courts may grant suppression motions in drug cases, they invariably deny them in murder cases.[227] The strongest refutation of the Task Force position, however, is that reversals of convictions on Fourth Amendment grounds appear to constitute only a tiny fraction of all reversals of criminal convictions by appellate courts.[228]

Undeniably, retrials of serious cases necessitated by an appellate court reversal may be difficult for past victims. But it seems unlikely that the degree of difficulty is necessarily related to the *reason* for the reversal and retrial, or that having to testify again because of a reversal resulting from Fifth or Sixth Amendment violations or instructional errors is less 'traumatic'. The attitudes of the police or prosecutor towards the grounds for the reversal might, however, exacerbate the situation if the prosecutor emphasizes to the victim the 'needlessness' of having to retry the case, or criticizes the appellate court's solicitude towards the guilty 'criminal'.

A second argument offered by the Task Force in opposition to the exclusionary rule is that it denies the victim justice. This argument appears to assume that a victim has a right to a conviction of the accused or, perhaps, a right to revenge.[229] But the history of the criminal process does not support a finding of such a right.[230] Whether victims have a right to a conviction should be examined in terms of whether they have a cognizable interest in participating in the sentencing of offenders and whether they have a 'right' to recovery from the wrongdoer, the subjects of the next section.

V. VICTIM PARTICIPATION IN SENTENCING

Ironically, the most politically visible activity in the victim's rights movement focuses on the end, rather than on the beginning, of the criminal process. Advocate groups such as MADD attend the sentencing of defendants;[231] formalized victim participation at sentencing frequently appears in victim's rights proposals;[232] and many states have recently adopted provisions allowing victims to participate in sentencing proceedings.[233] Leaving aside the question of restitution for the moment, the following discussion evaluates the desirability of such participation in terms of the justifications for imposing the criminal sanction and in terms of whether or not the justifications promote the interests of the victim.

A. The relevance of victim participation to the justifications for the criminal sanction

The classic justifications for the criminal sanction are deterrence, incapacitation, rehabilitation and retribution. At different times, different justifications are in ascendancy, but one single justification never entirely determines the imposition of the criminal sanction. Since each justification is analytically different, however, this part discusses each justification separately to determine whether each supports victim participation in sentencing.

1. Deterrence
The essentially utilitarian foundation of deterrence theory is the premise that punishment has the socially useful function of preventing crime.[234] Deterrence theory has two components: general deterrence where the punishment meted out for a criminal act discourages others from engaging in the specific wrong doing,[235] and specific deterrence where punishment of the individual wrongdoer dissuades him from engaging in further wrongdoing. General deterrence seeks to educate others; specific deterrence seeks to educate the individual offender.

General deterrence requires that the penalties for crimes be sufficiently severe – and certain – to prevent people from committing those crimes; it assumes that a rational person will 'trade off' the benefits of engaging in criminal conduct for the benefits of escaping punishment.[236] But despite increased penalties for crime, the rising crime rates of the past few decades seem to contradict the assumption that general deterrence is effective.[237] Indeed, complete general deterrence appears to be an unmanageable ideal, and the theory has fallen out of popular favour as a justification for the criminal sanction.[238] Nonetheless, the educational function of the criminal sanction remains a consideration, if only *sub silentio*, in criminal sentencing literature and in practice.[239] For general deterrence purposes, the participation of the individual victim seems to be of negligible value in determining sentences because this theory concentrates on the moral beliefs and behaviours of the community. It holds that the imposition of the criminal sanction deters crime, regardless of who the victim is. The focus of general deterrence is public and non-individualized; victim participation is not necessary to educate the community.

Specific deterrence is aimed at preventing the individual offender from engaging in future criminal activity.[240] Achieving specific deterrence does not require victim participation at sentencing, rather it requires a calculation of the appropriate level of punishment to teach the offender to abstain from wrongdoing in the future.[241]

2. Incapacitation

Proponents of the incapacitation approach believe that the best way to prevent a particular offender from committing future crimes is to remove him from society.[242] This belief is based on predictions or assumptions of future dangerousness or propensity to commit crimes that are not necessarily related to the actual crime for which the offender is sentenced.[243] In fact, the relationship between the actual offence and future dangerousness may be attenuated at best.[244] Although the *manner* in which the offender committed the crime might intuitively seem relevant to a determination of dangerousness, it may be of limited usefulness.[245] The factors examined in determining whether to incapacitate an offender are related to the characteristics of the offender, rather than to those of the victim.[246]

3. Rehabilitation

The rehabilitative goal of the criminal sanction has not received widespread support. But unless we are to incapacitate all offenders for all time, rehabilitation cannot be dismissed entirely because of our longstanding interest in reforming offenders in order to prevent them from committing future crimes. Rehabilitation, like incapacitation, is 'offender-oriented' rather than 'offence-oriented'. It concentrates on the offender, his nature, and what is needed to correct his undesirable behaviour.[247] To the extent that the offender's past behaviour offers a clue about what rehabilitative steps are necessary, the nature of the crime committed may be relevant to a sentencing decision. Yet unless the victim knows the offender, it is unlikely that he or she can supply the sentencer with helpful information about the crime or the offender that is not already available from other sources.

In a few instances, rehabilitation-oriented sentences may seem to depend upon, or benefit from, victim cooperation. For example, the successful rehabilitation of perpetrators of domestic violence or child abuse appears to necessitate therapeutic intervention that requires both victim and offender participation.[248] This is quite different, however, from giving the victim a role in determining *what* sentence to impose. Instead, it gives the victim a role in *implementing* the sentence.

4. Retribution

One meaning of retribution is associated with a theory of moral blameworthiness that justifies punishment. Although what constitutes appropriate punishment is both morally and culturally determined,[249] the guiding notion is that defendants must pay a 'debt' to society to make amends for their wrongs.[250] The other, perhaps more automatic meaning of retribution is simply that of revenge: society has a right to retaliate against those who have hurt it or failed to follow its rules.

The moral blameworthiness, or 'moral retributionist', view subdivides further into two general components: one view, associated with Kant, is that crime merits punishment simply because it is wrong;[251] the other view, identified by Herbert Morris, holds 'that society's members implicitly agree to an allocation of benefits and burdens',[252] and 'punishment serves the purpose of restoring the equilibrium of benefits and burdens'[253] upset by the wrongdoer. Both of these approaches embody a proportionality principle – a correspondence between the wickedness of the act and the suffering to be inflicted upon the actor. The arguments for this side of the retributionist thesis gain strength by using an 'innocent' victim to illustrate graphically the offender's blameworthiness. But importing the victim into the blameworthiness calculus logically requires courts to call into question the victim's relative blameworthiness – to measure the offender's actual moral culpability requires examining whether the victim 'deserved' what he got and whether '[t]he harm the criminal does to society by taking the law into his own hands could be insignificant in comparison to the benefaction . . . that would otherwise be left undone.'[254] Although the substantive criminal law does occasionally shift blame to the victim, as illustrated by the justification of self-defence, it does so only in a very narrow sense.[255] Considering the victim's blameworthiness at sentencing, rather than at adjudication, may act to distort the substantive law governing the initial determination of guilt.

A related question is whether 'victim precipitation' should be taken into account at sentencing. 'Victim precipitation' refers to victim conduct that induces or provokes another to commit a crime and is a broader concept than that of victim culpability.[256] One commentator has argued that certain types of victim precipitation *should* be considered at the sentencing stage because they 'make the crime more understandable and in many instances lessen the [offender's] moral culpability.'[257] While this may follow logically from an attempt to calculate the extent of someone's moral blameworthiness, it does result in a difficult inquiry as to 'relative badness'.

A determination of 'relative badness' at the sentencing phase closely resembles the concept of contributory or comparative negligence. These concepts may already explicitly or implicitly influence sentencing determinations,[258] but *formal* recognition of the victim's presence can produce unpredictable results. In a recent case, the defendant, convicted of driving under the influence and of manslaughter, received a minimal sentence for killing two drunken pedestrians, despite the arguments by the next of kin at sentencing for a harsh penalty. The sentencing judge observed that the pedestrians were 'more to blame' than the driver for their deaths.[259] Presumably, some explicit standards for measuring victim blameworthiness or victim precipitation could be devised to guide sentencing judges, but adopting such standards is ill-advised. No self-evident source for the development of these standards exists. An inquiry into comparative blameworthiness could increase the appearance of capriciousness in the criminal process. Such an inquiry could create a normative nightmare for both victims and society, because it necessarily would consider how the victims should have acted. The prototypical example of this problem is the crime of rape, where both law and society have traditionally 'judged' the victim on the basis of who she was, where she was, how she was dressed, and whether or not she resisted.[260] Finally, despite its fall from grace, general deterrence remains a goal of the criminal justice system. Taking the victim's blameworthiness into account weakens the educational value of the criminal sanction and thus lessens its general deterrent effect.[261]

Recent victim's rights proposals appear to be driven more by the retaliatory view of retribution than by the moral aspect of retribution. The victim who participates in sentencing might further the ends of the retribution-as-vengeance theory by providing specific and graphic information about the crime – information that will provoke outrage.

Despite its popularity among victim's rights proponents, retaliation has received relatively little support from philosophers or social scientists.[262] Vengeance is uncivilized,[263] and it certainly cannot be said to appeal to the 'higher nature' of man, yet the '*romantic version of the vindictive theory* . . . holds that the justification of punishment is to be found in the emotions of hate and anger, these emotions being those allegedly felt by all normal or right-thinking people.'[264] The retaliatory view of retribution ultimately is a utilitarian view, because its justifications are that it prevents mob violence, channels society's outrage, and preserves the legitimacy of the criminal justice system by paying heed to the community's sense of justice.[265] But none of these rationales adequately support retaliation, even from a utilitarian perspective. First, except in unusual or highly publicized cases, the likelihood of *mob* violence is almost nonexistent. Second, most crime – even core crime – does not provoke strangers to retaliate directly against the criminal. Third, although it may be proper to be angered by evil acts, it is not at all self-evident that vengeance or retaliation is the only available or appropriate response for channelling society's outrage – another perfectly appropriate response to outrage would be to renew efforts to prevent violent crimes. Finally, some crimes transcend even outrage and *any* response may be futile in an instrumental sense.

Nor is it a simple task to determine what constitutes the community's sense of justice, and to ascertain whether that sense comports with the retaliatory view of retribution in most, if not all, instances. Whatever community feeling does exist could be reflected in ways other than vengeance – for example, through jury condemnation, police and prosecutorial discretion, and legislative determination of penalties. In general, only a very narrow category of crimes raises the issue of the community's sense of justice, and even in these cases the community may not agree on what is just. The controversy in New Bedford, Massachusetts during and after a rape trial indicates that sharp divisions in a community's sense of justice exist even in serious cases.[266]

The utilitarian justifications for the retaliatory view of retribution are inadequate. But what of the individual's desire for vengeance? Although few people would suggest a return to the blood feud, many would argue that the victim is entitled to his or her 'pound of flesh'. In this way, the victim may be entitled to tell the judge what he or she thinks should be done to the offender. The first and immediate criticism of this type of participation is that the victim's desire for vengeance conflicts with two principles that apply even to retributive sentencing: proportionality and equality. In an extreme example, while a victim may believe that an auto thief should be hanged and may muster a variety of moral arguments in support of his position, proportionality requires a rejection of the victim's position. Second, the equality principle requires similar treatment of similarly situated offenders in order to eliminate capriciousness in outcome.

The underlying assumption that anger and vengeance are different aspects of the same phenomenon and that vengeance is the necessary and appropriate response to the anger many victims experience also does not withstand close examination. A victim may direct anger at the offender, at the offence, at him or herself, or at a combination of these elements. Although anger is a justifiable response to crime, vengeance as a formalized manifestation of anger is of questionable psychological value to the victim. The anger experienced may therefore have little relevance to retaliation. Second, while anger is a normal and understandable response to all kinds of harms, anger does not inexorably lead to retaliation as an appropriate response to harm. Even if we can distinguish intentional harms from accidents, we still react with anger to hurt. We may even retaliate. But direct retaliation towards the perceived source of the harm is only one of many possible responses to the anger engendered. Finally, retaliation may be the victim's *first* impulse but not the last or the definitive one.[267] While the passage of time may not end a crime victim's anger, it may diminish the retaliatory impulse. Thus, what people choose to alleviate their feelings of anger, particularly after the initial shock of the harm has passed, can vary enormously from physical retaliation to withdrawal, to efforts to prevent future harms, to forgiveness of the offender.[268]

Anger and its manifestation as blame certainly *are* normal responses to violent crime, but they are not necessarily tied to a desire, need or justification for retaliation. Disaster victims often try to assign responsibility for an evil, many times in a way that relieves them of responsibility for the outcome. Thus, victims of crimes often blame the perpetrator, 'the system', the police, the district attorney, the defence lawyer, or all of them for the victim's agonies.[269] But blame does not relieve a victim of responsibility for the criminal act, if any, and for what he or she chooses to do about it.[270] As discussed earlier, victims who assume a degree of responsibility for a crisis or disaster may suffer less stress and may reduce their sense of vulnerability and loss of control more successfully than those who do not.[271] Assigning responsibility to others may also help the victim to find an explanation for the victimization. The victim's question 'why' may be answered by blaming the parole officer of an offender who committed the crime while on parole,[272] or by blaming a judge for releasing an offender on bail.[273] But such explanations ultimately do not provide a lasting or sufficient answer to the broader question of meaning.[274] Indeed, the opposite of vengeance – forgiveness – is more likely to enable the victim to recover. As Hanna Arendt observes:

> [F]orgiveness is the exact opposite of vengeance, which acts in the form of re-acting against an original trespassing, whereby far from putting an end to the consequence of the first misdeed, everybody remains bound to the process . . . In contrast to revenge . . . the act of forgiving can never be predicted; it is the only reaction that acts in an unexpected way and thus retains . . . something of the original character of action. Forgiving, in other words, is the only reaction which does not merely re-act but acts anew and unexpectedly, unconditioned by the act which provoked it and thereby freeing from its consequences both the one who forgives and the one who is forgiven.[275]

Forgiveness alone retains the uncontested authorship essential to responsibility and resolution. Forgiveness rather than vengeance may, therefore, be the act that eventually frees the victim from the event, the means by which the victim may put the experience behind him or her.

Emphasizing individual vengeance and blame can undermine, rather than facilitate, recovery from a violent crime. This is not to say that victims can or should be indifferent to the sentence imposed; the rare disproportionately light sentence disaffirms the victim's experience and undoubtedly causes the victim more pain.[276] But even a harsh sentence does not end the matter for the victim. In a sense, sentencing does provide a recognizable event and possible opportunity for completion of a phase of the recovery process. But to say to a victim that after sentencing he or she can now put the experience to rest denies that any remaining questions of meaning, fears of death, or feelings of helplessness exist.[277] While the sentencing may signal the end of public concern with the crime, it surely cannot be expected to signal the end of the victim's recovery process.

If the harm to the victim is determinative of a particular sentence, then victim participation in sentencing would appear to be of use to the criminal process. But none of the rationales that underlie the criminal sanction are necessarily furthered by considering the *individual* harm in imposing a sentence. Moreover, concentrating on the harm to a specific victim may increase, rather than decrease, capriciousness in sentencing.

B. The relevance of harm

The Federal Victim and Witness Protection Act provides that the pre-sentence report 'shall contain. . . . information concerning any harm, including financial, social, psychological and physical harm done to or loss suffered by any victim of the offense.'[278] Although the record of the hearings before the Criminal Law Subcommittee of the Senate Judiciary Committee indicates that a major reason for including this information was for purposes of determining restitution,[279] the appendix to the hearings emphasizes that statements concerning the actual harm caused are 'useful tools in determining equitable penalties during the sentencing of a convicted offender'.[280]

Often the substantive law defines the criminal offence and the sanction to be imposed by the actual harm that has resulted. The definition of an offence frequently depends on the result of the conduct – simple battery, aggravated assault and murder all encompass particular results within their definitions. And legislatures provide for penalties that correspond in severity to the harm associated with the prohibited behaviour.[281] This emphasis on outcomes makes some sense, both intuitively and philosophically: the principle of proportionality requires us to punish murderers more severely than petty thieves, as does the principle of relative moral blameworthiness. Beyond these rather general formulations, however, the justifications for emphasizing the particular harm inflicted in determining the sanction to impose become more problematic.

One commentator has countered many of the arguments offered in support of taking the particular harm into account at sentencing by showing how this approach is inconsistent with the moral retributionist rationale for the criminal sanction,[282] how it does not necessarily further deterrence,[283] and how it does not influence the incidence of jury nullification or reduce the problems of discretion in the criminal justice system.[284] Moreover, the 'frugality principle' – the notion that punishment 'can be justified only by necessity and should be no greater than necessary to achieve its goal'[285] – cannot support reliance on the particular harm as the exclusive reason for imposing punishment.[286] Thus, the only rationale for the criminal sanction with which emphasizing the particular harm is consistent is that of retaliation.[287]

Focusing on the particular harm caused emphasizes retaliation. This appeal to personal vengeance may be necessary to elicit the victim's cooperation with the prosecution in some cases, but not all: victims may cooperate because of feelings of social duty or altruism as well. And whether formalizing individual retaliation at the sentencing stage is beneficial either to victims or to society is questionable.[288] Explicit encouragement of a victim's urge to retaliate does not necessarily aid the victim's recovery and, as noted earlier, may foreclose the possibility of taking responsibility for the experience. From society's perspective, the state attempts to mediate among individuals in order to prevent vigilantism and runaway vengeance, and a greater focus on individual retaliation may thwart this goal.

Thus, while retaliation is the only rationale for the criminal sanction with which victim participation at sentencing and an emphasis on the particular harm are consistent, this rationale is problematic for both the victim and society. And ironically, while victim's rights advocates have urged victim participation in sentencing for the purpose of apprising the sentencer of the specific harm caused, mandatory or determinate sentencing laws may render the information provided largely irrelevant.[289] Nonetheless, the victim may have an interest in being heard independent of the reasoning behind the criminal sanction.

C. Other possible justifications for victim participation

Although the individual contribution that a victim can or should make to the determination of the criminal sentence may be minimal at best, other justifications for victim participation may still exist. These justifications for a 'right' to participate fall loosely into three categories: 'fairness', 'due process' and 'recognition'.

1. Fairness
Victims of core crime are individuals, while the criminal justice process is an amalgam of public agencies and courts with their own agendas, bureaucracies and rituals. Yet the criminal justice process appears to ignore the concerns, wants and needs of victims while it simultaneously relies on victims to function.[290] Sacrificing individuals to society's goals seems 'unfair' to many; the treatment of victims as a means to an end seems wrong.[291] Victim participation in sentencing ostensibly cures this inequality by giving the victim 'equal time'. But if fairness or equality are the goals served by participation, waiting

until sentencing to recognize the victim does not seem to cure the perceived evil of using the victim as a means to an end. If the real reason for encouraging victims to speak at sentencing is the desire for harsher sentences, the process continues to use the victim for an instrumental purpose. The use of the victim can be more subtle, however, because in many cases the victim participates either to a limited extent, or not at all, after reporting the crime and agreeing to press charges.[292] At best, it may be several months before a sentencing proceeding occurs, assuming that there is a conviction.[293] Thus, the victim may continue to be 'used' without fair treatment for an extended period, because sentencing occurs at the end of the criminal process.

Symbolically, the defendant does appear to have an advantage in the criminal process: he has a lawyer, while the victim does not: he enjoys the protection of specific constitutional provisions, while the victim does not; he frequently is the focus of attention and concern – even if that attention and concern are entirely negative in orientation – while attention paid to the victim is typically nonexistent or dependent upon the victim's usefulness to the prosecution. The perception that defendants are somehow advantaged is thus difficult to dispel. The reality, however, is that most defendants have little or no real advantage either substantively or procedurally. And the fact that the defendant has one person ostensibly supporting and advocating his interests – his lawyer – may be considered an advantage by some,[294] but viewed another way, representation is less an advantage than a necessity. Without counsel, the defendant is at a distinct disadvantage in the system; having counsel lessens, but does not obliterate, that disadvantage.[295]

Another possible argument that can be made in support of victim participation in sentencing is that such participation renders the sentencing process more democratic and thus will make the sentence imposed more reflective of the community's response to a crime. But the fact that democratic legislative bodies set sentences detracts from this argument. Nevertheless, the democratizing function may arguably be better served by allowing the victim and his or her friends and relatives to participate in sentencing in order to provide the judge with a sense of the community's norms and values in a particular case. The legislature is probably a better measure of those norms and values than is a judge, however, particularly when the judge is faced with a self-selected group of individuals who do not necessarily represent the norms of the community. In fact, if ensuring that community norms prevail is the goal, jury sentencing would be more representative than victim participation.[296]

2. Due process

The 'due process' rationale focuses on the victim's natural law rights to 'life, liberty and property' and suggests according some procedural due process protection to victims.[297] The argument proceeds as follows: When an individual becomes a victim of a violent crime, that person's right to life or liberty (defined as security from harm) has been invaded. Although the due process clause is a check on government power, the government uses victims as witnesses, and victims can therefore claim a private interest in the outcome of a criminal matter. In this view, the government and the courts should provide procedural due process for victims.[298]

If the victim does have some right cognizable under the due process clause – natural, fundamental or substantive – that entitles him to a hearing, the question remains what kind of hearing. The procedural side of the due process clause arises in cases involving government attempts to deprive an individual of a constitutionally protected or legislatively granted right, or to burden this right in some way.[299] Procedural protections are generally required as safeguards against erroneous decision-making.[300] But the victim suffers no deprivation at the hands of the government during the sentencing process. The sentence does not formally foreclose any civil action for damages caused by the crime unless the victim agrees,[301] the sentence has no bearing on whether the victim's property will be returned,[302] and the sentence does not determine whether the state will restrain the victim's physical liberty.[303] Only the restitution context involves the adjudication of some cognizable claim belonging to the victim.[304] Thus, inquiry into the protection of a victim's due process rights because of an erroneous determination by the sentencing judge is unnecessary simply because the victim has no rights or entitlements at stake at sentencing.[305] To seek a justification for the incorporation of procedural due process rights for victims, despite the lack of identifiable *governmental* interference with an individual right, far exceeds the scope of even the Supreme Court's most expansive procedural due process applications.[306] And cluttering up sentencing hearings with additional procedures is not really what advocates of the crime control position seek. The protraction of sentencing proceedings runs contrary to the desire for efficiency and swift and sure punishment.

3. Recognition

'Recognition' is somewhat distinct from fairness or due process concerns. In one form, it may be defined as permitting the victim to speak in response to the appearance of unfairness of the present criminal process,[307] but it is largely a symbolic gesture. This type of recognition of the 'individual dignity' of the victim might have some merit in a utilitarian calculus. By giving victims a voice, this type of recognition could increase the social welfare by encouraging victims to report and prosecute crimes. But whether or not victims are encouraged to help the police and the prosecution may depend more on whether victims have been treated with dignity earlier in the process, or throughout the process, than on whether they participate at sentencing. Moreover, although recognition of the individual's experience in a formalized setting is theoretically possible, great care must be taken to ensure that any existing problems of victim alienation are not exacerbated by perfunctory treatment, or alternatively, by uninformed responses such as blaming victims for their predicaments or telling them that now they should 'put it all behind them'. Finally, because both practical and theoretical considerations may preclude the sentencer from implementing the victim's wishes, some victims may discover that their opinions are meaningless to the outcome and become more embittered.

Recognition also ensures some public validation of the victim's experience – the lending of a sympathetic official ear – but validation may not be a workable justification for victim participation, and it suffers from some of the same flaws as the symbolic gesture form of recognition. Moreover, public validation may not be very useful to many victims who are more interested in obtaining validation from a more specific reference group, such as their friends or family. Overall, there appears to be little justification for victim participation in the determination of the criminal sanction. However, victims may have a more limited role to play – that of helping the court to determine 'restitution'. Although determining the amount of restitution that an offender should pay may not necessarily mandate the victim's actual presence at sentencing, it certainly requires some victim involvement. The next section discusses victim participation in determining restitution, and observes that participation only serves to emphasize the problematic nature of 'victim's rights'.

D. The riddle of restitution

While many propositions advanced on the behalf of past victims may be of marginal concern to them, compensation for injuries can be of central importance. If crime victims have 'rights', the right to recover from the wrongdoer is the most tenable individually based right.

Restoration of the victim to the *status quo ante* is what the tort system is supposed to accomplish, and its failure to do so in instances of criminal harm has led many commentators and politicians to advocate grafting tort principles onto the criminal law, typically at the sentencing stage.[308] Both the California Victim's Bill of Rights,[309] and the Federal Victim and Witness Protection Act have made restitution an issue at the sentencing stage.[310]

1. Restitution as paradox

Few would quarrel with the proposition that, in an ideal world, the person who does harm should compensate the victim. This premise is the basis of the tort system, which in theory provides victims of crimes with compensation for their injuries.[311] As a theoretical matter, the civil courts are the proper forum for victims to claim damages.[312] The current emphasis on restitution has blurred the theoretical separation between crime and tort, although restitution is not a complete substitute for a tort action. Usually defined in terms of actual damages and restoration of property,[313] restitution generally does not encompass broader tort concepts such as damages for pain and suffering.[314] Nor do victim's rights laws expand restitution to include these broader damages.[315]

The Federal Victim and Witness Protection Act provides that the sentencing judge 'may' order restitution and 'shall' state his or her reasons 'on the record' if he or she does not do so.[316] The California Victim's Bill of Rights goes further, stating that '[r]estitution shall be ordered . . . in every case, regardless of the sentence or disposition imposed . . . unless compelling and extraordinary reasons exist to the contrary.'[317] The wording of both the federal and California provisions seems to suggest that the victim's right to restitution 'trumps' the state's right to impose the criminal sanction.[318] But a fundamental tension exists between the imposition of the criminal sanction and access to monetary remedies for victims – frequently the use of one negates the use of the other. If restitution is to be more than a symbolic but empty promise to past victims and an assurance for future victims, either the private interest in recovery has to prevail, or an accommodation between public and private interests has to be created.

When serious crimes are involved, the public interest will almost inevitably foreclose either allowing private interests to prevail or accommodation. As the criminal law has evolved, its nature and function has become increasingly social and public, and the criminal process now serves the frequently interrelated public tasks of preventing crime and punishing offenders. The justifications for the criminal process and the characteristics that distinguish criminal law from all other law focus on these two tasks.[319] The increasingly public nature of the criminal law is largely a result of our acknowledgment that many crimes have profound effects not only on individuals, but also on the community as a whole. While the distinction between public and private rights is not a particularly satisfactory one, in the instance of core crime, the distinction seems worth preserving.[320] The community has interests in its security and continued existence that are fundamentally affected by war, disasters and violent crimes. If individual victims are permitted to dictate the choice of sanctions, the community will be virtually excluded from protecting itself from the disruptive impact of crime.

The criminal sanction is the community's response to crime. Because core crime transcends the interests of the harmed individual, the criminal event 'belongs' to others as well. Accordingly, the larger community protects its interests by prohibiting private settlements of criminal cases,[321] encouraging community-wide participation in crime prevention,[322] and defining the appropriate sanctions or range of sanctions for particular crimes.[323] The community's protection of its right to exist, as manifested by its imposition of the criminal sanction, will therefore often negate the interest of the victim in recovering from the offender. This is the case, for example, when the community chooses to imprison someone on retributive or incapacitative grounds.

Any unspoken hesitancy to allow the victim's right to recover from the offender to dominate the sentencing determination may explain the attempts to define restitution concepts in terms of the traditional justification for the criminal sanction in an effort to resolve the paradox created. Proposals for restitution or state compensation for injuries have existed for centuries and these proposals have drawn heavily on the traditional justifications for the criminal sanction. Bentham's utilitarian scheme, for example, called for 'satisfaction', a combination of restitution and compensation: reparation for past injury and assurance to society, in order to promote a feeling of security, that suffering will not go unrecognized.[324] Garofalo argued that mandatory restitution would deter criminals by raising the crime tariff, save money, and lead to reformation of some criminals.[325] Thus Bentham and Garofalo suggest that even in the narrow sense of reparation, compensation to victims is not a good end in and of itself.

It also must serve the public purposes of the criminal law, particularly those of deterrence and rehabilitation.

In spite of the critiques of rehabilitation, some liberal supporters of restitution have stressed its value as a rehabilitative tool. Some have argued that restitution personalizes the context of a criminal sentence, keeping the offender in contact with the victim, so that he or she can see the consequences of the criminal acts. Restitution arguably personalizes the sentence and increases the offender's awareness of responsibility and remorse, thereby aiding his rehabilitation.[326] Whether restitution orders under the threat of imprisonment do serve a rehabilitative function is an open question. Other variables, such as availability of work and other sources of financial support for the offender, undoubtedly influence the effectiveness of restitution as a rehabilitative device.

The deterrence argument for restitution is based on a 'crime tariff' model that assumes that if the price of crime is high enough, potential offenders will refrain from committing crimes.[327] Perhaps offenders would be more deterred by the prospect of having to suffer financially rather than physically, but this hardly seems likely. Most offenders given the choice between making restitution and going to jail would probably opt for restitution.[328]

The retributionist impulse touched off by conservatives has taken the form of mandatory imprisonment for offences, longer prison terms and determinate sentencing. None of these enhance the likelihood of the offender making the restitution that conservatives also demand.[329] For example, although the Senate hearings on the issue of restitution reveal some recognition that the desire to punish offenders and the desire to compensate victims are frequently contradictory, the Senate ignored the contradiction in enacting the Federal Victim and Witness Protection Act.[330]

On the liberal side, some advocates of restitution have advocated using restitution as a fine-like punishment imposed instead of imprisonment, because restitution provides a direct method of reminding the criminal of the wrong and forcing an acknowledgment of moral responsibility.[331] At first blush, this seems ideally suited to moral retributionist goals, but in instances of serious crime it is unworkable. As a society, we want the rapist, mugger or robber imprisoned on proportionality and incapacitation grounds;[332] in many instances, the victim does also.[333] In cases in which we are indifferent about punishing offenders through imprisonment or fines, restitution through fines may make sense. But restitution is not so much a 'punishment' as it is an amends for wrongdoing. Punishment, by definition, should be an unpleasant 'extra' that serves no purpose other than to inflict pain or suffering.[334]

2. *California's attempt to resolve the paradox*

The California legislature explicitly recognized the paradoxical nature of restitution in 1983 when it had to reconcile the Victim's Bill of Rights amendment to the state constitution requiring restitution in all cases with California's constitutional and statutory requirements of increased and mandatory prison terms.[335] Conservative Republicans insisted that individual offenders be required to make restitution regardless of imprisonment or ability to pay.[336] Where necessary, they were willing to require payment of restitution as a condition of parole, essentially taking the position that the offender, and *only* the offender, is responsible for providing the victim with a financial remedy.[337] Under the conservative plan, and in the light of California's existing mandatory sentencing structure, a victim who suffered serious bodily injury as a result of a forcible rape in which the perpetrator used a deadly weapon would have to wait a *minimum* of approximately ten years, eight months, before the assailant would be eligible for parole[338] and, perhaps, be able to earn money to make restitution payments. Such a 'resolution' of the restitution paradox is no resolution at all.

Liberal Democrats sought to increase the amount of funds available to victims under the California Victims of Violent Crime Compensation programme[339] by recharacterizing it as a victim's restitution fund, financed by penalty assessments charged in addition to fines in all criminal cases.[340] The Democrats additionally proposed changes in the law involving tort suits for damages, including extending statutes of limitations, providing for punitive damages in wrongful death suits, and increasing the civil liability of parents whose children commit a crime.[341]

The 'restitution fund' places a tax on all criminal activity: a mandatory payment to the restitution fund of $5 assessed for every $10 of criminal fines in misdemeanour cases, a mandatory assessment for felony convictions ranging from $100 to $10,000, and a $20 assessment imposed on those convicted of driving under the influence.[342] Although conservatives initially opposed the plan in which traffic violators 'subsidized' rapists and murderers, the proposal eventually gained bipartisan support and became law. The programme that emerged was thus more like California's pre-existing victim's compensation programme, with increased funds to be supplied essentially by a tax on well-to-do offenders,[343] rather than a programme of restitution by offenders.

3. Some unanswered questions

In those cases in which direct restitution by the offender to the victim is possible and is a sentencing issue, neither federal nor state provisions offer much guidance on the procedures for determining the appropriate amount of restitution. One commentator has recently argued that once a person is convicted, his or her rights 'are merely conditional',[344] and therefore no formal trial is necessary to determine the amount of restitution required.[345] The argument uncritically accepts that restitution is compatible with the justifications for the criminal sanction.[346] Because this article asserts that restitution is analytically different, the problem of procedure cannot be so lightly dismissed.[347]

The Federal Victim and Witness Protection Act recognizes due process questions associated with restitution by placing the burden of proving the amount in question by a preponderance of the evidence on the prosecution and the same burden of proof on the defendant to show his or her inability to pay.[348] On the other hand, it leaves the burden of 'demonstrating such other matters as the court deems appropriate upon the party designated by the court as justice requires'.[349] The reference to 'appropriate matters' in this latter provision creates virtually complete judicial discretion in restitution proceedings. Moreover, the Act applies to harms resulting from 'the offence' without defining whether the offence means all the offences with which the defendant was charged, or simply the offence for which he or she was convicted.[350] Thus, the defendant could have to pay restitution for crimes of which he or she is not guilty.[351]

The situation on the state level may be worse than it is on the federal level. A recent article surveying restitution provisions throughout the United States found that many state plans failed to provide for due process protections for criminal defendants comparable to those available in civil actions against the criminal offender.[352] The option of restitution, either instead of a jail sentence or at least with the promise of a lesser term, makes it difficult for offenders to object to the amount of restitution awarded, however unfounded.[353] Moreover, many states have shifted the burden of proving the amount of reasonable restitution from the person seeking restitution to the offender.[354] The lack of procedural protection is troubling

because it is symptomatic of a general willingness to treat offenders as
'others' and not as persons entitled to the same consideration the law
provides other wrongdoers who cause harms.[355]

4. A final note on victim's compensation programmes

The California compromise led to increased funding for the already
existing victim's compensation programme.[356] Victim's compensation
statutes exist in almost every state[357] and are largely the product of a
liberal, social welfare ideology,[358] although some have argued that
compensation should be considered a right.[359] Still, no satisfactory
explanation exists for treating victims of crime as *more* entitled
to state-funded compensation than victims of other insolvent or
governmental tortfeasors. Several compensation advocates have
argued that because the state has taken responsibility for crime
prevention, it has a duty to compensate individual victims when it
fails to protect them.[360] This argument, however, does not explain
why crime victims are 'special'. Under this analysis, the state is
equally under a duty to compensate victims of uninsured motorists
because it controls the licensing of drivers and 'requires' insurance.[361]
Moreover, according victims of crimes a special status in society
above victims of governmentally inflicted harms – for example, civ-
ilians who are injured because of the dumping of toxic wastes by the
government, or who get cancer as a result of government testing of
nuclear weapons – seems to be insupportable.[362]

An argument that the state needs a victim's assistance to enforce
the criminal law, and therefore should reward victims for their cooperation, is problematic under most existing statutes. Many victim's
compensation programmes provide only for victims of violent
crimes,[363] and frequently require that the victims be 'innocent' –
excluding those who arguably precipitated the crime or are otherwise
'blameworthy',[364] or those who do not cooperate fully with law
enforcement.[365] This substantially narrows the field of victims encouraged to aid the system and provides few incentives to aid law
enforcement. Further, with normative language such as 'innocence'
in the statutes, those in charge of deciding which victims receive
compensation have enormous discretion. Finally, one of the major
complaints about victim's compensation programmes has been that
few victims know or are told of such programmes.[366] As a practical
matter, compensation falls woefully short as an incentive for many
victims to help the state enforce laws.

Another less instrumental approach to victim's compensation programmes might justify treating crime victims differently from other victims. The state has an expectation that crime victims will report crimes and assist in the prosecution of offenders, but this expectation does not extend to victims of many kinds of insolvent tortfeasors. Indeed, the state may *punish* a crime victim for non-cooperation by holding him or her in contempt for refusing to testify, or the state conceivably could prosecute victims for the obstruction of justice.[367] Although crime victims can and do choose not to report crimes, once they report a crime, they must accept the intrusion of the larger community into their experience. Victim's compensation may provide a symbolic recognition of the victim's contribution to the general welfare of the community. Perhaps by demonstrating our collective opposition to violent crime by compensating victims, the system gains moral credibility for its position against non-instrumental violence. But, to compensate such victims lacks coherence, and to characterize victim's compensation as symbolic of an opposition to non-instrumental crimes is to accept responsibility to contribute to the fund generally, rather than to tax offenders in order to compensate. The unwillingness of most advocates of compensation to abandon the premise that the wrongdoer should directly or indirectly pay the victim weakens the interpretation of victim's compensation as a community response.[368]

A final observation on restitution and compensation is appropriate before concluding. Neither compensation nor restitution provide for non-monetary loss. The secondary costs of victimization – pain and suffering, emotional distress, loss of status and security – are not easily quantified. And, except perhaps for loss of status, these 'costs' are not ultimately expunged by money, although as the common wisdom would have it, money certainly helps. But increased understanding of the meaning of the experience and willingness to overcome the ambivalence about victims might be of more value to them in the long run, particularly because of the reality of limited monetary resources.

VI. CONCLUSION

This article has briefly touched upon the complex issues raised by the victim's rights movement and the psychological phenomena resulting from victimization. It offers an outline of the current state of the law and does not discuss victim's rights proposals that do not relate

142   *Critical Views on Victimology and Victim Policy*

directly to changes in the criminal law of process.[369] Rather, the
concern of this article is to increase the understanding of the experience of victimization, and the manner in which the anguish of victims
has been reformulated or mistranslated into support for a particular
ideology. The co-optation of victim's concerns by crime control proponents has created a new mythology of victimization that fails to hear
those concerns. The following exchange, taken from the Senate
Subcommittee Hearings on the Omnibus Victim and Witness Protection Act, both exemplifies the inability of non-victims to hear past
victims and demonstrates the resulting translation of the anguish of
victimization into a condemnation of the offender:

Senator Heinz. Do you have any thoughts on how prosecutors can
be more sympathetic or more understanding, more humane in their
treatment of people such as yourself?
Mrs X. I certainly do have a lot of opinions. When I talked to the
police – I did a series of workshops in the Montgomery County
Police Department – the first thing I emphasized was that whether
a person is a prosecuting attorney, a judge, or the President of the
United States, I would urge him to examine his own feelings about
crime. In my particular case, about rape.
    What I feel is that most people are so afraid of being victims
themselves that when they are dealing with a victim they treat us as
anathema. *Our very existence* makes them uncomfortable. I imagine I
look like someone you know. Maybe I look like someone you love? I
might make you feel uncomfortable just by my existence. Rape
happened to me. It wasn't nice. It wasn't midnight, and I wasn't alone
or in a bar. I didn't ask for it.
    This makes people uncomfortable. I would ask prosecuting
attorneys not to hide behind sarcasm here, nor employ the games of
the law, not to be afraid of being somehow compassionate, not to
confuse cold with professional.
Senator Heinz. In other words, what you are really saying is that
although the *criminal* may have every step of the way explained to
him by his lawyer or, if he can't afford his own lawyer, by a
court-appointed lawyer – paid for by the *taxpayer*, there was no
one in your case who ever had the courtesy or the simple decency
to explain the process and sit down with you and let you know, no
matter how uncertain the process was, what it was comprised of.[370]

To whom, or to what, is he responding?

NOTES AND REFERENCES

1. See note 87.
2. See note 71.
3. The author draws on her experiences as both a public defender and a victim of a violent crime for insight as to effects of crime on the victim and of recent changes in the criminal process.
4. J. Goebel, *Felony and Misdemeanor*, 15–21 (1937); Berman, The background of the Western legal tradition in the folklaw of the peoples of Europe, 45 *U. Chi. L. Rev.* 553 (1978).
5. See, e.g., F. Pollock and F. Maitland, *The History of English Law Before the Time of Edward I*, at 449–51 (2nd edn, 1899); 1 J. Stephen, *A History of the Criminal Law of England*, 60 (1883); Berman, note 4, at 554–5.
6. Berman, note 4, at 557; see also J. Goebel, note 4, at 341. But even the blood feud had certain social rules and rituals: in the 'law' of homicide, for example, not all lives were of equal worth; thus a blood feud might require the deaths of several persons, or the expropriation of cattle or more assets, to atone for the loss of a single individual. See F. Pollock and F. Maitland, note 5, at 450; Berman, note 4, at 556–7.
7. See F. Pollock and F. Maitland, note 5, at 450. Under the idea of outlawry, a person who broke the law could be attacked by the entire community in which he lived. Because the lawbreaker was considered to have gone to war with the community, the community's response was to go to war with him – to banish him, pursue him, kill him, ravage his land, burn his house. Ibid. at 449. Thus, even in pre-modern Western society, a public as well as private form of reaction to crime existed.
8. Ibid. at 451. A killer, for example, was given a year to pay the victim's family the value of the victim's life, generally determined by a complex set of class-based rules, before the family could begin the blood feud. Ibid. The kin of the killer were exempt from the feud unless they had harboured him. Ibid.
9. Ibid. at 449, 451.
10. The crime tariffs were oppressive. Pollock and Maitland observed:

   From the very first, it was an aristocratic system; not only did it make a distinction between those who were 'dearly born' and those who were cheaply born, but it widened the gulf by improverishing the poorer folk . . . When we reckon up the causes which made the bulk of the nation into tillers of the lands of lords, bot and wite should not be forgotten.

   Ibid. at 460. While the system 'outwardly reconciled the stern facts of rough justice with a Christian reluctance to shed blood,' ibid., Pollock and Maitland submitted that the demand for money instead of life was essentially delusive, because few persons were likely to pay, and most were outlawed or sold into slavery. Ibid. at 460–1.
11. Ibid.
12. Ibid. at 457–8; J. Goebel, note 4, at 429–33.

144   *Critical Views on Victimology and Victim Policy*

13. F. Pollock and F. Maitland, note 5, at 457–61.
14. Ibid. at 458.
15. Ibid. at 458–9.
16. For example, wilful homicide became a capital offence, and the kin of the slain lost their right to wer and to compensation. Only later was a statute specifically enacted to create a claim for damages in homicide cases. Ibid. at 459. A felon's lands went to the king; his chattels were confiscated. Ibid. at 465–6.
17. Ibid. at 454–64; J. Stephen, note 5, at 102. Although this summary obviously simplifies a complex historical change, it does so to emphasize that the focus and function of criminal law shifted substantially from the individual to the state. See also Greenberg, The victim in historical perspective: some aspects of the English experience. 40 *J. Soc. Issues* 77 (1984).
18. Berman, note 4, at 553–4.
19. See Langbein, Albion's fatal flaws, 98 *Past and Present* 96, 102 (1983); Langbein, The origins of public prosecution at common law, 17 *American Journal of Legal History* 313, 317–23 (1973). But see Hay, Controlling the English prosecutor, 21 *Osgoode Hall Law Journal* 165, 167–80 (1983) (English private prosecution in eighteenth and nineteenth century was largely discretionary).
20. See Langbein, Shaping the eighteenth-century criminal trial: a view from the Ryder Sources, 50 *U. Chi. L. Rev. 1*, 47–51 (1980) (larceny victims had discretion both in bringing charges and in determining whether larceny would be a capital offence). But see ibid. at 55–6 (although victim or private accuser was called prosecutor and played an 'essential role' in prosecuting, prosecutor had official support of constables and justices of the peace; the coroner handled homicide cases).
21. See Goldstein, Defining the role of the victim in criminal prosecution 52 *Mississippi Law Journal* 515 (1982); Comment, Private prosecution: a remedy for district attorneys' unwarranted inaction 65 *Yale Law Journal* 209 (1955). Although the idea of having private prosecutions in the United States has been proposed as a remedy for victims of crimes, see Goldstein, above, at 558–61; Comment, above, and there are occasional 'private prosecutions' or instances of private aid to district attorneys, private prosecution has never really played a prominent part in American criminal justice.
    Goebel and Naughton's history of the development of a criminal justice system in colonial New York notes the system was a mixed one of public and private prosecutions, depending on the location of the prosecution. Officials frequently brought formal accusations, however, and the office of the attorney general conducted many criminal prosecutions in the name of the Crown by the 1700s. J. Goebel and T. Naughton, *Law Enforcement in Colonial New York* 329 n. 14, 330–1, 337, 619–21 (1944) (in Easthampton, offences were prosecuted on complaints of injured persons or informers; in New York City, the sheriff filled role of law enforcement official and prosecutor; the Attorney General's power increased throughout 1700s as direct representative of the Crown's interests). Public prosecution developed throughout the colonies,

apparently, and certainly was firmly in place by the time the English were debating the issue.

22. By the nineteenth century, the expense of conducting investigations and of bringing private prosecutions placed a heavy burden on victims, Kurland and Waters, Public prosecutions in England, 1854–79: an essay in English legal history, *Duke Law Journal* 493, 512 (1959), and while compensation and reward schemes were used to encourage prosecution, they frequently were insufficient, ibid. The poor could not prosecute at all. Ibid. at 515. Moreover, in serious cases the constable had played an important role, and the coroner had become largely responsible for prosecuting homicide. Langbein, note 20, at 55–6. Finally, the severity of criminal penalties in England for hundreds of crimes – death or transportation – effectively foreclosed any chance for victims to obtain tort damages. See also note 10.

23. Kurland and Waters, note 22. The English debates leading up to the institution of the public prosecutor's office are mostly silent on the burden private prosecution placed on crime victims. Instead, the conflict centred on abuse of authority and loss of lawyers' jobs and the need for coordination and effective prosecution. See ibid. at 528–60. The English use of private prosecutions to enforce criminal statutes for most of England's history may simply have been a peculiar result of inertia, vested interests that had grown over time, and suspicion of authority. Ibid. at 561–2.

24. See, e.g., R. Jackson, *The Machinery of Justice in England* 214 (7th edn, 1977) (people are usually 'content' to leave the conduct of the prosecution to the police); Hay, note 19, at 180 (fewer than three per cent of English prosecutions are conducted by private individuals; about nine per cent of shoplifting cases are prosecuted by retail stores). But see Proposed independent prosecuting service: the prosecutor's viewpoint, 48 *Journal of Criminal Law* 302 (1984); Independent prosecutors, 134 *New Law Journal* 1001 (1984) (both criticizing a government proposal to create a centralized national prosecution office). For a recent discussion of the English criminal process, see Hughes, English criminal justice: is it better than ours?, 26 *Arizona Law Review* 507 (1984).

25. Of course, crime victims retain a private right of action in tort against criminals. Today, just as in the fourteenth century, the tort right to compensation in damages theoretically addresses the harm to the individual, while criminal prosecution theoretically addresses the social or public harm of criminal acts. In theory, the law has recognized the harm that victims have suffered and has provided a mechanism for redress. The separation of the treatment of individual claims from that of societal claims for criminally caused harms, and the resulting separation into the private and public spheres, however, creates the appearance that the law virtually ignores victims of crimes. See R. Reiff, *The Invisible Victim: The Criminal Justice System's Forgotten Responsibility* xi (1979) ('Society – sensitive to the issues of social justice for the offender – spends millions of dollars on programs for offender-oriented court reform and rehabilitation. On the other hand, society fails to

protect crime victims, degrades them socially, and refuses them aid');
M. Hyde, *The Rights of the Victim* 4 (1983) ('for the most part, victims
are the innocent and neglected element in the criminal justice system');
Goldstein, note 21, at 519 ('the victim has been left to play a distinctly
secondary role' in the criminal justice system). And while in theory the
tort system provides redress for the individual, in fact victims often have
no hope of recovery because many identified offenders are unable to
pay damages. See notes 311–24 and accompanying text.

26. Those who do find a 'deep pocket' can and do pursue the offender in
actions for civil damages. See Rios, 'Drunken driving victim and family
get $11 million', *San Jose Mercury News*, 24 Sept. 1983, at 1A, col. 3;
'S.F. jury gives burgled homeowners $400,000', *San Francisco Chron-
icle*, 28 July 1983, at 2, col. 2.

27. Perhaps it is the influence of the crime control ideology, see notes 47–51
and accompanying text, that causes us to rely so heavily on tinkering
with law enforcement and the conviction process to eliminate crime.
Perhaps it is that the costs of doing so remain hidden, while the costs of
other crime prevention methods are more obvious and direct. It is far
easier for legislatures to enact 'tough' penalties than to consider what
might be done to prevent crime generally. Another reason why we
focus on the criminal justice system may be that it not only has a 'unique
visibility', but it also provides a powerful apparatus for the support of a
particular ideology. J. Reiman, *The Rich Get Richer and the Poor Get
Prison* 162–3 (2nd edn 1984). That ideology 'conveys the message that
there are no dangerous crimes unique to the wealthy' and that it is the
poor who are responsible for crime. Ibid. at 166. It conveys the image of
equal treatment of rich and poor, however, to avoid any charge of class
bias, and it 'conveys the message that crime is not the result of the
deprivations of poverty but rather of individual moral failings.' Ibid.
The implicit ideology of criminal law focuses on individual offenders,
diverting attention from the evils present in the social order and in
established institutions. Ibid. at 144.

28. See Kelman, Criminal law: the origins of crime and violence, in *The
Politics of Law* 214, 220 (D. Kairys ed. 1982); see also R. Clark, *Crime
in America* 3–4 (1970).

29. See, e.g., Bayer, Crime, punishment, and the decline of liberal opti-
mism, 27 *Crime and Delinquency* 169, 172 (1981) (the main current of
liberal thought is optimistic, focusing on social roots and psychological
bases of crime as remediable); Currie, Crime and ideology, *Working
Papers* May–June 1982, at 26 (in the 1960s, public debate about crime
was dominated by a liberal vision that linked violence to social disadvantage and held out promise that 'social rehabilitation programs'
would reduce the crime rate); see also C. Silberman, *Criminal Violence,
Criminal Justice* 227–30 (1978) (reflecting mainstream liberal ideology
and solutions throughout). See generally R. Clark, note 28.

30. See Bayer, note 29; Currie, note 29.

31. See Bayer, note 29, at 179–86; see also F. Allen, *The Decline of the
Rehabilitative Ideal: Penal Policy and Social Policy* (1981).

32. The Warren Court's concern for the rights of the accused and its

selective incorporation of provisions of the Bill of Rights amounted to a
'revolution' in criminal procedure. See L. Baker, *Miranda: Crime,
Law, and Politics* (1983); Allen, The judicial quest for penal justice:
The Warren Court and criminal cases, *U. Ill. L.F.* 518 (1975).
33. Indeterminate sentencing is a prime example of a failed experiment.
Based on a rehabilitative approach to the criminal sanction, the indeterminate sentence could not withstand criticism of rehabilitation itself as a
proper function of the criminal sanction. See text accompanying notes
247–8; see also C. Silberman, note 29, at 504–5.
34. See Bayer, note 29, at 170–9; Curtis, The conservative new criminology, *Society* Mar.–Apr. 1977, at 8, 12–13; Silver, Crime and conventional
wisdom, *Society* Mar.–Apr. 1977, at 9, 17. Longitudinal studies of social
welfare programmes instituted in the 1960s reveal that at least one
programme, Head Start, has had a salutary effect in reducing crime
rates. See Science and the citizen, Head Starts, *Scientific American*,
Mar. 1981, at 82 (commenting on Schweinhart and Weikart, Young
Children Grow Up: The Effects of the Perry Preschool Program on
Youths Through Age 15, in *The High/Scope Educational Research
Foundation* (1980) (pre-school-age students who participated in enrich-
ment programme had lower arrest rates up to age 15 than members of
control group)).
35. Saltzburg, Foreward: the flow and ebb of constitutional criminal procedure in the Warren and Burger Courts, 69 *Geo. L.J.* 151 (1980).
36. Penal reformer Margaret Fry first proposed victim's compensation in
1957. See Fry, Justice for victims, in *Considering the Victim: Readings
in Restitution and Victim Compensation* 54–6 (J. Hudson and B. Galaway eds. 1975) [hereafter cited as Readings]. Fry's efforts led directly
to the establishment of victim's compensation programmes in New
Zealand and Great Britain. The *Journal of Public Law* published a
symposium on victim compensation in 1959. The *Minnesota Law Review* followed suit in 1965. In 1965 California became the first state in
this country to adopt a victim's compensation programme. See S. Schafer, *Compensation and Restitution to Victims of Crime* 153 (2nd edn
1970).
37. See note 358.
38. As of 1970, California, Hawaii, Maryland, Massachusetts and New
York had adopted victim's compensation programmes. See Governmental compensation for victims of violence, 43 *S. Cal. L. Rev.* 1,
158–93 app. (1970). Wisconsin adopted its first compensation statute in
1975. See 1975 *Wisconsin Laws* ch. 344, s. 3. Minnesota enacted its
victim's compensation statute in 1974. See 1974 *Minnesota Laws* ch.
463, s. 3. New Jersey adopted victim compensation in 1971, Alaska in
1972. See 1971 *New Jersey Laws* ch. 317, s. 1; 1972 *Alaska Sess. Laws*
ch. 203, s. 1.
39. See, e.g. Compensation to victims of personal violence: an examination
of the scope of the problem, 50 *Minnesota Law Review* 213 (1965)
(symposium); Governmental compensation for victims of violence,
note 38, at 1 (symposium).
40. See M. Fleming, *Of Crimes and Rights: The Penal Code Viewed as a Bill*

of Rights 15 (1978); E. Van Allen, *Our Handcuffed Police: The Assault Upon Law and Order in America and What Can be Done About It* 35–6 (1968); J. Wilson, *Thinking About Crime* 4 (1975). All of these works contain conservatively oriented chronicles of rising crime rates. See also Currie, note 29 (rising crime rate of 1960s made liberal vision 'a shambles').

41. See C. Silberman, note 29, at 159–61.
42. Ibid.
43. 'No single event ticks off America's political schizophrenia with greater certainty than the case of a black man raping a white woman . . . Racism and sexism and the fight against both converge at the point of interracial rape, a baffling crossroads of an authentic, peculiarly American, dilemma.' S. Brownmiller, *Against Our Will: Men, Women and Rape* 230 (1975).
44. See *Institutional Racism in America* 58–77 (L. Knowles and K. Pewitt eds. 1970). When *Furman* v. *Georgia* was decided by the Supreme Court, some of the Justices relied on the obvious racial discrimination in death penalty cases to strike down Georgia's death penalty statute. *Furman* v. *Georgia*, 408 U.S. 238, 242–57 (Douglas, J., concurring); ibid. at 364–5 (Marshall, J., concurring).
45. See Bayer, note 29, at 178–9.
46. The crime problem became 'an official Republican campaign issue' by April of 1968. L. Baker, note 32, at 210 (1983); Currie, note 29, at 26–7.
47. I will be using Herbert Packer's description and definition of the crime control model when I refer to it throughout this piece. H. Packer, *The Limits of the Criminal Sanction* 149–73 (1968). The rhetoric and ideology of 'crime control' (or 'law and order') have changed little since Roscoe Pound first lectured on the issues of criminal justice sixty-one years ago. See R. Pound, *Criminal Justice in America* (1945). Then, as now, the complaints were that the courts were 'soft on crime' and that the crime rate had the good citizens of the nation terrified, yet the procedural protections afforded defendants then were far fewer than those available now.
48. H. Packer, note 47, at 158.
49. Ibid. at 160.

> The model, in order to operate successfully, must produce a high rate of apprehension and conviction. . . . There must then be a premium on speed and finality . . . [E]xtrajudicial processes should be preferred to judicial processes, informal operations to formal ones . . . The model that will operate successfully on these presuppositions must be an administrative, almost a managerial, model.

Ibid. at 159.

50. Ibid. at 160 ('presumption of guilt is what makes it possible for the system to deal effectively with large numbers').
51. Ibid. at 158. Packer observes that the values contained in the crime control model are grounded 'on the proposition that the repression of criminal conduct is by far the most important function to be performed

by the criminal process. The failure of law enforcement to bring criminal conduct under tight control is viewed as leading to the breakdown of public order. . . .' Ibid.

52. One conservative book attacking the Warren Court's decisions used this phrase for its title. E. Van Allen, note 40. The law enforcement and conservative communities launched a number of stinging attacks on the Court after it decided *Miranda*. See L. Baker, note 32, at 200–5.

53. See, e.g., E. Van den Haag, *Punishing Criminals* 157–63 (1975) (arguing that offenders are not caught or punished as a result of court decisions and that police and trial court judges are thwarted by laws and appellate decisions that favour defendants).

54. Van den Haag, Crime, punishment, and deterrence, *Society*, Mar.–Apr. 1977, at 11.

55. E. Van den Haag, note 53, at 155–7.

56. See Wilson, Thinking about crime, *Atl. Monthly*, Sept. 1983, at 72 [hereafter cited as Wilson, *Thinking*]; Wilson, Thinking about thinking about crime, *Society*, Mar.–Apr. 1977, at 10.

57. Van den Haag asserts: 'The probability of convicting the guilty is greatly reduced in the U.S. by (a) delay, (b) the exclusionary rule, and (c) literally endless appeals allowed defendants from state to federal courts.' E. Van den Haag, note 53, at 164.

58. One conservative author has been unwilling to abandon deterrence theory, entirely, however. See Wilson, note 56, at 72–84.

59. See, e.g., E. Van den Haag, note 53, at 184–91 (arguing that rehabilitation is impossible without retributive punishment and that rehabilitation does not affect recidivism rates).

60. When the California legislature enacted determinate sentencing after almost 60 years of indeterminate sentencing based on a rehabilitation premise, the determinate sentencing law began: 'The Legislature finds and declares that the purpose of imprisonment for crime is punishment.' California Penal Code s. 1170(a)(1) (West, 1984); S. Kadish, S. Schulhofer and M. Paulsen, *Criminal Law and Its Processes* 205 (4th edn 1983).

61. Renewed interest in incapacitation has resulted in 'habitual offender' or 'career criminal' statutes in many states. See, e.g., California Penal Code ss. 999b–h (West Supp., 1984) (establishing 'career criminal' programme); California Penal Code ss. 667, 667.5, 667.7 (West, 1982) (increasing sentences for 'habitual offenders'); *Ky. Rev. Stat. Ann.* s. 532.080 (Baldwin 1984) (providing that the jury determine whether the offender is a 'persistent felony offender' and allowing imposition of life imprisonment on such finding); *La. Rev. Stat. Ann.* s. 15:529.1 (West 1981) (making life imprisonment without possibility of parole a possibility for people convicted of a prior felony); New York Penal Law s. 70.10 (McKinney, 1975) ('persistent felony offender' may be sentenced to a minimum of 15–25 years or a maximum of life imprisonment).

62. The oft-cited example is the change in California's indeterminate sentencing law in 1976, when the penal code was revised to declare 'that the purpose of imprisonment is punishment.' California Penal Code s. 1170(a)(1) (West, 1984). Governor James Thompson of Illinois recently

wrote that '[t]he tough sentencing laws I fought for in the General Assembly and which are now law . . . are not the primary causal factor in prison overcrowding.' Thompson, Introduction: Illinois' response to the problem of prison crowding, *University of Illinois Law Review* 203, 204 (1984). Those 'tough sentencing laws' became effective in 1978. Casper, Determinate sentencing and prison crowding in Illinois, *University of Illinois Law Review* 231, 237 (1984); see also B. Jackson, *Law and Disorder* 25–26, 151–4 ('tough on crime' postures used by New York gubernatorial candidates in the 1970s; legislators respond to the level of fear and anger transmitted to them by their constituents).

63. In 1970, there were approximately 196,000 persons incarcerated in prisons in the United States, or 97 prisoners per 100,000 in the population. In 1980, there were approximately 321,000 prison inmates, or 142 prisoners per 100,000 people. By 1983, the number of prisoners had grown to 455,000. Since the beginning of 1983, the prison population in this country has increased by approximately 222 inmates per day. See Bencivenga, Book Review, *Christian Science Monitor*, 14 Mar. 1984, at 18, col. 1.

64. After nearly a decade in which no one was executed in the United States, the Supreme Court upheld Georgia's death penalty statute. *Gregg* v. *Georgia*, 428 U.S. 153 (1976): The pace of executions did not accelerate, however, until 1983, after the Court decided four cases that arguably overruled its decision in *Furman* v. *Georgia*, 408 U.S. 238 (1972). See Weisberg, Deregulating death, 1983 *Sup. Ct. Rev.* 305 (explaining the Court's doctrinal retreat from death penalty cases); Press, Rate of executions picks up in U.S., *Christian Science Monitor*, 15 Nov. 1984, at 3, at col. 2 (six persons executed between 1977 and 1983, five executed in 1983, and nineteen executed as of 8 November 1984).

65. The crime rate has, for the moment, decreased slightly. Explanations for the slight decrease in index offences vary enormously, depending on ideology. Criminologists have observed that the ageing of the population accounts for much of the decrease, while political conservatives attribute the phenomenon to tougher law enforcement and penalties.

66. See Gross, Some anticrime proposals for progressives, 234 *Nation* 137 (1982) (after 1980 election, President Reagan made 'sweeping attack' on ideology of 1950s and 1960s and proposed that the exclusionary rule be reformed, preventive detention statutes be enacted, and longer prison terms be imposed). See generally L. Baker, note 32.

67. In 1968, for example, Van Allen wrote: 'What good are our police . . . if a court like the U.S. Supreme Court continues to put what is tantamount to a premium on lawlessness while it in effect penalizes the victim . . . We have seen what the criminal-protecting U.S. Supreme Court decisions have done to the cause of justice. They have made the criminal's rights superior to those of their victim.' E. Van Allen, note 40, at 119. Most of the political rhetoric of the late 1960s and the 1970s, however, focused on public fear of crime – a 'future victim' posture – and largely overlooked the symbolic value of past victims.

68. As the women's movement gained strength, focus on deconstructing the

mythology of rape grew in both medical and legal circles. See, e.g., Berger, Man's trial, woman's tribulation: rape cases in the courtroom, 77 *Colum. L. Rev.* 1, 3 (1977) ('[I]t is fitting that the "rediscovery" of rape should coincide with the growth of the Women's Movement . . . Women have . . . played a key role in lobbying for reforms in the law of rape.'); Rape: 'the ultimate violation of the self', 133 *American Journal of Psychiatry* 436, 437 (1976) ('Recent attitudinal shifts have been largely due to the initiative taken by countless numbers of women who have begun to sensitize our medical, social and legal institutions about the extent to which cultural biases have determined the maltreatment of the [rape] victim').

69. See note 76 and accompanying text.
70. The forces of 'law and order' have been quite receptive to the lobbying by groups representing specific classes of victims. For example, the California rape shield statute, *Cal. Evid. Code* ss. 782, 1103 (West 1974), was titled the Robbins Rape Evidence Law after its co-sponsor, conservative Republican Senator Alan Robbins. The name of liberal Senator George Moscone, a co-author, is not associated with the rape shield law in California. Note, California Rape Evidence Reform: An Analysis of Senate Bill 1678, 26 *Hastings Law Journal* 1551, 1554 n. 15 (1975).
71. See, e.g., President's Task Force on Victims of Crime, *Final Report* (1982) (recommendations for action by governmental agencies) [hereinafter cited as Task Force]; New York State Compensation Board, A Bill of Rights for Crime Victims, in 5 *Victimology* 428 (1980) (recommendations similar to those of the President's Task Force); Task Force on the Victims of Crime and Violence, Executive Summary: Final Report of the APA Task Force on the Victims of Crime and Violence, 40 *American Psychologist* 107 (1985) (recommending, *inter alia*, greater victim participation in criminal process).
72. See, e.g., L. Forer, *Criminals and Victims* (1980); M. Hyde, note 25; R. Reiff, note 25; Carrington, Deterrence, death, and the victims of crime: a common sense approach, 35 *Vand. L. Rev.* 587 (1982); Goldstein, note 21; Harland, Monetary remedies for the victims of crime: assessing the role of the criminal courts, 30 *UCLA Law Review* 52 (1982); R. Elias, *Victims of the System: Crime Victims and Compensation in American Politics and Criminal Justice* (1983) (empirical study of victims and victim compensation programmes in New Jersey and New York); Burgess and Holmstrom, Coping behavior of the rape victim, 133 *American Journal of Psychiatry* 413 (1976) (stages of coping with the event); Notman and Nadelson, The rape victim: psychodynamic considerations, 133 *American Journal of Psychiatry* 408 (1976) (discussing reactions to victimization of rape victims); Reactions to victimization, 39 *J. Soc. Issues* 1 (1983) (collection of articles and studies dealing with effects of criminal victimization and of victimization by disaster or disease). See generally *Victimology*, a journal, started in 1976, which specializes in criminal victimization topics.
73. Pub. L. No. 97–291, 96 Stat. 1248 (1982) (codified at 18 U.S.C. ss. 1501, 1502, 1512–15, 3579–80 (1982)).

152   *Critical Views on Victimology and Victim Policy*

74. See, e.g., *Mass. Gen. Laws Ann.* ch. 258B (West 1983); *R.I. Gen. Laws* ss. 12–28–1, 12–28–8 (Supp. 1983); *W. Va. Code* ss. 61–11A–7 (Supp. 1984).
75. See Task Force, note 71.
76. Mothers Against Drunk Driving (MADD) was founded in 1980 by a California woman, Candy Lightner, after her daughter was killed by a drunk driver. See Lightner to speak in Palo Alto, *Peninsula Times Tribune*, 17 May 1984, at E–1, col. 4. MADD now has at least 258 chapters nationally and approximately '300,000 supporters'. President's Message, 3 *MADD National Newsletter* 1 (Spring 1984).

    Bob and Charlotte Hunninger of Cincinnati, Ohio, founded 'Parents of Murdered Children' in 1978, for the purpose of providing support for parents whose children had been killed. See Miller, Read this if you have kids, *San Jose Mercury News*, 17 Apr. 1984, at 1B, col. 1.
77. Arizona Constitution art. I, s. 22(2), (3); California Constitution art. I, s. 28(e), (g) (as amended on 8 June 1982); Colorado Constitution s. 19(1)(b); Michigan Constitution art. I, s. 15; Nebraska Constitution art. I, s. 9; Texas Constitution art. I, s. 11a; Wisconsin Constitution art. I, s. 8(3); *Ga. Code Ann.* s. 17–6–1(b)(2), (c) (Supp. 1984); *Utah Code Ann.* s. 77–20–1 (1980).
78. The California initiative passed in 1982 instituted radical changes in California law. See note 87. And in New Mexico, for example, a murder victim's mother has been successfully lobbying for changes in criminal procedure similar to those contained in California's victim's rights initiative. See *Outrage: crime victims strike back*, broadcast by KPIX in San Francisco (13 Apr. 1984); see also Frymer, Documentary details crime victims' outrage, *San Jose Mercury News*, 18 Aug. 1983, at 9C, col. 1.
79. See notes 315–17; see also Schmalz, Crime Victims Seek a Greater Voice, *New York Times*, 6 Mar. 1985, at 17, col. 2 (describing recent lobbying efforts of crime victims in New York).
80. Conservative Republicans were the progenitors of Proposition 8, California's victim's rights initiative. Galante, Exclusionary rule struck in California, *National Law Journal*, 18 Feb. 1985, at 11, col. 1. Proponents of the sweeping constitutional amendment, mainly conservative Republicans, said the initiative was meant to stop California's traditionally liberal Supreme Court from giving defendants greater rights under the state constitution than they enjoy under the US Constitution. Ibid. And, in *In re Lance W.*, a divided California Supreme Court held that Proposition 8 effectively abolished independent state grounds for the exclusion of evidence seized by the police. *In re Lance W.*, 37 Cal. Adv. Sh. 3d 873, 210 Cal. Rptr. 631 (1985). See also Turpen, The criminal injustice system: an overview of the Oklahoma victims' bill of rights, 17 *Tulsa Law Journal* 253 (1981) (the Oklahoma District Attorneys Association drafted the state's victim's rights legislation; lobbying by district attorneys, law enforcement officers, and 'citizens' through petition led to eventual passage).
81. See notes 170–84, 214–25 and accompanying texts.

82. L. Strauss, *Natural Right and History* 181–2 (1959); Berlin, Two concepts of liberty, in *Four Essays on Liberty* 165–6 (1970).
83. J. Feinberg, *Social Philosophy* 58–9 (1973).
84. See texts accompanying notes 181, 220–9.
85. The rhetoric in support of Proposition 8 repeatedly emphasized the fear of future victimization and the handcuffing of law enforcement by the courts. By contrast, the text of Proposition 8 mentions victims in only 3 of its 21 substantive provisions: Section 3(b) provided the victim a 'right to restitution', section 6(a) promised the victim a 'right to a hearing' at sentencing, and section 6(b) provided the victim a right to a hearing at parole proceedings. See *Brosnahan* v. *Brown*, 32 Cal. 3d 236 app., 651 P.2d 274 app., 186 Cal. Rptr. 80 app. (1982) (ballot statements and provisions of Proposition 8).
86. At least one liberal explicitly ignored the contradictions in trying to regain the momentum liberal programmes had enjoyed in the 1960s by asserting that '[a] logical next step would be a Victim's Bill of Rights, which could provide for witness compensation, protection against reprisals, prompt return of confiscated property, progress reports on the prosecution of offenders, free legal services and restitution payments by *the criminal* or, failing that, by the government.' Gross, note 66, at 139 (emphasis added).
87. The California referendum, for example, effectively abolished the right to bail in noncapital cases, California Constitution art. 1, ss, 12, 28(c), attempted to abolish the Fourth and Fifth Amendment exclusionary rules, ibid. at art. 1, s. 28(d), increased minimum mandatory sentences, see, e.g., *California Penal Code* s. 667 (West 1982), and attempted to abolish plea bargaining, ibid. at s. 1192.7. The act also requires restitution to victims, California Constitution art. 1, s. 28(b), provides for victim participation at sentencing hearings, California Penal Code s. 1191.1 (West 1982), and allows victims to oppose parole of offenders, ibid. at s. 3043 (adult offenders); Cal. Welf. and Inst. Code s. 1767 (West 1982) (juvenile offenders). These changes seem to reflect reforms advocated by conservatives. See note 66.
88. Hans von Hentig is usually credited with founding this subspecialty in H. von Hentig, *The Criminal and His Victim: Studies in the Sociology of Crime* (1948). See also S. Schafer, *The Victim and His Criminal, A Study in Functional Responsibility* 39–59 (1968). See generally *Victimology* (I. Drapkin and E. Viano eds. 1974). The victimologists now have their own scholarly journal entitled *Victimology*.
89. Explicitly recognizing the relative lack of psychological studies of the consequences of victimization, the *Journal of Social Issues* has published one symposium on the effects of various types of victimization, see Symposium, reactions to victimization, 39 *J. Soc. Issues* 1–227 (1983), and another exclusively addressing the effects of criminal victimization, see Symposium, criminal victimization, 40 *J. Soc. Issues* 1–115 (1984); see also Fischer, A phenomenological study of being criminally victimized: contributions and constraints of qualitative research, 40 *J. Soc. Issues* 161 (we know more about reported fear of

crime and indices of fear than experience of victimization); Burgess and Holmstrom, Rape trauma syndrome, 131 *American Journal of Psychiatry* 981 (1974) (literature on rape provides little information on physical and psychological effects of rape).

90. The basic theory this piece proposes is not original, but rather follows closely the concepts and analysis developed by Dr Irvin Yalom. See I. Yalom, *Existential Psychotherapy* (1980); see also R. May, *Discovery of Being: Writings in Existential Psychology* (1983); R. May, *Power and Innocence: A Search for the Sources of Violence* (1978) [hereinafter cited as R. May, *Power*]; R. May, *The Meaning of Anxiety* (rev. edn, 1977); R. May, *Man's Search for Himself* (1953); R. May, *Love and Will* (1969); B. Bettelheim, *Surviving and Other Essays* (1979); V. Frankl, *Man's Search for Meaning* (3rd edn, 1984); K. Erikson, *Everything in Its Path* (1976).

91. Throughout the piece, I will discuss only the effects of 'core' crimes on victims, because the effects of other crimes are unlikely to be as severe in most instances and because the victims of core crimes provide the symbol that gives force to the entire victim's rights movement.

92. Objective writing does not, and perhaps cannot, capture the nature of experiences relating to death, meaning, freedom and responsibility, and existential isolation as well as perhaps fiction or poetry can. What follows is an effort to sketch a simple analytical framework, rather than an effort to impart a complete understanding of these issues.

93. See, e.g., Burgess and Holmstrom, note 89 (rape victims experience acute stress reaction to life-threatening situation; fear of death is the primary component of the experience of rape); Janoff-Bulman and Frieze, A theoretical perspective for understanding reactions to victimization, 39 *J. Soc. Issues* 1 (1983) (studies indicate that victimization causes the destruction of the assumption of invulnerability and the loss of a sense of meaning and of control); Silver, Boon and Stones, Searching for meaning in misfortune: making sense of incest, 39 *J. Soc, Issues* 81 (1983) (studying whether finding meaning aided incest victims in coping with experience).

94. See K. Erikson, note 90, at 184. This assumption persists to some extent today. The *Diagnostic and Statistical Manual* of the American Psychiatric Association notes that 'Post-Traumatic Stress Disorders' caused by severe trauma are influenced by prior adjustment: '[P]reexisting psychopathology apparently predisposes to the development of the disorder.' 3 American Psychiatric Association, *Diagnostic and Statistical Manual* 237 (1981). But this somewhat glib conclusion has been contradicted by some prominent psychiatrists. Bettelheim, for example, rejects the hypothesis that reactions to extreme trauma are necessarily defined by pre-existing emotional problems. B. Bettelheim, note 90, at 28–35. And the evidence from studies of Vietnam veterans suffering from the disorder is inconclusive as well. See M. MacPherson, *Long Time Passing: Viet Nam and the Haunted Generation* 192–3, 197–207 (1984); see also Lyons, More Vietnam veterans are turning to therapy, *New York Times*, 13 Nov. 1984, at Cl, col. 1 (American psychiatrists refused to believe that Post Traumatic Stress Disorder existed at all for

a long time, despite studies and speculation dating back to World War I that war and other catastrophes leave deep traumatic scars).

95. See, e.g., R. Lifton, *Thought Reform and the Psychology of Totalism* (1961) [hereinafter cited as R. Lifton, *Thought Reform*]; see also R. Lifton, *Home From the War* (1973).

96. See, e.g., B. Bettelheim, note 90, at 24–33, 105–11. By making the comparison and noting the similarities, I do not wish in any way to trivialize the monstrous horror of the death camps, nor the long-lasting consequences of the camp experience for survivors.

97. Kai Erikson's study of the effects of a flood that destroyed several small towns in West Virginia and killed many people contains the same themes as do other studies of extreme experiences. See K. Erikson, note 90. Accounts of other forms of disaster – no matter how relatively horrifying to outsiders – also reflect reactions of loss, grief, fear and disorientation in the aftermath of the experience. See R. Lifton, *History and Human Survival* 117–94 (1970) (detailing reactions of Hiroshima survivors); Quanstrom, Burning Memories, *San Jose Mercury News*, 26 Sept. 1983, at 1A, col. 3 (detailing reactions of neighbourhood in San Diego, California, five years after a jet crashed).

98. In some instances, prior experiences do impede recovery from a disaster. When an individual 'has undergone too severe or too frequent early traumatic experiences' and later experiences sudden and severe trauma, recovery from the later experience may be extremely difficult. See F. Fromm-Reichman, *Psychoanalysis and Psychotherapy* 93–4 (1959). But even 'normal' people depend on dissociation of traumatic events to master their existence. Ibid. Although a recent study of rape victims indicated that pre-assault psychological symptoms were the most likely predictors for long-term retention of symptoms, the relationship diminished over time. Sales, Baum and Shore, Victim readjustment following assault, 40 *J. Soc. Issues* 117, 122–3 (1984). Moreover, the authors found that other variables influenced manifestations of symptoms at various times. Ibid. at 129. Cf. R. Lifton, *Thought Reform*, note 95, at 86 (personal responses, while similar, depended 'largely upon' character traits, 'emotions and identities developed within [the person] during . . . entire previous life'); Lyons, note 94, at 21, col. 1 (Veterans Administration estimates that 350,000 to 400,000 Vietnam veterans suffer from disorder in some form: '"every patient is different"'.

99. Compare Notman and Nadelson, The rape victim: psychodynamic considerations, 133 *American Journal of Psychiatry* 405 (1976) (rape is traumatic external event that breaks balance of ego adaptation and environment, resulting in guilt, phobic reactions, anxiety and depression), with K. Erikson, note 90, at 156–7 (medical terms for conditions present in 93 per cent of flood survivors include depression, anxiety, phobia, post-traumatic neurosis; Erikson's terms include confusion, despair, hopelessness).

100. Strikingly common themes run through confidential conversations that I have had with crime victims and their families. Although each person with whom I have talked has had various behavioural responses to the crime and its aftermath, all of these people experienced feelings of fear,

anxiety and loss of security or control. Many have asked why they were victimized; those who have not explicitly asked 'why', devised their own explanations for their victimization. Most have attempted to find some meaning in the event, whether by blaming themselves or by searching elsewhere. A few have become totally isolated from others. But all have limited their activities in one way or another.

101. The sexual assault victims with whom I have spoken experienced reactions similar to those reported in formal studies. Some of the victims had specific fear reactions to the location of the assault, and others experienced a more generalized fear reactions. All but one had moved from the area where the assault had taken place. Similar reactions were found by Scheppele and Bart. Scheppele and Bart, Through women's eyes: defining danger in the wake of sexual assault, 39 *J. Soc. Issues* 63 (1983). See generally K. Erikson, note 90; Metzger, It is always the woman who is raped, 133 *American Journal of Psychiatry* 405 (1976); Maganini, Crime victim aid plan suffering from neglect, *San Francisco Chronicle*, 17 Oct. 1983, at 1, col. 5 (statements by assault, mugging, and rape victims about experiences); rape, *Stanford Campus Report*, 27 Jan. 1983, at 5 (anonymous interviews with two victims of sexual assaults).

102. B. Bettelheim, note 90, at 28.

103. K. Erikson, note 90, at 253.

104. I. Yalom, note 90, at 159.

105. Bettelheim has observed that the worst situation for an individual is '[w]hen we are abandoned and immediate death is possible and likely . . . Then the effects are catastrophic. The combined sudden breakdown of all . . . defenses against death anxiety projects us into . . . an *extreme situation*.' B. Bettelheim, note 90, at 11 (emphasis in original). In his study of Westerners imprisoned by the Chinese and subjected to 'thought reform', Lifton found that four years after the experience, 'my subjects still bore marks of both fear and relief. The fear was related to . . . the fear of total annihilation.' R. Lifton, *Thought Reform*, note 95, at 238.

106. I. Yalom, note 90, at 159. Studies of the impact of near-death experiences have not concentrated as much on victims of violent crime as they have on accident victims, unsuccessful suicides and people with terminal illnesses. Some of these studies indicate that *positive* changes may result from the experience – that realization of the previous nature of life may sharpen one's awareness, see ibid. at 33–8, result in a change in priorities, and lead to enhanced relationships with others, ibid. at 35. This may not be as true for crime victims, however. A failure of crime victims to benefit from their confrontation with death may be an effect of being labelled a 'victim' or may be a result of a lack, caused by society's intense ambivalence toward crime victims, of any social support. See notes 139–47. Whether crime victims experience an enhanced appreciation for life because of their confrontation with death is an open question at this time.

107. I. Yalom, note 90, at 41.

108. See Perloff, Perceptions of vulnerability to victimization, 39 *J. Soc.*

Issues 41 (1983) (non-victims tend to underestimate likelihood or frequency of negative life events and appear to maintain illusion of unique invulnerability). Dr Yalom borrows from Tolstoy's *Death of Ivan Ilych* to illustrate the belief in special protection from death and harm:

> The syllogism he had learnt from Kiezewetter's Logic: 'Caius is a man, men are mortal, therefore Caius is mortal,' but certainly not as applied to himself. That Caius – man in the abstract – was mortal, was perfectly correct, but he was not Caius, not an abstract man, but a creature quite, quite separate from all others . . . It cannot be that I ought to die. That would be too terrible.

    I. Yalom, note 90, at 117–18 (quoting L. Tolstoy, *The Death of Ivan Ilych and Other Stories* 131–2 (1960)).

109. Scheppele and Bart found that women who had followed 'the rules of rape avoidance' were more likely to have severe reactions to the assault than those who knew that they were in a dangerous situation at the time of the attack. To be assaulted when one has taken all appropriate measures to avoid assault is a horrifying reminder that one is not in control of one's fate. Scheppele and Bart, note 101, at 76–8. The severity of the reaction to being attacked in 'safe circumstances' is related to the loss of control, not just of the attack itself, 'but for the future as well'. Ibid. at 79. Peterson and Seligman suggest that criminal victimization may increase feelings of helplessness or reinforce already existing learned helplessness, for 'when uncontrollable bad events *precede* helpless behavior, and when the helpless individual expects future responding to be futile, it may well be that learned helplessness is operative.' Peterson and Seligman, Learned helplessness and victimization, 39 *J. Soc. Issues* 103, 107 (1983).

110. See R. Lifton, Thought Reform, note 95, at 148–9 (apparent resisters to thought reform used denial and repression as coping strategies); see also I. Yalom, note 90, at 44–5.

111. See Krupnick, Brief Psychotherapy with Victims of Violent Crime, 5 *Victimology* 347, 348 (1980). Once the illusion of invulnerability is shattered by an assault, victims may even overestimate the likelihood of another assault. Tyler, Assessing the Risk of Crime Victimization: the integration of personal victimization, 40 *J. Soc. Issues* 27, 45 (1984).

112. See Peterson and Seligman, note 109.

113. See Scheppele and Bart, note 101.

114. See C. Silberman, note 29, at 19–21.

115. Suicide paradoxically 'relieves' death anxiety by giving the individual ultimate control over his or her own death. I. Yalom, note 90, at 122, 197–9. Numerous rape victims, Vietnam veterans and survivors of Hiroshima have responded to their victimization with suicide attempts or successful suicides. See, e.g., T. Beneke, *Men on Rape* 164 (1982) (suicide attempts by rape victims are not uncommon); M. MacPherson, note 94, at 239 (detailing suicide rates of Vietnam veterans); R. Lifton, note 97, at 117–94 (discussing suicide as a response to the nuclear attack on Hiroshima); see also Stipp, Cancer threat seen for Vietnam vets in

study of deaths, *Wall Street Journal*, 29 Jan. 1985, at 42, col. 6 (suicide rate among Vietnam veterans in Massachusetts is 58 per cent above the expected rate).

116. One recent study of 94 sexual assault victims found that 91 per cent of women who were raped in a 'safe situation' – at home with the doors locked, for example – suffered from either a 'diffuse' fear reaction – a view of numerous situations as dangerous – or a 'total fear' reaction – a life characterized by constant, 'almost unbearable' fear. Scheppele and Bart, note 101, at 78. These extreme reactions are not surprising given the intrusiveness of the crimes described; such an invasion could easily shatter the victim's illusion of invulnerability and her confidence in her ability to control life.

It is not atypical for a victim of a sexual assault to state, 'I wish he'd killed me' or 'if it happens again, I hope I die.' See S. Brownmiller, note 43, at 406; see also Frazier and Borgida, Rape trauma evidence in court, 40 *Am. Psych.* 984, 990 (1985) (a recent survey found sexual assault victims five times as likely to attempt suicide as non-victims); Dowd, Rape: the sexual weapon, *Time*, 5 Sep. 1983, at 27, 28 ('Studies show that . . . suicide attempts are fairly common after rape').

117. See I. Yalom, note 90, at 356.
118. Ibid. at 43. This form of dread – of fear of nothingness – causes the world to become foreign. It is a sensation of falling, of not perceiving, of being lost. It is more than anxiety or panic in the classic meaning of those words; it is, indeed, dread.
119. P. Tillich, *The Courage to Be* 111 (1952). Tillich sees death and meaning as separate existential issues, but acknowledges that the question of life's meaning is related to the consciousness of mortality. Ibid. at 170. See also B. Bettelheim, note 90, at 4.
120. I. Yalom, note 90, at 466.
121. The questions asked by the crime victim may range from the simplest inquiries to the anguished cry of Job. They may transcend causal explanations or attributions, encompassing the search for life's ultimate meaning. Human suffering seems to demand an explanation and, as Frankl observes, a victim's search for meaning in the aftermath of the event may operate at two levels: on one level is a search for meaning in one's own suffering; on the other level is a search for meaning to human suffering in general. V. Frankl, note 90, at 178–88. Not all victims consciously pursue meaning, however. See Silver, Boon and Stones, note 93, at 94.
122. Most commonly, victims will blame the perpetrator, but they also frequently blame the police for failing to protect them and blame society for creating the circumstances leading to the crime.

If the word 'attribution' is substituted for 'blame', the questions of meaning become more apparent. See Miller and Porter, Self-blame in victims of violence, 39 *J. Soc. Issues* 139 (1983) (self-blame is defined as attribution; control and meaning are supplied for victims through attribution).

123. See Peterson and Seligman, note 109.
124. John Walsh, the father of a boy who was abducted and murdered in

1981, has worked diligently and successfully to publicize the need for effective law enforcement in locating missing children and to obtain federal support for a national system for locating abducted children. See Anderson, Missing children's center gets funding, *San Jose Mercury News*, 19 Apr. 1984, at 2A, col. 5. Many rape victims eventually become involved with rape crisis counselling. Moreover, one of the factors motivating the founders of Mothers Against Drunk Driving was a desire to help families of victims.

125. Although much publicity has been given to Mothers Against Drunk Driving and their 'tough' policies against drunk driving, some relatives of victims may choose to remedy what they perceive to be a greater evil. The daughter-in-law of a homicide victim, for example, chose to start a group to oppose the death penalty because '[w]e simply wanted to prevent violence from being added to violence.' See Deans, Murder most foul, but vengeance kills the soul, *San Jose Mercury News*, 17 July 1983, at 4C, col. 1.

126. A near-death experience can result in a reorganization of priorities and a desire to concentrate on what one finds to be meaningful. See I. Yalom, note 90, at 33–5. Occasionally, however, crime victims will identify with the aggressor and court danger or enter a criminal life. Scheppele and Bart, note 101, at 71 (one rape victim became a prostitute, thief and drug abuser; another carried a knife and 'became promiscuous'). The case of Patricia Hearst, who was kidnapped, tortured and raped, only to be convicted of armed robbery, may be the most widely known example of the phenomenon of identifying with the aggressor. Ideologically the 'perfect' victim symbol, Ms Hearst received remarkably little sympathy for her plight.

127. Just as with other traumatic events, such as the loss of a significant and loved other person, there are stages of recovery and reintegration. See Burgess and Holmstrom, note 89, at 981, 982–4 (1974) (acute phase during first several weeks after sexual assault; long-term reorganization took place at different rates for different victims); see also B. Bettelheim, note 90, at 36 ('Personal integration, and with it achievement of meaning, is a highly individual, lifelong struggle').

128. B. Bettelheim, note 90, at 34–35; V. Frankl, note 90, at 121–3. A study of father–daughter incest victims found that, even after an average time of twenty years since the crime, over 80 per cent of the victims responding stated that they were still searching for an understanding of the experience. See Silver, Boon and Stones, note 93, at 99. Those victims who had found at least some meaning coped with life significantly better than those who could not find any meaning, ibid. at 93, even though the search for meaning might not have produced a totally sufficient explanation for them.

129. See I. Yalom, note 90, at 218–21.

130. J.P. Sartre, *Being and Nothingness* 633 (1956).

131. I. Yalom, note 90, at 218. Dr Yalom adopts Sartre's definition. Ibid. In a section titled 'Responsibility Awareness American Style – Or, How to Take Charge of Your Own Life, Pull Your Own Strings, Take Care of Number One, and Get "It",' Yalom quotes an exchange between an

EST (Ehrhard Sensitivity Training) trainer and a participant that illustrates 'that one is responsible for being mugged.' Ibid. at 256.

> EVERYTHING THAT YOU EXPERIENCE DOESN'T EXIST UNLESS YOU EXPERIENCE IT. EVERYTHING A LIVING CREATURE EXPERIENCES IS CREATED UNIQUELY BY THAT LIVING CREATURE WHO IS THE SOLE SOURCE OF THAT EXPERIENCE. WAKE UP, HANK.

Ibid. at 257 (quoting L. Reinhart, *The Book of EST* 142–4 (1976) (emphasis in original)).

132. While this concept of responsibility sounds very abstract, it actually exists even at an everyday level: you see a friend on the street, you smile and say hello, but the friend does not acknowledge you. You respond by deciding that the friend is angry with you, or did not notice you, or is preoccupied. *How* you saw the friend was a matter of choice: you may have missed the friend's sad expression or failed to see that he or she was looking in another direction.

133. Burgess and Holmstrom, Coping behaviour of the rape victim, 133 *American Journal of Psychiatry* 413, 416 (1976) (some women denied the event; some dissociated the experience; some suppressed it). One sexual assault victim captured this phenomenon perfectly: 'You don't want to believe it happened. . . . It's so unreal that you don't want to believe it happened or that it can happen.' Rape, note 101, at 5, col. 3.

134. See note 131.

135. Robert Lifton's formulation of responsibility postulates that adjustment occurs in three phases. The first is 'confrontation', a recognition of the impact of external forces and of the potential for choice. The second is 'reordering', an exploration of existential guilt and a testing of new ideas and behaviours. The third is 'renewal', the choice of an ideological path. R. Lifton, *Thought Reform*, note 95, at 463–7.

136. See W. Ryan, *Blaming the Victim* (rev. edn, 1976). Blaming victims for their plight tends to make them feel guilty. The trap of blame and guilt creates a bond between the victim and the event that may come to dominate the victim's life, making it impossible for the victim to live independent of the criminal event. See notes 268–75 and accompanying text.

137. In discussing innocence, Rollo May distinguishes between two kinds of innocence. One is 'authentic innocence' – 'a quality of imagination . . . [F]rom this innocence spring awe and wonder . . . It is the preservation of childlike attitudes into maturity without sacrificing the realism of one's perception of evil, or as Arthur Miller puts it, one's "complicity with evil."' R. May, *Power*, note 90, at 48–9. Naivete characterizes 'pseudoinnocence', the second kind of innocence: 'It is childishness rather than childlikeness . . . [which leads us to] make a virtue of powerlessness, weakness, and helplessness.' Ibid. at 49. This second form of innocence is a defence against responsibility. Ibid. at 63–4. To May, pseudoinnocence is a profound problem in American culture. Ibid. at 50, 56–7. To emphasize this form of innocence may be to discourage crime victims from taking responsibility for their experi-

ences and lives and to encourage them to engage in ultimately self-defeating attitudes of helplessness, powerlessness, denial or repression.

138. If the victim becomes a stereotype, an 'it', to other people, the potential for relationship is negated; the victim becomes objectified and relationship of the kind that mitigates isolation is precluded.

139. See I. Yalom, note 90, at 353.

140. Ibid. at 356. It may be the common wisdom that 'the one thing that victims of crime would cherish most: to somehow wipe out the moment when assailant and victim came together; to turn back the clock 10 seconds before the crime and allow the victim to walk away . . .' Greene, A violent stranger becomes a lifelong companion, *San Jose Mercury News*, 7 May 1984, at 14B, col. 3. But ultimately victims cannot be free from the assaut until they acknowledge that it happened.

141. 'Being' is both internally and externally defined. J.P. Sartre, note 130, at 303. Even the hermit, who eschews human contact, relates to his environment and thereby realizes his existence.

142. M. Buber, *Between Man and Man* 11 (1965).

143. See generally W. Ryan, note 136 (describing American proclivity for blaming victims for their misfortunes). Blaming victims may serve a protective function for others: if one can perceive a difference between a victim and oneself, it may be possible to maintain one's own illusion of invulnerability. A concrete example of this phenomenon appears in the book *The Onion Field*, which chronicles the kidnapping of two police officers, one of whom was murdered. The victims were blamed officially and indirectly for their fate. J. Wambaugh, *The Onion Field* 235–41, 368–72 (1973).

144. In a perhaps misguided effort to console a person who has been victimized, friends or relatives frequently make such remarks as 'it could have been worse,' 'at least you're alive,' 'at least they caught the guy,' or 'its over with; you're safe now.' These statements are less than comforting when one realizes the nature of severe trauma. See Coates and Winston, Counteracting the deviance of depression: peer support groups for victims, 39 *J. Soc. Issues* 169, 174–75 (1983) (summary of studies of reactions of nonvictims to victims).

145. Ibid. Our culture places a great emphasis on 'happiness' and the absence of distress. Seeing another's distress makes us uncomfortable, so we often withdraw contact.

146. See notes 108–9 and accompanying text.

147. Coates and Winston, note 144, at 175 ('It would appear, then, that when victims fail to quickly "snap out of it," others try to enforce standards indicating they should do so').

148. Given the profound nature of the experiences of victims, it would be foolish to say that there is one 'right' way to cope with the experience. Although some generalizations about the effect of extreme trauma on individuals are possible, the resolution of the crisis depends on an infinite number of external and internal variables influencing the individual. Moreover, as Bettelheim observes, '[a] survivor has every right to choose his very own way of trying to cope.' B. Bettelheim, note 90, at 37.

149. See notes 70–1, 266–7 and accompanying texts.
150. Ironically, the hysterical reaction is the one most likely to give the victim credibility in the eyes of the police. Although a lack of a perceptible response or affect is not unusual, it may lead the police to believe no crime occurred. See Berger, note 68, at 23–4 and n.150; see also Burgess and Holmstrom, note 89, at 982 (discussing two forms of immediate emotional response to rape: one, 'the expressed style, in which feelings of fear, anger, and anxiety were shown through such behavior as crying, sobbing, smiling, restlessness, and tenseness'; the other, 'the controlled style, in which feelings were masked or hidden and a calm, composed, or subdued affect was seen').
151. One study of assault and robbery victims in Brooklyn and Newark found that the motivations of victims differed from the goals of the criminal process and that victims were often dissatisfied with the performance of prosecutors, judges and police. R. Elias, note 72, at 83–140. Twenty per cent of those surveyed had negative feelings toward the 'system' that manifested a transfer of blame. Typical comments included: '"The law doesn't protect the citizen,"' and '"I'm frustrated. I won't deal with the . . . system anymore. Next time I'll just kill him and when they take me to court I'm going to tell the judge that I want the same treatment as this guy got!"' Ibid. at 134. Although many of the victims surveyed saw a need for better law enforcement or stricter sentencing, 26 per cent had no suggestion for improving the situation for future crime victims because they were apparently satisfied with the way in which their cases were handled. Ibid. at 135.
152. Task Force, note 71.
153. Ibid. at 3–13.
154. The President's Task Force admits as much: 'Based on the testimony of . . . victims, we have drawn a composite of a victim of crime in America today.' Ibid. at 3. It nonetheless asserts, however, that the composite victim 'is every victim'. Ibid.
155. Senator Edward Kennedy heard 'horror stories of murder, rape and torture' from witnesses advocating the abolition of parole in a hearing before the Senate Judiciary Committee, for example. See Crime victims' agony, *San Francisco Chronicle*, 24 May 1983, at 8, col. 1. One seldom hears from victims for whom the system has 'worked'. But see Silverberg, My mugging: justice is done, *Newsweek*, 4 July 1983, at 13 (arguing that the press may have overemphasized those instances where malfunction in the criminal justice system have occurred).
156. See, e.g., Wisconsin Constitution art. I, s. 8 (1981); Task Force, note 71, at 22.
157. See, e.g., Task Force, note 71, at 57–68, 75–6.
158. See, e.g., *California Penal Code* s. 1192.7 (West 1983); R. Reiff, note 25, at 114–17; Task Force, note 71, at 65–6; Gifford, Meaningful reform of plea bargaining: the control of prosecutorial discretion, 1983 *U. Ill. L. Rev.* 37, 90–2.
159. See, e.g., Task Force, note 71, at 21 (recommending that victims not be required to appear at preliminary proceedings and that hearsay testi-

mony of police or other law enforcement officers be admissible instead).

160. See, e.g., California Constitution art. I, s. 28(d); Task Force, note 71, at 24 (fourth amendment exclusionary rule only); see also California Legislative Assembly Committee on Criminal Justice, *Analysis of Proposition 8*, at 9–10, 14–17 (1982).
161. See, e.g., note 233.
162. See, e.g., notes 315–17.
163. See *Brosnahan* v. *Brown*, 32 Cal. 3d 236, 305–6 app., 651 P.2d 274, 319 app., 186 Cal. Rptr. 30, 75 app. (1982) (reprinting ballot statements); Victim rights bill fuels get-tough stand, 68 *A.B.A.J.* 530, 530 (1982) ('George Nicholson, a candidate for California attorney general and a member of a five-man committee pushing the initiative, said the move is an effort to counteract liberal decisions by the California Supreme Court').
164. As of this writing, the Supreme Court has declined to decide whether preventive detention statutes violate the Eighth Amendment. See, e.g., *Murphy* v. *Hunt*, 455 U.S. 478 (1982) (vacated as moot); *United States* v. *Edwards*, 430 A.2d 1321 (D.C. 1981), cert. denied, 455 U.S. 1022 (1982). See generally Note, The Eighth Amendment and the right to bail: historical perspectives, 82 *Colum. L. Rev.* 328 (1982) (arguing that the historical meaning and development of a right to bail and the intent of the Framers precludes the use of preventive detention).
165. See note 164. The Court did seem to approve preventive detention of juvenile offenders last term. See *Schall* v. *Martin*, 104 S. Ct. 2403 (1984). No suggestion of incorporating Eighth Amendment concerns appears in the opinion; however, Justice Rehnquist, writing for the majority, may have indicated a broader interest in preventive detention by emphasizing the existence of a '"legitimate and compelling state interest" in protecting the community from crime' while, at the same time, stating that 'the harm to society may even be greater . . . given the high rate of recidivism among juveniles.' Ibid. at 2410 (quoting *De Veau* v. *Braisted*, 363 U.S. 144, 155 (1960)). The majority also concluded that detention of juveniles in a juvenile facility is not 'punishment', ibid. at 2414, a conclusion sharply disputed by the dissenters, ibid. at 2429 (Marshall, J., dissenting).
166. These justifications are characteristic of crime control ideology, see H. Packer, note 47, at 210–14, and of conservative ideology as well, see, e.g., Borman, The selling of preventive detention, 1970, 65 *Nw. U.L. Rev.* 879, 881–4, 926–8 (1971); Mitchell, Bail reform and the constitutionality of pretrial detention, 55 *Virginia Law Review* 1223 (1969).
167. See Mitchell, note 166 (Nixon's Attorney General John Mitchell arguing in favour of preventive detention); The case for pretrial detention, address by Kleindienst, ALTA Midwinter Meeting (Jan. 30, 1970), reprinted in *Preventive Detention: Hearings before the Subcommittee on Constitutional Rights of the Senate Committee on the Judiciary*, 91st Cong., 2d Sess. 1187, 1190 (1970) [hereinafter cited as *Preventive Detention Hearings*] ('We in the Department of Justice believe that

pretrial detention is essential to any serious effort to reduce crime in the District of Columbia').

168. For example, the argument of then Attorney General John Mitchell in support of preventive detention rested in part on an analogy to civil commitment of the mentally ill. See Mitchell, note 166, at 1233–4, 1241. The analogy is not entirely appropriate, however, because civil commitment is based on a treatment model rather than a punitive model. Moreover, subsequent decisions by the United States Supreme Court and other courts have required the state to prove, by at least clear and convincing evidence, dangerousness as a result of mental illness. Compare *Addington* v. *Texas*, 441 U.S. 418 (1979) (clear and convincing evidence required in civil commitment proceedings), with *Estate of Roulet*, 23 Cal. 3d 219, 590 P.2d 1, 152 Cal. Rptr. 424 (1979) (proof beyond a reasonable doubt required for civil commitment). In *O'Connor* v. *Donaldson*, 422 U.S. 563 (1975), the Supreme Court indicated that civil commitment of the mentally ill *without* treatment might violate the due process clause. Ibid. at 577. Thus, a purely preventive detention rationale, even in the context of civil commitment, might not pass constitutional scrutiny.

169. D.C. Code Ann. s. 23–1322 (Supp. 1982). The statute provides that defendants accused of crimes of violence can be detained for 90 days if the prosecution certifies that the detention will 'protect the community' or if the defendant has been convicted of a violent crime within ten years of the current offence charged. Ibid.

170. Past victims who were victimized by someone released on bail are a perfect symbol of what can happen to the innocent public and are therefore used to raise fears of future victimization. The fact that some innocent people become victims of persons released either on bail or on their own recognizance has provided ample symbolic support for pretrial detention. See Task Force, note 71, at 22–3.

   The Justice Department recently concluded that approximately 16 per cent of offenders released on bail were rearrested for another offence while they were out of jail. National Institute of Justice, US Department of Justice, *Pretrial Release: A National Evaluation of Practices and Outcomes* (1981). The study does not indicate what type of offences resulted in the rearrest of persons on bail, nor does the percentage seem significant as a raw figure. A 1970 study by the the National Bureau of Standards showed that 11 per cent of defendants released before trial in the District of Columbia were rearrested for subsequent offenses, 25 per cent of those charged with 'dangerous' crimes were rearrested for a second misdemeanour or felony, and 17 per cent of those defendants charged with 'violent' crimes who were released were rearrested for a subsequent felony or misdemeanour. Borman, note 166, at 898–9. Thus, it may not be true that most innocent victims are victimized by persons who are out of custody awaiting adjudication of serious charges. But statistics do not respond to the emotions of fear and loathing that are raised when a person released on bail is subsequently rearrested for a serious offence.

171. See, e.g., California Constitution. art. I, s. 12; Michigan Constitution

art. I, s. 15; Wisconsin Constitution art. I, s. 8(3); *Utah Code Ann.* s. 77–20–1 (1980).
172. Bail Reform Act of 1984, s. 203, Pub. L. No. 98–473, 98 Stat. 1976 (codified at 18 U.S.C. s. 3141 (1985)).
173. See, e.g., G. Deukmejian, *Of Judges, Justice, and Crime Victims* 7–8 (1980); Graham, Lecture: witness intimidation, 12 *Florida State University Law Review* 238, 239 (1984) ('[w]itness intimidation is an extremely serious obstacle in the *quest for law and order* that is only now receiving the attention which it deserves') (emphasis added). Cf. Task Force, note 71, at 19 (asserting that 'threats and actual retaliation are not uncommon' in justifying proposal that addresses of witnesses not be available to defence absent 'a clear need'). Ironically, intimidation of victims and witnesses was not an issue in the debates over the enactment of the District of Columbia preventive detention statute. See *Preventive Detention*, note 167.
174. The President's Task Force asserts that 'many victims and witnesses are threatened or intimidated by defendants and others.' Task Force, note 71, at 61, but this conclusion is based on a carefully selected and impressionistic sample. By contrast, a careful study of crime victim compensation programmes in Brooklyn, New York, and Newark, New Jersey, found that a total of 30 per cent of the victims participating in the study had been threatened. However, only 19 per cent had been threatened 'sometime' after the crime had occurred; 11 per cent were threatened at the crime scene. Moreover, 70 per cent of the victims said that 'they had never been threatened.' R. Elias, note 72, at 99 (1983).
    George Deukmejian relied on a study by the ABA Commission on Victims that found 'nearly' one-third of all non-cooperating witnesses 'cited fear of reprisal as the reason for non-cooperation' to justify his conclusion that victim intimidation seriously impedes law enforcement and prosecution. G. Deukmejian, note 173, at 7–8. Deukmejian's failure to distinguish between victims and witnesses – the latter category being broader than the former – weakens his argument. Moreover, other studies contradict the ABA study. For example, Robert Elias found that the release on bail of an assault or robbery defendant had little influence on whether victims pursued their cases in court. See R. Elias, note 53, at 106 (81 per cent of respondents said release had no effect at all, and 18 per cent said release had an effect; of those affected, about half said release made them fearful, and about a quarter said it made them angry). Cf. W. Spelmen and D. Brown, *Calling the Police: Citizen Reporting of Serious Crime* 181–2 (1981) (while delay in reporting crimes is largely attributed to inconvenience, fear of reprisal, and embarrassment and culpability, authors argue that '[o]ffenders do not retaliate against victims and witnesses very often').
175. See notes 112–16 and accompanying text.
176. See note 109.
177. See note 182.
178. See notes 319–24.
179. The House Report on the Comprehensive Crime Control Act of 1984 states that pre-trial detention does not violate due process nor does it

constitute punishment, because preventive detention 'is not intended to promote the traditional aims of punishment such as retribution or deterrence.' H.R. Rep. No. 1030, 98th Cong., 2d Sess., 8–9, reprinted in 1984 U.S. Code Cong. and Ad. News 473. Former Attorney General John Mitchell's article in support of preventive detention never discusses the precise issue of punishment and only gives passing notice to the related problem of the 'presumption of innocence'. Mitchell, note 166, at 1231–2. But see Tribe, An ounce of detention: preventive justice in the world of John Mitchell, 56 *Virginia Law Review* 371, 378–80, 394–6 (1970) (arguing that preventive detention is unavoidably a form of punishment because it relies on determinations of moral culpability).

180. See, e.g., Pub. L. No. 98–473, tit. II, ch. I, 98 Stat. 1979–1980 (1984) (pre-trial detention includes consideration of nature of offence, prior convictions and evidence against accused); California Constitution art I, s. 12 (bail may be denied in felony cases where facts are evident or the presumption great and clear evidence exists that the accused is likely to cause great bodily harm to others if released); Michigan Constitution art. I, s. 15 (where proof is 'evident', bail may be denied if a violent felony has occurred and accused has prior convictions for violent felonies, or if a particular felony, such as robbery, was committed).

181. Public safety has been the predominant justification for preventive detention statutes. The preventive detention portion of the Victim's Bill of Rights adopted by initiative in California bore the headings 'Public Safety Bail'. *Brosnahan* v. *Brown*, 32 Cal. 3d 236, 300 app., 651 P.2d 274, 314 app., 186 Cal. Rptr. 30, 70 app. (1982). Justice Rehnquist's opinion in *Schall* v. *Martin*, 104 S. Ct. 2403 (1984), a juvenile preventive detention case, emphasizes the legitimacy of a governmental interest in public safety as a justification for pre-trial detention of juveniles.

182. See Task Force, note 71, at 22–3 ('Victims of violent crime have expressed with outrage and indignation their dissatisfaction with bail laws . . . Victims who have been robbed or raped, and the families of those murdered by persons who were released on bail while facing serious charges and possessing a prior record of violence, simply cannot understand why these persons were free to harm them'). Elias found that, although the vast majority of victims in his study were opposed to granting bail, the opposition in part was because of confusion about pre-trial detention: 'Many seemed to think that pretrial detention was part of the defendant's punishment for committing the crime, and that by being released, he was "getting off" from his crime.' R. Elias, note 72, at 105.

183. This characterization is Kelman's. Kelman, note 28, at 216. The President's Task Force embraces this theory: 'In deciding issues of bail, the court must . . . balance the defendant's interest in remaining free on a charge of which he is presumed innocent *with the reality that many defendants have proven, by their conviction records, that they have committed and are likely to commit crimes* while at large.' Task Force, note 71, at 23 (emphasis added).

Despite the Supreme Court's recent acceptance of the notion that psychiatrists can predict future dangerousness for the purposes of imposing the death penalty, the ability of anyone to predict future dangerousness with much accuracy is questionable. Compare *Barefoot* v. *Estelle*, 463 U.S. 880 (1983) (psychiatric testimony that capital defendant is likely to commit future dangerous acts if not executed is admissible in penalty phase of capital trials), with ibid. at 916 (Blackmun, J., dissenting) (there is no evidence that psychiatrists can accurately assess future dangerousness; use of such expert testimony in penalty phase is unjustifiably prejudicial to defendants). See also Slobogin, Dangerousness and expertise, 133 *University of Pennsylvania Law Review* 97, 109–27 (1984) (clinical and actuarial predictions of dangerousness, while more accurate than random decisions, produce a significant number of false predictions of serious assaultive behaviour); Wilson, Dealing with the high-rate offender, 72 *The Public Interest* 52, 61–3 (1983) (the nature of the present offence and prior record are not accurate predictors of who is a high-rate offender; factors that do identify likelihood of person being especially dangerous may lead to substantial errors when applied to a specific individual).

184. For example, the President's Task Force characterizes the Eighth Amendment right to bail as a mere 'interest' in remaining free. Task Force, note 71, at 23. The transformation of a constitutional right into an interest may be justified because constitutional rights only attach to 'us'. Since the accused is seen as a 'criminal', not as a human being, it is relatively easy to treat him differently. Negative labels have long served the purpose of justifying atrocities against others: 'Gook', 'Nigger', and 'dirty Jew', all have taken their place as labels inescapably linked to atrocity.

185. H. Packer, note 47, at 162–3.

186. In 1978, Charles Silberman observed that 'a jail sentence constitutes far more severe punishment than comparable time in prison' because of the terrible conditions in many local jails. C. Silberman, note 29, at 351–2. In my experience as a public defender, clients often preferred 'the joint' to the Santa Clara County main jail, and would plead even if it meant a prison term. Conditions at the jail were seen to be worse than conditions in the California prison system at that time. This may not hold true today as prison populations increase, and it may not be true in all jurisdictions, but the fact remains that many jails are so dreadful that defendants will be anxious to get out as quickly as possible.

187. In several cases, I had clients who were questioned by police officers while they were in custody, despite the fact that the officers knew they were represented by the Public Defender's Office. In one juvenile case, for example, I explicitly informed the investigating officer that my client did not wish to talk to him, only to find the officer attempting to interview my client in the detention facility a day or two later. In another case, an investigating officer persisted in asking an adult client about an offence, despite the fact that I had told the officer the client was represented by the Public Defender.

188. Task Force, note 71 at 63, 67–8, 75–6.

189. Ibid. at 67–8, 75–6, 99.

190. In the book *Helter Skelter*, for example, the prosecutor admits that had Charles Manson insisted on his statutory right to a speedy trial after his indictment on multiple murder charges, the prosecution would have been 'in deep trouble' because it did not yet have sufficient evidence to convict Manson at trial. V. Bugliosi and C. Gentry, *Helter Skelter* 279 (1975).

191. Some rapid process advocates argue that Anglo-American criminal law causes artificiality in guilt determinations and that an 'inquisitorial' model would 'cure' the problem of delay. See, e.g., M. Graham, *Tightening the Reins of Justice in America: A Comparative Analysis of the Criminal Jury Trial in England and the United States* (1983); J. Langbein, *Comparative Criminal Procedure: Germany* (1977). This is an inaccurate assumption, however. Under continental systems, preparation and investigation are also subject to the constraints of time.

192. As Packer suggests, the presumption of innocence is honoured more in the breach; the criminal process actually operates on an assumption of guilt. H. Packer, note 47, at 160, 239. As a result, the rush to judgment can result in erroneous conviction and imprisonment of the innocent before an error is discovered or admitted. For example, Lenell Geter, a black engineer tried and convicted of armed robbery, was sentenced to life in prison in Texas, despite the fact that he had no record and several of his co-workers had insisted to the prosecutor that Geter was at work at the time of the robbery. Geter served 14 months in a Texas prison before the efforts of his supervisor, co-workers and others induced the District Attorney to acknowledge his error; the apprehension of another suspect probably also helped to convince the prosecutor. See Applebome, Wedding on again after mistaken life sentence, *New York Times*, 23 Mar. 1984, at A14, col. 1.

In Seattle, a man was tried and convicted for a rape he insisted he had not committed. The man contacted a reporter for assistance in proving his innocence, and eventually the police arrested another suspect who confessed. The reporter won a Pulitzer Prize for his investigative work; the innocent man lost his job and his reputation as a result of the conviction. See Curry, The wrong man, *San Francisco Chronicle*, 23 Jan. 1983 (Sunday Punch), at 2, col. 2; see also Jones, Drifter's lies lead to nightmare for 2 innocent black men, *San Francisco Chronicle*, 16 Oct. 1983, at A15, col. 1 (drifter lied to police about having been robbed by two blacks, one of whom was then convicted of robbery; drifter admitted lying before sentencing). Mandell, Justice system goes astray: victim loses job, self-respect, *San Francisco Chronicle*, 24 June 1984, at A2, col. 1 (charges against a woman accused of embezzling $50,000 were dropped after persistent efforts by defence lawyers and reporter to point out numerous defects in investigation leading to the charges).

193. In one well-publicized case involving numerous rapes of women in their homes in Columbus, Ohio, an innocent man was convicted for two rapes and served five years in prison, while the real culprit remained at large and continued to attack women until police noted the similarities in the incidents and apprehended the guilty person. See Doctor guilty in

rapes of 21 Ohio women, *San Francisco Chronicle*, 23 Sept. 1983, at 25, col. 1.

194. The President's Task Force asserts that '[v]ictims . . . are burdened by irresolution and the realization that they will be called upon to relive [*sic*] their victimization when the case is finally tried. The healing process cannot truly begin until the case can be put behind them.' Task Force, note 71, at 75. This assertion simply is not supported by existing psychological evidence: the healing process begins immediately after a traumatic experience, although it may easily be interfered with if the victim receives improper signals from others. See notes 144–220 and accompanying text. Moreover, re-experiencing the event is itself part of the healing process. In re-experiencing the event, the victim can gain perspective and control over the experience.

195. It is, of course, not beneficial for victims to arrive at the courthouse only to learn that their matter has been continued to a later time. This problem, however, exists more because of miscalculations, problems of coordination and poor communication than because of fundamental defects in the process. It can be controlled by allowing the victim-witnesses to be 'on-call', see, e.g., Task Force, note 71, at 68, or by an effort on the part of prosecutors to make sure that the victim-witness is aware of possible delays. An explanation of structural problems such as the availability of courtrooms, the need for preparation, and the nature of the procedural steps that need to be taken is more likely to be of benefit to victims than is rushing the case through the system without regard for preparation by either side or for the victim's psychological state.

196. Cf. Sales, Baum and Shore, note 98, at 130 (study found rapid return to normal behaviour followed by increase in symptoms; further research necessary to clarify significance); Burgess and Holmstrom, note 89, at 985 (victims who had not reported previous molestation or assault and who were subsequently raped had not processed earlier trauma).

197. There are three general types of plea bargains: a plea to some charges in return for the dismissal of others; a plea to a lesser included offence in exchange for dismissal of more serious charges, with a corresponding reduction in penalty; or a plea to charges with some sentencing considerations.

198. As high as 90 per cent of the convictions in the United States may be the result of guilty pleas, a great number of which are undoubtedly the result of plea bargaining. See S. Kadish, S. Schulhofer and M. Paulsen, note 60, at 154–5 (1983) (empirical studies show a wide range of guilty plea rates; in one study, New York had a 92.7 per cent rate, while Pennsylvania only had a 65.5 per cent rate); Y. Kamisar, W. LaFave and J. Israel, *Modern Criminal Procedure* 1222 (5th edn, 1980) (quoting Chief Justice Burger's estimate that approximately 90 per cent of defendants plead guilty); Judicial Council of California, *1983 Annual Report*, 120–1 (1983) (in 1981–1982, 78 per cent of the felony cases filed in California superior courts, other than in Los Angeles County, were disposed of by guilty plea; Los Angeles had a ratio of 82 per cent); see also H. Zeisel, *The Limits of Law Enforcement* 34 (1982). But see

Schulhofer, Is plea bargaining inevitable?, 97 *Harvard Law Review* 1037 (1984) (arguing that Philadelphia courts have largely and success-fully abolished plea bargaining as chief method of disposition of cases).

199. For example, the prosecution offered immunity from prosecution to Linda Kasabian, an accomplice in the murders of seven people, if she agreed to testify truthfully against Charles Manson at trial. See V. Bugliosi and C. Gentry, note 190, at 342.

200. A prosecutor in Santa Clara County related the following case that he had been assigned for trial: a mentally ill, but not legally insane, man who lived in his car apparently was hungry and decided to steal some food to eat. His solution was to enter a house at night, and 'walk past the stereo, the television, and the cameras' to the kitchen. He opened the refrigerator and took 'a jar of Skippy peanut butter and a loaf of Buttertop bread' and left. The police found him not long afterwards in his car; during the search they found a jar of crunchy Skippy peanut butter and a partial loaf of Buttertop bread. The defendant admitted that he had taken them. Although the deputy district attorney assigned to try the case felt that he would have problems proving exactly whose peanut butter and bread the defendant had, he was more troubled by the fact that a strict interpretation of case law and the California Penal Code made this offence a first degree burglary, with a mandatory state prison term. The plea-bargaining policies of the office were very strict; the defendant's choice of private refrigerator instead of a grocery store made him technically guilty of a felony carrying a mandatory prison term, rather than a misdemeanour petty theft, and the deputy district attorney felt such a result was unjust. Moreover, court time would be taken up in a jury trial, and apparently the victim wasn't too upset about the loss of the food. The deputy finally persuaded his supervisor to allow him to reduce the charge to misdemeanour burglary, to which the defendant pled guilty. (Confidential communication.)

201. See *Brosnahan* v. *Brown*, 32 Cal. 3d 236, 305 app., 651 P.2d 274, 319 app., 186 Cal. Rptr. 30, 75 app. (1982) (reprinting Proposition 8 ballot statements); Y. Kamisar, W. LaFave and J. Israel, note 198, at 1224 n.m (quoting statement of New York Police Commissioner Patrick Murphy attacking plea bargaining and the court system and implying that plea bargaining as to felony gun possession leads to many mur-ders); E. Van den Haag, note 53, at 157–63, 171–3 (attacking courts and liberals for making plea bargaining a tool for allowing even serious offenders to go unpunished, thereby raising the crime rate).

202. *California Penal Code* s. 1192.7 (West 1982).

203. Ibid.

204. For narrow interpretations of California's provisions regarding witness availability, see *People* v. *Enriquez*, 19 Cal. 3d 221, 233–7, 561 P.2d 261, 269–71, 137 Cal. Rptr. 171, 178–81 (1977); *People* v. *Williams*, 93 Cal. App. 3d 40, 51–5, 155 Cal. Rptr. 414, 419–22 (Cal. Ct. App. 1979); *People* v. *Gomez*, 26 Cal. App. 3d 225, 230, 103 Cal. Rptr. 80, 83–4 (Cal. Ct. App. 1972).

205. Gifford, note 158, at 73. Needless to say, considerable controversy exists in the psychotherapeutic community as to whether catharsis is

helpful or necessary to recovery from trauma. See, e.g., A. Beck, *Cognitive Therapy and Emotional Disorders* (1979) (cognitive approach to helping relieve emotional distress); F. Fromm-Reichman, *Principles of Intensive Psychotherapy* (1960) ('catharsis' and insight overrated as therapeutic devices; process and relationship more likely to relieve emotional distress).

206. The lay witnesses and victims I have talked with certainly were *relieved* after they testified. Their relief was less related to the tension created by having to think about the crime than to the tension produced by the mere prospect of testifying, however.

207. As Yalom points out, Freud saw catharsis as the release of repressed effect that produced psychiatric symptoms 'symbolically provid[ing] an outlet for the tension'. I. Yalom, note 90, at 304. Yalom observes 'this formulation is so beautiful in its simplicity that it has persisted . . . Certainly it is the popular view incarnated in innumerable Hollywood films'. Ibid. The image of the hysteric rising from her sick bed – 'Sigmund, I am cured!' – persists despite the fact that 'psychotherapy is "cyclotherapy" – a long, lumbering process.' Ibid. at 307 (footnote omitted).

208. Moreover, simply reliving the experience is not enough – the experience then must be re-integrated into the person's consciousness in the form of 'rewriting' history, if you will. J. Coleman, *Psychology and Effective Behavior* 405 (1969).

209. One indication that testifying is not cathartic in terms of resolving the experience of the criminal event is the failure of many victims to experience a strong emotional reaction when they tell police about the crime and when they testify. See note 150. This separation of emotion and description is neither unusual nor necessarily harmful. In fact, 'telling what happened' is all that the trial process requires of the witness. Description of the factual occurrences *may* be of aid to a victim by providing a way of organizing the cognitive aspect of a criminal event, but this is a highly speculative observation, because there simply is not enough available information about the experiences of victims who have testified.

210. As is discussed below, see text accompanying note 212, one argument in favour of curtailing the defendant's right to examine the victim at trial is that such testimony is too traumatic for the victim-witness. Although I dispute the generalization, it is true that some crime victims indeed may be too psychologically traumatized by their victimization to be able to testify. The extreme nature of a violent criminal experience occasionally does produce a psychotic episode or a lasting breakdown of emotional functioning. See, e.g., Burgess and Holstrom, note 89, at 985. Abolition of plea bargaining may thus cause the prosecution to lose a conviction of the defendant for *any* offence and allow the guilty to go free.

211. See *Model Code of Professional Responsibility EC 7–13* (1979) (duty is to seek justice, not merely to convict).

212. See Task Force, note 71, at 7, 9–10 (composite model). The Task Force recommends that hearsay be admissible against defendants in

preliminary hearings and grand jury proceedings and that the victim not be required to 'relive his victimization . . . Within a few days of the crime, some victims are still hospitalized or have been so traumatized that they are unable to speak about their experience. Because the victim cannot attend the hearing, . . . the defendant is often free to terrorize others.' Ibid. at 21. Ironically, the California victim's rights provision which sharply curtails plea bargaining, and therefore increases the number of trials in which victims must testify, apparently disregards the Task Force's claim that testifying produces undue trauma.

The Task Force seems untroubled by the fact that if a victim attends a preliminary hearing, she might realize that the police and prosecutor have charged the wrong defendant, or that some victims of allegedly horrible crimes are not telling the truth. The presumption of guilt, intrinsic to the crime control model, seems especially prominent here. Moreover, the Task Force seems unaware that an opportunity to testify once before trial, if there should be a trial, is likely to help the victim familiarize herself with the process. Finally, the confrontation clause of the Sixth Amendment might place some limit on the extent to which the victim's testimony can be introduced through hearsay evidence or statements not made under oath.

213. Preparation of lay witnesses through a mock direct and cross-examination can help them understand the process. To the extent that we understand something, we are less likely to fear it and less likely to feel helpless about the outcome. When information about something can be obtained, anxiety will likely be reduced even if the experience itself cannot be fully grasped ahead of time. M. Seligman, *Helplessness* 107–33 (1975). Explaining how the preliminary hearing, grand jury or trial is conducted can give victims a better feeling of mastery and control. I have suggested to several rape victims that they watch part of another trial, civil or criminal, before they themselves testify in order to get a picture of what a courtroom proceeding is like. With this experience behind them, the prospect of testifying is not so intimidating. Those who have tried this have found it helpful. I have also advised victims to obtain a copy of the transcript of their testimony at any preliminary hearings to review before the trial, especially if there has been a long delay between the preliminary hearing and the trial. No reason exists for prosecutors not to do their best to prepare witnesses in a like manner. Although many deputy district attorneys have heavy caseloads, they should be able to take the time to acquaint their lay witnesses with the basics of the process.

214. See note 80.

215. California Constitution art. 1, s. 28(d) (West 1983).

216. Task Force, note 71, at 24–28.

217. Amsterdam, Perspectives on the Fourth Amendment, 58 *Minnesota Law Review* 349 (1974) (containing major arguments for and against the exclusionary rule and an analysis of the historical reasons for the Fourth Amendment).

218. Ibid. at 400. The German experience, as well as the more recent examples of Chile, see, e.g., Chavez, Church says civil rights in Chile

The Wrongs of Victim's Rights

are eroding, *New York Times*, 1 Nov. 1984, at 13, col. 1, and Argentina, see, e.g., J. Timmerman, *Prisoner Without a Name: Cell Without a Number* (1981), should serve as a warning against giving authorities too much power as a result of fear or economic instability.

The tendency to consider a criminal as an 'other' or 'it', rather than as a human being, leads many conservatives to overlook the potential for tyranny. Denying the humanity of offenders is the easiest way to dismiss the problem of human actions that are evil, and it permits an us–them paradigm to dominate thought and action in response to crime. Accordingly, the right to freedom from unreasonable searches and seizures does not attach to offenders: offenders are simply not included in 'the people'.

219. Task Force, note 71, at 27–8. Chief Justice Burger has long opposed the exclusionary rule, see *Bivens* v. *Six Unknown Agents*, 403 U.S. 388, 416 (1971) (Burger, C.J., dissenting) ('Some clear demonstration of the benefits and effectiveness of the exclusionary rule is required to justify it in view of the high price it extracts from society – the release of countless guilty criminals'); L. Baker, note 32, at 56–8.

220. For a discussion of immediate reactions to the exclusionary rule, see Kamisar, Public safety v. individual liberties: some 'facts' and 'theories', 53 *Journal of Criminal Law and Criminology* 171 (1962). After the California Supreme Court adopted an exclusionary remedy, then Attorney General Edmund C. Brown stated that the police had done better investigatory work and that investigations 'are more thorough and within American constitutional concepts . . . I believe the overall effects of the . . . decision . . . have been excellent'. Ibid. at 179. The US Attorney for the District of Columbia also opined that the exclusionary rule improved police preparation of cases. Ibid.

221. See Allen, note 32, at 535–7; Halpern, Federal habeas corpus and the Mapp exclusionary rule after *Stone* v. *Powell*, 82 *Colum. L. Rev.* 1, 5–12 (1982); Mertens and Wasserstrom, The good faith exception to the exclusionary rule: deregulating the police and derailing the law, 70 *Geo. L.J.* 365, 373 (1981).

In *United States* v. *Leon*, 104 S. Ct. 3405, 3421–3 (1984), the majority opinion emphasized the question of specific deterrence of particular police officers who obtained a search warrant from a superior court judge in concluding that the officers had relied on the warrant in good faith and that the evidence obtained should not have been suppressed, despite the fact that the affidavit submitted in support of the warrant failed to provide enough information to establish probable cause. See also LaFave, The Fourth Amendment in an imperfect world: on drawing 'bright lines' and 'good faith', 43 *University of Pittsburgh Law Review* 307 (1982) (arguing that the good faith exception will encourage police to engage in conduct otherwise impermissible under the Fourth Amendment).

222. The empirical studies available contradict the prevailing wisdom that countless guilty people go free as a result of the suppression of evidence. See, e.g., Davies, A hard look at what we know (and still need to learn) about the 'costs' of the exclusionary rule: the NIJ study and

other studies of 'lost' arrests, 1983 *Am. B. Found. Research J.* 611
(criticizing a National Institute of Justice study for concluding that the
exclusionary rule had 'major impact' on criminal prosecutions in California on the basis of data that indicates the opposite conclusion; only
2.4 per cent of felony arrests in California are not pursued by the
prosecution as a result of unlawful searches and seizures); US Comp-
troller General, *Report on Impact of the Exclusionary Rule on Federal
Criminal Prosecutions* (1979) (only 1.3 per cent of all cases studied had
evidence suppressed as a result of a successful suppression motion);
Nardulli, The societal cost of the exclusionary rule: an empirical assessment, 1983 *Am. B. Found. Research J.* 585 (motions to suppress evidence were filed in less than 5 per cent of all cases; of those motions
filed to suppress physical evidence, only 17 per cent were granted; thus
only 0.7 per cent of all cases included a successful motion to suppress
physical evidence obtained through an illegal search or seizure; only
0.56 per cent of all cases were 'lost' because of a motion to suppress
physical evidence); see also Carlsen, California's Appeal Court reversal
rate, *San Francisco Chronicle*, 25 Aug. 1983, at 12, col. 1 (detailing
study by California Judicial Council finding that only 75 of 604 criminal
appeals in California resulted in reversal and that over one-fourth of
these were the result of sentencing errors). But see National Institute of
Justice, *The Effects of the Exclusionary Rule: A Study in California*
(1982) (concluding that 5 per cent of all felony cases in California were
rejected by prosecutors because of search and seizure problems and
that from 1976 to 1979 30 per cent of all felony drug cases were rejected
because of the exclusionary rule).
223. Task Force, note 71, at 25.
224. Ibid. at 28 (emphasis added).
225. Because so few cases are 'lost' because of the exclusionary rule, see
note 222, it is very unlikely that police will be discouraged to the point
of inaction. While I am aware of instances where the police have not
asked the district attorney to issue a complaint because they are aware
that the evidence seized during a search would probably be suppressed,
those instances did not involve violent crimes, and they certainly did not
involve 'inaction'.
226. See note 222.
227. See Nardulli, note 222, at 602 and Table 13 (of the cases that were 'lost'
because of suppression of physical evidence, less than 20 per cent were
'serious', involving unarmed robbery, arson and burglary); Davies,
note 222, at 667 ('while there are not truly comprehensive statistics on
the number of arrests rejected or dismissed because of illegal searches,
all the pieces of data we do have show the general effect of the rule to
be quite low, and the effect in nondrug arrests and violent crime arrests
to be quite low').
228. Of 75 criminal writs and appeals decided by the California courts of
appeal in both published and unpublished opinions between 1 January
1981 and 28 February 1981, only 12.4 per cent resulted in a reversal. Of
the reversals, only nine cases, or 5.1 per cent of the total appeals,
involved errors in motions to suppress evidence, and a few of those

were reversed for improper *suppression* of evidence; one of the nine cases involved a *Miranda* issue. Judicial Council of California, *1983 Annual Report* 7–8 (1983); see also Carlsen, note 222.

229. See notes 262–373 and accompanying text.

230. See notes 13–23 and accompanying text.

231. See Rios and Yeochum, Making sure drunk drivers pay, *San Jose Mercury News*, 18 Dec. 1983, at 1A, col. 4 (reporting the effect of MADD monitoring on sentencing judges in Santa Clara County, California); cf. Magagnini, Drunk case judges mad at 'monitors', *San Francisco Chronicle*, 16 May 1983, at 1, col. 2 (San Francisco County judges found MADD monitoring inappropriate; MADD advocate quoted as saying, 'There are judges . . . who failed to get re-elected because MADD is all over their tails').

232. See, e.g., Task Force, note 71, at 76–8.

233. See *Ariz. Rev. Stat. Ann.* s. 13–702(F) (1983); *California Penal Code* s. 1191.1 (West Supp. 1985); *Conn. Gen. Stat. Ann.* s. 54–91c (West Supp. 1984); *Fla. Stat.* s. 921.143 (Supp. 1985); *Me. Rev. Stat. Ann.* tit. 17–A, s. 1257 (Supp. 1983); *Mass. Ann. Laws* ch. 258B, s. 3(h), ch. 279, s. 4B (Michie/Law. Co-op. 1985); *N.H. Rev. Stat. Ann.* s. 651: 4–a (Supp. 1983); *R.I. Gen. Laws* s. 12–28–4 (Supp. 1984); *Tenn. Code Ann.* s. 40–35–209 (Supp. 1984); *West Virginia Code* s. 61–11A–2 (1984).

234. Cesare Beccaria repeatedly emphasized deterrence as the justification for punishment of offenders in *An Essay on Crimes and Punishments*, published in 1819; the purpose was social betterment: 'The degree of the punishment, and the consequences of a crime, ought to be so contrived as to have the greatest possible effect on others, with the least possible pain to the delinquent.' C. Beccaria, *An Essay on Crimes and Punishments* 75 (1819 & photo. reprint 1953) (emphasis deleted). Jeremy Bentham is probably the most well-known spokesman for the utilitarian theory that punishment is an evil in and of itself and only is justifiable if it serves the greater social good of preventing 'some greater evil'. J. Bentham, *An Introduction to the Principles of Morals and Legislation* (1876), reprinted in S. Kadish, S. Schulhofer and M. Paulsen, note 60, at 189. See generally H. Packer, note 47, at 39–45 (summary and critique).

235. H. Packer, note 47, at 39; E. Van den Haag, note 53, at 181–3.

236. Kelman characterizes this premise as a 'variety of economic theories that correspond in the philosophical literature to arguments justifying punishment as necessary to deter crime' and notes that '[p]olitically, the central method of the economic view of crime has focused less on optimal criminality than on the observation that we can reduce crime by upping its price.' Kelman, note 28, at 214, 216.

237. The rise in crime, including violent crime, might have been attributable more to an increase in the population of people at a crime-prone age than to anything else, but fear has caused a shift in thinking from deterrence to incapacitation and retribution. See, e.g., An eye for an eye, *Time*, 24 Jan. 1983, at 28, 28–9 (discussing the influence of rising rate of violent crime on re-emergence of capital punishment); Currie,

note 29, at 32–3 (failure of deterrence has caused a shift in focus from deterrence theory to incapacitation theory).

238. This is true despite efforts of conservative criminologists to demonstrate that the threat of increased incarceration can affect the behaviour of marginal individuals. See note 235; Currie, note 29, at 32.

239. As Packer notes, 'the symbolic richness of the criminal process is a powerful deterrent' that serves to reinforce societal values. H. Packer, note 47, at 44. The stigmatization of guilt and social condemnation still exerts a powerful force on behaviour. Consider, for example, the transformation in social attitudes about driving under the influence currently being undertaken by the media, MADD and insurance companies. At one point, driving under the influence was not a crime taken seriously, and a conviction carried little stigma.

240. See Ibid. at 39, 45–8.

241. Ibid. at 45. The common wisdom is that, by putting an offender in jail or prison, we demonstrate to him that his behaviour will not be tolerated. He should consequently learn not to repeat that behaviour. Recidivism rates would seem to deny the efficacy of special deterrence, however, ibid. at 46, but as Packer notes, 'we are certainly not in a position now to say that the concept has no utility,' ibid. at 47. Special deterrence, or 'intimidations', may be very effective on some individuals, or on some types of crime, and its efficacy may depend in part on the level of brutality of the prison experience. Ibid.

242. Ibid. at 48. Incapacitation is enjoying renewed popularity. See note 237; see also Wilson, note 183, at 52, 61 (selective incapacitation is the 'most rational way to use the incapacitative powers of our prisons').

243. See Wilson, note 183, at 61–2. But see Cohen, Selective incapacitation: an assessment, 1984, *University of Illinois Law Review* 253, 281 and n. 67 (data in a Washington, DC, study indicated that 15.3 per cent of auto thefts were committed by specialists, 19.8 per cent of burglaries, and 28 per cent of robberies).

244. Cf. Slobogin, note 183, at 119–23 (1984) (comparing usefulness of clinical assessments to predict future dangerousness that rely on nature of present offence and psychological variables with usefulness of predictions based on demographic variables that have been statistically demonstrated to correlate with violent behaviour).

245. See ibid. at 119–23, 153–4 ('The fact that a homicide is committed in a particularly vile manner does not necessarily mean that its perpetrator is more likely to commit a second violent act than a more fastidious murderer . . .').

246. Wilson, note 183, at 62–3, 65 (predictive factors for high-rate offenders include, among other things, a prior criminal record, a history of drug or alcohol abuse, and a documented inability to secure a job).

247. As Packer observes, however, 'we do not know how to rehabilitate offenders, at least within the limit of the resources that are now or might reasonably be expected to be devoted to the task.' H. Packer, note 47, at 55. In a general sense, this is true, although knowledge about the relationship of substance abuse and criminal activity, for example, does provide some direction for 'rehabilitative' efforts.

248. If an agency or organization is willing to work with a child abuser, it may be preferable to maintain the family unit and have all family members participate in therapy if they are willing, rather than to send the offender to jail. Parents United, for example, has been successful in counselling sexually abused children and the abusing parents.

249. See Cohen, Moral aspects of the criminal law, 49 *Yale Law Journal* 987, 990–4 (1940). H.L.A. Hart argues, for example, that:

> a person may be punished if, and only if, he has voluntarily done something morally wrong; . . . his punishment must in some way match, or be the equivalent of, the wickedness of his offence, and . . . the justification for punishing men under such conditions is that the return of suffering for moral evil voluntarily done, is itself just or morally good.

H.L.A. Hart, *Punishment and Responsibility* 231 (1982). Normative words and phrases haunt this formulation: what referents exist for determining 'wickedness' or 'moral evil voluntarily done'? A moral code in one culture may be vastly different from that in another. Similarly, the 'wickedness' of a given act may be greater in one society than in another. Lloyd Weinreb has found the concepts of 'deserts' and 'moral responsibility' to have normative components; he is, however, unable to find other concepts to replace them. See Weinreb, The complete idea of justice, 51 *U. Chi. L. Rev.* 752 (1984).

250. Punishment of those who deserve it is, under classic retribution theory, self-justifying. See, e.g., H.L.A. Hart, note 249, at 231 ('suffering for moral evil voluntarily done, is itself just or morally good'). But the infliction of pain is not something that we can universally agree is 'good', so we seek other justification as well. Some have argued that punishment for wickedness is a means to 'atone' for the wicked deed. See, e.g., H. Packer, note 47, at 38. Others see the punishment as a 'payment' of a 'debt'. See, e.g., H. Morris, *On Guilt and Innocence* 34–6 (1976).

251. See I. Kant, *The Metaphysical Elements of Justice* 99–102 (J. Ladd trans. 1965), quoted in S. Kadish, S. Schulhofer and M. Paulsen, note 60, at 187–8.

252. Morris, Persons and punishment, in *Punishment* 75 (J. Feinberg and H. Gross eds. 1975).

253. Ibid.

254. Commentary, Constitutional law: the death penalty: a critique of the philosophical bases held to satisfy the Eighth Amendment requirements for its justification, 34 *Oklahoma Law Review* 567, 594 (1981). Criminal activity may be a self-help device to impose social control. *See* Black, Crime as social control, 48, *Am. Soc. Rev.* 34, 36 (1983) ('Like the killings in traditional societies described by anthropologists . . . most intentional homicide in modern society may be classified as social control, specifically as self-help, even if it is handled by legal officials as crime'). And there may be a tendency for legal officials to respond less harshly in the self-help situation where the victim arguably 'deserved'

his or her victimization. Ibid. at 40, 42. One recent, and extreme, example of this form of social control/self-help involved the fatal shooting of a man who had bullied residents of a small town in Missouri. Investigation of the homicide was stymied by the refusal of any of the town's citizens to identify the killer or to admit that they had seen anybody fire at the victim. The case received a great deal of media attention and dramatically illustrates the use of self-help by a community that believed its existence to be threatened. While it may very well be that the person or persons who shot the victim would legally be guilty of murder, the behaviour of the victim – carrying a gun and terrorizing the community – seems to be equally 'blameworthy'. See Widow of slain 'town bully' seeks $11 million for death, *San Jose Mercury News*, 11 July 1984, at 9A, col. 1.

255. See G. Fletcher, *Rethinking Criminal Law* 855–75 (1978) (discussing tensions in the law of self-defence created by theoretical and pragmatic concerns with choice, culpability, and rights).

256. Gobert, Victim precipitation, 77 *Colum. L. Rev.* 511, 514 (1977).

257. Ibid. at 535.

258. Ibid. at 539–40. A 19-year-old man, who shot and killed his father, was found guilty of voluntary manslaughter following a court trial in California. Apparently the victim had beaten his wife and sexually abused his daughters; the morning the victim was shot, he beat his wife and threatened to kill his 19-year-old son. In sentencing the defendant to five years' probation, the judge commented that the victim was 'the scum of the earth' and 'a man the planet Earth can rotate without quite nicely'. Father-killer sentenced to 5 years' probation, *San Francisco Chronicle*, 25 Feb. 1984, at 5, col. 4; Judge seeks sentencing ideas, *San Jose Mercury News*, 29 Jan. 1984, at 12A, col. 1. On the other hand, Richard Jahnke, a 17-year-old who shot his abusive father and was convicted by a jury of manslaughter, was sentenced to serve five to fifteen years in prison by the trial court, which refused to take the victim's behaviour into account in imposing sentence. The Governor of Wyoming subsequently commuted the sentence to three years in a juvenile detention facility, noting that 'the court record characterized the father as a cruel, sadistic man'. Jahnke was portrayed as a victim. Father killer's sentence reversed, *San Francisco Chronicle*, 15 June 1984, at 30, col. 4.

259. See Cohn, Oakes gets 90 days in driving deaths, *San Jose Mercury News*, 13 Aug. 1983, at 1A, col. 5.

260. T. Beneke, note 115, at 6–33 (language and cultural symbols influencing beliefs about rape); Berger, note 68, at 7–32 (1977) (summary of the history and rationale of the law of rape); Comment, Police discretion and the judgment that a crime has been committed – rape in Philadelphia, 117 *University of Pennsylvania Law Review* 277 (1968) (reflecting the old common law assumption that rape is a charge easily made and hard to defend, and recommending that police consider time between occurrence and report, physical appearance of 'complainant', medical evidence, the complainant's conduct prior to the offence, evidence of weapons or struggle, information derived from a record check

on every complainant, the opinion of the complainant's husband or parents as to the truthfulness of her allegations, and the results of a polygraph examination of the complainant). See generally S. Brownmiller, note 43.

261. Although principles of comparative or contributory fault may justify the reduction of damages in intentional tort cases, see Dear and Zipperstein, Comparative fault and intentional torts: doctrinal barriers and policy considerations, 24 *Santa Clara Law Review* 1, 26–32 (1984), we may not be willing to incorporate notions of comparative fault in determining criminal penalties. The notion of general deterrence in tort is slightly different from the general deterrence justification in criminal cases; the state may be unwilling to weaken the educative effect of punishment by explicitly making criminal sentences dependent on the behaviour of the victim.

On the other hand, California has provided that certain types of victim precipitation may be considered by a judge in determining what sentence to impose under the determinate sentencing law. A sentence may be mitigated if '[t]he victim was an initiator, willing participant, aggressor, or provoker of the incident,' or if the defendant was reacting to 'an unusual circumstance, such as great provocation . . .' California Rules of Court Rule 423(a)(2), (3) (1985).

262. Revenge or retaliation is enjoying a renaissance, however. For example, a recent book advocates the use of revenge as a legitimate justification for the criminal sanction. See S. Jacoby, *Wild Justice* (1983). Conservative columnist George Will writes '[t]he element of retribution – vengeance, if you will – does not make punishment cruel and unusual, it makes it intelligible.' Will, The value of punishment, *Newsweek*, 24 May 1982, at 92. Advocates of the retaliation model of retribution tend to advocate its use for utilitarian reasons, however. See notes 264–76 and accompanying text.

263. To the extent that vengeance is associated with vigilantism, barbarity, lynching and other pejoratives, the tendency has been to reject it as a justification for punishment. Similarly, to the extent that it is associated with historical punishments such as drawing and quartering and other forms of torture, it seems reflective of a less enlightened state.

264. Feinberg, Punishment, in *Punishment*, note 252, at 8.

265. See Schulhofer, Harm and punishment: a critique of emphasis on the results of conduct in the criminal law, 122 *University of Pennsylvania Law Review* 1497, 1508–14 (1974).

266. The New Bedford case involved a sexual assault that polarized the largely Portuguese-American community. The issues included age-old beliefs about rape and ethnic prejudices. See Rangel, Thousands march to protest bar rape convictions, *New York Times* 24 Mar. 1984, at 7, col. 1; Friendly, Naming of victim in rape trial on TV and in newspapers prompts debate, *New York Times*, 24 Mar 1984, at 7, col. 5; Beck and Zabarsky, Rape trial: justice crucified'?, *Newsweek*, 2 Apr. 1984, at 39.

Another justification for retaliation is that it is necessary to ensure public respect for the law: The 'law has an expressive function, expressing and thereby sustaining certain values.' Will, note 262, at 92. By deferring to 'a common sense of justice', retaliatory punishment maintains respect for the law. See Schulhofer, note 265, at 1513. This is really no more than a general deterrence argument in retributive clothing, however, and it is not altogether clear that public, ritualized retaliation serves the function of enforcing respect for the law: Recall the public executions of pickpockets in England, where the brethren of the condemned circulated in the crowds, picking pockets. See also M. Foucault, *Discipline and Punish* 58–65 (1979) (public executions used to solidify authority of sovereign more than to express 'common' sense of justice).

267. The wife of a Stanford University mathematics professor who was murdered observed: '"My own personal philosophy based on my spiritual beliefs and on my psychological beliefs is that there is no point in hanging on to hatred and fear . . ."' Madison, No hatred for killer, widow says, *Peninsula Times Tribune*, 24 Jan. 1984, at B1, col. 1. George Wallace has stated that he has forgiven the man who tried to assassinate him. Wallace: Bremer is forgiven, *San Jose Mercury News*, 15 May 1984, at 3A, col. 4. Relatives of victims, on the other hand, frequently do become intensely involved in seeking vengeance. See, e.g., Burress, Angry son tries to attack mother's killer in court, *San Francisco Chronicle*, 11 Feb. 1984, at 3, col. 1 (son of murder victim tried to attack defendant after judge overruled jury verdict to impose death penalty); Foley, 'Trailside' trial to begin in L.A., *San Jose Mercury News*, 9 Oct. 1983, at 1A, col. 4 (mothers of victims expressing rage at criminal justice system and supporting death penalty).

268. Compare Bilby, Maximum drunk-driving term given, *Denver Post*, 6 June 1984, at 9A, col. 1 (mother of victim of drunk driver 'said her feelings for the man who killed her son have turned from hate to pity'), *with* Anderson, Missing children's center gets funding, *San Jose Mercury News*, 19 Apr. 1984, at 2A, col. 5 (John Walsh, father of murder victim, became 'crusader on behalf of missing kids' and lobbied for legislation), and sources cited in note 267.

269. A man who survived a murder attempt, but whose fiancee was killed during the attack, remains outraged at the criminal justice system. The outrage has generalized to anger at defence lawyers in general. See Mandel, Crime victim, legal victim, turns crusader, *San Francisco Chronicle*, 16 Jan. 1983, at A2, col. 1.

270. See notes 129–36 and accompanying text. At the time of this writing a considerable amount of controversy surrounds the shooting of four black teenagers on a New York subway by Bernhard Goetz, a man who had been mugged by three blacks several years before. Did Goetz shoot the four young men because of rage, an urge to retaliate or fear produced by the prior incident? It would be foolish to speculate on the effect of his prior victimization at this time; the shooting of four people in a subway appears to be an extreme response, particularly if it is true that Goetz fired a second shot into an apparently disabled youth. Stengel, A troubled and troubling life, *Time*, 8 Apr. 1985, at 35.

271. See text accompanying notes 129–35; *cf.* Miller and Porter, note 122 (acknowledging that their own behaviour may have contributed to assault enabled victims to reassert control and autonomy).

272. See, e.g., Crime victims' agony, note 155 (detailing testimony at Senate Judiciary Committee subcommittee hearing by victims and relatives of victims advocating abolition of parole).
273. The bail issue has also led to the adoption of preventive detention statutes. See notes 170–2.
274. See notes 119–37 and accompanying text. The questions of good and evil are not easily answered; indeed, most explanations fall woefully short of providing any lasting understanding. Each individual is ultimately responsible for answering his or her own 'why'.
275. H. Arendt, *The Human Condition* 240–1 (1958).
276. Compare Cohn, note 259 (daughter of a man killed by a drunk driver, who was 'on the verge of tears' after apparently lenient sentencing, was quoted as stating, 'He'll never, ever realize what he did'), with Bilby, note 268 (mother of the victim said the judge '"did all he could do"').
277. See notes 146–8 and accompanying text.
278. Pub. L. No. 97–291, 96 Stat. 1248 (1982) (amending Fed. R. Crim. P. 32(c)(2)).
279. *Omnibus Victim's Protection Act: Hearing on S. 2420 Before the Subcomm. on Criminal Law of the Senate Comm. on the Judiciary*, 97th Cong., 2d Sess. 55 (1982) [hereinafter cited as *Senate Hearings*].
280. Ibid. at 171.
281. Within wide limits, the Eighth Amendment prohibition against cruel and unusual punishments may require legislatures to maintain the relationship between harm and punishment. See, e.g., *Solem* v. *Helm*, 463 U.S. 277 (1983) (life sentence without possibility of parole under habitual offender statute disproportionate when underlying offences are not serious or violent); *Coker* v. *Georgia*, 433 U.S. 584 (1977) (death penalty is grossly disproportionate punishment for rape).
282. Schulhofer, note 265, at 1515.
283. Ibid. at 1519–22.
284. Ibid. at 1522–62.
285. Ibid. at 1562 (citing J. Bentham, *An Introduction to the Principles of Morals and Legislation* 194 (1876).
286. Ibid. at 1562–85.
287. Ibid. at 1508–10.
288. See notes 264–76 and accompanying text.
289. Although judges may have a range of sentencing options, that range is becoming increasingly narrowed by the legislatures. The change in focus from rehabilitation to retribution as the primary justification for the criminal sanction has led to the end of indeterminate sentencing. See S. Kadish, S. Schulhofer and M. Paulsen, note 60, at 205; O'Leary, Criminal sentencing: trends and tribulations, 20 *Criminal Law Bulletin* 417 (1984); see also Casper, note 62, at 233–7. Legislatures now set minimum mandatory penalties, often with precise detail, to limit judicial discretion in imposing sentences. See, e.g., *Penal Code* s. 1170 (West Supp. 1985); *Ill. Rev. Stat.* ch. 38, ss. 1005–5–3(2), 1005–8–1 (1982); New York Penal Law ss. 60.05, 70.00, 70.02 (McKinney Supp. 1984); 42 *Pa. Cons. Stat. Ann.* ss. 9712–17 (Purdon Supp. 1984); I. Schwartz, *New York Sentence Charts* 6–7 (1985). See generally Casper, note 62.

Indeterminate sentencing and discretionary probation thus have been replaced by determinate sentences and mandatory prison provisions. As more and more statutes sharply circumscribe the judge's discretion, the issues of the specific harm to the victims and victim participation become increasingly irrelevant.

290. See *Senate Hearings*, note 279, at 83 (statement of Marlene A. Young, Executive Director of the National Organization for Victim Assistance); ibid. at 187–92 (statement of Deborah P. Kelly, Department of Government and Politics, University of Maryland).

291. See, e.g., Task Force, note 71, at 60, 64. The Task Force's *Final Report* recommends that victims be allowed to participate throughout the process. In its recommendations for prosecutors, the report emphasizes a victim-centred prosecutorial model. Ibid. at 63–71. See also Goldstein, note 72.

292. Although some have argued that the victim should have a greater role throughout the process, see note 291, and some victims or relatives of victims have also wanted a more active role in prosecution, see Foley, note 267, it is not self-evident that all, or even most, victims want to be so involved.

293. This is a rough figure, as each state has different provisions for speedy trials, sentencings and other criminal procedures.

294. One victim is quoted as saying: 'Why do criminals have more rights than victims? They get to choose counsel and have these continuances . . . You are stuck with a lawyer they give you, you are left out of what's going on . . .' *Senate Hearings*, note 279, at 189. In many instances, however, it is a total misperception that the 'criminal' got to choose his or her own lawyer. An indigent defendant is assigned counsel by the court, and has little to say in the matter. Even though an accused has a right to counsel, the Supreme Court has made it clear that that right does not include the right to a 'meaningful attorney–client relationship.' *Morris* v. *Slappy*, 461 U.S. 1, 14 (1983). Indeed, I found that asking defendants if they had an attorney in a prior case usually produced the response, 'No, I had a PD (public defender).'

295. The majority of defendants have no reason to perceive themselves as advantaged, especially if they remain in custody or are represented by public defenders – often referred to as 'dump trucks' by clients who see their lawyers as only wanting to strike a quick deal. And when an indigent defendant does not meet his public defender until the day of his trial or has appointed counsel who does not know how to conduct a trial, 'having a lawyer' is more illusory than real. Cf. Babcock, Fair play: evidence favourable to an accused and effective assistance of counsel, 34 *Stanford Law Review* 1133, 1163–74 (1982) (discussing adversary model as undermined by failure of courts to assure effective representation for indigent defendants).

296. The jury trial is unique to Anglo-American criminal procedure. It is a way of presenting at least the appearance of democratic, rather than hierarchical, decision–making. Cf. Damaska, Structures of authority and comparative criminal procedure, 84 *Yale Law Journal* 480, 492, 532–42 (1975) (comparing 'liberal' English criminal procedures to

hierarchical continental methods). While the use of the jury is not exclusively ideological – by now, it has become custom or habit in the United States – there is an overlay of belief that a jury better reflects community values than does a judge.

297. Cf. M. Fleming, note 40 (arguing that the proper focus of criminal law is protection against crime, not protection of criminals).

298. Ibid. see also R. Reiff, note 25.

299. See P. Brest and S. Levinson, *Processes of Constitutional Decisionmaking* 719–46 (1983).

300. See *In re Winship*, 397 U.S. 358, 371–2 (1971) (Harlan, J., concurring); Friendly, 'Some kind of hearing', 123 *University of Pennsylvania Law Review* 1267, 1278 (1975).

301. A sentence might, however, practically preclude recovery. *See* notes 316–24 and accompanying text. A plea bargaining arrangement might ease recovery in some jurisdictions, however. California, for example, permits the use of a guilty plea or a 'no contest' plea in a subsequent civil suit to prove that the defendant committed a felony. See *Cal. Evid. Code* s. 1300 (West Supp. 1985); *California Penal Code* s. 1016 (West Supp. 1985).

302. For example, the Santa Clara County, California, District Attorney's Office had a general policy of photographing the property of victims and returning the property to them whenever possible. By contrast, the San Mateo County, California, District Attorney's Office would retain property until after a conviction was affirmed on appeal.

303. The President's Task Force seems to imply that a victims's physical safety and liberty may be affected by the release of an offender, at least in the context of parole. Task Force, note 71, at 30, 84. Again, however, the *Final Report* vacillates confusingly among past victims who have a 'deep and real' fear of retaliation and may want 'to take precautions', and society's 'responsibility for protecting the innocent'. Ibid. at 84.

304. See notes 311–18 and accompanying text.

305. In a few instances, the release of an offender may pose a direct danger to the individual victim, but those instances will be rare. Even if we had criteria for determining general dangerousness – e.g., the likelihood that the interest in protecting future victims dictates that a given offender be incapacitated – general dangerousness is decidedly different from dangerousness to a specific individual. The difficulty of separating a victim's understandable fear of, and perception of threats from, the offender from actual threats to the individual would make rational sentencing very difficult, if not impossible, in the vast majority of cases. In cases involving domestic violence, where the offender has clearly directed his behaviour toward a given individual or individuals, dangerousness may be more predictable.

306. Perhaps this is why the President's Task Force recommended amending the Sixth Amendment to the United States Constitution to provide explicitly for victim's rights. See Task Force, note 71, at 114–15.

307. This basis for recognition could be characterized as an 'individual dignity' argument. As Jerry Mashaw has observed:

> State coercion must be legitimized, not only by acceptable substantive policies, but also by political processes that respond to a democratic morality's demand for participation in decisions affecting individual and group interests . . .
>
> To accord an individual less [than a hearing] when his property or status is at stake requires justification . . . because a lack of personal participation causes alienation and a loss of that dignity and self-respect that society properly deems independently valuable.

Mashaw, The Supreme Court's due process calculus for administrative adjudication in *Mathews* v. *Eldridge*: three factors in search of a theory of value, 44 *U. Chi. L. Rev.* 28, 49–50 (1976) (footnotes omitted).

308. See, e.g., California Constitution art. I, s. 28(b); 18 U.S.C. ss. 3579, 3580 (1982); *Alabama Code* s. 15–18–67 (1982); *California Penal Code* ss. 1191.1, 1191.2 (West Supp. 1985); *Iowa Code Ann.* ss. 910.2, 910.3 (West Supp. 1985). See generally Harland, note 72, at 69–75.
309. California Const. art. I, s. 28(b).
310. 18 U.S.C. ss. 3579, 3580 (1982).
311. See, e.g., note 26.
312. Many advocates of mandatory restitution have asserted that requiring the victim to pursue a civil remedy is unnecessarily burdensome and duplicative, and have disputed the historical distinction between criminal and civil law. *See, e.g.,* S. Schafer, note 36; Laster, Criminal restitution: a survey of its past history, in *Readings*, note 36, at 19–28; Note, Victim restitution in the criminal process: a procedural analysis, 97 *Harvard Law Review* 931, 933–7 (1984).
313. Harland, note 72, at 60–4.
314. Ibid. at 86–9.
315. The federal restitution provision, enacted as part of the Victim and Witness Protection Act of 1982, provides for restitution of non-compensated costs, including damage or loss of property, payment of medical and psychiatric care, funeral expenses and lost income. 18 U.S.C. s. 3579(b), (e) (1982). But see *Ala. Code Ann.* s. 15–18–65—66 (1982) (all perpetrators of criminal activity are to compensate for 'pecuniary loss', damage or injury; 'pecuniary loss' is defined as 'all special damages which a person shall recover against the defendant in a civil action'); *Ariz. Rev. Stat. Ann.* s. 13–603(c) (Supp. 1984) (requiring restitution 'in the full amount of economic loss as determined by the court and in the manner as determined by the court after consideration of the economic circumstances of the convicted person'); *Me. Rev. Stat. Ann.* tit. 17-A, s. 1322(6) (1983) ('restitution' defined as monetary or in-kind reimbursement for 'economic loss').
316. 18 U.S.C. s. 3579a(2) (1982).
317. California Constitution art. I, s. 28(b). It further provides that victims be heard at sentencing for the purpose of determining restitution. *California Penal Code* s. 1191.1 (West Supp. 1985).
318. Cf. Dworkin, Liberalism, in *Public and Private Morality* 113, 136 (S. Hampshire ed, 1978) (preservation of a true liberal system requires that individual rights occasionally trump the economic market and political democracy).

319. Deterrence, rehabilitation and incapacitation are all aimed at crime prevention, a public function. Retribution also serves a public function, either as a utilitarian means of handling public outrage or as an irreducible, morally good public response to wickedness. See notes 251–3, 262–4 and accompanying texts.

320. In fact, the University of Pennsylvania found the subject vexing enough to publish an entire symposium on the public/private distinction. The public/private distinction, 130 *University of Pennsylvania Law Review* 1289 (1982). It *may* be of note that none of the participants in the symposium addressed the public/private distinction in the area of criminal law; on the other hand, Duncan Kennedy acknowledged two critiques of criminal law in his comment on Paul Brest's contribution. Kennedy, The stages of the decline of the public/private distinction, 130 *University of Pennsylvania Law Review* 1349, 1350 and n. 2 (1982). Perhaps we are all so acculturated into believing that criminal law is public that we don't really think of it automatically when we think of attempts to distinguish 'private' from 'public'. Or at least I am so acculturated that I am convinced that criminal law is inescapably collectivity oriented rather than individually oriented. Nozick's argument that compensation to one person does not reassure others who are frightened and does little to stabilize the environment in which individuals live is a good one in so far as it recognizes the importance of the distinction. See R. Nozick, *Anarchy, State, and Utopia* 57–87 (1974); see also H. Arendt, *Eichmann in Jerusalem* 260–1 (revis. edn, 1965) (crime is a wrong against the community whose law is violated).

321. Many criminal codes forbid such things as 'misprision' or 'obstruction of justice', often in broad terms. See, e.g., 18 U.S.C. ss. 1503–1512, 1515 (1984); *Ariz. Rev. Stat.* s. 13–2409 (Supp. 1984); *Mass. Ann. Laws* ch. 264, s. 4, ch. 268, s. 13B (1970); cf. *California Penal Code* s. 153 (West Supp. 1985) (compounding or concealing a crime).

322. One frequent criticism of the Uniform Crime Index is that it fails to reflect the 'true' rate of crime because of non-reporting, among other things. Linked to the problem of non-reporting is the belief, if not the certainty, that crimes that go unpunished lead to an increase in the crime rate. Thus, studies are conducted to determine how to increase citizen reporting, see W. Spelman and D. Brown, note 174, and victim's compensation has been justified in part because of a posited incentive to increase reporting of crimes and to increase victim cooperation, see R. Elias, note 72, at 254, 259 n.24.

   A relatively recent development that encourages public participation in crime prevention is the 'Neighbourhood Watch' programme, in which members of the community monitor suspicious activity. But neighbourhood watch programmes, citizen patrols and other community-based, public responses to the crime rate do not appear to have substantially reduced crime, although they 'can at the very least help pull a neighborhood together and improve its sense of security.' Currie, note 29, at 23.

323. Thus, the Supreme Court has granted legislatures wide latitude in determining what sanctions to impose for what crimes. *Rummel* v. *Estelle*, 445 U.S. 263, 274–6 (1980) (reluctance to review legislatively

mandated terms of imprisonment under Eighth Amendment). But see
Solem v. *Helm*, 463 U.S. 277 (1983) (while courts should grant 'substantial deference' to legislatures, no penalty is *per se* constitutional).

324. Bentham, Political remedies for the evil of offences, in *Readings*, note
36, at 29.
325. Garofalo, Enforced reparation as a substitute for imprisonment, in
Readings, note 36, at 43.
326. See, e.g., L. Forer, note 72, at 299 (1980). Forer also points to the
debilitating effects of prison and the expense of imprisonment as further
reasons to adopt restitution schemes. Ibid. at 136–8, 307.
327. Kelman, note 28, at 215–16.
328. Restitution has been used most frequently as a condition of probation.
See Harland, note 72, at 57, 69–75. But it might also be used to escape
criminal liability altogether under a so-called 'civil compromise' statute.
See, e.g., *California Penal Code* s. 1378 (West 1982) (victims may
'compromise' misdemeanours by acknowledging satisfaction for injury); see also Harland, note 72, at 65. Most offenders, given the choice
between jail and probation, probably prefer probation and restitution.
Although I found no empirical evidence on this subject, my own clients
almost always chose restitution over jail.
329. At present, a person in prison has no opportunity to earn the money
necessary to make restitution. Even where prisoners do work, the
profits are used primarily to defray the expense of feeding and housing
inmates, and prisoners' wages are minimal. Moreover, private industry
and labour resent the competition of prison industries. '[N]obody wants
to see prison shops opened in their market.' See Schilling, Prison shops
have 'edge,' foes say, *Rocky Mountain News*, Dec. 25, 1983, at 97,
col. 1.
330. A submission to the Subcommittee on Criminal Law of the Senate
Judiciary Committee by Ronald A. Zweibel, Chairman of the New
York State Crime Victims Board and President of the National Association of Crime Victim Compensation Boards, provides a good example
of this tendency. The submission noted the problems of both civil and
restitutive recovery but utterly failed to acknowledge that restitution is
often no more than an unrealistic goal: '[T]he realities of recovering
losses from a criminal offender, who may be judgement proof, incarcerated or indigent, are not particularly promising . . . Although encum-
bered by some of the same practical problems as encountered with civil
recoveries, restitution at least provides an alternative avenue for securing this basic right.' *Senate Hearings*, note 279, at 172.
331. See L. Forer, note 72, at 303. But see Dittenhoffer and Ericson, The
victim/offender reconciliation program: a message to correctional reformers, 33 *University of Toronto Law Journal* 315, 346–7 (1983) (community programme in which offender and victim meet and agree on
restitution amount and terms is not a clearly better alternative to jail).
332. There are other problems with restitution as well. For one thing, many
offenders lack legitimate means to pay restitution, and may resort to
other methods of providing for the money to meet restitution payments
rather than go to jail. Second, if an offender legitimately lacks the

means to make restitution, it may not be possible to incarcerate him. See *Bearden* v. *Georgia*, 461 U.S. 660, 668–9 (1983) (state may not imprison probationer who has made 'all reasonable efforts' to pay fine or make restitution as condition of probation "without considering whether adequate alternative methods' of punishment are available).

333. Given a choice between receiving restitution or seeing the offender punished or incapacitated, the victim of a core crime is likely to *want* both, but will settle for something less. Given the cultural association of crime with punishment, many victims will arguably prefer punishment; some victims may want the offender incapacitated for more 'altruistic' reasons such as the protection of the community. Thus, even from a pure 'victim' orientation, restitution may not be as important as is often assumed.

334. Although physical torture has largely been replaced by deprivation of rights and wealth, M. Foucault, note 266, at 7–15, the deprivation is still punishment, reaffirming power relationships and social control, and inflicting pain. It is a negative stimulus. As such, pain or suffering, however short, is a part of punishment.

335. The Victim's Bill of Rights made restitution mandatory, see California Const. art. I, s. 28(b), and lengthened sentences in cases where an offender had a prior conviction for a felony, no matter how old the prior felony conviction, see ibid. at s. 28(f); cf. *California Penal Code* s. 667 (West Supp. 1985) (requiring a five-year sentence for each prior 'serious felony' conviction to run consecutively to sentence for new 'serious felony' conviction); see also California Legislative Assembly Committee on Criminal Justice, *Analysis of Proposition 8*, at 28, 31–2, 42–3 (1982) (arguing that '[s]ignificantly [l]onger [s]entences' would result under Proposition 8). The California Determinate Sentencing Law, together with individual provisions requiring *mandatory* prison sentences for a number of offences, already existed when Proposition 8 passed. See *California Penal Code* s. 1170 (1977).

336. Paul Gann, a co-author of the Victim's Bill of Rights, stated that 'he favors just about any effort to get restitution money from convicted felons, including confiscating money or property,' and went on to observe: "'If they commit a heinous crime, like rape or murder, as far as I'm concerned they can get the money selling their blood if somebody will buy it.'" Norman, Traffic tickets may help pay the bills for victims of crime, *Peninsula Times Tribune*, 4 June 1983, at Al, col. 1, A8, col. 1. Republican legislators 'introduced legislation that would require convicted adults and juveniles to repay their victims, either directly with money or goods, or indirectly through community service,' Stanton, A proposal to pay victims of crime, *Peninsula Times Tribune*, 23 Mar. 1983, at A4, col. 1, but they ultimately agreed to Democrat-sponsored legislation, see notes 340–3 and accompanying text.

337. Senate Bill 593, introduced by Senator Dolittle and co-authored by Republican Assemblyman Nolan, would have provided that courts impose a mandatory 'restitution penalty' of between $50 and $100,000. S. 593, 1983, Cal. Legis., Regular Session, at 5 (17 June 1983) (amended in assembly, 15 July 1983). If the offender were sentenced to

prison, the Director of Corrections would have been required to with-hold 50 per cent of the prisoner's income and transfer it to the State Board of Control to be placed in a restitution trust account. Ibid. at 8–9. The Board of Prison Terms, in considering parole, would have to determine a payment schedule for 'remaining restitution penalty'; parole could be revoked if the restitution payments were not made, and parole terms could be extended up to 15 years in order to assure payments. Ibid. at 8. The majority leader of the Assembly referred to the Republican proposals as 'unworkable' and 'hoax-like', concluding that the Republican package 'offers a false hope that everybody will get restitution for a crime.' Demos would make criminals pay 'tax' for restitution funds, *San Francisco Examiner*, 23 Mar. 1983, at B12, col. 1, 3; accord *Should a Restitution Penalty Be Assessed in Criminal and Juvenile Cases to Be Paid into a Separate Account for the Benefit of the Victim?*, Memorandum by Byron D. Sher, Chairman of the California Assembly Committee on Criminal Law and Public Safety (1983) (on file with author).

338. This is based on the maximum, 'aggravated', eight-year term, see *California Penal Code* s. 264 (West Supp. 1985), for violation of the statute, see ibid. at s. 261 (West Supp. 1985), a five-year consecutive enhancement for great bodily harm, see ibid. at s. 12022.8 (West 1982), and a three-year enhancement for use of a deadly weapon, see ibid. at s. 12022.3. The maximum sentence is thus 16 years. With one-third of the sentence reduced by good time/work-time credits, ibid. at ss. 2931, 2933 (West Supp. 1985), 10 years and 8 months would be the minimum sentence the offender would have to serve.

339. *California Government Code* ss. 13960–13974 (West. Supp. 1985).

340. See *California Government Code* ss. 13959, 13960.1, 13967 (West Supp. 1985); H.R. 1485, 1983–1984 Cal. Legis., Regular Sess., 56–68; Ashby, Assembly passes bills on restitution to crime victims, *Los Angeles Daily Journal*, 10 June 1983, at 1, col. 2.

341. See Press Release by California Assemblyman Byron Sher (12 Sept. 1983) (on file with author) [hereinafter cited as Sher]. In the press release, the sponsors of the 'Crime Victim Restitution Program of 1983' stated: 'The Restitution Fund would be financed by doubling current fine limits, ordering a restitution fine in every criminal case, and impos-ing heavy fines on drug offenders.' Sher, ibid. at 1. California law now provides that restitution fines may be paid by withholding 20 per cent of a prisoner's wages, a peculiar blend of the Republican's direct restitu-tion idea and the Democrat's compensation fund model. *California Penal Code* s. 2085.5 (West Supp. 1985). See also Lynne, Of parking violators and victims of violence, *Peninsula Times Tribune*, 31 Mar. 1983, at A2, col. 1.

342. See *California Government Code* s. 13967 (West Supp. 1985); *Califor-nia Penal Code* ss. 1463.18, 1464 (West Supp. 1985); *Cal. Welf. and Inst. Code* s. 729.6 (West Supp. 1985).

343. One author has argued that this type of funding scheme furthers the goals of punishment and rehabilitation, see Friedsam, Legislative assist-ance to victims of crime: the Florida Crimes Compensation Act, 11

The Wrongs of Victim's Rights 189

Florida State University Law Review 859, 872 (1984), presumably because it is a form of quasi-restitution. But the distinction between payment of a restitution 'fine' and other 'fines' seems nonexistent. Moreover, it is not clear that restitution functions either as a rehabilitative device or as a punishment. Nor does 'taxing' well-to-do offenders, primarily white collar criminals or drug dealers, seem to add to general deterrence.

344. Note, note 312, at 944.
345. Ibid. at 944–6.
346. Ibid. at 937–41.
347. I take issue with this argument for two reasons. First, as I have argued *see* notes 324–34 and accompanying text, restitution is *not* supported by any of the rationales for the criminal sanction. Second, this argument ignores the fact that if a convicted offender is sued in tort, he does not sacrifice the procedural and evidentiary benefits that other tort defendants have. To treat him differently in the criminal context undermines the purpose of the safeguards in the civil context.
348. 18 U.S.C. s. 3580(d) (1982). For an argument that the determination of restitution should take place in the adjudicatory phase of the criminal process in order to protect the rights of defendants, see Note, Restitution in the criminal process: procedures for fixing the offender's liability, 93 *Yale Law Journal* 505, 516–17 (1984). The courts have also been unwilling to dispense with due process protections in the restitution area, although they have disagreed on what process is due. Compare *U.S.* v. *Welden*, 568 F. Supp. 516 (N.D. Ala. 1983) (restitution order under Federal Victim and Witness Protection Act violates due process clause, seventh amendment right to jury trial, and eighth amendment prohibition against cruel and unusual punishment, because it might result in imprisonment for debt), with *In re D.G.W.*, 70 N.J. 488, 361 A.2d 513 (1976) (due process encompasses a right to be heard at the sentencing hearing), and *State* v. *Pope*, 107 Wis. 2d 726, 321 N.W.2d 359 (Wis. Ct. App. 1982) (due process requires notice, an opportunity to be heard, and a right of confrontation).
   The procedures for determining restitution that have been developed by courts and legislatures are not as protective as are existing procedures for civil cases. See Harland, note 72, at 99–108.
349. 18 U.S.C. s. 3580(d) (1982).
350. See Note, note 348, at 509–11.
351. Ibid. at 517.
352. Harland, note 72, at 99–108.
353. Ibid. at 73–4, 105.
354. Ibid. at 100–8. Similarly, California's Victims's Bill of Rights did not address any substantive or procedural questions, but simply left it up to the legislature to determine how the restitution provisions should be implemented. Although the legislature has created the Crime Victim's Restitution Fund, it has yet to provide a procedural framework for reaching a restitution decision at sentencing.
355. Harland's thesis is that the use of restitution is grounded more on convenience and practicality than on any particularly 'profound

190   *Critical Views on Victimology and Victim Policy*

    reconsideration of the fundamental purposes of civil versus criminal
    courts or tort-crime differences.' Ibid. at 120.
356. See *California Government Code* ss. 13959–13974 (West 1980 and Supp.
    1985).
357. See, e.g., *Alaska Stat.* s. 18.67.010–.180 (1981 and Supp. 1984); *Fla.
    Stat. Ann.* s. 960.01–.28 (West 1985); *Mass. Ann. Laws* ch. 258A, ss.
    1–9 (Michie/Law. Co-op. 1980 and Supp. 1985). In 1984, Congress
    established a federal victim compensation programme. Victims of
    Crime Act of 1984, Pub. L. No. 98–473, 98 Stat. 2170 (1984). The
    federal law enacts a tax on offenders – $25 for individuals convicted of a
    misdemeanour, $50 for individuals convicted of a felony – similar to the
    'penalty assessment' scheme used in California. Ibid. at s. 1405, 98 Stat.
    at 2174–5. The fines are to be distributed to state victim's compensation
    programmes.
358. See, e.g., Yarborough, S.2155 of the Eighty-Ninth Congress – The
    Criminal Injuries Compensation Act, 50 *Minnesota Law Review* 255,
    256–57 (1965). English penal reformer Margaret Fry argued, for exam-
    ple, that the state, having taken on the responsibility of controlling
    crime and adjudicating guilt, also had the responsibility to compensate
    those injured when the state failed to control crime. See Fry, note 36;
    cf. Mueller, Compensation for victims of crime: thought before action,
    50 *Minnesota Law Review* 213, 216–17 (1965) (characterizing victim's
    compensation as 'compulsory government insurance, comparable to
    workmen's compensation, social security, or medicare'); Schafer, Res-
    titution to victims of crime – an old correctional aim modernized, 50
    Minnesota Law Review 243, 249 (1965) (emphasizing the need for the
    state to fulfill 'an important social welfare function' through victim's
    compensation). But see R. Elias, note 72, at 27–9 (victim's compensa-
    tion is motivated by the desire to 'buy off' civil unrest); Weeks, The
    New Zealand Criminal Injuries Compensation Scheme, 43 *S. Cal. L.
    Rev.* 107, 107–9 (1970) (victim's compensation was a politically conve-
    nient way to offset objections to liberalization of penal system).
        Although inspired by liberalism, several statutes did incorporate
    conservative values, such as requirements that the victim be 'blameless'
    and cooperate with law enforcement officials. See, e.g., *California
    Government Code* s. 13961 (West Supp. 1985) (State Board of Control
    empowered to promulgate eligibility rules); *Cal. Admin. Code* tit. 2,
    Rr. 648.3, 649.9 (1985) (for claims arising before 1 July 1974, victims
    could be required to cooperate with law enforcement in the
    apprehension *and* conviction of the criminal in order to recover; for
    claims arising 1 July 1974 or thereafter, applicant has burden of proving
    by a preponderance of the evidence to Board's 'satisfaction' that in-
    juries or death arose 'from a crime of violence which was promptly
    reported' to law enforcement agency, and that victim did not, 'by his
    acts, contribute to his own injuries', among other things); *Minn. Stat.
    Ann.* s. 611A.53(2) (West Supp. 1985) (reparation unavailable if victim
    failed to report the crime to the police within five days, 'failed or
    refused to cooperate fully' with law enforcement, or is related to the

offender); *Wis. Stat. Ann.* s. 949.08 (West 1982) (compensation unavailable if victim 'engaged in conduct which substantially contributed to' injury or death, 'has not cooperated with law enforcement', is related to the offender, or committed a crime himself or herself).

359. R. Elias note 72, at 237, 252–3 (social welfare model may increase victim discontent); Elias, The symbolic politics of victims compensation, 8 *Victimology* 213, 217–20 (1983) (compensation should be based on a theory of rights).

360. See, e.g., Fry, note 36; Wolfgang, Social responsibility for violent behaviour, 43 *S. Cal. L. Rev.* 5, 6 (1970); Yarborough, note 358, at 256.

361. See generally Starrs, A modest proposal to insure justice for victims of crime, 50 *Minnesota Law Review* 285 (1965) (criticizing special treatment of crime victims inherent in state compensation schemes and advocating private insurance as a remedy). I am unaware of any proposals in which states compensate victims of uninsured motorists; the farthest that states seem willing to go in this direction is to require that drivers be insured. See, e.g., California Vehicle Code ss. 16020, 16021 (West Supp. 1985); *Fla. Stat. Ann.* ss. 324.011–.021, 627.733 (1984 and Supp. 1985). The sanctions imposed on uninsured drivers who are involved in accidents, see California Vehicle Code s. 16070 (West Supp. 1985); *Fla. Stat. Ann.* s. 324.051(2) (West Supp. 1985), typically suspension or revocation of a driver's licence or vehicle registration, do nothing to compensate victims.

362. For an excellent attempt to find a theoretical and practical justification for government compensation to victims of toxic waste dumping, see Note, The inapplicability of traditional tort analysis to environmental risks: the example of toxic waste pollution victim compensation, 35 *Stanford Law Review* 575 (1983).

363. See, e.g., *Fla. Stat. Ann.* s. 960.03(3),(7) (West 1985); *Okla. Stat. Ann.* tit. 21, s. 142.3(13) (West 1983); *Wis. Stat. Ann.* ss. 949.01, .03 (West 1982 and Supp. 1985).

364. See note 358.

365. See, e.g., *Cal. Admin. Code* tit. 2, R. 648.3 (1985); *Minn. Stat. Ann.* s. 611A.53(2)(b) (West Supp. 1985); *Ohio Rev. Code Ann.* s. 2743.60(C) (Page Supp. 1984); *Okla. Stat. Ann.* tit. 21 s. 142.10(c) (West 1983); *Wis. Stat. Ann.* s. 949.08(d) (West 1982); *W. Va. Code* s. 14–2A–14(d) (Supp. 1985).

366. See R. Elias, note 72, at 111–12, 180. Elias, note 359, at 218.

367. In 1982, the Santa Clara County courts held two minor victims in contempt for their refusal to testify in sexual abuse cases. Both victims were confined in juvenile hall. Despite the negative publicity, the District Attorney's office supported the imprisonment of the victims. See Letter from William Hoffman, Chief Assistant District Attorney for Santa Clara County, to Lynne Henderson (25 May 1982) (on file with author); see also Nakao, 12-year-old-girl held in solitary for not testifying is freed, *San Francisco Examiner*, 8 Jan. 1984, at 1, col. 1 (molestation victim held in contempt for refusing to testify against stepfather).

368. *See* notes 137–47 and accompanying text.
369. For an article that discusses changes in the law of evidence as a result of the California Victim's Bill of Rights, see Mendez, California's new law on character evidence: evidence code section 352 and the impact of recent psychological studies, 31 *UCLA Law Review* 1003 (1984).
370. *Senate Hearings*, note 279, at 65–6 (emphasis added).

Part Two
The Victim's Role in the Penal Process: Critical Views

5 The Victim's Role in the Penal Process:
A Theoretical Orientation
Leslie Sebba

The attention which has been directed in recent years to that '"poor relation" of the criminal law', the victim,[1] has led to the crystalliza-tion of professional and public opinion in favour of alleviating the predicament of this forgotten figure of the contemporary criminal justice system. The impetus for reform has concentrated primarily on improving the material situation of the victim by means of schemes for compensation or restitution, and reducing his psychic trauma – particularly where victims of sexual assaults are concerned – by means of crisis intervention and the provision of other services for the victim.[2]

While it is clear that new areas of victim-oriented reforms continue to be identified and even acted upon, as illustrated by the District Attorney's Victim-Witness project,[3] the approach seems to be piecemeal, and has not taken the form of a systematic search for areas where a reorientation may be desirable. Further, the study of victim-related topics in this area has not fully exploited the know-ledge accumulated in two tangential areas of criminology and the criminal law: (a) the research into the exercise of discretionary powers by police and public prosecution, which has been oriented entirely towards the offender, although it has direct relevance to victimology; and (b) the literature of the procedural lawyers, particu-larly in continental Europe, which deals with the respective roles of civil and criminal actions and the possibilities of their combination.[4] What is lacking, therefore, is an integrated view of these problems – a truly victim-oriented examination of the criminal process.[5]

A comprehensive evaluation of the victim's role in the penal pro-cess, however, must also take account of the recent shift on the part of criminologists, politicians and other sections of the public in the realm of the philosophy of punishment – the shift away from the rehabilitative aim towards a system of proportionality which, while ostensibly based on the objectives of deterrence on the one hand, and humanity and justice on the other, nevertheless bears a startling resemblance to the principle of retribution. These two contemporaneous developments, the victimological revolution on the one hand, and the collapse of the rehabilitation model of corrections on the other, have each individually consumed gallons of printers' ink but attempts to reconcile and integrate them are practically unknown. A theoretical reorientation in relation to the victim's role in the penal process cannot, however, ignore the philosophical basis of the sanctions whose ultimate imposition constitutes the climax to that process. In the present article we shall hazard a formulation of a theoretical approach – or rather two alternative approaches – to the victim's role in the penal process. Much of the article, however, will be taken up with a consideration of the historical ideologies which such a formulation should take into account, as well as the identification of some of the practical issues to which the theoretical approaches will have to be applied. We shall start with a summary of these issues, drawing upon various legal systems – in particular Israel[6] – for purposes of illustration.

A SUMMARY OF THE ISSUES[7]

Making a complaint

The initiation of the penal process normally depends in the first instance on the filing of a complaint by the victim. Both self-report and victimization surveys indicate that many offences go unreported.[8] The decision *not* to report is not always freely made, but may be based on ignorance of the proper mechanism, as well as disillusion with official agencies.[9] Clearly, methods should be found to overcome these obstacles. There remains an ideological problem of criminal policy: should the victim be legally obligated to report the offence, exposing himself to the stigma of criminality if he fails to do so?

Citizen's arrest

Should the victim or potential victim (as well as the bystander) be granted a more active role in law enforcement than the mere lodging of a complaint? In England a citizen may make an arrest (without a warrant) for an 'arrestable offence' (punishable by at least five years' imprisonment), although the mere suspicion that such an offence has been committed (unless it in fact has been), or that it *will* be committed, serves only as a justification for police arrest.[10] In Israel the legacy of the former colonial-style regime remains, and a private citizen may only arrest an offender who commits a felony *in his presence*.[11] It is clear that this question calls for careful consideration of the respective roles of citizen-victim on the one hand, and law-enforcement officer on the other.

Police arrest and investigation

The discretionary nature of the decision of a police officer to make an arrest or to open an investigation has been well documented in the criminological literature.[12] The secondary role of the victim in these studies has already been alluded to, yet his predicament is readily apparent. For example, the downgrading of a battery to a 'disturbance'[13] or the refusal to arrest because the victim also is considered to be guilty of misconduct[14] could be perceived as an infringement of his rights.

The issue to be faced here is whether it is legitimate for the investigating body to refrain from pursuing its investigation on the ground of 'want of public interest',[15] and what weight in the 'public interest' equation is to be given to the victim's conduct and attributes. In particular, can there be a lack of 'public interest' even where the victim expresses an insistent *private* interest in pursuing the investigation?

Welfare of complainant

It is increasingly recognized that society's interest in the victim at this stage should not be confined to regarding him as a supplier of testimony against the offender, but to consider that he may be entitled to benefit from more positive interventions. The growing literature in this area has already been referred to.

Pre-trial detention

Provisions for pre-trial detention of suspects and defendants and for release on bail vary considerably from system to system, and the grounds for decision-making on the part of the police and courts in this area are even more multifarious. Inevitably, however, a consideration that frequently affects the decision whether to release a suspect/defendant in some jurisdictions is the estimation of the

198   *Victim's Role in the Penal Process: Critical Views*

danger of his 'tampering with the evidence', including, of course, exerting pressure on the victim. The prevailing consideration here is traditionally the threat to the 'case against the defendant'; but what of the threat of the well-being of the victim, and how is this to be measured against the infringement of the suspect's liberty inherent in his continued incarceration?[16]

The decision to prosecute

There has been a developing literature in recent years on prosecutorial discretion but, here again, the victim's attitude is usually a secondary topic. The question is closely related to that of police investigation for three reasons: (a) in some countries the police are themselves the prosecuting authority, especially with respect to minor offences; (b) the police decision not to conduct an investigation may itself be based on the desire of the victim to refrain from prosecution;[17] (c) the other victim-related factors which influence the decision not to arrest or investigate are similar to those operating at the prosecution stage.[18]

Here, again, the question arises whether the prosecution should have the power, notwithstanding the victim's insistence on prosecution, to close the case, to 'divert' it away from the courts, or to plea-bargain.[19] The converse question also arises whether prosecution should be instituted where the victim wishes the matter to be dropped.

From earliest times there have been some offences which were regarded as being within the special province of the victim, who was empowered to pardon the offender or to waive prosecution. The most notable example is adultery, whereby the husband was granted this power under the Code of Hamurabi – a provision which has survived into modern systems of European law.[20] It must be asked whether either the long history of this type of provision or the current rebirth of the victim constitute sufficient justification for entrusting to the latter this form of prosecutorial control.

Remedy against non-prosecution

Most legal systems provide for a mechanism, whether by means of a preliminary hearing or a grand jury, to prevent an arbitrary instigation of prosecution that would subject an innocent suspect to unnecessary suffering. Is the victim also entitled to a controlling mechanism to prevent an arbitrary *non*-prosecution of his complaint? The Israeli Criminal Procedure Law provides for an application for review on the part of the Attorney General.[21] Such control is, of course, internal, in that the prosecution is in any case subject to the general supervision of the Attorney General. A still dissatisfied complainant may apply to the High Court, which will interfere only where the prosecution's discretion was exercised in bad faith or for extraneous motives. Similarly, in the US, an application for mandamus almost never succeeds.[22] The attribution of a greater significance to the victim in the penal process would require a reevaluation of these remedies.

Private prosecutions

Should the complainant himself be empowered to instigate a criminal proceeding on the failure of the prosecutor to pursue the matter, or even without the necessity to await the decision of that body? In some US jurisdictions such a power lies with the individual complainant, although it is fraught with problems.[23] The English situation is somewhat paradoxical in this matter; prosecutions are nearly all nominally private,[24] but are in fact instigated by public officials acting in a private capacity.[25] The genuinely private prosecution (such as the libel action conducted by Sir James Goldsmith against the satirical journal *Private Eye*) are comparatively rare.[25a]

Israel, together with a number of other states,[26] has adopted a compromise in this matter. Certain offences – such as assault and trespass – are regarded as being of a somewhat private nature, and they, and they only, may be prosecuted by the complainant himself.[27] In these cases, moreover, there is no administrative appeal against inaction by the public prosecutor. All other offences, however, are within the exclusive powers of the public prosecutor.

The issue here is fundamental: is there a place in the contemporary penal system for private initiatives in the matter of prosecution, or do we prefer to rely on the institutionalized framework of the state? In other words, is the prosecution of offenders exclusively a matter of public policy, or does it concern the victim as well? Finally, if the form of compromise described above is adopted, what are the criteria for determining which offences merit victim prosecution and which do not?

Joinder of civil parties

Whether or not the victim instigates a criminal proceeding in his own right, should he be entitled to be a *civil* party to a criminal prosecution brought by the agents of the state? This practice is entirely foreign to the common law tradition, but is a recognized feature of the civil law systems.[28] These systems, while granting the victim no formal standing in the criminal process as such, assist him in achieving the goals of the civil process – financial compensation or restitution – without the need for additional litigation.

It may be that the considerations for allowing or disallowing this practice are above all practical and pragmatic, since all systems allow the victim to bring a civil action following the criminal process. Yet such practical considerations may be decisive in enabling the victim to assert his rights, for to launch into the complexities of civil litigation may be beyond the abilities of most victims, as well as being futile in many cases in which the offender will either have disappeared or have been incarcerated – his assets inaccessible or nonexistent. Moreover, under common law rules of evidence, the criminal conviction would not even be admissible as evidence in the civil proceedings.[29] It is thus an irony that the European approach, which notionally places the victim in a more subservient role in the criminal prosecution, by comparison with the common law, in practice places him in a superior position by means of the joinder device.

The court hearing

Here also the victim encounters problems: gruelling cross-examination by the defence counsel (the rape victim, again, being the most vaunted case of this), and delays in court such as will deter many from filing a complaint in the first place. Proposals are now being heard for legal representation for the victim; at the same time the Victim-Witness project is also designed to improve the situation of the witness at this juncture.

Should consideration for the victim at the trial stage be taken further, and result in a diminution of the right to confrontation and cross-examination and the exclusion of hearsay, as is illustrated by the Israeli provisions under which the evidence of a child victim of a sexual assault is admitted without the need for his or her presence in court?[30] Current developments designed to reduce the vulnerability of the sex victim to character assassination in the courtroom may be an indication that compromises with the common law heritage may be considered in other jurisdictions within the common law tradition.

The sentence

Modern practice does not give the victim direct input in the matter of the sentence to be imposed upon the offender. However, victim-related aspects of the offence may influence the court's determination of the sentence, such as the offender-victim relationship subsequent to the offence.[31] Finally, evaluation of the risk to be incurred in leaving the offender at large in the community may depend on the perceived continuing vulnerability of the victim.

On the other hand, some forms of disposition may be specifically victim-oriented. Some jurisdictions, including Israel, provide for court-ordered compensation to be paid by the offender to the victim (thereby obviating the need for a civil action by joinder or other-wise), although the effectiveness of this is probably limited.[32] Moreover, the statutory provisions for fines specify that the court should, in determining the size of the fine, consider, *inter alia*, the effect of its imposition on the capacity of the offender to compensate the victim.[33]

The recent victimology literature has been most inventive in developing ambitious suggestions for incorporating court-ordered compensation into the rehabilitative programme laid out for the offender.[34] However, the respective merits of individual schemes cannot be assessed independently of the larger question of the aims of the penal process as a whole, and the role of the victim in that process.

Post-sentencing correctional decisions

Questions raised in connection with the victim's influence on the sentencing decision recur when the offender is a candidate for parole or clemency. Here, again, some consideration may be given to the victim's predicament; but US courts have ruled that the victim has no standing to prevent clemency.[35]

There is a tradition in most countries, however, to the effect that neither pardon nor amnesty may jeopardize the rights of 'third parties' – including, of course, victims. Could it be argued that this principle should be taken a stage further by extending the protection to the victim's *sensibilities*, thereby reversing the rule in *Eacret* v. *Holmes*?

The preceding account, which makes brief reference to a number of areas of penal decision-making in which the victim is or might be involved, and identifies the main issues arising in each case, indicates not only a variety of solutions to these issues under different legal systems, but also some of the underlying ideological questions respecting the relationship between offender and victim, and the relationship of both to society as a whole. The fundamental anomaly of the penal process is that it is instituted in the name of the state, and ostensibly because of an injury to the state, but that it arises directly from the grievance inflicted upon the individual victim. What, then, is the proper role for the victim in that process, and how can a cohesive response – or alternative cohesive responses – be forthcoming on the variety of issues raised above? Such cohesion cannot be hoped for without an understanding of the background and development of modern systems of criminal justice, which will be considered in the next section.

THE NATURE OF CRIMINAL PROCEEDINGS

Von Hentig, Schafer and other learned scholars have documented in some detail the evolution of early penal systems from the stage at which the course of justice was the exclusive domain of the victim himself or his clan (private vengeance). They considered how such vengeance came to be regulated by the state and frequently translated into a scale of composition between the parties – finally evolving to a stage where the significance of the victim's role effectively disappeared – a process described by Schafer as 'the decline of the victim'.[36]

However, the evolution of the civil–criminal dichotomy, whereby the state is seen as the injured party in criminal cases while the victim fulfills this role only in civil cases, appears to be less well documented – or at least is more controversial. It is generally held that this dichotomy was unknown in early societies[37] – the vengeance-composition motif serving both purposes simultaneously. This view, however, which presupposed that conduct was judged by external criteria and that concepts of intentionality and moral obloquy were foreign to these systems, has been rejected in at least one analysis.[38]

More significantly, even in modern times it has been difficult to subject the civil–criminal dichotomy to scientific criteria of differentiation.[39] The same conduct may frequently constitute both a tort and a crime, and attempts to distinguish the two systems in terms of the substantive characteristics of the conduct giving rise to the respective actions[40] have not been entirely successful, since the notions of intentionality or foreseeability, popularly thought to supply the basis for this differentiation, are sometimes required even by the civil law – and are frequently absent in the criminal law.

Other criteria distinguishing crimes from torts, whether based on procedural considerations or on the ultimate objective of the proceedings, have been even more problematical. The notorious illustration of this was the 'penal action' in England, abolished only in 1951, whereby a common informer could claim a penalty for persons guilty of certain criminal acts. The acts were criminal, and the penalty punitive in nature, but the action and the judgment were civil, and the beneficiary was not the state but a private individual – although not necessarily a victim. Other commonly cited examples of confusion are the notion of punitive damages in a civil action and, of course, the provision for the ordering of compensation or restitution to the victim in criminal trials. The eminent jurist, Kenny, after grappling with the problem in his famous essay, 'What is a crime?', concluded that the only truly valid criterion for differentiating between a crime and a tort was that the sanction for a crime was remissible only by the state.[41] This, however, was not unduly helpful, since when one enquires as to the delimitation of the power to pardon and remit sanctions, one is informed that this power applies to 'crimes'![42]

It follows from the absence of total differentiation between the civil and criminal spheres that the view that the victim is totally forgotten by the penal system and is left exclusively to his remedies under the civil law, is an oversimplification. This is borne out most forcefully by a feature of the English common law referred to earlier in this article – that criminal prosecution in England is conducted, at least notionally, exclusively by private individuals. Except for a few offences, the prosecution of which is undertaken by the Director of Public Prosecutions, the criminal process is instigated by the laying of an information before the magistrate by a complainant (or 'prosecutor'). Any citizen may fulfill this role, and historically the natural candidate would have been the victim. Thus, while in practice the establishment of a professional police force has resulted in a near-monopolization of the complainant role by the police (or other public officials), a victim formally has the power to make one of the most critical decisions in the penal process – the decision to prosecute.[43]

Indeed, the crucial role bestowed – at least potentially – upon the victim under common law constitutes an integral part of what is generally considered to be the main identifying characteristic of the common law trial, namely the *adversary* nature of this process. The main features of the adversary system are that the two parties – prosecutor and defendant – have equal standing before the court, and that it is for the parties rather than the court to submit all the relevant evidence at their disposal and to examine and cross-examine the witnesses – the role of the court being predominantly passive.[44] This adversarial (or accusatorial)[45] system is contrasted in this respect with the inquisitorial system prevailing on the European continent.[46]

It is a fundamental principle of the adversary system that proceedings should be brought by an individual complainant, whether or not he is the victim. The concept of the equivalence of parties is surely predicated on the identity of the prosecutor as a private individual rather than a public official, and the invocation of the Crown in whose name the prosecution is generally brought does not deprive the trial of its duel-like character. Indeed, in this respect the form of criminal trial prevailing in England can be seen as the direct successor of trial by compurgation or trial by battle, the latter institution having formally disappeared only with the abolition of 'appeals of felony' in 1819. Further, when the justices of the peace assumed a less prosecutorial and more judicial role, 'the failure of the state to recognize its changing character and create public agencies, other than the police, to undertake the task of managing criminal proceedings, was responsible for another partial reversion to the principles of private warfare in the form of privately instituted and conducted prosecutions. One of the salient results of this long process of institutional development has been to make the investigation and determination of questions of fact in criminal cases similar both in spirit and practice to that employed in the trial of civil actions.'[47] This is further illustrated by the failure of the state until recent times to bear the costs of the prosecution, which devolved upon the prosecutor himself.

Thus, while early developments of the concept of the King's Peace preclude an unreserved acceptance of Howard's view that 'the notion that the commission of a crime is an offense against the state itself as well as a mere private injury to one of its members is, at least so far as the English criminal law is concerned, of modern origin,' one can surely endorse his comment that the new idea of the role of the state 'has not as yet wholly supplanted the old idea,' as 'evidenced by the extent to which the principle of private prosecution pervades the theory and practice of English criminal procedure . . .'

Thus, the historic looseness of the differentiation between civil and criminal law and the adversary nature of the proceedings can be regarded as different sides of the same coin. The developments in the United States and Israel, on the other hand, where the establishment of a public prosecution have been grafted onto an adversary system, although more in keeping with our contemporary concepts of the role of the state, in fact create an anomaly; for is it not a severe strain on the concept of equal adversaries, to match the poor defendant against the monolithic totality of the state?

Disappearance of the victim

In the present context, however, emphasis is laid not on the inequality of the duel, but on the disappearance of one of the original parties, namely the victim. Since, however, the preceding historical and comparative analysis reveals that notionally, at least, the failure of the victim to play an active role in the penal process is an illogical deviation from the principles of justice on which the American criminal trial is based, the reinstitution of the victim to his erstwhile role would remove that deviation.[48]

However, before any conclusions may be drawn as to the appropriate role of the victim in the criminal trial, and whether the time is ripe for a return to 'first principles' of victim prosecution (thereby achieving a purer form of adversary proceedings), an eye must be cast towards the outcome of these proceedings. What should the role of the victim at the trial be in the light of prevailing notions of sentencing? Without prejudice to the presumptive innocence of the defendant, there should surely be some consistency between the role and expectations of both society and the victims at the two stages of the penal process – namely, the trial and the sentencing.

This is not the place to consider the vast and voluminous literature on the philosophy of punishment. What is clear is that the recognized objectives of punishment in modern times have not directly been concerned with the victim, but have primarily been concerned with society as a whole, on the one hand, and the offender on the other. Thus, retribution and general deterrence lay stress mainly on the needs of society; reform and rehabilitation are concerned with those of the offender, while individual deterrence and social defence may be regarded as taking into account the mutuality of the interaction between offender and society.

Inclusion of the victim in the above concepts places something of a strain upon the analysis, whether by regarding him as a member of society, and thus a beneficiary under this heading,[49] or by developing some form of rehabilitative programme which will benefit the victim, as well as the offender. The concept of 'creative restitution'[50] is a case in point. Indeed, the main concern of Professor Schafer in his first edition of *Compensation and Restitution to Victims of Crime* in 1960,[51] was how to reconcile the need to compensate the victim with the then prevailing objective of the correctional ideology – rehabilitation of the offender: 'The tendency of modern criminology, after considering the importance of the crime itself, is to allow an increasingly dominant part to the possible reform and rehabilitation of the offender. In accordance with this development the victim's injury may lose importance, and on top of his lack of material restitution, spiritual restitution to the victim may also show a tendency to decrease.'[52] Schafer contrasted the rehabilitative ideology with the classical era of penal philosophy 'when criminal justice throughout the world adjusted the punishment roughly to the quality and quantity of the victim's injury.'

During the intervening years, however, as is well known, there has been a volte-face in this respect; if 'retribution' is still not quite a respectable word, 'rehabilitation' has become almost an obscenity;[53] and if it is only the baser forces of 'public opinion' that actually favour retribution *per se*, the more academic notions of a 'justice model'[54] and of 'fair and certain punishment'[55] have a greater external resemblance to a retributive scheme of punishment than to any other.[56] If to allow the victim a greater role at the punishment stage may also be regarded as retributive in character,[57] there emerges an implicit alliance of public opinion, academics and the victim – all tending in the same direction. Whether it is desirable to head in this direction depends upon which model of criminal justice society seeks to adopt.

TWO ALTERNATIVE MODELS OF THE PENAL PROCESS

'The kind of model we need is one that permits us to recognize explicitly the value choices that underlie the details of the criminal process.' With these words Herbert Packer introduced his famous 'two models of the criminal process',[58] the 'Due Process Model' and the 'Crime Control Model'. Packer's models, however, have two drawbacks in the present context: first, they are not directly appli-

cable to the issue of punishment (which Packer analyzed independently of his models), but only to the procedural aspects of criminal
justice;[59] second, these models illuminate the relationship between
the state on the one hand and the defendant on the other, but are of
no assistance in determining the role of the victim *vis-à-vis* the two
leading parties in the *dramatis personae* of the penal process.

In order to overcome the above limitations, and in the light of the
preceding discussion, we propose an *Adversary-Retribution Model*,
on the one hand, and a *Social Defence-Welfare Model*, on the other.
The first model emphasizes the role of the victim both at the trial and
sentencing stages of the penal process. It suggests, in the first place,
adhesion to the basic structure of the common law trial, i.e. a confrontation between aggriever and aggrieved, and in the second place,
a determination of sentence which would 'fit the crime' – wherein the
injury to the victim is the main component. At the same time,
differences between civil and criminal proceedings would be
minimized.[60] In this model the state plays a somewhat subsidiary role
as overseer and enforcer – acting primarily on behalf of the victim.
The second model, on the other hand, essentially eliminates the
victim–offender confrontation. Instead, the state plays a critical and
mediating role *vis-à-vis* each party, endeavouring so far as possible to
control the threat to society represented by the offender, whether by
incapacitation or rehabilitation, and simultaneously to cater to the
needs of the victim. In a sense the criteria here for social action are
utilitarian, for the overriding and optimal objective of the totality of
the proceedings is to maximize the benefits and minimize the harm to
all parties concerned – the victim, the offender and the community.

Let us illustrate the applicability of these models to various stages
of the penal process. It is to be noted that certain developments of
Israeli law will be particularly helpful here.

The adversary-retribution model would maximize the role of the
victim in prosecuting the offence. Indeed, in England, the provision
for adequate legal aid for this purpose, coupled with the dissemina-
tion of information as to the existing system, would be all that were
needed to achieve this goal. The American system of private prosecutions as an alternative option would be the minimum goal. The
inquisitorial system, under which criminal justice is almost wholly a
'public' matter, can clearly be subsumed only under the social
defence-welfare model, the matter of prosecution being exclusively a
matter of public policy. Israel represents a compromise in which a
distinction is made between 'public' and 'private' offences; the latter

can be prosecuted privately.[61] However, a true social defence-welfare model would also provide the victim with an adequate mechanism for appeal against non-prosecution, as illustrated by Israel's provisions cited above. Furthermore, while the adversary-retribution model would emphasize the granting of legal aid for prosecutorial purposes, the state would provide a gamut of services for the alleviation of the victim's distress under the social defence-welfare model.

Similarly, while the adversary-retribution model would lead to an efficacious system of retributive sentences, reflecting the debt owed by the offender to the victim, under the social defence-welfare model, the court might, in appropriate circumstances, provide for 'creative restitution' where indicated as a rehabilitative measure. However, the fundamental obligation of the state would be to provide for the victim's loss and suffering by a system of state compensation.

The key to the dynamics of these two models is in the following: under the adversary-retribution model the state provides the machinery for the victim himself to achieve the desired objectives, whether prosecution or compensation-restitution; under the social defence-welfare model the state would not only stand in the shoes of the victim in prosecuting the offender, but would also stand in the shoes of the offender in compensating the victim.[62] The victim would then have no direct claim against the offender in the matter of punishment, which would be left exclusively to the state.

Another good example of the social defence-welfare model is found in the continental system of the joinder of the victim as a civil party. Here the victim is placed in an advantageous situation for making his civil claim – the proceedings having been instituted by the state; yet the criminal proceedings as such remain within the exclusive domain of the state.

Here, again, the case of Israel is an interesting one. In 1965 Israel discarded Ottoman law, which provided for the joinder of the civil party and which had in any case become a dead letter following the importation of English legal principles. Further, the English rule of evidence laid down in *Hollington* v. *Hewthorn*[63] was followed, to the effect that the judgment in a criminal proceeding could not be relied upon in a subsequent civil action.[64] The victim could thus neither join the criminal action as a civil party, nor even rely upon its outcome, but had to prove his case *ab initio*. A recent legislative amendment has introduced a twofold reform: (a) the criminal judgment is now prima facie evidence in a subsequent civil action, both as to the guilt of the defendant and as to the findings upon which his guilt is based;

(b) the judge who heard the criminal case may, immediately following its determination, entertain the civil case.[65] The result is that the victim-plaintiff has his case effectively proved for him, and even has the benefit of a judge familiar with the facts of the case. Thus, while the principle of state control of criminal proceedings has not been touched, the victim's situation for the purpose of civil proceedings has been considerably improved.

One final, but pertinent, example of the social defence-welfare model will be recalled here – the Israel child victim law that provides, as mentioned earlier, for indirect testimony by the child victims of sexual assault. Here the principle of adversary proceedings is totally rejected in the interests of the welfare of the victim – it is hoped, without undue sacrifice of the defendant's interests.

DERIVATIVE MODELS

The above models were developed in the light of historic and current trends in the development of the criminal justice system. In recent years, however, new utopian-sounding models have appeared in the professional literature, ostensibly designed to serve as radical alternatives to the existing scheme of things. Yet while these proposals are in many respects highly innovative, they can nevertheless be reconciled with the framework of the two models outlined above.

One of these proposals was that put forward by Griffiths for a 'Family Model' of criminal justice.[66] Griffiths regarded Packer's two models as being in fact variations of a single model – the so-called 'battle' model – since both crime control and due process models were predicated on a basic antagonism between the parties to the criminal proceedings, namely the state and the defendant. The family model, on the other hand, regarded the offender not as an enemy to be contended with, but rather as a wayward son whom the parent might reprove – but ought not to reject.[67]

This approach very properly lays emphasis on the fact that in the criminal process the state is taking action not against an outside enemy, but against one of its own members.[68] However, apart from the possible practical objections to this model (Griffiths does not spell out its detailed operation), it suffers from the glaring omission of any reference to the victim. When this omission is taken into consideration, the 'family' orientation appears rather forced, involving as it does, the symbolic 'parent' to whom the misdemeanant is accountable, namely society – but not the all too corporeal 'brother', namely the victim.[69]

Be that as it may, the family model is nevertheless consistent with the social defence-welfare model described above. Both the social defence movement and welfare philosophy, like Griffiths, regard the offender essentially as an erring member of society, rather than as its enemy.[70] Conversely, under Griffiths' family model, the criteria for decision-making would involve a balance between the interests of 'parent' society and misdemeanant son similar to that described above. The chief innovation in the Griffiths model is in applying social defence-welfare philosophy *vis-à-vis* the offender at the *trial* stage, whereas prevailing practice would tend to limit its application to the post-verdict proceedings (although this is less true of the inquisitorial system). Thus, Griffiths is in effect describing a social defence-welfare model, applied exclusively to the offender.[71]

A very different approach, but one which appears to be gaining increasing support, is one which advocates a *conciliation* model of criminal justice, whereby the courtroom is essentially a forum for enabling two contending parties – offender and victim – to reconcile their differences and arrive at an outcome agreeable to both.[72] This approach has been most explicitly advocated by Hogarth,[73] Graecen[74] and Sheleff,[75] and is in effect being implemented in the framework of such experiments as the Urban Court in Dorchester, Boston, the Philadelphia Municipal Court, and the Night Prosecutor Program at Columbus, Ohio.[76] In these experiments a judicial or para-judicial officer is in effect acting as an arbitrator in a dispute between citizens.[77]

While this approach has been related both to the literature on conflict resolution techniques and to the existing informal practices of an overburdened criminal justice system,[78] it has also been inspired by two considerations of immediate relevance in the present context: (a) concern for the victim and the state of oblivion in which he finds himself in the contemporary scheme of criminal justice; and (b) recognition of the lack of historic or scientific differentiation between civil and criminal proceedings – themes developed in the earlier part of this article.[79]

It thus becomes evident that this model is a variant of the adversary-retribution model described above.[80] For under the reconciliation model, the judicial or quasi-judicial proceeding is essentially predicated on a confrontation between the parties; thus, the main criterion posited above for the adversary-retribution model is fulfilled.[81] Moreover, the emphasis on reconciliation rather than retribution, for all its more civilized connotations, in fact amounts to a distinction without a difference. It is true that 'reconciliation' implies that the judge functions more as an arbitrator, actively seeking a compromise between the parties,[82] whereas 'adversary-retribution' suggests proceedings of a more formal character and an outcome of a more punitive nature. Yet for both, the ultimate objective is to arrive at a remedy consistent with the gravity of the case and agreeable to the victim.[83] Moreover, a single system may be retributive in relation to the motivation of the victim in initiating the proceedings, but reconciliative from the point of view of its procedural mechanics – or even in the nature of its ultimate outcome. The paradigm model for an approach that is both retributive and conciliatory would be the erstwhile system of a tariff of compensation – a 'sanction' which in its historical context may be perceived to have been retributive,[84] but which today is identified as a remedy of a manifestly civil character.

Thus, for all the novelty and importance of the reconciliation approach, analytically it has much in common with the adversary-retribution model described in this article. The dichotomy between the so-called battle model on the one hand, and the reconciliation model on the other,[85] may be seen in this context not as reflecting polarized extremes, but rather as the extreme ends of a continuous range of alternative procedures,[86] all of which fall within the same overall conceptual model.

CONCLUSION

One of the purposes of this article has been to show that the current interest in taking account of the victim's interests in the course of the criminal process does not constitute an innovation, but has strong historical roots in the common law heritage. The second purpose has been to discuss two distinct models of the penal process whereby the victim's role may be determined: the adversary-retribution model, which revives pristine concepts of the criminal trial, and the social defence-welfare model, which builds rather on the type of positivistic thinking that has predominated over the past century.

The two models presented here are more comprehensive than those offered by Packer and Griffiths, which deal exclusively with the nature of the relationship between state and defendant but ignore the victim. At the same time, radical proposals for a 'new' type of criminal proceeding based upon the reconciliation of the conflicting interests of the parties are entirely consistent with the first of the two models portrayed here (the 'adversary-retribution' model).

The value of such model-building is not so much in providing alternative blueprints for a criminal justice system (a somewhat utopian role for the academic jurist), but in providing a useful perspective when considering practical issues.[87] Thus, by developing models of the penal process that take account of the role of the victim, a framework is provided for the evaluation of his function at the successive stages of this process: initiation of complaint, arrest, investigation, bail, decision to prosecute, conduct of prosecution and disposition – as well as for the consideration of solutions related to the welfare and treatment of the victim himself. Moreover, adoption of alternative models will frequently produce differing solutions to these issues. The appropriate solution may then be selected not on an *ad hoc* basis, but with an awareness both as to the philosophical approach upon which it is based and as to the overall structure of the criminal justice system of which it forms a part.[88]

Finally, the question inevitably arises which of the two models is preferable? The unlimited resources and expertise available to the modern state should guarantee an advantage to the social defence-welfare model, whereby the state is directly responsible both for the correction and rehabilitation of the defendant and for the welfare of the victim. Nevertheless, current trends in penal philosophy seem to indicate the ascendency of the adversary-retribution model. As noted above, disillusion with the rehabilitative role of the state *vis-à-vis* the offender is at a peak, and the inevitable result has been the resort to a quasi-retributive model. As to the victim, state schemes providing for compensation are still in an early stage of development, and the scope and success of their ultimate application is in doubt.[89] At the same time, some writers seem to believe that in essence the pre-medieval adversary model of criminal justice may perhaps be successfully applied in the twentieth century. Moreover, the risk that the distinction between criminal law and tort will be eliminated is not tantamount to disaster.[90] Indeed, a tortious remedy may be the optimal outcome for both defendant and victim alike, for in a quasi-penal setting such a remedy would be more energetically enforced than under contemporary civil law.[91] Finally, the interaction of defendant and victim implied in this model may on occasion be of therapeutic value to both parties.

At the same time, there remain two categories of cases for which the adversary-retribution model seems to be inappropriate. In the first category fall the more heinous crimes,[92] such as offenses involving extreme forms of violence, etc. Here a solution based upon the adversary model may be inadequate. For, if the retributive urge of the victim is to be satisfied, the penalty exacted (especially if not restricted to tortious remedies) may be excessive; on the other hand, if the victim were reconciled to the defendant without any significant social intervention, the failure to protect society from recurrence of the offense might be too great a cost to pay.[93] In such cases it may therefore be desirable to maintain a social-defense-welfare system operating within a separate judicial structure – just as the criminal-civil systems have generally functioned separately in recent times. One advantage of such a scheme would be that the resources of the state – both for rehabilitating the offender and for compensating the victim – would be concentrated on a relatively small number of serious cases.

The second problematical category involves the cases in which there are no direct personal (or even corporate) victims. It is not necessary here to raise the issue of whether the so-called 'victimless crimes' should be decriminalized, for there would still remain offences against the machinery of state (sedition, bribery of officials, etc.), as well as those against the public at large (pollution, tax evasion, traffic offences, etc.). The adversary model, as depicted in this article, would be inappropriate here, too, by reason of the absence of one of the adversaries.[94] On the other hand, to invoke the machinery of the social-defence model for a minor fiscal offence or for the infringement of a by-law would seem to be unjustified, if such machinery were no longer invoked for traditional offences such as theft.

The following solution is proposed for such cases. Where the offence was of a heinous nature[95] the case would indeed be dealt with under the specialized social defense-welfare system retained for such offences (although without the need to provide for a victim). In other cases, exclusive reliance would be placed on a non-penal framework of adjudication. Even today many offences which are technically criminal are dealt with on an administrative level.[96] Procedures here are informal, and in some respects even resemble the reconciliation techniques referred to earlier.[97] Moreover, proceedings for road traffic and municipal offences, although they take place in a judicial setting, do not generally involve the stigma of criminality, and are sometimes considered to be only quasi-criminal in nature.[98] These areas of the law could be integrated into a system of administrative tribunals that would be the equivalent of the courts operating under the 'adversary-retribution' model, but where the role of victim was reserved to the state.

NOTES AND REFERENCES

1. Schafer, *The Victim and His Criminal* 21 (1968).
2. See, generally, Drapkin and Viano (eds), *Victimology: A New Focus*, Vols, II and III, (1974/5); Viano (ed.), *Victims and Society* (1976); and the journal *Victimology*.
3. See also Knudten *et al.*, *Victims and Witnesses: Their Experiences with Crime and the Criminal Justice System* (1977).
4. See, however, Fisher, 'The victim's role in criminal prosecution in Ethiopia', in Drapkin and Viano, n. 2, Vol. III at 73 for a broader victimological perspective on these matters in an Ethiopian socio-legal context.
5. Two pioneering publications which deal with this topic are the following: Hill, 'The role of the victim in the prosecution and disposition of criminal cases', 28 *Vand. L. Rev.* 931 (1975), which analyzes the views of criminal justice personnel in Nashville, Tennessee, as to the role of the victim at various stages of the penal process; McDonald (ed.), *Criminal Justice and the Victim* (1976). These publications, however, are more concerned with the specific problems which arise than with overall concepts.
6. Israel has the merit in this context of endeavouring, in spite of a general commitment to the common law approach to criminal procedure, to adopt selectively provisions from other systems also; cf. in this respect also Fisher's analysis of Ethiopian Criminal Procedure, n. 4.
7. No attempt will be made here to deal with these issues comprehensively. The purpose of the following section is merely to raise some of the pertinent questions in order to illustrate the type of problems which arise and with a view to developing a typology of models within a framework in which they might be solved.
8. See Nettler, *Explaining Crime* (1978).
9. *The Challenge of Crime in A Free Society*, Report by the President's Commission on Law Enforcement and Administration of Justice 22 (1967).
10. Criminal Law Act 1967, s. 2.
11. Criminal Procedure Ordinance (Arrest and Search) (New Version) 1969, s. 6. A citizen may also arrest a person who has escaped from lawful custody, or on the instructions of a judge. Ibid.
12. See e.g., Piliavin and Briar, 'Police encounters with juveniles', 70 *American Journal of Sociology*, 206–14 (1964); LaFave, *Arrest* (1965).
13. See Parnas, 'The police response to the domestic disturbance', *Wisconsin Law Review* 914 (1967).

14. LaFave, n. 12 at 123.
15. In Israel such a power is expressly vested in the police, where the offence is not a felony under s. 53 of the Criminal Procedure Law 1965.
16. In 1974, Israeli law was amended to enable evidence to be adduced from a prostitute against a suspected pimp immediately after the latter's arrest, such evidence subsequently becoming an integral part of the court record. This provision was later expanded to apply to blackmail and to narcotics offences. (See ss. 31A and 111A of the Criminal Procedure Law 1965). These provisions enable the suspect to be released (of particular importance in cases under the prostitution law, where detention is mandatory) while ensuring that the victim is free from the threat of intimidation – if not from the infliction of vengeance!
17. See LaFave, n. 12 at 114.
18. Compare LaFave, op. cit., with Miller, *Prosecution* (1969). The Israel Criminal Procedure Law 1965 (s. 56), specifies 'lack of public interest' as a basis for closing a file at the prosecution stage, too.
19. See McDonald, 'Notes on the victim's role in the prosecutorial and dispositional stages of the American criminal justice process', paper presented at the Second International Symposium on Victimology, Boston (1976); Hill, n. 5 at 948–66. The possibility of involving the victim in the plea-bargaining process has been discussed by these writers, as well as in Morris, *The Future of Imprisonment* 55–7 (1974).
20. See Tartaglione, 'The victim in judicial proceedings', in Drapkin and Viano, n. 2, Vol. III at 5.
21. Criminal Procedure Law 1965, s. 58.
22. Miller, n. 18 at 331–4. See also Hill, n. 5 at 967–8.
23. See Ward, 'Private prosecution – the entrenched anomaly', 20 *N.C.L. Rev.* 117 (1972); a discussion more favourable to this institution appears in the note 'Private prosecution: a remedy for district attorney's unwarranted inaction', 65 *Yale Law Journal*, 209 (1955).
24. In a few selected cases, proceedings are brought by the Director of Public Prosecutions.
25. R.M. Jackson, *The Machinery of Justice in England* (1972).
25a.See *Goldsmith* v. *Pressdram* [1977] QB 83.
26. See Fisher, n. 4 at 75–7 and n. 25. For a discussion of the West German provisions on this topic, see Kaiser, 'Role and reactions of the victim and the policy of diversion in criminal justice administration', in Jasperse *et al.* (eds) *Criminology Between the Rule of Law and the Outlaws*, 159, 162–3 (1976).
27. See s. 62 of the Criminal Procedure Law 1965. However, in these cases a prosecution instigated by the District Attorney will take precedence over a private prosecution. Moreover, the Attorney-General will then be empowered to issue a *nolle prosequi*, thereby effectively terminating the private prosecution. Cf. n. 43.
28. See: Tartaglione, n. 20; Howard, 'Compensation in French criminal procedure', 21 *Modern Law Review* 387 (1958).
29. But see n. 64.
30. See Reifen, 'Court procedures in Israel to protect child victims of sexual assaults', in Drapkin and Viano, n. 2, Vol. III at 67.

216   *Victim's Role in the Penal Process: Critical Views*

31. See Bein, 'The impact of the victim's behavior on the severity of the offender's sentence', in Drapkin and Viano, n. 2, Vol. III at 49. Williams, 'The effects of victim characteristics on the disposition of violent crimes', in McDonald (ed.), *Criminal Justice and the Victim*, n. 19, at ch. 8; Kress, 'The role of the victim in sentencing', paper presented at the Second International Symposium on Victimology, Boston (1976).
32. See Hasson and Sebba, 'Compensation to victims of crime: a comparative survey', in Drapkin and Viano, n. 2, Vol. II, at 103, and the other articles on the same topic in this volume.
33. See s. 63(c) of the Crimes Law 1977.
34. See n. 50.
35. See *Eacret* v. *Holmes*, 333 P.2d. 741 (1958) where the parents of the murdered victim sought to prevent commutation of the death penalty imposed upon the murderer.
36. Schafer, n. 1 at 21–31.
37. See Laster, 'Criminal restitution: a survey of its past history and an analysis of its present usefulness', 5 *University of Richmond Law Review* 71–98 (1970).
38. See Mueller, 'Tort, crime and the primitive', 46 *J. of Crim. L. Crimin. & P.S.* 303 (1955).
39. See on this topic: Kenny, 'The nature of a crime', in Turner (ed.), *Kenny's Outlines of Criminal Law* 530 (1952); Williams, 'The definition of crime', 8 *Current Legal Problems* 107 (1955); Hadden, 'Contract, tort and crime: the forms of legal thought', 87 *L.Q.R.*, 240 (1971). The common ground between the fields of tort and crime was also emphasized by Holmes, whose views on this topic were analyzed exhaustively by Hall, in his article: 'Interrelations of criminal law and torts', 43 *Columbia Law Review* 753, 966 (1943).
40. von Bar, *A History of Continental Criminal Law* 524 (1916).
41. See Kenny, n. 39 at 539.
42. Cf. Turner's comment on Kenny, ibid. at 547.
43. The Director of Public Prosecutions, however, has the power to 'take over' a prosecution, even where his objective is to let it lapse by offering no evidence (cf. n. 27). This was confirmed by the High Court case of *Turner* v. *DPP* See *The Times*, 8 Aug. 1978. The would-be prosecutor in that case may perhaps be described as a *secondary* victim of the defendant's crime – a co-principal perpetrator, who had been convicted on the defendant's testimony, the latter having turned State's witness! The DPP's intervention thus came about in order to ensure that the state's promise of immunity would not be nullified by a private prosecution motivated by vengeance.
44. Harnon, 'Criminal procedure in Israel – some comparative aspects', 115 *University of Pennsylvania Law Review* 1091, 1093 (1967). Harnon also specified an additional feature, namely, the presumption of innocence and right to silence; but see in this respect the following note.
45. Although these terms are frequently used interchangeably, it has been pointed out that the term 'adversary' should be limited to the procedural features referred to here, whereas the expression 'accusatorial' should be employed more generally to describe the fundamental characteristics of

the common law system, such as the presumption of innocence and the right to silence; see Goldstein, 'Reflections on two models: inquisitional themes in American criminal procedure', 26 *Stanford Law Review* 1009, 1016–17 (1974). In the framework of the present discussion it is precisely the adversary features of the system that are of greater interest, since it is these that are more directly concerned with the victim–offender interaction – the other accusatorial features being concerned in a more general way with the status of the accused.

46. See Howard, *Criminal Justice in England* (1931). Goldstein, op. cit., however, has pointed out that American law has incorporated a number of inquisitorial features.

47. Howard, ibid., at 8.

48. Cf. the forgotten call of the author of the *Yale Law Journal* note of 1955 ('Private prosecution' etc., n. 23): 'Expansion of the private citizen's role in criminal law enforcement is dictated both by his significant experience in American and foreign criminal law and by the historic policies which have supported his right to participate' (Ibid. at 218). It is interesting to note that written in a 'pre-victimological' age, this note regards the private prosecutor simply as a private citizen, with almost no intimation that he is probably the victim, or any discussion of the implications of this fact.

49. See Schafer, *Compensation and Restitution to Victims of Crime* (1970).

50. See Eglash, 'Creative Restitution,' 48 *J. of Crim. L. Crimin. & P.S.*, 619 (1958); see also: Laster, n. 37; Schafer, n. 49; and the report by Edelhertz, *Restitutive Justice* (1975).

51. Schafer, n. 49.

52. Ibid. at 121.

53. See, e.g., American Friends Service Committee, *The Struggle for Justice* chs. 3 and 6 (1971); Frankel, *Criminal Sentences* 90–1 (1973); von Hirsch, *Doing Justice* ch. 2 (1976).

54. See Fogel, *We Are the Living Proof – The Justice Model of Corrections* (1975).

55. See Twentieth Century Fund, *Fair and Certain Punishment* (1976).

56. Thus, the proposal for 'presumptive sentencing' put forward by the Twentieth Century Fund Task Force posits 'that a finding of guilty of committing a crime would predictably incur a particular sentence unless specific mitigating or aggravating factors are established' (ibid. at 20–1). If such a system does not necessarily imply a retributive *aim* of punishment, it is certainly consistent with retributive principles of *distribution* (cf. Hart, *Punishment and Responsibility* 9, 11 (1968).) Moreover, the Goodell Community for the Study of Incarceration (von Hirsch, n. 53) supported the retributive concept as the basis both for the aim of punishment (ch. 6) and its distribution (ch. 8) – notwithstanding their preference for the term 'desert' rather than 'retribution'!

57. Retribution is of course defined and described in the literature of penal philosophy in a variety of ways. According to one approach, a man's punishment is justified on retributive grounds because, *inter alia*, 'his penalty will give satisfactions equivalent to the grievance he has caused' (Honderich, *Punishment: The Supposed Justifications* 43 (1971)). See

also n. 84. The Goodell Committee Report, on the other hand, suggests that retribution implies rather that the 'offender should somehow be *"paid back"* for his wrong' (von Hirsch, n. 53 at 45–6 [emphasis added]).

58. See Packer, *The Limits of the Criminal Sanction* 153 (1968). (The models were originally introduced in 'Two models of the criminal process,' 113 *University of Pennsylvania Law Review* 1 (1964).

59. It has, however, been doubted whether the 'crime control model' is truly a procedural one; see Goldstein, n. 45 at 1015, and cf. Damaska, 'Evidentiary barriers to conviction and two models of criminal procedure: a comparative study', 121 *University of Pennsylvania Law Review* 506, 575–7 (1973).

60. 'It would be well to begin by abandoning traditional concepts concerning the 'state's interest' in the suppression of crime. In spite of theoretical distinctions, criminal law and civil law seem to be more integrated than ever before. It is unnecessary to distinguish between civil damages and punishment in effecting restitution' (Schafer, n. 49 at 121–2). Cf. supra at 225–6.

61. See above at p. 222; however, as noted above, this category of 'private' offences for which prosecution by the victim is permitted, is not unknown in continental Europe (see Kaiser, n. 26).

62. The dilemma of selecting the preferred model was epitomized in the conclusions adopted by the 11th International Congress of Penal Law (Budapest, 1974) on the topic of victim compensation:

> The majority of the participants of the congress recommend that the primary compensation for a victim of a crime should be made from public funds by the state or some other public institution . . . The minority of the participants favour compensation from public funds but recommend that such compensation should occupy only a subsidiary position, leaving primary responsibility with the offender.

(Cited in European Committee on Crime Problems, *Compensation of Victims of Crime* Appendix II, (1978).)

63. [1943] KB 587 (CA).

64. This rule was subsequently modified by s. 11 of the Civil Evidence Act 1968.

65. See s. 35 A of the Courts Law 1957 (as amended).

66. Griffiths, 'Ideology in criminal procedure or a third "model" of the criminal process,' 79 *Yale Law Journal* 359 (1970).

67. The similarity between Griffiths' typology and Karl Llewellyn's dichotomy between 'parental' and 'arm's length' justice has been pointed out by Damaska, n. 59 at 570–3.

68. The logic of this approach is borne out by the so-called 'self-report' studies conducted by criminologists which reveal that almost all members of society are not only potential law-breakers, but actually infringe the law; see, e.g., Nettler, n. 8 at 98–9.

69. Thus, Griffiths appears to have forgotten when attributing his 'battle' image to Packer's models that such a description of the criminal process was once more than a metaphor!

70. Admittedly, social defence philosophy is not unequivocal in this respect, for while it posits a belief in the rehabilitation of the offender, it also emphasizes the 'protection of society' – as though from an outside threat. Further, the concept of social defence is open to different interpretations: see Ancel, *Social Defence* (1965), esp. ch. 1.

71. One can assume that Griffiths would apply the same philosophy in relation to the victim, who would surely be entitled to benefit from a paternalistic attitude no less than the offender. It seems to follow that the social defence-welfare model could be subsumed under Griffiths' family model. However, one would thereby lose sight of an essential characteristic of the former, namely, the *independent* concern on the part of the state for the offender on the one hand and the victim on the other. The dynamics of a family may not necessarily follow this pattern. While the notional parent under Griffiths' scheme would doubtless mollify the victim on a separate occasion from his chastisement of the errant son, another type of parent may attempt to preside over a confrontation between the two clashing members of his family. This approach would, as the forthcoming discussion will clarify, render the family model an offshoot, not of the social defence-welfare model, but of the adversary-retribution model; the family model concept is thus fraught with ambiguity, at least in the current context.

72. Griffiths, n. 66 at 410–11, regards reconciliation as the basis of his family model too, but under his model such reconciliation is to take place between the offender and society.

73. Hogarth, 'Alternatives to the adversary system,' in *Studies in Sentencing*, 35–89 (1974).

74. Graecen, 'An arbitration approach to criminal justice,' in 4 *Law in American Society* (1975) (cited in Sheleff, n. 75).

75. Sheleff (Shaskolsky), 'Victimology, criminal law and conflict resolution', paper presented at the Second International Symposium on Victimology, Boston (1976).

76. See: US Dept. of Justice, *Citizen Dispute Settlement* (1974); Sheleff, op. cit. See also the conciliation proceedings conducted prior to the private prosecution under German law (Kaiser, n. 26).

77. Studies on 'Alternatives to conventional criminal adjudication' have been conducted in recent years at the Criminal Law Education and Research Center at New York University, and at the Institute on Advanced Studies in Justice at the American University.

78. See especially Sheleff, n. 75.

79. Hogarth, however, based his arguments rather on the need for greater flexibility in the accommodation of competing interests in the criminal justice field. Moreover, the alternative models that he proposes focus as much on the dynamics whereby the system may be changed as on the nature of the optimal system to be adopted.

80. This conclusion was reached by the author subsequent to the delivery of his original paper on this topic at the Second International Symposium of Victimology, in the course of which the reconciliation model was classified as a third (or compromise) approach.

81. See above at p. 227. It is true that the second criterion, namely the

passive role of the adjudicator, may be modified under the reconciliation model. However, this feature is not always linked specifically with the epithet 'adversary' (see Hogarth, n. 73 at 55). Moreover, it is given to modification under the so-called adversary systems prevailing today; see Harnon, n. 44 at pp. 1093–5.

82. The literature does not always differentiate clearly between reconciliation, which appears to imply a voluntary meeting of minds, and arbitration, which implies the possibility of an *imposed* settlement. Thus at least four gradations would be possible within an essentially adversary framework: (a) a private (criminal) prosecution; (b) a civil suit; (c) arbitration; (d) reconciliation. Hogarth also proposes (e) 'mediation'. In the case of reconciliation or mediation techniques, alternative machinery must be available in case of failure; cf. the German procedure whereby a private prosecution may be instigated only if reconciliation proceedings (misnamed 'arbitration') are unsuccessful. (See Kaiser, n. 26.)

83. Whether there is a need to maintain a degree of proportionality between the gravity of the offence and the outcome of the proceedings is a question which has not been adequately dealt with in the reconciliation literature. Indeed, it is not altogether clear how far composition between the parties under early law could deviate from the tariff which had been laid down (see Laster, n. 37 at 73). Naturally, if the proceedings are viewed as purely civil, any agreed settlement between the parties would in principle be legitimate.

84. Cf. n. 57. See also the dictionary definition of retribution 'recompense . . . from Latin *retribuere* – to repay' (*Webster's New Twentieth Century Dictionary* (2nd edn 1975). Under early law pecuniary penalties paid to the victim were often of greater amount than the damage caused; see, e.g., Cohn, 'Fines', in Elon (ed.) *The Principles of Jewish Law* 545–6 (1975).

85. See, e.g., Hogarth, n. 73 at 82.

86. Cf. n. 82. It should be observed that similar discussions regarding alternative techniques of dispute settlement are currently taking place within a purely civil law context, reconciliation procedures being presented as an alternative to the established institutions, namely formal adjudication and arbitration. Thus at the 10th International Congress of Comparative Law (Budapest, 1978), a section was devoted to the topic of 'The Use of Conciliation for Dispute Settlement'. This parallel development in civil and criminal law lends added weight to the approach presented here, namely that the critical question is whether criminal proceedings should be substantially merged with civil proceedings (on the basis of an 'adversary-retribution' model), or whether they should rather be dominated by the role of the state.

87. Cf. above at p. 231.

88. This does not necessarily mean that one or another system must perforce be adopted in its totality. There may be merits in a compromise solution on any particular issue – such as the Israeli provision for private prosecutions not on a general basis, but for a limited number of offences. (Cf. also the mixture of accusatorial and inquisitorial models perceived by Goldstein in the American criminal process.) Alternatively, it may be

desirable to operate two distinct models that apply to different areas of the law.

89. See Miers, *Responses to Victimization* (1978); Forer, 'The law: excessive promise and inadequate fulfillment', 24 *Crime and Delinquency* 197, 208 (1978) (see also n. 91). Paradoxically, however, the foundations for a victim-initiated tort-type action against the defendant (under the adversary-retribution model) may have been laid by the state victim compensation schemes (operating under the social defence-welfare model); the schemes are developing a jurisprudence in the area of the principles of liability *vis-à-vis* victims of crime. (See Miers, op. cit., chs. 4 and 6.)

90. See Hadden, n. 39 at 259; Sheleff, n. 75; Shuman, 'Responsibility and punishment: why criminal law?', 14 *American Journal of Jurisprudence* 25, 58–60 (1970). Cf., however, the strong objections to any such development expressed in an earlier day by Hall, n. 39 at 755.

91. Even orders to pay compensation issued by a *criminal* court are usually civil in their execution, and thus are often of little value, since victims lack the means to enforce them. Further, a study conducted in Israel (Hasson and Sebba, n. 32) showed that a large proportion of the defendants so ordered to pay were simultaneously sent to prison!

92. Appropriate criteria would have to be adopted for determining the cut-off point for 'heinousness'. One possibility would be to make use of a scale based upon the perceived relative seriousness of different forms of criminal conduct, such as that developed by Sellin and Wolfgang, *The Measurement of Delinquency* (1964), which is now being replicated across the US on a national scale.

93. An analogy may be drawn here with the 'non-amendable' or 'botless' crimes under Anglo-Saxon law, crimes which had come to be regarded as too serious to be dealt with on the basis of compensation between the parties. (See Plucknett, *A Concise History of the Common Law* 402, 428 (1948).)

94. Sheleff, n. 75, has pointed out that since a reconciliation model is impractical for this type of case, the paradoxical result may be that rather than *abolishing* 'victimless crimes,' the criminal law may henceforth be concerned *exclusively* with victimless crimes (in the wide sense – including offences against the state or the general public.).

95. Cf. n. 92.

96. The ambiguity here resulted in the famous controversy between Edwin Sutherland and Paul Tappan as to whether 'white-collar crime' was in fact crime. (See Sutherland, 'Is 'white collar crime' crime?', 10 *Am. Sociol. Rev.* 132 (1945); Tappan, 'Who is the criminal?', 12 *Am. Sociol. Rev.* 96 (1947).)

97. In Israel certain fiscal authorities are empowered to negotiate an agreed penalty to be paid by an offender in lieu of court proceedings.

98. See Ginossar, 'Autonomy of correctional law', 9 *Israel Law Review* 24 (1974).

6 The Victim's Role in the Penal Process:

Recent Developments in California*

Donald D. Ranish and David Shichor

One of the most important recent public concerns about the criminal justice process is the victim and his place within the complex of due process standards and procedures. The focus has for so long been on those who violate the standards of societal behaviour and not on those who have suffered the consequences of criminal activity. Some have argued, therefore, that the criminal justice system is unbalanced since it ignores the needs and concerns of victims.

This pattern is changing, however. Both scholars and the public have begun to recognize the problems facing victims of criminal acts. This concern was manifested in forceful terms in June 1982 when California voters approved an initiative known as Proposition 8, the so-called Victims' Bill of Rights. Its leading sponsor and advocate was Paul Gann who, with Howard Jarvis in 1978, wrote the now-famous Proposition 13, which cut property taxes in California by more than half. Given this notoriety, Gann and his supporters were easily able to qualify the amendment to the California constitution. The voters approved it by more than 55 per cent of the votes cast.

The new constitutional initiative is actually a complex of procedures and alterations to California's penal code.[1] This article focuses on two interrelated provisions of the Gann initiative. The first is the right of a victim or his next of kin to appear at the sentencing hearing of the criminal defendant in order to present to the court his views regarding the defendant's criminal behaviour and the impact of that behaviour on the victim. The law provides the victim with the opportunity to address whether the defendant should be sentenced to state prison or be granted probation. The second component of this initiative allows a victim or his next of kin to appear before a panel of the

* A previous version of this paper was presented at the 35th Annual Meeting of the American Society of Criminology, 9–13 November 1983, Denver, Colorado.

Board of Prison Terms – commonly known as the parole board – which considers a release date for the prisoner guilty of the particular criminal act or acts in question.

While these are not new provisions in the criminal justice system in California or elsewhere, the Gann initiative has provided a structural and operational scheme by which victims of serious crimes can communicate to the authorities charged with dealing appropriately with the criminal about the crime, the offender, and the meaning of the criminal act to the victim's life.

Given the new reality in California, this article focuses on the rights of victims to participate in sentencing and parole procedures, by first addressing the specific elements of the California law now in place and then by reviewing the appropriate victimological literature. The authors' purpose was to ascertain where these California procedures fit within the theoretical criminological research, as well as to review other efforts to assist the victim. The authors analyse the law's actual impact on the sentencing and parole systems in California and determine what kinds of victims are taking advantage of these options. Finally, this article attempts to examine and evaluate these procedures within the context of a variety of criminological, constitutional and political issues which are raised by the use of the options now available to victims in California's criminal justice system. What is important to address is the degree to which these possibilities for victims are beneficial to all involved in the disposition of criminal defendants, not only for California but for the nation as a whole. This entire enquiry, it must be noted, must be developed within the context of California's determinate sentencing law which provides the parameters for sentencing in the criminal courts.

The ultimate question, of course, is whether society is better served by the two related procedures for victims described here. Is it clear that the community is safer, and are victims of crime better able to deal with and understand their misfortune? What are the benefits to individuals involved and society at large? Finally, is there an underlying political motive for the advocacy of these kinds of provisions now developing in the criminal law?

PROVISIONS OF THE LAW

The provisions of the Gann initiative under examination involve two separate but interrelated elements. First, the law provides that a victim of any crime or the next of kin, if the victim has died,[2] has the right to attend all sentencing proceedings to present to the judge his views about the crime, the criminal defendant and the possible need for restitution. The court is required to consider the statement made by the victim which becomes part of the permanent record of the criminal case. The prosecuting attorney, a deputy district attorney for the county in which the trial has occurred, notifies the victim (or victims) of the actual sentencing hearing at which the victim may appear. The law also allows the victim to retain private counsel to present the victim's position on the issues in question. The actual language of the law indicates that the county probation officer involved in the case is responsible for notifying the victim regarding the sentencing hearing (California Penal Code, Section 1191.1).

The other element of the Victims' Bill of Rights allows or provides for the victim, his next of kin, or retained counsel to be notified of any parole eligibility or setting of a parole date for any prisoner in state custody 30 days before the actual hearing by a panel of the Board of Prison Terms. At this hearing, the victim or counsel has the right to 'adequately and reasonably' express his or her views regarding the crime and the offender. This statement becomes part of the record of the Board of Prison Terms and must be considered as part of the decision-making process regarding the disposition of the defendant (California Penal Code, Section 3043). The same procedure is available for victims of young offenders under the Youth Offender Parole Board (California Welfare and Institutions Code, Section 1767).

Before the new law was instituted in July 1982, victims had opportunities to appear informally at sentencing hearings. Judges rarely denied a victim in California the opportunity to express his point of view. Parole release decisions likewise have been subject to public comment. Citizens have organized letter and petition campaigns to seek the retention of a prisoner in state prison. These developments need victimological perspective; therefore, a brief theoretical review of the victimological literature is appropriate.

VICTIMOLOGY: SOME THEORETICAL THOUGHTS

Historically, the victim has been an integral part of the criminal justice process. Schafer (1977) in his review of the victim's role in this process notes that in ancient times social control was in the hands of individuals. At that time, social organization was not sufficient, thus individual members of society were forced to take the law into their own hands. The individual 'made the law, and he was the victim, the prosecutor and the judge' (Schafer, 1977: 7). He revenged harms committed against him and demanded compensation for them. When people began to live in kinship groups, an offence against an individual was considered to be against the whole group. This development facilitated the emergence of the concept of collective responsibility, which in turn led to the practice of blood feuds. This custom increased the cohesion of the kinship unit and served as a social defence mechanism against outsiders. With the development of a more stable economic system and higher level of material culture, the arrangement of compensation has emerged.

In fact, ancient law is more a law of torts than a law of crimes (Maine, 1887). For instance, most offences that in modern societies are considered to be criminal violations – such as, theft, robbery and assault – were handled as torts in Roman law (Meiners, 1978). Similarly, the law in primitive societies 'contained monetary evaluations for most offenses as compensation to the victims, not as punishment of the criminal' (Laster, 1975: 20).

During these historical periods, the victim was a major focus of interest in the law. The victims' role in the offence was not questioned; victims were assumed to be innocent and passive, and their major role in the proceedings was to be compensated for the harm suffered. The importance of the victim started to decline with the rising political and economic power of the kinship. Eventually the concept of criminal law has developed to consider most offences committed by one individual against another as offences against the state, rather than as offences to the individual who was actually harmed. The victim's relation to the crime was viewed as a civil rather than a criminal matter, hence he could find remedies only through the civil law. These developments underline the 'decline of the victim' (Schafer, 1977: 15).

In the twentieth century the interest in the fate of the victim started to increase. Schafer (1977: 24) writes:

There has been renewed recognition during the past few decades that crime gives rise to legal, moral, ethical, and psychic ties not only between the violator and society, but also between the violator and his victim.

But this increase in interest was gradual, and until recently, to many the victim was the forgotten link in the criminal justice process. This state of affairs was connected with the rehabilitative ideology prevalent in the criminal justice system during the greater part of the century. During this time the focus of criminological interest was on the offender. The main concern was with his personal and socio-economic characteristics, his legal rights, and the effect of the criminal justice system on him. In comparison, professional literature dealing with crime victims was limited until the 1970s. Since the 1970s, an increasing number of theoretical and empirical works have been written about victimization, the victim's role in crime, typology of victims, victim compensation and restitution, and other related topics. The Bureau of the Census conducted yearly victimization surveys, several victimology conferences were held, and the World Society of Victimology was established.

The victim's role in the criminal justice process also came under scrutiny. In their review of the victimological literature Decker, Shichor and O'Brien (1982) found several works which pointed out that the criminal justice system takes into consideration the identity of the victim. Historically, the identities of both the offender and the victim have been determining factors in the administration of justice (Pritchard, 1955; Barnes and Teeters, 1959). To a degree this is still true today, although it happens in more subtle ways. Newman (1966) found that the behaviour and personal characteristics of the victim are important variables in the conviction or the acquittal of an offender.

On the other hand, Williams (1976) has found that although the personal characteristics of the victim affect the way in which a violent case is being processed (that is, the prosecutor's decision to screen or to continue a case), such characteristics did not appear to have an influence on whether the defendant was found guilty or not. According to this research, the only factor which had an effect on the guilty verdict was the existence of a personal relationship between the victim and the defendant. The likelihood that a case will be dismissed or dropped altogether (except in the case of homicide) when there is a familial or friendship relation between the victim and the defendant is much higher than under any other circumstances.

Another study has indicated that 'victim precipitation' and the image projected by the victim appear to influence the judge in the sentencing process (Denno and Cramer, 1976: 224). While the ways in which the victims were dressed and behaved were important in the courtroom, their ascribed characteristics (i.e. sex, age and race) seemed to have even greater impact on the proceedings.

The victim's importance in the courtroom is demonstrated also through the proliferation of victim-witness programmes. These were established as an outcome of a 'new' trend in criminological thinking which claimed that the criminal justice system disproportionally paid too much attention to the offenders (i.e. protecting their constitutional rights), while their victims receive much less attention. Furthermore, victims often go through very negative experiences in the criminal justice process. They can be summoned numerous times to court, can be questioned rigorously and often even offensively on the witness stand, and can be harassed by the accused or the accused's relatives and friends. Because victims also often feel that the authorities are indifferent to their plight, they often decide not to report crimes. This situation has prompted the launching of victim-witness programmes which are meant to, first, satisfy 'the emotional and social needs of crime victims and witnesses', and secondly, ' . . . increase the willingness of victims and witnesses to cooperate with police and prosecutors after they have reported a crime' (Rosenblum and Blew, 1979: 3). In addition, these programmes are meant to underscore that victims and witnesses are important participants in the criminal justice process.

McDonald (1982) has reviewed recent developments regarding the victim's role in the American criminal justice system. He mentions two special programmes designed to increase the victim's participation in the criminal justice process. For instance, in a programme established in Miami, victims were invited to participate in the plea-bargaining session at which the judge, the prosecutor, the defence attorney, and – if the victim wanted – the defendant were present. It was found that victims attended these sessions in only one-third of the cases. These sessions, which lasted an average of 10 minutes, did not delay the court proceedings. When victims did attend the proceedings, they hardly said anything and thus their participation was minor. They usually approved the agreements which were already discussed between the lawyers and did not demand vengeance. The impact of the presence of the victim on changing the agreement was found to be minimal.

Another example is McDonald's own small-scale study of 37 victims in Detroit. In this project the victims were asked by the prosecutor what kind of sentences they wanted for the defendant if he were found guilty. Forty-six per cent of the victims requested the maximum possible sentence. McDonald attributes the major difference between the Miami and the Detroit projects to the different settings in which the victims made their recommendations. In Miami, since the victim was physically present with the defendant in the same room where the lawyers were negotiating, he might have been reluctant to speak his mind. On the other hand, in Detroit the victims made their recommendations in a private discussion with the prosecutor. Nonetheless, in Detroit the victims of violent personal crimes were less likely to request the maximum sentence than were the victims of property offences.

Questions regarding these two projects linger. The victims in Miami possibly wanted harsher sentences but were afraid or too embarrassed to request them. Indeed, they might have found the new procedures frustrating. Another possibility is that the active participation in the negotiations provided them with a more humanizing experience; it might have dampened their demand for revenge. In Detroit, while victims had the opportunity to recommend a sentence, they did not actually participate in the proceedings and therefore may have become frustrated. Writes McDonald (1982: 401):

> The victim will recommend the maximum but probably will get less. The criminal justice official will regard the request for the maximum as unrealistic and he will see the victim's involvement as not worthwhile.

Finally, a study conducted at Georgetown University addressed the degree to which victims convey to prosecutors what they believe to be the appropriate plea bargain or disposition of the case in question. Fifty-nine per cent of the prosecutors claimed that they very seldom heard from the victims. Another 15 per cent indicated that when they heard from victims, it was usually in the case of serious violent crimes. As to how much weight prosecutors gave to the victim's opinions, 15 per cent indicated none at all, while 32 per cent indicated a significant amount. Some respondents claimed that they would not plea bargain if the victim opposed this kind of arrangement. Finally, 43 per cent declared that they give a significant weight to the victim's wishes: however, a number of factors played a part in the decisions. These included the nature of the offence, the extent of the harm done to the victim, and the credibility of the victim. Thus, 74 per cent of the prosecutors in this survey claimed that the victim's opinions and wishes were important for their decisions. In a simulated plea-bargaining situation, 41 per cent of the prosecutors took into consideration the victim's attitude toward the plea bargain.

This brief review of the literature reveals that victims can and do have an impact on the judicial process. Clearly, victims can and often do influence the sentencing process in some way, although to empirically establish and evaluate this is not a simple task. Whether this is true for the newly implemented Gann initiative in California is the subject of the next section.

THE VICTIMS' BILL OF RIGHTS IMPLEMENTED: HOW HAS IT WORKED? – THE FIRST YEAR

Any law's effect must be measured by the degree to which it changes or makes a difference in the policy matter in question. The evidence is clear that the two procedures examined here have not had any dramatic impact on the way in which sentencing and parole decisions are rendered. This is because of the limited numbers of victims who have sought to appear before the court at sentencing hearings or present themselves to a Board of Prison Terms panel reviewing a petition for a prisoner's release.

Before the Gann initiative, California law already provided that in sentencing, a judge has before him a probation report prepared by the county probation department, the position of the deputy district attorney, the defendant's attorney and the sentencing rules mandated by the legislature. In essence, the practical reality is that judges use two criteria in sentencing beyond the requirements of the law: the facts of the particular crime and the defendant's prior criminal record.

It must also be noted that about 90 per cent of the criminal cases are disposed of through plea bargaining. This is true in spite of the limitation of plea bargains under the Gann initiative.[3] The new law disallows plea bargains in superior or felony court for most serious crimes; however, plea bargains can still be accomplished in municipal court where a preliminary hearing occurs. Since the parties involved make an arrangement – a plea bargain – affecting the charge to which the defendant will plead and the sentence to be imposed, there is little discretion left. Judges do, however, know the 'going rate' of a sentence to be imposed in any given jurisdiction for any particular crime and can evaluate the plea bargain before them in those terms. And there is the determinate sentencing law in California which must be upheld. Regardless of this law, there is judicial discretion in the application of a sentence to a defendant, and this is where the Victims' Bill of Rights provisions might provide for a victim to make a difference in the judge's sentencing decision.

Victims' requests to appear before panels of the Board of Prison Terms for release determinations have been few. Indeed, during the first year of the law's effect, only 32 victims or next of kin filed requests in 14 different cases with the state board (Cavanagh, 1983). During this time, there were a total 818 parole consideration hearings held (California Board of Prison Terms, 1983: 7). It must be noted that many of the state's prisons are in central and northern California; one-third of the state's population is in Los Angeles County. The distance for a victim to travel might be prohibitive and therefore deter individuals from seeking an audience before the parole panel holding hearings at one of the state's prisons. By definition, then, it would appear that victims appear less before the parole board panels than before a judge conducting a sentencing hearing.

In summary, it is difficult to conclude that the provisions of the Victims' Bill of Rights have had any major impact on the sentencing and parole decisions made regarding felony offenders in California.[4] The criteria and systemic dynamics had been well established before the implementation of the Gann initiative. The actors within the criminal justice system – the prosecuting attorney, defence counsel, the judge, probation authorities and correctional officials – continue to conduct themselves as always. The only exception might be in highly publicized cases for which exist a high degree of public interest in the criminal offender and the disposition of his sentencing or parole determination.

Although the Gann procedures have minimally affected criminal justice process in California, the intention of this legislation should still be explored. What has been incorporated into California criminal law is an effort to provide a mechanism by which criminal victims can have more direct input and impact on the criminal justice system. This new reality in California raises criminological, constitutional and political issues, the subjects of the next sections.

SOME CRIMINOLOGICAL ISSUES

There are a number of criminological issues raised by the provisions of the Gann Victims' Bill of Rights. First of all, if a victim's participation in the sentencing and parole decisions has an impact, is disparity introduced into the criminal justice system since only some of the victims exercise this right? Very likely, middle and upper-middle class persons will be more inclined to participate in these proceedings, either directly or through legal representation.

In a somewhat similar vein, Black (1976: 95) suggests:

The more organized the victim of a crime, . . . the more serious is the offense. Accordingly, the police are more likely to hear about a robbery of business than the robbery of an individual on the street. If they do, they are more likely to make an investigation and an arrest, prosecution is more likely, and so is a conviction and a severe sentence.

In essence, the more 'important' the victim is, the more participation there will be in the sentencing and parole hearing process, and the victim's impact on the criminal justice system will grow in direct proportion.

The provision of the Bill of Rights which provides that there must be a consideration of whether the person would pose a threat to the public safety if released on parole would be very speculative. The prediction of 'dangerousness' is predicated more upon subjective and emotional factors than objective evidence and criminal justice procedures. The Gann initiative is clearly designed to intimidate judges and parole board members. It attempts to influence these professionals in one specific policy direction – toward harsher punishment or denial of parole. It is openly based upon the claim that judges and parole boards (and perhaps others within the criminal justice system) by and large do not do an adequate job of carrying out their responsibilities.

Since the Gann bill is devised to bring about more severe sentences, the result will be an increase in prison population, a trend evident before the passage of this proposal. There is now a serious overcrowding problem in the California correctional system. Since the implementation of the determinate sentencing law in July 1977, the California prison population has grown by more than 75 per cent, from just under 20,000 inmates to almost 37,000 in late 1983 (Ingram, 1983: 3). The problem of overcrowding is so servere in California that in the spring of 1983 inmates were 'housed' in tents in the maximum correctional facility of San Quentin. While there are other reasons for the large increase in the prison population, the underlying assumptions and attitudes of the Gann Victims' Bill of Rights can only contribute to an already difficult situation for correctional authorities.

SOME CONSTITUTIONAL ISSUES

There are a number of constitutional issues as well. Specifically, how do the Gann procedures conform to well-established standards of due process? That is, do the statements by the victims at sentencing and parole hearings meet the evidentiary standards otherwise required by criminal procedures? Gann provides no direction. What about the concerns regarding hearsay, biased witnesses and the application of the exclusionary rule? Of course, there is no jury hearing the victim's statement; nevertheless, the comments of the victim become part of the defendant's record which might have an impact at the appellate court level if an appeal is filed.

Another consideration is that a judge might be unduly influenced by the emotional appeals of the victim. This is very understandable. Yet it must be remembered that the court's responsibility is to insure that standards of justice are not altered by emotional statements by victims. The legal process must be upheld, for it is legal guilt, not factual guilt, that is the foundation of the criminal justice system. It must be remembered that the judge has the probation and sentencing report, the statements of the attorneys, the testimony of the actual case (if there has not been a plea bargain), and his own perceptions of what justice requires in a given case.

The question still remains as to what degree a victim should participate in the sentencing process under a rule-of-law system. Sentencing has been formulated through the legislative process and reviewed by the courts. Does the victim's contribution benefit constitutional standards, hinder them, or have a neutral effect? That is the serious essential question from a constitutional standards perspective.

Regarding the Board of Prison Terms hearings, the situation is somewhat different. The rather informal hearing process provides for the defendant to have an attorney present. A representative of the district attorney's office of the county from which the commitment to state prison has occurred can also attend. The question of guilt or even of the initial sentence is no longer the issue. There is really a very subjective process occurring as the panel evaluates the prisoner's progress and establishes options including the setting of a release date. The victim's contribution to this process might be both important and limited. A victim can rarely contribute any substantive information regarding the offender's current status or the degree to which there has been any rehabilitation by the criminal in question. It seems clear that the victim's participation in the hearing is designed to put pressure on the board. While members of the parole panel will most likely be impressed by the victim's attendance – and may be witness to an emotional presentation – the members of the board are professionals who deal with not only criminal offenders but correctional personnel. The panel might not be as moved as one might assume or expect.

SOME POLITICAL ISSUES

The sponsors of the Gann initiative rightly believed that the public would respond to a proposal which appeared to provide strongly written criminal penalties and an acknowledgment of the needs and concerns of victims. Given crime's central concern among so may citizens, the proposal's provisions allowing victims to participate in the criminal justice process beyond the traditional roles of witnesses and jurors is appealing. It makes for good political rhetoric to be against crime – because who can be for crime, for coddling criminals, for not being concerned about the plight of the victims of criminal behaviour?

At the same time, however, these procedures have not had the practical effect hoped for by the advocates and many in the public. In purely practical terms, the process formalized by the Gann initiative has serious problems. First of all is the problem of notification. While the law is specific in the requirement that the authorities notify the victim or the next of kin regarding a sentencing or parole hearing, the evidence clearly demonstrates that there has developed an informal network of notification and communication regarding the sentencing hearing in particular. Quite often, the deputy district attorney assigned to the case calls the victim or the victim's family. Similarly, often deputy district attorneys notify victims about parole hearings. These practices violate the standards of the formal Gann procedures which stipulate that the probation department will be in charge of victim notification.

Secondly, the question must be raised whether fashioning criminal justice procedures through the initiative process is productive or appropriate. While public contributions and support are vital in a democratic society to ensure a criminal justice system which provides for equal access and protection, to what degree should the public – rather than legislators – write criminal procedures? This goes to the very essence of the public policy-making process. Is there some positive political function in the public's perception that it is dealing with the problems of criminal offenders in a direct manner? Is the community better served because of direct public input, and does this increase the support of the criminal justice system among the public because of this avenue of expression?

The ultimate question is whether the community (in this case, California) is safer because of the implementation of these two procedures in the Victims' Bill of Rights. Furthermore, are the victims of crimes better able to handle the trauma associated with being a crime victim? The answer to the first question is probably no; the answer to the second is a qualified yes.

The complexity of the criminal justice system which is bound up within the political process forecloses any real ongoing impact among the public at large. The system functions with professionals who deal with criminal defendants daily. The citizen's input is minimal and cursory, although there might be well-publicized cases in which a plea by a victim at a sentencing hearing or parole review makes a difference.

At a more specific level, however, the opportunity for a victim to speak before the court at a sentencing hearing or before a parole panel can have a cathartic effect. Given the forum to speak out about what harm has been done, a victim can perhaps improve his emotional health and recover more quickly from the difficulties associated with being a victim. Since victims do not have to participate in this process, the election of taking part or not allows for the victim to make his or her own specific judgment. In this way, then, the Gann options can be beneficial to the victim as well as to the criminal justice system in general.

SUMMARY AND CONCLUSIONS

This article has examined the procedures instituted in California which allow a victim or his next of kin to appear at a sentencing hearing or a parole board panel to state his position regarding the crime, the criminal, and the possible options that should be considered for the offender. These procedures now are part of statutory law in California because of a political process which allows the writing of legislation by initiative. The results of this new procedure have been minimal in the first year of implementation; so far, the criminal justice system has not been affected by the new procedures. This is especially true given the limited number of victims who have taken advantage of the opportunity now available to them.

In a more general sense, the Gann initiative must be examined in terms of the political milieu in which it evolved. There is no question that the foundation upon which the Gann procedures are built is a conservative crime control model (Packer, 1964). The goal of the initiative is to limit the options for criminal suspects and defendants and ensure a greater control over the sentencing and the release of offenders. In ultimate terms, this entire effort is a political one, an attempt to direct public policy toward a specific, conservative direction. It demonstrates the ability of special interest groups.

It is possible to argue that the victims in this so-called Victims' Bill of Rights are a 'trojan horse'; that is, victims have been used as a vehicle to gain public support for the initiative which is a grand attempt to restructure the criminal procedure of the state of California. If so, this is a very adept political effort, one that might be duplicated in other states and other fields of not only criminal law but other public policies as well. This might prove to be the most important legacy of the California Victims' Bill of Rights. The demonstration that the public can be convinced to support alterations in criminal procedure in the quest to 'do something' about crime is important. However, the result is the manipulation by special interest groups to achieve their own policy ends. The only continuing check against violations of constitutional standards of due process is judicial review, something that no doubt will continue to occur regarding the Victims' Bill of Rights.

NOTES

1. The Victims' Bill of Rights has a number of interrelated provisions dealing with the criminal justice process in California. These include evidence standards, testimony regarding previous felony convictions, the limitation of the diminished-capacity defence, and restrictions on plea-bargaining. There are other sections involving the right to safe schools, youthful offenders and a restitution system for victims.
2. The Gann initiative provides that the next of kin shall be defined, in the

following order, spouse, child or children, grandchild, parent, brother, sister, niece, or nephew.
3. The Victims' Bill of Rights restricts plea bargaining at the felony or superior court level; however, there is no such limitation at the municipal court level. This is where preliminary hearings are held and the place where plea bargains are being accomplished. In this instance, the Gann initiative has simply shifted the plea-bargaining process from the superior or trial court to the preliminary hearing court.
4. In correspondence with the authors, Terence W. Roberts, Director of the Victims of Crime Assistance Center of the McGeorge School of Law, writes: 'Given the rather limited nature of an appearance of a victim at a board [Board of Prison Terms] hearing, I don't believe that there will be much impact on the decision making of the panels' [regarding parole release decisions].

REFERENCES

Black, Donald, *The Behavior of Law*. New York: Academic Press, 1976.
Barnes, Harry E. and Teeters, Negley K., *New Horizons in Criminology*. Englewood Cliffs, New Jersey: Prentice-Hall, 1959.
California Board of Prison Terms. 'Life prisoner report annual, 1 July 1982 through 30 June 1983.' Sacramento, California: State of California, 1983.
California Penal Code 1982.
California Civil and Criminal Court Rules 1981.
'California Journal ballot proposition analysis', *California Journal*, May 1982.
California Welfare and Institutions Code 1972.
Cavanagh, Joan W., Executive Director, California Board of Prison Terms 1983.
Chen, Edwin and Rohrich, Ted, 'Prop 8 – A legacy of confusion', *Los Angeles Times*, 19 April 1983.
Decker, David L., Shichor, David and O'Brien, Robert M., *Urban Structure and Victimization*. Lexington, Mass.: D.C. Heath, 1982.
Denno, Deborah and Cramer, James A., 'The effects of victim characteristics on judicial decision making', in William F. McDonald (ed.), *Criminal Justice and the Victim*. Beverly Hills, California: Sage, 1976.
Hughes, Wesley G. and Farr, Bill, 'Victims' wives confront killer at parole panel', *Los Angeles Times*, 10 June 1983.
Ingram, Carl, 'Deukmejian names new prisons chief', *Los Angeles Times*, 18 October 1983.
Ingram, Carl and Farr, Bill, 'Governor stops parole for murderer-rapist', *Los Angeles Times*, 6 April 1983.
Laster, Richard E., 'Criminal restitution: a survey of its past history', in Joe Hudson and Burt Galaway (eds.), *Perspectives On Crime Victims*. Springfield, Illinois: Charles C. Thomas, 1975.
McDonald, William J., 'The victim's role in the American administration of

criminal justice: some developments and findings', in Hans Joachim Schneider (ed.), *The Victim in International Perspective*. Berlin: Walter de Gruyter, 1982.

Maine, Henry S., *Ancient Law*. London: John Murray, 1887.

Meiners, Roger F., *Victim Compensation: Economic, Legal, and Political Aspects*. Lexington, Mass.: D.C. Heath, 1978.

Newman, Donald J., *Conviction: The Determination of Guilt or Innocence Without Trial*. Boston: Little, Brown, 1966.

Packer, Herbert L., 'Two models of the criminal process', *University of Pennsylvania Law Review*, 1964, 113, pp. 1–68.

Paltrow, Scot J., 'New anti-crime law in California is helping some accused felons', *Wall Street Journal* 26 November 1982.

Pritchard, J.B., *Ancient Near Eastern Texts Relating to the New Testament*. Princeton, New Jersey: Princeton University Press, 1955.

Roberts, Terrence W., Director, Victims of Crime Assistance Center, McGeorge School of Law, Sacramento, California .

Rohrlich, Ted, 'Jenny Kao's slayer gets life as mother asks for execution', *Los Angeles Times*, 11 August 1983.

Rosenblum, R.H. and Blew, C.H., *Victim/Witness Assistance*. Washington, DC: US Government Printing Office, 1979.

Schafer, Stephen, *Victimology: The Victim and His Criminal*. Reston, Virginia: Reston Publishing Company, 1977.

Thomson, Richard, 'How trial judges are coping with the "victims' Bill of Rights"', *California Journal*, January 1983.

Williams, Kristen M., 'The effects of victim characteristics on the disposition of violent crimes', in William J. McDonald (ed.), *Criminal Justice and the Victim*. Beverly Hills, California: Sage, 1976.

7 Victim Participation in Sentencing Proceedings
Howard C. Rubel

At present, the effects of the crime on the victim are appropriate factors for the court's consideration in sentencing.[1] Within the last five years, a far more controversial claim, that of the victim to go beyond the mere presentation of these effects and actually participate in or influence the disposition itself, has arisen with some force. The whole area of 'victim's rights' has been gathering force during the last few decades and is a continually pressing issue, achieving publicity and support from quite divergent areas of the social-political structure. As the process has continued, victim's rights has expanded into areas beyond its initial compensatory focus, and now encompasses demands by victims to be informed of the progress of the trials they are involved in, to be guaranteed protection from harassment, to be granted the right not to be excluded from parts of the trial, to be granted the right to make representations at bail hearings, and numerous other proposed responses to victim complaints. While most of these may be regarded as responses to practical problems encountered by persons 'performing one of their civic duties', demanding participation in the process of sentencing the offender goes beyond this and appears rooted in moral and ethical considerations.

The growth of victim's rights groups in Canada has been a hasty one and since 1979 at least 28 groups have formed in Canada, comprising 150 chapters across the country.[2] Such organizations have existed for a longer time in the United States and, partially in response to them, certain states have regularized systems for victims to participate in the decision-making process.[3] No such formalized processes exist in Canada as yet.

The traditional response of the courts to involvement of the victim in the sentencing process has been quite negative:[4]

> . . . there is also another principle which recognizes that Courts are not to be constrained to meet the views and wishes of complainants. It is not a question of maintaining a Judge's prestige;

Judges are indifferent as to that, I am sure. It is however a question of discarding all considerations of retaliation, vengeance and indemnities in the application of the criminal law, when judgments and sentences are in order, and of following the dictates of justice solely. The only interests are those of society and of the criminal.

There are few legislative guidelines to sentencing procedure and the primary procedural rule in both Canada and England is informality,[5] with great judicial discretion, regulated mainly by the common law doctrine of fairness.[6] Recently, the amount of publicity the media have given this issue, the lobbying of victim's rights groups and increased public scrutiny of what happens to offenders and victims in the justice systems has created an undeniable pressure on the legislature and the courts, with perceivable effects. Some judges have acknowledged and reacted to this pressure,[7] and the government of Canada has proposed legislation allowing not only the supplying of information necessary for restitution orders by the victim, but also for communication of the victim's 'views' of the matter.[8]

This article will examine both the supportive and the adverse theories behind victim input in sentencing and then more closely examine our current legal position against this theoretical background. Much of the theoretical analysis of the topic will rely on the interrelations between victim input and public or community input. It is important to realize that victim input may be viewed, especially from a relevance perspective, as an extension of public opinion, and legal attitudes towards public opinion will prove to be most useful in examining the theory behind individual victim input. Finally, it is important to note that both the victim and the public can influence the courts directly, by oral or written evidence, and also indirectly, through criticism, publicity and expressions of discontent.

In the following examination of first supportive and then adverse theoretical bases for victim participation in sentencing, the discussion will progress from the abstract to the more practical factors.

In spite of the historic legal trend opposing victim participation in the sentencing process, quite a divergent body of support for it has developed. Perhaps a good starting point is the theory behind punishment. One writer has related the historic development of sentencing to the dominant underlying theory of the time.[9] When the retributive theory was most prevalent, the sentencing process was a fixed one, with set punishments for each type of offence and little if any variation allowed on the basis of circumstances or the offender's character.

As retribution gave way to humanism, a large judicial discretion arose and sentences were generally individualized, with a few exceptions. Extending this theory to the present, the rise of demand for victim input seems capable of being attributed in part to the current favouring of a denunciatory theory of punishment. The Law Reform Commission of Canada has set out the current philosophy behind sentencing as a desire 'to register our social disapproval, to publicly denounce [crime] and to re-affirm the values violated by them'.[10]

In an article which in part discusses the relation of victim and public influence on sentencing, E. Kunen refers to the fact that one aim of sentencing is to effectuate 'the goal of community condemnation or the reaffirmation of societal norms'.[11] Such condemnation would naturally be strongly affected by the victim of the crime, who not only has a unique qualification to voice the evils of the crime, but may be more effective in getting this message across to the offender, due to his personal involvement, than a distant and non-involved manifestation of public discontent.

A more individual-oriented justification for victim involvement in the sentencing process is presented in an abstract yet interesting view of conflicts between the victim and the accused as property.[12] This property right is appropriated from the victim by the state. Ignoring the classical reasons as to why the state should pursue such actions rather than the victim himself, one reason the author puts forward is that by adopting the conflict, the state de-emphasizes it,[13] which may help to achieve a state goal of creating the appearance of the most stable, secure and peaceful society possible. This same goal may be the reason why the victim is given a reduced role at trial, as the victim's role is the factor most likely to re-emphasize the social problems surrounding crime in general.

Using the theory of conflicts as property, appropriated partly as a de-emphasizing function, we can explain the recent demands for more victim involvement on the basis of a re-emphasis of the victim's role in the conflict, as a result of increasing societal demand for focusing on the crime problem that exists today. The state appears no longer able to 'tone down' this problem to a marginally recognized level, as the public in many ways, through the media, the growth of social sciences and a trend for thought to shift back to the individual rather than the social being, has become involved in and fascinated with crime. In light of strong public pressure, the state is slowly allowing more exposure of the conflicts as a phenomenon affecting recognizable individuals, as opposed to only a faceless mass. The victim, as part of the enlightenment process, is regaining a role in the process of conflict resolution. Whether the public forces behind this trend are calling specifically for exposure of the crime problem through the victim's involvement, recognizing that the victim's role represents the state of government repression of the crime problems, or that this has just turned out to be the most logical way for the government to answer these demands, is open for debate.

Even if we do not view crime as giving rise to property rights, we could say that the recognition of responsibilities toward a party incorporates acknowledging that certain rights arise as a corollary of these responsibilities.[14] Thus, by recognizing governmental responsibilities to protect citizens, aid victims and, as in Canada, attempt to recompensate them for their losses, certain rights may be seen to arise as part of the 'victim' status, including a role in the conflict resolution.

While theories of legal rights may be countered by concepts of the 'greater' right of the state to act in the best interests of society as a whole, such logic is less effective if victim participation is rooted in a function of the society as a whole. J.W. Little has traced the history of punishment and found justification for involvement of non-officials as a function of public ceremony in the justice system.[15]

Little postulates that the public execution of the sentence was an important societal ceremony, involving the community in the criminal law process. In addition, the period of public executions was also one of fixed sentences, so in theory the punishments of offenders could be traced to the public's wishes as expressed through Parliament. As public execution of sentences was replaced by private execution, the humanistic theories behind this also resulted in judicial discretion in sentencing, to a large degree. This mode of public involvement in sentencing, apart from further supporting denunciatory theories of punishment, would seem to justify some form of involvement of representatives of the community in the punitive process as a concrete connection between the crime and social abhorrence of it. The victim's role in the court proceedings as to disposition of the offence may be viewed as a symbolic act bringing the hearing back into the context of social condemnation on a moral as opposed to a legal level.

In the above theories, emphasis has been placed on the interrelation between victim and community input in sentencing proceedings. The connection is quite commonly acknowledged and it has been stated that public opinion 'often parallels the voices of those least heard by the criminal justice system: the victims'.[16] The current demand for victim input may be viewed as merely a manifestation of the demand throughout our legal history for public input. This would-be public influence has been rejected for the most part by the courts but has been constant. Pressures, however, can change form and with the strong governmental rejection of the public sentiment over the past decade, a good example of which is the death penalty controversy,[17] those demanding some participation of community representation sought new methods by which this goal could be realized. The victim was an obvious choice as a new form of expression for public pressure, as society had become more individual-oriented, and the government recognized formal rights of the victim to compensation. The retribution laws under the Criminal Code gave the victims at least some standing in the criminal courts,[18] which is more than any other representative of the public has received. Both law and policy have recognized some rights in the victims, and so only a development of this role is necessary for the victim to become a reification of the public desire to have input into and be a part of the sentencing process.

When discussing victim input, it is also possible to regard victims as a class and their attempts to influence the disposition of cases as distinguishable from that of the public at large. In this manner the victim of an intoxicated driver may be seen as representing all victims of such crimes, which may be one level easier for objectors to public input to accept. It is then possible to see 'increasing judicial awareness of the impact on a victim's life [as] one step toward giving voice to large segments of the community who are routinely targeted for specific types of crime.'[19]

If the victim can be accepted as a reflection of public attitudes towards sentencing of offenders, more entitled to participate than the public at large due to proximity, this participation may reflect back to relieve public dissatisfaction with the justice system. Many commentators feel that one major shortcoming in the sentencing process is its 'estrangement from influences by . . . the interests and values of the community',[20] which prevents it from truly realizing the objectives of the denunciatory theory of punishment. Manifestations of public discontent, while perhaps oddly contradictory on the surface, reflect a consistent dissatisfaction with whoever has the discretion in sentencing.[21] Whether a particular segment of the public believes the court's response to crime is too weak or too strong, 'the criminal justice system is held in public disrepute largely because the public's right to express the correct degree of social disapproval has been arrogated elsewhere'.[22] Victim participation in sentencing hearing may help achieve one of the goals behind denunciation, placation of the public.

While the courts claim to take public sentiments towards crime and offenders into consideration in sentencing, this is only done through the courts' perception of an alienated factor. With the Charter of Rights has come a guarantee against 'cruel and unusual' punishment. In the United States, this same protection has been interpreted as one against a sentence that 'shocks the conscience and sense of justice of the people'.[23] Needless to say, the 'people' are never consulted in determining if a particular sentence reaches this standard. There have already been cases in Canada where courts have interpreted the Canadian right along the same or similar standards as the US Supreme Court did.[24] Determining the standards set by the public, not just the judicial impressions of it, may even be argued as constitutionally guaranteed. Apart from the mere potential of public influence on the sentencing process, there are examples where it has been relied on heavily by the courts.[25] Of course the reliance is strictly, if illogically, limited, as will be discussed later in this article. The courts have acknowledged that the public does participate in the sentencing part of criminal law, even if only through the medium of Parliament.[26]

It may be concluded that the victim's input into the disposition of a criminal trial may be 'morally' justified as a representation of public input, and public input has to a certain degree been acknowledged as having a place in the proceedings.

Moving from the abstract to a more functional approach to this topic, many of the claims by victims to rights of participation in sentencing can be attributed to the court and the law's treatment of the victim. A very simplified version of the victim participation controversy can be stated as the question of whether to treat the victim as a witness or as a party. While a witness is merely a source of information for the court, a party has standing to make requests of the court, to be informed of all facets of the process, to be consulted and to give its opinion on the evidence and the situation as a whole. While the court 'takes' information from a witness, it is obliged to give a party its ear. Of course, a party also has the right to be represented in court by counsel.

Some commentators empathize with the victim's demand of party status largely because the system goes far in making the victim feel like a party.[27] Apart from usually being the complainant, the victim is often attacked by defence counsel as the 'opposite party'. While the Crown is the actual opposite party, the victim and indeed the general public see no client sitting behind the Crown attorney's table. The Crown attorney appears to be protective of the victim and to express indignation at the victim's losses as if they were his own. Most legal observers would agree that if the victim's testimony can be overcome, the accused will win his case. The victim naturally may feel responsible for the initiation of the prosecution, and so may consider it mainly his responsibility to see that it succeeds. In being treated so similarly to a party in the trial process and bearing many of the responsibilities of one, the victim can hardly be criticized for demanding the rights of one.

A more psychological foundation for allowing victims to take part in sentencing proceedings is as a response to victim dissatisfaction and frustration. The Law Reform Commission of Canada mentions the resolution of frustration as one goal our criminal law should address.[28] In a recent report of the Federal-Provincial Task Force On Justice for Victims of Crime, the task force comments that one major reason for victim dissatisfaction with sentences is the apparent disparity in sentencing which the victim cannot understand, and suggests that the victim would understand why his case resulted in a certain disposition if he were involved in the trial process other than through giving testimony only.[29]

While some express a simple concern for the need to give victims the dignity of an explanation,[30] others see victim participation as more than a mere courtesy, as a necessary release to frustrations the victim acquires throughout his involvement with the crime and the court.[31] Indeed, it is easy to recognize the sentencing of the offender as a catharsis to the numerous embarrassments, inconveniences and frustrations the victim must suffer, and if such a cathartic process is not realized, the psychological harm to the victim may largely detract from the benefit achieved by bringing the offender to trial.

While the court allowing the victim to participate in the sentencing proceeding in order to alleviate his frustrations may be seen as a sociological function for the court, it may also be a very practical one. It had long been presumed that the major reason for victim (and witness) non-cooperation in the prosecution of the accused was the cost to the victim in time and money. In a very recent study, R.C. Davis has found that while non-cooperation is to a large extent related to costs, the main reason was a lack of understanding on the part of the justice system that victims are interested parties in their cases.[32] This is aggravated by the fact that the victim's participation in the trial process is a necessary, though minimal one, and so officials demand the victim's full participation and cooperation, but only for a limited use and time, and then all but discard them.[33] This can lead to a lack of cooperation in repeat victims and anyone who has heard of or experienced such treatment. A bad experience in court may as much as dissuade a victim from reporting a crime the next time. Davis proposes that allowing more participation of the victim, especially in being permitted to give his concerns and opinions on the disposition, will create better cooperation on the part of victims and allow better results from the system as a whole.

At the most practical level, victim participation may help lead to more justice and accuracy in the sentencing process. The victim's statement as to the facts during the trial has always been taken account of by the judge in considering the best disposition for the case. In spite of this, there is much speculation as to how well the victim can communicate the details and ramifications of his experience under the pressures of direct and cross-examinations, contending with the formalities of the evidentiary rules and generally in the face of natural nervousness. The sentencing procedure is a much more relaxed and informal one than the trial procedure, and this may present a better atmosphere for the victim to satisfy his fact-disclosing function. A more accurate picture of the events seems quite probable.

Edward Greenspan suggests that the defence counsel may want to involve the victim in the sentencing, contrary to popular notions. He points out that it may be quite advantageous to be able to show the court the victim's satisfaction with restitution, victim penitence, etc., or that the victim feels sympathy or clemency towards the accused.[34]

Even though the victim's statement may appear to be as much an emotional or subjective statement as a factual one, this will not necessarily lead to an impression of undue influence on the court. While the victim's submissions or representation may be viewed as biased, the Ontario Court of Appeal has pointed out that it is not uncommon for judges to act merely on the statements of counsel,[35] who may also be viewed as quite subjective on the topic of sentencing. In a recent article in a periodical for judges, it is stated that it is 'alarmist and inaccurate to equate [asking the victim's view before sentencing] with letting laymen do the sentencing'.[36] In response to arguments that victims' views of appropriate sentences will always be strongly retributive, two authors have found that while in probation and pre-sentence reports victims most often asked for a sentence of jail or prison, usually they were not aware of any alternatives, or the costs or problems associated with incarceration.[37] Probation officers were found merely to solicit opinions, without informing the victims of the possibilities available.[38] In sum, the victim's input into the sentencing process may be the best way to clarify for the court the events that took place and need not be routinely retributive. On occasion, the victim's input has been known to be the most beneficial factor on the offender's behalf.[39]

As indicated above, quite a broad spectrum of theory supportive of victim involvement in sentencing can be found. This support touches not only on notions of fair play, moral right and duties owed to the victim, but also on concrete areas of the justice system that may be improved through the implementation of such a process. While in a purely legal perspective practical considerations, including fairness to the accused, are predominant on this topic, a surprising level of practicality is addressed by parts of the theory. Of course, the negative and adverse perspectives on victim participation in the disposition of a case must equally be considered to allow one to fully come to grips with the numerous and contradictory concepts of this subject.

Theory adverse to the idea of victim participation in sentencing proceedings tends to lean more to the practical realm than the academic one although, in criticizing certain supportive positions, the concept is challenged from a variety of perspectives. Critics of a role for victims in the process of determining the appropriate disposition take the same liberties in relying on interconnections between victim and community sentiments as those in favour of the idea.

A fundamental objection to victim involvement in sentencing arises from the view that conflicts are appropriated from the victim by the state.[40] The reasons behind such state action, that government can more effectively, economically and objectively resolve the conflict than the individual can, in a fair manner that avoids the negative social impacts of individual revenge and mob violence, are quite easily accepted as worthwhile ones. It is, then, reasonable to consider the accentuating of conflicts on an individual level, through increased involvement of the individual victim in the process and the emphasis of the individual rights in dealing with offenders, as acting to defeat the stabilizing effects of state appropriation of conflicts, to some extent. Victim publicity always leads to social agitation, but victim publicity in the context of an acknowledged right of victims to have a say in the implementation of the justice system may inspire community demands for action and involvement based more on emotions than rational consideration, appearing more as a demonstration of the right to social involvement in the court process than as a demonstration of the need for more effective governmental response to the social causes of crime.

Another basic criticism of providing for victim participation in sentencing submissions surrounds the concept of maintaining the court as an institution insulated from the public pressures. There appears to be considerable value placed on the independence of courts and many commentators have identified a lengthy history of a divergence between public sentiment and the actual state of the law.[41] It is commonplace to argue on the basis of the court's expertise and experience in dispositional matters and the general public's lack thereof, and the courts have openly acknowledged this, commenting that it is inappropriate for sentencing judges to take into consideration the 'general satisfaction of the public'.[42] While the courts are manifestly acting for the public benefit and so may, as an extension of the state, be said to be accountable to the public, the public's influence on the courts has been relegated to input channelled through Parliament.[43] Further, some courts have gone beyond separating their own functions from the influence of the public and have viewed themselves as an influence on public opinion: "'The courts do not have to reflect public opinion . . . Perhaps the main duty of the court is to lead public opinion.'"[44]

While victim input may not overcome the court's powers of objectivity, it will create the tension of direct victim and community pressure that our preference for appointed rather than elected judges seeks to avoid.

Critics of victim participation also focus on the justice system's impact on the individual victim. While all parties agree that a problem exists in the level of victim dissatisfaction and frustration with the process, many warn that further participation of the victim in that process may intensify rather than alleviate these feelings. The Federal-Provincial Task Force on Justice for Victims of Crime raises the issue of the potential for requiring victims to verify their losses as part of the restitution procedure to be received as a challenge to the victim, rather than satisfaction of his need to have input.[45] Also to be considered are the victim's reactions to cross-examination on his version of the facts after the accused, his gainsayer, has already been found guilty. To be fair, the defence must have an opportunity to challenge the bias of the information the court receives.[46]

In a Toronto study done between 1976 and 1978, it was found that victims who attended court, were informed of the outcome of the trial or both, responded very similarly to those who did neither.[47] The information and experience made no real difference in the victims' demands for severity in dealing with the offender, or their reactions to the sentence imposed.[48] In interpreting the results, the author found that the victim's contacts with defence counsel, Crown prosecutors and police aggravated tensions between the victim and the accused.[49] There seems at least to be sufficient doubt cast on claims that victim participation (as opposed to being more fully informed and generally treated with more consideration) will lessen negative reaction victims have to the justice process. One final comment on this humanistic perspective on victims and the sentencing process is that one may question, independent of problems and negative effects such as those just discussed, the appropriateness and practicality of a purely legalistic institution such as the court as a main participant in a social function of the state.

Focusing on a more legalistic view of victim participation, it is possible to denounce such schemes as doing violence to the appearance of justice in the courts. While disagreeing, E.E. Younger admits that some 'judges equate sensitivity to victim problems with lack of fairness to the defendant.'[50] It can certainly be stated that the defence bar supports this statement even more than the judiciary,[51] and we can only hypothesize as to the empathy for such sentiments among the general public.

This concern for the appearance of justice may be just as valid for actual justice. The sentencing procedure in Canada is based on a principle of informality, with a corollary principle that where the offender challenges any representations the process must be formalized,[52] to ensure fairness and accuracy. If victims testify in sentencing proceedings or submit written evidence and do more than present common knowledge or factual statements, there can hardly be a standard, or even a process for that matter, of qualifying him, as is done with expert witnesses. The victim may be seen as an *amicus curiae* (though the term is often applied to a non-interested person), a relatively controversial status made increasingly so by the victim's obviously interested status. As one giving information (and perhaps opinion) to the court, the victim's testimony at the sentencing stage must be considered in terms of objectivity. While expert witnesses, professionals, police, etc., can usually be relied on to suppress emotionalism to acceptable levels in making statements to the courts, no such security can be found regarding the victim. As would be expected, in the excitement of the process and having to encounter the accused face to face in the courtroom, victims may feel more intensely their victimization, may accentuate the facts of the occurrence and may request or demand a more highly punitive disposition. As one study has shown, the victim's state of knowledge of the sentencing options available may lead him to rely on more severe options.[53] In the same study, the amount of time elapsed since the occurrence was found to have a large effect on victims' positions regarding sentencing.[54] This demonstrates a lack of capacity in the victim to be objective which, while most natural, does create a potential for injustice, especially if what the victim says in the sentencing hearing does not truly reflect his feeling toward the crime. This may become known to him only in a less anxious state, after proper consideration and time.

The American Bar Association, in a discussion of victim-witness legislation, concludes that even victim impact statements will most likely result in stiffer sentences, on the average.[55] A second concern is that allowing oral presentations from victims presents the potential and opportunity for emotional outbursts which could unfairly bias the judge.[56] While Kunen maintains that these are not sufficient reasons to exclude victim input, due to the fact that judges are often hardened by years on the bench, and probably would not be swayed by such to violate their consciences, she does suggest that written rather than oral submissions would be useful in preventing displays of emotions.[57] While judges may not willingly 'violate their consciences', the possibility of judges being affected, emotionally and subconsciously, is hard to rule out. In standard evidentiary matters testimony and evidence can be excluded as being too prejudicial and appeals may be launched on such material's improper admission or consideration.

Finally, on the point of fairness, Stuart has pointed out the injustice that could arise if two offenders who committed the same offence under similar circumstances received disparate sentences, due mainly to the fact that the victim in one case was vengeful, while the other was merciful.[58] Inequalities could also arise from a victim choosing not to testify in one case, or a victim not being located. In all, adding such a subjective factor to the already complicated and subjective enough sentencing procedure may create difficulties for sentencing judges trying to balance factors of uncertain or ambiguous weights.

A last consideration of the factors adverse to a more prominent role for victims in the sentencing process is simply that there may be better methods and opportunities to achieve the same goal, with fewer of the collateral dangers and disadvantages. A cost-benefit analysis may show that victim-offender reconciliation projects more effectively relieve victim frustration and aggression, facilitate restitution and create victim satisfaction with the course of justice.[59] Sentencing institutes for judges, where representatives of segments of the community can meet with them and communicate ideas or sentiments on types of crime, etc., would allow some satisfaction of the desire of the general public and classes of victims to have input into the disposition of cases under neutral circumstances, avoiding the danger of the full weight falling on a single convenient offender. Numerous diversion techniques offer a vastly unexplored potential to address all of the concerns of victim's rights groups and current supporters of increased victim participation. These techniques, along with further education and information services to the victim in particular and the public in general may prove to be such that a rational society cannot subordinate to riskier, less effective measures.

Having explored the theoretical justifications and condemnations of victim participation in the sentencing procedure and in the process revealed a proliferation of perspectives from which to view victim input, it is now possible to view the current legal position on this subject. While a thorough precedential review and analysis of the law is beyond the scope of this article, it is submitted that certain trends may be discovered which coincide with various theories presented earlier. Through analysing the court's consistency or inconsistency with the theory surrounding victim input, a clarified position may emerge, reflecting the true legal position of the victim in sentencing hearings and the court's response to recent demands.

In directly addressing the question of victim participation in sentencing proceedings, the courts generally take a strictly conservative position. The British Columbia Court of Appeal has stated:[60]

The *Criminal Code* contemplates prosecution of the accused by the Crown. It does not accord to persons affected by an offence status as parties to the proceeding against the accused apart from the provisions relating to restitution . . . Nor does it grant to them the right to make representations against the accused independent of those which the Crown chooses to put forward.

The court concluded that the applicant, desirous of making separate sentencing submissions through her own counsel as to the emotional effects of the crime perpetrated upon her, had no *locus standi*.

In *R.* v. *Lauzon*,[61] the court distinguished between the interests of complainants and those of society. While this issue will be examined below in light of theory equating, for some purposes, victim and society, here it will suffice to state that however impractical or obtuse, this distinction appears to be generally relied upon.

Regarding representations by persons claiming to act on the victim's behalf, the courts have been equally stolid in declining to allow participation, as in a recent Ontario High Court of Justice decision where the application of the parent of a deceased victim was not received, on the ground that it was not relevant and would not be helpful.[62] In total, the courts seem mainly supportive of the theories adverse to victim participation. Much reliance is placed by them on arguments of fairness and notions of the appearance of justice.[63] They also tend clearly to follow the theory that society, as separate from the victim, will suffer if the victim's role is increased.

In spite of the preponderance of decisions, there does seem to be much concurrence with theories supportive of victim involvement in the court's treatment and discussion of the issue. In an Ontario case, while refusing the victim's parents the right to make a statement, Reid J. stated that he could imagine circumstances in which a statement from parents or friends might be useful and helpful.[64] In that case the court stressed fairness to all, including the accused, as a main consideration.[65] One case Reid J. was probably referring to was the Quebec Superior Court case of *R.* v. *Hardy*, where the court received written submissions from the family of the deceased victim, asking the court to sentence the accused to the most lenient sentence possible for his manslaughter conviction.[66] If Reid J. and the Quebec Superior Court can be stated to concede the propriety of receiving representations from victims or their families when they are appeals for clemency, they have acknowledged a role for the victim or his representatives in the sentencing. The restrictions on this role cannot stand, however, as it would not be possible to justify giving the victim standing depending only on whether he were forgiving or vengeful. In addition, such a proposition would require some pre-disclosure of the nature of the statement to the judge before he could rule on it.

Other cases have also left the door open for victim participation if the fairness question is adequately dealt with. It may be said that when victims wish to ask for clemency, no accused would feel unfairly dealt with. In addition, there is a possibility that if all counsel are unopposed to the victim's input, it may be permitted. Indeed, the

British Columbia Supreme Court, in declining a victim participation application, distinguished a case where such an application had been approved, on this ground.[67]

While the above cases are exceptions to the norm, a common mode of victim influence on the disposition of a case is through probation and pre-sentence reports. Stuart comments that there 'seems little doubt that the victim's perspective does at present find itself into some pre-sentence reports',[68] and often the inclusion of the attitude of the victim toward the crime is a part of the report's analysis of the situation.[69] This situation was commented on in *R. v. Arsenault*,[70] and such inclusions in the report were criticized as not being appropriately presented to the court in this form. However, such a practice is common, and does seem to satisfy the court's concerns about fairness since both counsel have access to the report and rights to challenge or question it. One could conclude from the above that victim participation could be allowable when the dangers of unfairness are sufficiently guarded against. This is, in fact, the situation in some of the United States, where regularized systems for victims as participants in the decision-making process exist.[71]

Theory supporting victim participation in sentencing hearings frequently refers to the relationship between the victim and the general public, and views the victim as a representative of public sentiment necessary for the social condemnation of crime in accordance with current denunciatory theories of punishment. Indeed, courts have at times seen the public or classes within it as the 'victims' of crime, as exemplified in recent cases involving hate literature and the spreading of false news.[72] Unfortunately, courts rarely have the opportunity to comment on such abstract ideas.

The court's reception of public input into the sentencing procedure is extremely difficult to categorize, as it often appears confused and contradictory and certainly is ambiguous. In *Re Gamester and The Queen*, the Prince Edward Island Supreme Court granted an application of prohibition to prevent a provincial court judge from calling for and receiving members of the public's submissions as to the appropriate sentence for the accused. The court stated that:[73]

There are very definite dangers inherent in the procedure proposed . . . The submissions could conceivably interfere with his independence as a Judge. It could usurp his role as sentencer; it could raise new and irrelevant facts and people biased against the applicant might appear and attempt to influence the Judge with respect to the sentence he should impose.

The Alberta Court of Appeal, on the other hand, has stated that the 'community demands that certain conduct be heavily punished and when the Courts fail to satisfy this demand to support core values, the public . . . can justifiably complain that the Courts have failed in their duty'.[74] It appears that the court is under a duty to consider public values and sentiments in deciding upon a sentence, but is not allowed to attempt to discern exactly what these are. In *R. v. Henein*, the Ontario Court of Appeal relies in part on perceived public abhorrence to justify a custodial term being imposed for a crime often punished by a suspended sentence plus treatment for a lengthy probationary period.[75] In another case,[76] the same court commented that it is inappropriate for a sentencing judge to consider *'the reaction of the public* if excessively light sentences are given' or 'the general satisfaction of the public.'[77] The distinction between giving due regard to the public reaction to the crime and giving due regard to the public's reaction to a light sentence imposed for the crime is a fine one, to say the least.

Finally, in an older British Columbia Court of Appeal case,[78] it was held that a petition by members of the community, asking for leniency in sentencing the accused, was improperly relied on by the trial judge. The court did not comment on whether the evidence would have been admissible if presented by one of the parties, as part of submissions in the sentence hearing. Character evidence is commonly admissible on sentencing matters and so it could be concluded that it is not the information but the manner in which it is conveyed to the court that is most important, relating again to fairness.

It appears that there is much uncertainty as to what extent the court should rely on public input and in what manner the court should receive public input. What is clear, however, is that some public input is accepted and relied upon, and so support for victim input based on analogies of that to public input may be read into the case law.

Characteristic of the court's current position on victim input is a split between viewing the victim as a witness procedurally and as a party substantially. By this it is meant that while no formal recognition or procedural rights are given to victims, the courts all seem to acknowledge their special positions in the trial and in deciding on sentence give consideration to public sentiments and reactions which naturally reflect those of the victim and his family. The courts may be said to expose indication, especially in *obiter dicta*, that they acknowledge the theory behind supporting victim input. However, the rigours of the process and procedural fairness preclude any formal consideration being given to such factors.

In conclusion, an accurate assessment of victim's rights in the courts in relation to the process of sentencing is one of an inappropriate institution attempting to accommodate the demands of a sociological development without compromising its own fundamental characteristics. The court primarily views victims as witnesses, while the victims perceive themselves as parties. At this stage the courts are partially deferring to what they see as justified demands of a class of society, if just to alleviate certain social tensions which are most illuminated in the court's sphere of influence. Consequently, as the victim's situation is being recognized more and more, especially by official institutions, such as the court which are looked to by the victim for relief, pressure upon the court to give victims a stronger role in determining dispositions of their cases is increasing. The victims now hold what Myers refers to as 'unofficial party' status.[79] The courts, however, appear to have gone as far as they can in attempting to accommodate victim's demands, as the underlying theory in cases dealing with victim's demands is heavily restricted by concepts of judicial fairness and adherence to recognized procedure. In sum, the courts are only able to respond to a certain extent and are unable to satisfy victims' full needs. While it is important that legal institutions give recognition to the victim's situation, in order to avoid aggravating the problem, and to placate the victim to some extent, more flexible and appropriate remedies to victim dissatisfaction and frustration are necessary. Even though both the provincial and federal governments have adopted policies favouring official accommodation of victims' demands in part through the court, the courts are always an independent arbiter as to what is permissible in a fair and structured trial process. The additional scope of review given to courts through the Charter of Rights increases this independence from governmental attempts to placate the public and victims in a simple manner, by relegating official response to existing institutions such as the courts.

Other responses to problems which victims encounter include victim–offender reconciliation projects, increased victim compensation programmes, the availability of counselling services, a facilitation of civil remedies against convicted offenders, and more generally increased governmental recognition of the crime victim's situation. While court-related factors such as witness information programmes, better police–victim communications and exposure of the victim to the costs and difficulties of the legal system as a whole are important and helpful to the problem, improvements in these areas can only serve to supplement what is a social, not a legal problem. Courts will always remain highly technical institutions, applying doctrines and principles rigidly, and so the positive aspects of courts attempting to deal with social situations outside their realm will always be outweighed by the detriments caused to an already troubled judicial system.

In the end, we must look at the gains victims may achieve through the court process, and considering the court's limited abilities, the added frustration and dissatisfaction the victim often develops through interaction with the court process. These appear to be minimal. Courts can go only as far as treating the individual victim's interests in the same manner in which they treat the public interest, relying on their own perception of it, but not having the ability or the legal flexibility to accurately investigate its reality.

The current status of the victim in the criminal court, as a witness and a source of factual information, provides the victim with involvement in the process and an opportunity to see the process through. No additional gains are sufficient to justify any additional involvement in light of the potential of detrimental effects to the fair trial of the accused and the appearance of fairness of our legal system.

It is the recommendation of this article that victims and victims' rights associations should look to the political community, such as the Ministries of Justice and Social Services, for satisfactory responses to victim-related problems and not to the courts. In the past, as victim's rights groups continually emphasize, the government has spent tremendous amounts of money on supplementing and improving legal services but hardly any at all on the victim-related aspects of the system. Dealing with victims has, to a large extent, been foisted upon the courts and current indications such as the reports of the Federal-Provincial Task Force on Justice for Victims of Crime and Government of Canada publications are that such a trend continues and is being relied upon further by the government to respond to growing pressure. Only when the government attempts a complete response to victim-related societal problems that is separate and distinct from the court can the potential for realistic and adequate resolution of such phenomena exist.

NOTES

1. Clayton C. Ruby, *Ruby on Sentencing*, 2nd edn (Toronto, Butterworths, 1980), pp. 130–2, 161–3, 202–3.
2. Kathy English, 'Victims of violence: too many to ignore', *The Toronto Star*, 11 November 1984, p. A-1.
3. E.A. Zeigenhagen, *Victims, Crime, and Social Control* (New York, Praeger, 1977), p. 100.
4. Walsh J. in *R.* v. *Lauzon* (1940), 74 C.C.C. 37 at p. 52, [1940] 3 D.L.R. 606 at p. 619 (Que. C.A.).
5. John A. Olah, 'Sentencing: the last frontier of criminal law', 16 C.R. (3d) 97 (1980), at p. 103.
6. *Re Gamester and The Queen* (1978), 38 C.C.C. (2d) 548, 2 C.R. (3d) 6, 17 Nfld. & P.E.I.R. 297 *sub nom. Gamester* v. *Fitzgerald* (P.E.I.S.C.).
7. *Re Gamester*, note 6; and *R.* v. *Porter* (1976), 33 C.C.C. (2d) 215, 75 D.L.R. (3d) 38, 15 O.R. (2d) 103 (C.A.).
8. Canadian Dept. of Justice, *Sentencing* (Ottawa, February, 1984), pp. 39–40.
9. J.W. Little, 'The law of sentencing as public ceremony', 35 *University of Florida Law Review* 1 (1983).
10. *Our Criminal Law* (Ottawa, Minister of Supply and Services, 1976), p. 3.
11. Eve Kunen, 'Effects of external pressures on sentencing judges', 11 *For. Urb. L.J.* 263 (1982), at pp. 273–4.
12. Christie, Nils, 'Conflicts as property', in *Perspectives on Crime Victims*, B. Galaway and J. Hudson, eds (Toronto, C.V. Mosby, 1981).
13. Ibid., at p. 237.
14. A. Normandeau, 'For a Canadian and International Charter of Rights For Victims', 25 *Can. J. Crim.* 463 (1983).
15. See note 9, at pp. 5–9.
16. Kunen, note 11, at p. 265.
17. C.H.S. Jaywardene and H. Jaywardene, 'The public opinion argument in the death penalty debate', 22 *Can. J. Crim.* 404 (1980).
18. See Criminal Code, ss. 653, 654, 655.
19. Kunen, note 11, at p. 266.
20. Little, note 9, at p. 1.
21. Ibid., at p. 28.
22. Ibid.
23. *Furman* v. *Georgia*, 408 U.S. 238 (S.C.).
24. E.g., *Collin* v. *Kaplan* (1982), 1 C.C.C. (3d) 309, 143 D.L.R. (3d) 121, 2 C.R.R. 352 (F.C.T.D.).
25. *R.* v. *Henein* (1980), 53 C.C.C. (2d) 257 (Ont. C.A.).
26. Ibid., at p. 267.
27. Lois G. Forer, *Criminals and Victims* (New York, W.W. Norton, 1980), pp. 28–45.
28. See note 10, at p. 2.
29. Canadian Federal-Provincial Task Force On Justice for Victims of Crime, *Report* (Ottawa, Canadian Government Publication Centre, 1983), p. 54.

30. E.E. Younger, 'Are judges responsible for victims too?', 6 *P.J.J.* 2:28 (1982), at p. 2:29.
31. James Burns and Joseph Mattina, *Sentencing* (Nevada, National Judicial College, 1978), p. 205.
32. R.C. Davis, 'Victim/witness noncooperation: a second look at a persistent phenomenon', 11 *Journal of Criminal Justice* 287 (1983).
33. Ibid.
34. E.L. Greenspan, 'The role of the defence lawyer', in *New Directions in Sentencing*, Brian A. Grosman QC, ed. (Toronto, Butterworths, 1980), at pp. 267–8.
35. *R.* v. *Cary* (1952), 102 C.C.C. 25 at p. 28, 13 C.R. 333 at p. 336, [1952] O.R. 1 at p. 4 (C.A.).
36. Younger, note 30, at p. 2:29.
37. J. Henderson and G.T. Gitchoff, 'Using experts and victims in the sentencing process', 17 *Criminal Law Bulletin* 226 (1981).
38. Ibid.
39. See *R.* v. *Hardy* (1976), 29 C.C.C. (2d) 84, 33 C.R.N.S. 76 (Que. S.C.).
40. Christie, note 12.
41. See E.A. Fattah, 'Public opposition to prison alternatives', 24 *Can.J. Crim.* 371 (1982), and Jaywardene, note 17.
42. *R.* v. *Porter* (1976), 33 C.C.C. (2d) 215 at p. 220, 75 D.L.R. (3d) 38 at p. 43, 15 O.R. (2d) 103 (C.A.).
43. *R.* v. *Henein*, note 25, at p. 267.
44. *R.* v. *Sargeant* (1974), 60 Cr. App. R. 74 at p. 77, cited in *R.* v. *Atkinson, Ing and Roberts* (1978), 43 C.C.C. (2d) 342 at p. 344, 5 C.R. (3d) S-30 at p. S-32 (Ont. C.A.).
45. See note 29, at pp. 104–6.
46. *People* v. *Summer*, 40 Ill. App. 3d 832 (Ill. C.A.).
47. John Hagan, 'Victims before the law', 73 *Journal of Criminal Law and Criminology* 317 (1982).
48. Ibid., at p. 329.
49. Ibid., at p. 328.
50. See note 30, at p. 28.
51. See American Bar Association, 'Victim witness assistant project, victim witness legislation', *Sec. Crim. Justice* VIII, 1981.
52. Olah, note 5, at p. 103.
53. Henderson and Gitchoff, note 37.
54. Ibid., at p. 231.
55. See note 51, at p. 47.
56. Ibid.
57. See note 11, at p. 305.
58. See Don Stuart, 'Annotation', 38 C.R. (3d) 256 (1984).
59. Dorothy McKnight, 'Victim–offender reconciliation project', in *Perspectives on Crime Victims*, B. Galaway and J. Hudson eds (Toronto, C.V. Mosby, 1981).
60. *Re Regina and Antler* (1982), 69 C.C.C. (2d) 480, 29 C.R. (3d) 283 at pp. 283–4.
61. (1940), 74 C.C.C. 37 at p. 52, [1940] 3 D.L.R. 606 at p. 619 (Que. C.A.).
62. *R.* v. *Robinson* (1983), 38 C.R. (3d) 255 at p. 260.

63. Ibid.
64. Ibid., at p. 259.
65. Ibid., at p. 260.
66. See note 39.
67. *Re Regina and Antler*, note 60.
68. See note 58.
69. Ziegenhagen, note 3, at pp. 81–2.
70. (1981), 21 C.R. (3d) 268 at p. 274, 30 Nfld. & P.E.I.R. 489 at p. 495 (P.E.I.S.C.).
71. Ziegenhagen, note 3, at p. 100.
72. Such as the Ernst Zundel matter in July, 1984.
73. See note 6, at pp. 554–5 C.C.C., p. 14 C.R.
74. *R.* v. *Wood* (1975), 26 C.C.C. (2d) 100 at p. 107, [1976] 2 W.W.R. 135 at p. 143.
75. See note 25.
76. *R.* v. *Porter*, note 42.
77. Ibid., at p. 220 C.C.C., p. 43 D.L.R.
78. *R.* v. *Lim Gim* (1928), 49 C.C.C. 255, [1928] 1 D.L.R. 1038, 39 B.C.R. 457.
79. M.A. Myers, 'Offended parties and official reaction: victims and the sentencing of criminal defendants', 20 *Soc. Q.* 529 (1979), at p. 539.

BIBLIOGRAPHY

American Bar Association, 'Victim witness assistance project, victim witness legislation', *Sec. Crim. Justice* VIII, 1981.

A. Blumstein and J. Cohen, 'Sentencing of convicted offenders: an analysis of the public's view', 14 *Law & Soc. Rev.* 223 (1980).

J. Burns and J. Mattina, *Sentencing* (Nevada, National Judicial College, 1978).

Canada (Dept. of Justice), *Sentencing* (Ottawa, February, 1984).

Canadian Federal Provincial Task Force On Justice For Victims of Crime, *Report* (Ottawa, Canadian Government Publication Centre, 1983).

N. Christie, 'Conflicts as property', in *Perspectives on Crime Victims*, B. Galaway and J. Hudson, eds (Toronto, C.V. Mosby, 1981).

R.C. Davis, 'Victim/witness noncooperation: a second look at the persistent phenomenon', 11 *Journal of Criminal Justice* 287 (1983).

K. English, 'Victims of violence: too many to ignore', *The Toronto Star*, 11 November 1984, p. A-1.

E.A. Fattah, 'Public opposition to prison alternatives', 24 *Can. J. Crim.* 371, (1982).

L.G. Forer, *Criminals and Victims* (New York, W.W. Norton, 1980).

E.L. Greenspan, 'The role of the defence lawyer', in *New Directions in Sentencing*, Brian A. Grosman QC, ed. (Toronto, Butterworths, 1980).

J. Hagan, 'Victims before the law', 73 *Journal of Criminal Law and Criminology*, 317 (1982).

J. Henderson and G.T. Gitchoff, 'Using experts and victims in the sentencing process', 17 *Criminal Law Bulletin* 226 (1981).

C.H.S. Jaywardene and H. Jaywardene, 'The public opinion argument in the death penalty debate', 22 *Can. J. Crim.* 404 (1980).

E. Kunen, 'Effects of external pressures on sentencing judges', 11 *For. Urb. L.J.* 263 (1982).

Law Reform Commission of Canada, *Our Criminal Law* (Ottawa, Ministry of Supply and Service, 1976).

J.W. Little, 'The law of sentencing as public ceremony', 35 *University of Florida Law Review* 1 (1983).

D. McKnight, 'Victim–offender reconciliation project', in *Perspectives on Crime Victims*, B. Galaway and J. Hudson eds (Toronto, C.V. Mosby, 1981).

M.A. Myers, 'Offended parties and official reaction: victims and the sentencing of criminal defendants', 20 *Soc. Q.* 529 (1979).

A. Normandeau, 'For a Canadian and International Charter of Rights for Victims', 25 *Can. J. Crim.* 463 (1983).

J.A. Olah, 'Sentencing: the last frontier of criminal law', 16 *C.R.* (3d) 97 (1980).

D.J. Porich, 'The sentencing dilemma', *Canadian Lawyer*, 1:12 (1980).

C.C. Ruby, *Ruby on Sentencing*, 2nd edn (Toronto, Butterworths, 1980).

R. Stortini, 'The role of the Canadian jury', 24 *Canadian Law Quarterly* 244 (1981–82).

D. Stuart, 'Annotation', 38 *C.R.* (3d) 256 (1984).

E.E. Younger, 'Are judges responsible for victims too?', 6 *P.J.J.* 2:28 (1982).

E.A. Ziegenhagen, *Victims, Crime, and Social Control* (New York, Praeger, 1977).

8 The Alleged Molestation Victim, the Rules of Evidence and the Constitution:

Should Children Really Be Seen and Not Heard?
Thomas L. Feher*

INTRODUCTION

The problem of child sexual abuse is now frequently brought to our attention. Various factions of the media,[1] law enforcement agencies[2] and social scientists,[3] as well as a plethora of law review authors, frequently write and speak on the subject. Presumably, the main purpose of this attention is to foster the protection of children. Concern for the molested child's welfare is not new,[4] but the recent attention has kindled a public outcry for greater protection of children. State legislatures,[5] courts[6] and welfare systems[7] have responded to this concern in a variety of ways.

The nature of the responses indicate that their promoters harbour two major assumptions. The first is that the present system is actually inadequate in sending guilty offenders to jail. This is based on a belief that prosecutors do not bring offenders to trial because the courts' rules of procedure make conviction too difficult to justify trying the cases.[8] The next, and more critical, assumption is that the occurrence of sexual abuse will decrease if the convictions of those accused increase. There is no empirical data to support this assumption.

The problem perceived by the populace at large is that child abuse is on the rise.[9] In actuality, we only know for certain that the reporting of suspected incidents of abuse is on the rise.[10] The increase in

* The author wishes to express his gratitude for the helpful comments of Professor Janice Toran, Cleveland Marshall College of Law.

reporting may or may not indicate an increase in occurrence,[11] but it must certainly mean that more people are now the focus of child sexual abuse investigations.

The increase in media attention has produced an atmosphere startlingly reminiscent of the Salem witch hunts and McCarthy's 'Red Scare'.[12] As a corollary to the dramatic rise in the reporting of sexual abuse cases, there is also a disturbing rise in the number of false accusations of child sexual abuse.[13] The passion surrounding this issue makes the lot of the accused a particularly undesirable one. Even if the case ends before it reaches trial, the defendant may spend thousands of dollars on legal fees and suffer irreparable damage to his reputation, regardless of the truth of the accusation.[14] Far worse is the lot of the innocent accused at trial. Due to current characteristics and procedures peculiar to the investigation and prosecution of child sexual abuse, the tools provided by the system for the protection of one's liberty and reputation are particularly ineffective in these cases. Thus, there is a real danger that a disproportionately large number of innocent defendants are going to jail.

The potential for stripping innocent citizens of their liberty is the basic foundation for the constitutional guarantees of due process. Our legal system demands that certain prerequisites be met before any person may be convicted and sent to jail. On this issue the constitution is clear: the state may not deprive the defendant of his liberty without due process of law.[15]

This Article explores the unusual difficulties faced by the defendant in a child sexual abuse case: first, by displaying certain aspects of a child's psyche which make children particularly susceptible to suggestive influences; next, by demonstrating that child abuse investigations today are extremely suggestive and ill-suited to their proper goals because they can often inhibit a child's ability to testify 'truthfully', in an objective sense. Finally, the article suggests that, under these circumstances, allowing the child to testify is contrary to common rules of evidence and violates constitutionally guaranteed rights.

THE NATURE OF THE CHILD'S PSYCHE

When a person testifies about the occurrence of past events, he must do so from present memory of such events. Memory does not exist as a concrete item, like a book or a stone tablet. There is no guarantee that it can be read back accurately at trial.[16] Rather, memory is a process[17] subject to a variety of influences that can alter its accuracy.

The process of memory is generally divided into three stages,[18] sometimes referred to as the 'tripartite model'.[19] These stages consist of acquisition, retention and retrieval.[20]

The 'acquisition' stage relates to the contemporaneous perception and encoding of the event. If the formation is encoded into the memory imperfectly, recollections of the event through later testimony will necessarily be imperfect as well. Children, like adults, store only fragments of their experiences. But children are more problematic in this area because they store less of their experiences than adults.[21] The resulting memory is therefore less rich. Studies show that the less complete someone's memory is, the more susceptible that person is to suggestion.[22]

Completeness of memory may also suffer in the 'retention' stage, during which the memory simply sits in storage, untapped. Just as a muscle will atrophy through non-use, so may portions of a person's memory deteriorate through non-use. All people are subject to this process, but children forget faster than adults,[23] resulting in a lessening of the memory and 'clearing the way for suggestive influences'.[24] This is especially a problem in child sexual abuse cases where the investigation and trial often occur long after the occurrence of the alleged event.

Even in the unlikely event that encoding and retention were perfect, a child's susceptibility to suggestion can be heightened during the 'retrieval' process. Children have more difficulty than adults retrieving information from long-term memory.[25] Thus, Loftus postulates that children might 'be prone to rely on new (retrievable) information in their reports'.[26] The interview and investigation process provides numerous opportunities for suggestion.

Distortions may occur within any of the three component parts of memory described above. Everyone, regardless of age, is subject to distortions, particularly those caused by suggestion.[27] Many types of interviewing techniques qualify as 'suggestive'. The questions, by their form, their repetition, or other cue, will often suggest what appears to the interviewee to be the 'right' answer. These techniques convey a message that a particular response, often harmful to the defendant, is desired or 'correct'.[28] The interviewer may not intend to suggest an answer; indeed, he may not even know that he is doing so, but the effect of such questions is unchanged by their purpose.[29]

Aside from failures in the memory process, the power of suggestive questioning may be intensified by the interviewee's perception of the interviewer's 'status'.[30] This is a problem because children generally perceive that most adults occupy a high status.[31] Almost certainly, police officers, social workers or parents speak from a position of 'power' from a child's perspective. Landsman notes that:

> To avoid appearing foolish, confused, ignorant or unhelpful some witnesses will seek to give what they think the examiner considers the 'right' answer. Frequently, the questioner will further this objective by communicating her views either in the wording of the questions or in the non-verbal cues accompanying interrogation. Such distortion is especially likely to occur when the witness has a high regard for the examiner or wants to please her.[32]

Interviewer status may be especially troublesome in child sexual abuse cases because the child's first conversation about the abuse is often had with a parent, the child's ultimate status symbol. The parent may harbour hard feelings toward the suspected abuser, or have preconceived notions of what 'abuse' may have occurred. Studies show that when interviewers entertain such notions, the accuracy of the interview suffers.[33] Parents, lacking the requisite training, will not be able to avoid supplying significant suggestion. The first discussion about the abuse is the most influential, and as such, the most potentially devastating to defendants.[34]

Another factor that intensifies the possibility of suggestion is the fact that the interviewing process is also a learning process and can actually change what exists in the child's memory.[35] Once such a change takes place, it is virtually irreversible.[36] These changes in memory will often be 'recent' in relation to any testimony at trial if the allegations involve abuse covering a long time span. Therefore, the time-related memory failures that allowed the initial changes in the child's memory will not be present for subsequent interviews conducted by defence personnel.

Repeated interviewing reinforces these altered perceptions.[37] The repeated reinforcement of these ideas creates in the child a 'subjective reality' that an event did happen even if it never did.[38] This enables the child to relate such experiences on the witness stand without 'lying'. She actually believes the event happened, and no conventional trial tactics should be able to show that she is 'lying', because she is not.[39]

From the foregoing, it is apparent that all humans are more susceptible to suggestive influences when their memory is incomplete because of poor encoding or memory deterioration, or when they perceive that the interviewer has a high status in relation to themselves. In the abstract, then, children may be no more susceptible to suggestion than adults. But child abuse investigations typically involve: (1) sexual acts that children do not encode well; (2) lapses of time that cause more memory deterioration in children than in adults; and (3) interviewers with a highly-perceived status. Thus, it may well be that children who are the subject of such investigations are more susceptible to suggestion than adults. While bearing in mind the significant impact of repetitive questioning, it must then be asked: are alleged victims of child sexual abuse subjected to repetitive, suggestive interviewing techniques?[40]

THE REALITIES OF THE INTERVIEWING PROCESS

There exists today an assumption on the part of many professionals that children who allege sexual abuse must be believed.[41] This stands in opposition to the earlier held conviction that such allegations should be initially disbelieved.[42] Current research suggests that, indeed, children probably do not often 'lie' about instances of sexual abuse.[43] From such research has been spun a 'presumption of accuracy' with regard to children's allegations.

Theories of abuse assessment

Several theories exist on ways to evaluate the circumstances surrounding a child sexual abuse case. One of the most prominent treatises on the subject of child sexual abuse assessment is 'The child sexual abuse accommodation syndrome'.[44] Author Roland Summit, a psychiatrist, postulates that a child alleging abuse is not lying,[45] that the family will put pressure on the child to recant the accusation,[46] and that the proper place of the professional interviewing the child is to support the child in her accusations[47] and help her bring the hidden truth to the fore.[48] He also urges that any subsequent retractions by the child should be disbelieved.[49]

The assumptions underlying this theory are problematic if one seeks to rely on its followers for assessment.[50] The model is based on the classic family model, intact and harmonious.[51] It assumes, possibly correctly, not only that the perpetrator will pressure the child to recant, but that the mother and other family members will also. Under such conditions, it would not be surprising to see an actual victim recant.

But in practice, the theory is flawed. These cases now arise frequently during divorces and custody fight situations.[52] Here, the initial allegation may either be made by the parent or by the child as coached or conditioned by the parent. Without the initial allegation actually originating from the child, the rest of Summit's analysis fails. The theory is that the child will be under pressure to recant or not to tell. Summit says that the mother[53] will try to keep the allegations secret.[54] This would not be the case in custody fights where such allegations, if true, would mean automatic denial of custody to the perpetrator.

Summit feels that once the mother has denied the child's claim, the pressure of keeping the family together is then placed upon the child, and that the child will recant to maintain the stability of the home.[55] But in a divorce or custody situation, the family will not be intact anyway, or, if one outside the home is accused, it has no bearing on the family situation.

Summit also feels that the mother will have to make a choice between the words of the child and the accused, and that she will usually choose to believe the father, because to do otherwise would reflect poorly on her 'choice' of mate.[56] But in a divorce or custody situation, the mother has either already rejected him, or it has no bearing on her 'choice' of mate.

Although patently inapplicable in a large number, if not the majority, of situations, Summit's views are still applied to a wide variety of cases.[57] The job of the health care professional, says Summit, is to accept and validate the claims of the child, lest that child suffer psychological harm.[58] He seems to urge that competent, modern professionals believe the child[59] and help convince the courts that the child is sincere.[60]

Another popular tool in the assessment of child sexual abuse is *The Handbook of Clinical Intervention*.[61] In the section entitled 'Validation of child sexual abuse', Suzzane Sgroi suggests that claims of abuse may be validated through behavioral indicators,[62] many of which are contradictory of themselves, or merely indicative of innocent behaviour.[63] Coleman finds that these 'indicators' are generally non-specific in nature: they are so general and sweeping that at least one or more could apply to almost any child.[64] The use of such non-specific indicators, when coupled with a bias to accept accusations of abuse at face value, 'could bring the current witch hunt for child molesters to a fever pitch.'[65]

Practical applications of the theories

Significant questions exist as to the reliability of these theories as tools for the accurate diagnosis of child abuse. Yet, followers of these people are training 'cadres of police, protective service workers, and rank and file mental health care professionals'.[66] As a result, reports of the use of highly questionable interviewing techniques are now coming to light.

There are reports of the misuse of 'anatomically correct' dolls;[67] of the failure to complete interviews and pursue investigation once an 'admission' has been made;[68] of interviewer threats not to allow children to go home before admitting abuse;[69] of narrowly focused interviews that ignore what the child is trying to say and emphasize anything remotely related to sex;[70] of rewards for 'admissions';[71] of anger when the child will not 'admit' abuse;[72] and of the frequent use of leading questions.[73]

Interviewers often ignore statements made by the child that do not conform to their own theory about the abuse.[74] They may blatantly ignore improbable and incredible portions of some children's assertions which might otherwise indicate a lack of validity in the claim.[75] Repeated interviews often occur.[76] The child views these phenomena as a demand for more, or different, information, feeling that the interviewer was not satisfied by what the child already said.[77] If false allegations are repeated often enough, the child may well come to believe them.[78]

The most significant problem may be that the interviewer is unaware that a false memory is being created in the child. The interviewer is most likely trying to get the child to admit what the interviewer thinks is 'the truth' in order to protect the child's best interest.[79] These procedures, whether intentional or not, bear significantly upon the child's testimony at trial. Child witnesses, who are already susceptible to suggestion, undergo highly coercive interviewing techniques and then relate the results of these interviews as evidence at trial.[80] It is not, then, a great leap to assume that some children are undergoing the type of permanent memory alteration discussed in the section above on 'The nature of the child's psyche'.

Present testimony consists of a review of memory.[81] Therefore, what takes place in the interviews may be the most important issue in a sexual abuse trial. And yet, the interviewing process is not always well-documented.[82] Without a record of the interview process, there is no way to determine whether the child's memory and later testimony are products of actual experience or of suggestion.

The case of Jordan, Minnesota

During the latter part of 1983, in the small town of Jordan, Minnesota, allegations arose regarding crimes committed against children, ranging from gross sexual abuse to murder.[83] Twenty-four people were accused:[84] one pleaded guilty, two were acquitted,[85] and the charges were dismissed against twenty-one others.[86] According to County Attorney Kathleen Morris, the charges were dismissed in order to shield the children from the trauma of trial[87] and to prevent the disclosure of evidence relating to an ongoing murder investigation.[88]

The investigation of the allegations was then picked up by the Minnesota Bureau of Criminal Apprehension and the Federal Bureau of Investigation, acting jointly. On 12 February 1985, the Minnesota Attorney General's Office issued 'The Report on Scott County Investigations', which detailed the results of this joint investigation. The Report serves as a tragic example of the manner in which an investigation of child sexual abuse can go awry, permanently tainting the testimony of alleged victims.[89] The Report found that no credible evidence existed for the multifarious allegations lodged against the residents of Jordan.[90] Further, it found that any evidence, or testimony, that may have existed was ruined by the investigation.[91]

It noted that the authorities did not conduct a thorough search for evidence that would corroborate the allegations.[92] The Report recognized the need for such evidence, especially in child sexual abuse cases due to the underlying investigatory techniques.[93]

The Report made specific findings regarding the use of repetitive questioning techniques,[94] recognizing that repeated interviews seriously undermined the reliability of any subsequent testimony.[95] One child was interviewed nine times before the joint investigation began; another child endured at least thirty interviews in the course of the original investigation.[96] The Report also cited examples of separating children, who steadfastly refused to admit that any abuse took place, from their parents for several months. These children were repeatedly interrogated by their foster parents about the alleged abuse.[97] There were even examples where the children were told that their reunion with their parents would be fostered by 'admissions' of their parents' abuse.[98]

The Report found that there was a permeating lack of recording or documentation of the interviews.[99] The Report recognized that recording is necessary to determine the consistency of the child's statements.[100] The Report also condemned the 'cross-germination' effect that occurred when the authorities informed interviewees of allegations made by others[101] and conducted joint interviews.[102] Such practices too readily provide children with information that they can adopt as their own.[103]

The Report concluded that no evidence existed for the majority of the accusations and that the careless manner of the investigation not only ruined the prospects for the successful prosecution of any valid cases, but may have 'created' invalid cases as well.[104]

This prima facie evidence of the potential for abuse in the interviewing process must not go unheeded. To those who doubt that professionals in this area could be so reckless in the performance of their duties, the Scott County report shows not only that it can happen, but that it already has.

THE REALITIES OF SEXUAL ABUSE TRIALS

The problem created by the interaction of the child's psyche and the interviewing process is not only that the child may be made to falsely believe that she has been abused,[105] but that, in many situations, the defendant will be unable to convince a jury of his innocence in the course of the trial. Several factors contribute to this situation.

In many jurisdictions, it was once required that the testimony of alleged rape victims be corroborated in order to protect against false accusations.[106] Almost all states have relieved the prosecution of the burden of providing corroboration of the rape accusations.[107] Child sexual abuse is a crime that will often leave no physical evidence even when it actually has occurred.[108] In the context of an *actual* occurrence of abuse, the repeal of this rule would appear beneficial. But in the context of a man on trial for accusations which are the product of the interviewing process, the result is that one more procedural safeguard to incorrect convictions has been removed.

Rule 608 severely inhibits a defendant's ability to cross-examine the child witness. Rule 608(a) provides that the credibility of a witness can be attacked with opinion or reputation evidence that relates to his character for truthfulness only, rather than by evidence of his character in general.[109] This has generally been accepted to mean that, when seeking to impeach a witness's credibility through the testimony of others, the character testimony should relate only to the primary witness's general character for truthfulness in the community.[110] Rule 608(b) focuses this requirement. The basic gist of the rule is that one may not impeach a witness's veracity by a showing of prior specific acts which would tend to impeach credibility through extrinsic evidence.[111] Defence counsel may ask the witness about prior acts, if the judge is so inclined, but will be stuck with whatever the witness's response is.[112] Thus, if a child has been of the type of character to have repeatedly lied or made false accusations in the past, but because of age or some other circumstance has not developed a 'reputation' for untruthfulness, the defendant would not be allowed to produce witnesses to testify about those prior instances of lying, because it would be inconsistent with 608(b).[113]

The purposes of Rule 608 are: (1) to protect the witness from undue embarrassment;[114] (2) to avoid confusion of the issues;[115] and (3) to avoid overextending the trial.[116] Although admirable, these rationales are not persuasive in the context of child sexual abuse trials. First, the embarrassment of having a rebuttal witness called cannot outweigh the value to the jury of having some probative evidence of the victim's possible lack of veracity.[117] Second, it must be apparent that, in a case without corroborating physical evidence, where it is simply the word of the child against the word of the defendant, given the presumption of innocence, the child's veracity may be the only issue to be decided by the jury. Testimony bearing upon the victim's veracity, therefore, cannot be said to go to 'collateral issues'.[118] Third, for the same reasons as above, the state's interest in keeping trials manageable must be outweighed by the defendant's need to present such evidence to the jury. Because of its impact on a defendant's constitutional rights, the applications of Rule 608 should be scrutinized. If it is to remain in effect, an exception must be created for cases involving testimony by the victim or other pivotal witness against these defendants.

Should the defendant wish to ascertain what influences may be playing upon the child through psychiatric examination, he may encounter significant obstacles. No state currently recognizes the power of defendants to compel psychiatric examinations for complaining witnesses in sex offence cases.[119] Some states recognize that the judge may, in certain situations, order an examination in the exercise of judicial discretion.[120] Still others hold that the court does not, even in its discretion, have the power to so order.[121] When a defendant is unable to compel a psychiatric examination, expert evaluation of the child's testimony is limited to an analysis based upon existing documentation. Unfortunately, such documentation is not always made.[122]

Another consideration in trial analysis is the perception of the child and her testimony by the jury. Research in this area is relatively sparse.[123] There exists a belief that, as a rule, jurors tend to be biased against believing a child's testimony.[124] But, as seen below, biases a juror brings into the courtroom can clearly be altered through the course of a sexual abuse trial.

The hypothesis that jurors tend to disbelieve child witnesses is founded upon the notion that, as a group, child witnesses tend to lack the confidence and consistency that jurors generally link with believability.[125] General biases against believing child witnesses may not apply across the entire spectrum of crimes.[126] Sexual assault may result in less prejudice against believing the child witness than other crimes.[127] Other factors which generally influence juror bias may, in child sexual abuse cases, weigh in the child's favour. For example, a child may be more readily believed if his testimony involves a detailed description, if he was exposed to the defendant over a long period of time, or if the crime was violent.[128] The juror will also be influenced by the amount of evidence. If it is weighted to one side, any bias against believing the child should disappear.[129] The prosecution will obviously have already tipped the scales in its favour once the child has testified. Once again, where the case is often the child's word against the adult's, only an effective means of rebutting the child's testimony will tip the scales back toward the defendant. Aside from those limitations already discussed, it has also been noted that traditional, aggressive methods of cross-examination will not work, because such tactics will promote sympathy for the child and ire at the defence.[130]

The further removed in time the testimony is from the jury's decision-making process, the more persuasive it becomes.[131] If not first, the child will certainly testify during the prosecution phase of the case, guaranteeing a lapse of, at minimum, the length of the defence case, closing arguments and jury instructions. Thus, even the subsequently discredited testimony of the child may often impact on the jury's decision.[132]

The judge's instructions also influence the jury's view of the child's testimony. It is said that giving specific instructions as to the credibility of child witnesses lowers the jury's perception of their credibility.[133] Conversely, an instruction that children are considered competent could result in undue emphasis on the value of the child's testimony.

In short, it appears that in many sexual abuse trials the defendant will be at a decided disadvantage. Even though theoretically presumed innocent, he will be so hard pressed to rebut the prosecution's prima facie case that the presumption is worthless. These facts must not go unconsidered when evaluating the admissibility of a child's testimony.

THE ADMISSIBILITY OF CHILDREN'S TESTIMONY

Evidentiary prohibitions

The federal and state rules of evidence can be used to exclude evidence that is unreliable or unduly prejudicial. The testimony of children that is the product of suggestion should fall within these prohibitions.

Rule 403
Federal Rule of Evidence 403[134] and its state counterparts[135] should provide for the exclusion of child testimony. The 'Prejudice Rule' has as its goals, *inter alia*, the avoidance of misdecision by the fact-finder and the promotion of real and perceived fairness in the judicial process.[136] Trials cannot be viewed as scientific processes in which abstract evidence will be weighed and accorded its just value. The true realist must recognize that jurors, as human beings, are susceptible to undue influences.[137] As such, it is paramount that the trial judge guard against the admission of evidence that will lead juries to decisions not solidly founded upon reliable evidence.

The first part of a Rule 403 analysis is the determination of the evidence's probative value. Probative evidence is '[t]estimony carrying quality of proof and having fitness to induce conviction of truth.'[138] Where a witness's testimony is the product of suggestion instead of actual memory, it does not accurately reflect upon real events[139] and as such shed little or no light upon facts at issue in the case. The testimony's probative value, then, is low.

If a defendant is not able to prevent prejudicial or unreliable testimony, or is impaired in his ability to cross-examine or impeach the child, he may find himself the object of the jury's rage. A defendant must present evidence of the interviewing process if he hopes to exclude the child's testimony on the ground that it is the product of suggestion, but there is generally no documentation of the interview process.[140]

Testimony may be excluded when its probative value is outweighed by danger of unfair prejudice. Unfair prejudice occurs when evidence appeals to the biases or dislikes of the jurors.[141] To be sure, at least the majority of jurors are not fond of the sexual abuse of children. This prejudice takes on the requisite unfairness when, at trial, the defendant has no effective means of cross-examination and becomes the focus of the jury's outrage.

As a product of the defendant's inability to adequately cross-examine, the child's testimony may also come under the rule's prohibition against misleading the jury. Misleading the jury occurs when it is likely that the jury will accord the evidence more weight than it merits.[142] It is obvious that, where the child's testimony does not accurately describe the actual occurrences, yet the defendant has no effective means to rebut the given testimony, the jury will accord the evidence more weight than it deserves. Therefore, the danger of unfair prejudice and misleading the jury should mandate the exclusion of the evidence. To do otherwise ignores a judge's responsibility to ensure fair trials and accurate fact-finding.[143]

Rule 601

The general rule of witness qualification is that the witness must both possess requisite competence and have actual knowledge of the matters to which she will testify.[144] Each state requires some degree of competency as a qualification to testify at trial. The traditional test of competency for a witness is that the witness must: (1) have actual knowledge of the matter to which he or she will testify, (2) have a recollection of those events, (3) be able to communicate the information to the trier of fact, and (4) be able to appreciate the gravity of the oath or the importance of telling the truth.[145] The states vary as to their definitions of competence, but a significant number require that children possess these traditional capacities by denying competency where the child appears incapable of receiving accurate impressions of the matter about which he or she will testify or of relating those impressions truthfully.[146]

It seems clear that, once the child has undergone excessively suggestive interviewing techniques, she is patently unable to meet these qualifications. First, it is at least questionable whether there were any events which she could have perceived. Second, and more importantly, she is now permanently unable to retrieve accurately from her memory the knowledge of any related events which did occur. She would then be unable to 'relate such events truthfully'. Thus, the child would not pass even these rudimentary tests of competency.

Rule 602

The notions embodied in Federal Rule of Evidence 602[147] may provide the most significant obstacle to the introduction of testimony that is the product of suggestion. Aside from its applicability in the federal arena, the requirement of personal knowledge of the facts which will be testified to is statutorily required in at least a majority of the states.[148] The rule is derived from the common law's preference for the most reliable evidence.[149] The purpose of the rule is to prevent the witness from testifying as to what he has merely learned from the statements of others because he cannot 'satisfy the present requirement of knowledge from observation'.[150]

The requirement is not a stringent one on its face. It provides that the basis for knowledge may be supplied by the witness's testimony or otherwise. Thus, by merely testifying as to her presence during the alleged acts, the child may satisfy the facial requirements of Rule 602. Further, evidence of circumstances indicating that she was there[151] would also suffice.[152] But where such evidence is lacking, the mere fact that the child testifies that she was there should not always be sufficient. If it appears that the testimony constitutes mere repetition of what the child has been told by others, then the child lacks the personal knowledge required by Rule 602.[153]

In a recent case, *State of Hawaii* v. *McKellar*,[154] a trial judge granted the defendant's motion to disqualify two children alleged to be the victims of sexual abuse. The court found repeated violations of proper interviewing techniques, a lack of corroborating evidence, and a failure to record key interviewing sessions.[155] The judge found that 'personal knowledge' requires both that the witness perceive the event when it occurs and have a present recollection thereof, and that the state bears the burden of proving that this is the case.[156] Under the facts of the case, the court found that the state could not meet this burden, and that as such, the children's testimony was incompetent and inadmissible.

It may certainly be argued that the child's simple statement that the sexual abuse occurred should suffice to defeat an objection based upon 'personal knowledge'. But in cases such as these, it is clearly within the trial judge's discretion to find that this assertion is so lacking in reliability as to not meet the fundamental burden.[157] This is especially true where, in cases such as *McKellar*, there is a lack of corroborative evidence.[158]

Constitutional prohibitions

Even where a state's competency rules would allow the child to take the stand, her testimony may still not be admissible, regardless of the state rules.[159] This is so because securing a criminal conviction through testimony that is tainted by suggestion violates the due process clause of the United States Constitution.[160]

The due process clause of the Fourteenth Amendment[161] prohibits sending a defendant to jail without providing a trial that is fundamentally fair.[162] This fairness may be violated in a variety of ways, either through the use of procedures which lack fairness, or through the denial of specific rights guaranteed by the Constitution and applicable to the states through the Fourteenth Amendment.[163]

The confrontation clause of the Sixth Amendment,[164] applicable to the states through the Fourteenth Amendment,[165] guarantees the defendant the right to *effective* cross-examination.[166] It has been maintained that, as long as the defendant is present when the witness testifies, and is able to cross-examine her, he has received the rights accorded him under the Sixth Amendment.[167] But such an analysis is superficial. It ignores the question of what constitutes 'cross-examination' under the Constitution. As stated above, in order to pass constitutional muster, the state must allow *effective* cross-examination. Where a hypersuggestible witness undergoes a highly suggestive interviewing process, it is highly possible that a new memory will be created. '[T]he resulting memory may be so fixed in [his] mind that traditional legal techniques such as cross-examination may be largely ineffective to expose unreliability.'[168] The courts are now beginning to recognize that, in these situations, meaningful cross-examination may not be achieved.[169] If the defendant cannot effectively subject such testimony to cross-examination, the jury must not hear it.[170]

The constraints placed upon prosecution-produced evidence by the confrontation clause are not necessarily coextensive with those in the due process clause. Indeed, the due process clause may be even more stringent.[171]

Due process requires that the state not convict a defendant upon evidence which is the product of suggestion. In *United States* v. *Wade*,[172] the court overturned the conviction of a defendant who was identified in court by a witness who had previously identified the defendant under suggestive conditions. Reversal is mandated when the totality of the circumstances indicates that the 'procedure was so impermissibly suggestive as to give rise to a substantial likelihood of irreparable misidentification.'[173] Where there is such a likelihood of misidentification, failure to exclude the evidence violates the defendant's right to due process.[174] Evidence of this type is certainly admissible in some situations.[175] Child witnesses are highly susceptible to suggestion and often undergo severely suggestive interviews. It is hard to imagine that the testimony of such a person could ever bear enough indicia of reliability as to not violate due process.

Further, there seems to be no basis for limiting the use of these standards to cases where the witness's testimony consists of an identification. *Wade* and its progeny have provided guidance for the admissibility determination to other types of testimony,[176] and their logical congruence to the situation at hand is too compelling to be ignored.

Due process is also violated when a defendant is convicted upon evidence which, in the cumulative, cannot lead the reasonable juror to an affirmative finding of guilt, as to every element of the crime, *beyond a reasonable doubt*.[177] Because defendants are presumed innocent and have a transcending interest above that of the state (i.e. their liberty), this rule is necessary to overcome the natural margin of error inherent in human fact-finding.[178] Where a conviction is not based upon requisite evidence, it constitutes a violation of due process.[179] If a man charged with sexual abuse were truly presumed innocent, but was tried upon the virtually uncorroborated testimony of a child which is the product of suggestive interviewing, then it is a natural conclusion that he could not be guilty beyond a reasonable doubt.

Unlike the right to counsel, the right to due process does not depend upon the commencement of judicial proceedings to attach. Procedures used by the government during both the investigatory and trial stages must conform with due process. The police may not engage in investigatory practices that 'offend a sense of justice'.[180] This is especially so where offensive techniques yield unreliable results.[181] As discussed on pp. 261–4 in the section on 'The nature of the child's psyche', there are reports of cases where sexual abuse investigators have been so bent upon eliciting inculpatory statements that they engaged in practices which they at least should have known were impermissibly suggestive. It must certainly 'offend a sense of justice' purposely to try to elicit incorrect statements from a child in order to convict the defendant.

The state, in the conduct of its trials by judges, as well as in the presentation of its cases by prosecutors, 'must comply with established rules of procedure and evidence designed to assure both *fairness* and *reliability* to the ascertainment of guilt or innocence.'[182] But the use of suggestive questioning techniques and the allowance of blanket competency for all witnesses does not foster either of these goals.

Subjecting a man to a term in prison for a conviction of child sexual abuse is a severe sanction by the state. Before it is taken, the methods used in acquiring the conviction should be subjected to extreme scrutiny. To be sure, a defendant's constitutional rights are not absolute and must be weighed against the state's interests.[183] Arguably, the state has a significant interest in the effective prosecution of child molesters. The Supreme Court has recognized that the states have 'a strong interest in effective law enforcement'.[184] But the states' interest in effective law enforcement cannot be translated into a need which is paramount to the defendant's need adequately to defend himself.[185] It must be borne in mind that traditional analyses of this problem can often yield faulty results. This is so because the rules of evidence and procedure were formulated for adult witnesses and victims who have not undergone intensive suggestive interrogation. This situation raises too strong a possibility of wrongful conviction. No state interest as vaguely couched as 'the need for law enforcement', or Summit's 'need for validation',[186] could be compelling enough to override the defendant's right to effective cross-examination and due process of law.

Our rule-makers today seem to have forgotten one of the basic tenets of our legal system. As Justice Harlan wrote in his concurrence to *Winship*, there exists in our criminal system an underlying assumption that 'it is far worse to convict an innocent man than to let a guilty man go free.'[187] It is incumbent upon our system to eradicate procedures that lead to a substantial likelihood of wrongful convictions.

PROPOSALS

What are we to do with a problem of this stature? One option, used in many of the hypnosis cases, is simply to exclude the evidence.[188] This is too harsh a rule because a significant degree of sexual abuse does occur, and the state has a responsibility to itself and its citizens to bring actual offenders to justice. The state's interest must be balanced against the defendant's significant interest in not being incorrectly convicted.

The problems in this area are twofold. First, suggestive interviewing techniques are sometimes used upon hypersuggestible individuals. Second, we have no way of determining which cases have used such techniques and which have not.

We must first endeavour to stop the use of these practices. This would best be accomplished by appropriate re-education of those who conduct investigations as to what constitutes proper, effective and neutral questioning techniques. We must then seek to ensure that the interviewing process is adequately documented. This will allow the courts to make proper competency and admissibility rulings, as well as allowing the defence an effective mode of rebuttal and impeachment.

What are the proper forums for these reforms? As to proper technique training, the enlightened approach should be extolled by the institutions which train the people who do the interviewing. Continued adherence to the proper standards should then be monitored by police and social welfare agencies which employ the interviewers.

The second solution is more problematic in its application. It is questionable whether the courts may force the interviewing agencies to conform to a policy of documentation. If it can be done, it would be by the court's refusal to admit this type of testimony without proper documentation.

This might be accomplished through a number of legal frameworks. The court might adopt an exclusionary rule similar to that adopted in some states regarding hypnotically refreshed testimony, refusing admission without adherence to predetermined standards, including documentation, during the interviewing process.[189]

It might also be accomplished by analogy to *Wade* and its progeny. Here, the court could exclude the testimony because it is inherently unreliable and, when weakly corroborated or uncorroborated, lacks sufficient indicia of reliability. A basis for this might be found in the

Wade opinion, where, although deciding the issue on right to counsel grounds, the Court noted that the problem with the lineup was that the defendant would be unable to 'effectively reconstruct at trial any unfairness that occurred at the line-up [thus depriving] him of his only opportunity meaningfully to attack the credibility of the witness' courtroom [testimony].'[190] It should be remembered that this was a 1967 case, long before the advent of inexpensive videotape equipment. At that time, the presence of counsel was probably the most reliable way for a defendant to be made aware of what procedures were used.

In some states, the courts might, as in *McKellar*, use Rule 602 to force documentation as the only means sufficient to meet the state's burden for proving actual knowledge.

At best, these are makeshift rules used to safeguard what should be monumental concerns for any justice system. Truly, the onus should fall upon state legislatures to enact laws which would mandate such procedures. State legislatures, especially those who have come to the aid of the 'innocent' victim should now also come to the aid of the 'innocent' defendant.

VII. CONCLUSION

The psyche of the child, the type of interrogation techniques used, and the realities of jury trial present a significant possibility that innocent people are going to jail. The system of investigation must be reorganized to provide juries with the proper tools to make accurate decisions. The legal profession, prosecution, defence and judiciary must be made knowledgeable about the psychological realities of the situation.

Our legal system is generally effective in keeping innocent people out of jail. But it is presently failing in this rapidly growing area of prosecution. Our job as legal scholars, advocates and activists must be to push the system back into achieving equitable and just results. Only after the introduction of these safeguards may we ever be confident in rendering verdicts of guilt, and comfortable in the act of depriving these defendants of their liberty.

NOTES AND REFERENCES

The author wishes to express his gratitude for the helpful comments of Professor Janice Toran, Cleveland Marshall College of Law.
 1. See, e.g., Leo, Some day, I'll cry my eyes out, *Time*, 23 Apr. 1984, at 72; The youngest witnesses, *Newsweek*, 18 Feb. 1985, at 72.
 2. See, e.g., McGrath and Clemens, The child victim as a witness in sexual abuse cases, 46 *Montana Law Review* 229 (1985). The authors are, respectively, the County Attorney and Assistant County Attorney of Lewis and Clark County, Montana.
 3. See, e.g., Goodman, The child witness: conclusions and future directions for research and legal practice, 40 *J. Soc. Issues*, Summer 1984, at 157.
 4. This concern was exhibited in the legal area as early as 1969. See Libai, The protection of a child victim of a sexual offense in the criminal justice system, 15 Wayne *Law Review* 978 (1969).
 5. Between 1982 and 1986 eighteen states enacted statutes providing for hearsay exceptions in child abuse cases. See Galante, New war on child abuse, National Law Journal, 25 June 1984, at 1, col. 1; Slicker, Child sex abuse: the innocent accused, Case and Com., Nov.–Dec. 1986, at 12 n.7.
 6. See, e.g., Galante, note 5.
 7. See Elshtain, Invasion of the child savers: how we succumb to hype and hysteria, 49 The Progressive 23 (1985).
 8. See Note, Elimination of the resistance requirement and other rape law reforms: the New York experience, 47 *Alb. L. Rev.* 871, 897–8 (1983) (suggesting that the conviction rate is low for these alleged offenders because the alleged victims are poor witnesses).
 9. Data exists supporting the contention that the incidence of child abuse is rising, but the incidence of crime in general is rising as well. See Note, note 8, at 897 n.160.
10. With heightened media attention and public awareness, perhaps only the percentage of actual occurrences which are subsequently reported has risen. See Note, The young victim as witness for the prosecution: another form of abuse?, 89 *Dick. L. Rev.* 721, 729 (1985) (noting that in Pennsylvania between 1982 and 1983 reported child sexual abuse rose 32 per cent). Reports of child sexual abuse in 1982 numbered approximately 56,000, compared to 7,600 in 1976, indicating an approximate increase in reporting of 700 per cent. Ibid. at 729, Table I.
11. See J. Kroth, *Child Sexual Abuse*, 3–4 (1979) (suggesting that the rise may be due either to an increased occurrence rate or to an increased social awareness.
12. Professor Elshtain suggests that this type of overdone reformist craze is a uniquely American phenomenon. 'What we are witnessing is . . . the rapid transformation of a genuine social concern into a media fad and political issue. It has happened before; prohibition, marijuana, and pornography come readily to mind. Now we have a crisis of confidence that centers on the safety of our children.' Elshtain, note 7, at 23. She also suggests that many of the statistics promulgated by interested

parties (i.e. psychologists, criminologists, bureaucrats, academic researchers and legislators) are misleading or incorrect; the statistics are suspect because these parties have an interest in defining the problem, and its solutions, in a way that will enhance their own influence and power. Ibid. at 24.

13. Douglas Besharov, formerly a prosecutor from New York, who helped write the state's first child abuse reporting law, and who was head of the Federal National Center on Child Abuse and Neglect from 1975 to 1979, notes that 'what was hidden 20 years ago isn't today, and that's good. But we're now also getting reports that are just junk.' The youngest witnesses, note 1, at 72. Besharov is quoted elsewhere as saying that the nation's child protection system is 'out of control' and that, by some estimates, sixty to seventy per cent of reported cases are unfounded. Karlson, Child protection system said out of control, *St. Paul Pioneer Press Dispatch*, 15 Nov. 1985, at 1D, col. 1. See also Slicker, note 5, at 14–15 (listing examples of false accusation).

14. The mere issuance of an indictment is sure to make headlines. The youngest witnesses, note 1, at 72; see also Schetky and Boverman, *Faulty Assessment of Child Sexual Abuse: Legal and Emotional Sequelae* 10 (paper presented to the Annual Meeting of the American Academy of Psychiatry and the Law, Albuquerque, N.M., 10 Oct. 1985) (detailing story of an acquitted father who accrued a debt of $30,000 in the defence of a child sexual abuse charge).

15. See, e.g., *Davis* v. *Alaska*, 415 U.S. 308 (1974) (using Fourteenth Amendment to apply Sixth Amendment right of confrontation to the states).

16. See E. Loftus, *Eyewitness Testimony* 21 (1979).

17. Ibid.; See also Loftus and Davies, Distortions in the memory of children, 40 *J. Soc. Issues*, Summer 1984, at 51 (1984) (detailing studies revealing that new information accrued from conversation, questions, or other sources 'can do more than simply supplement in recollection: it can occasionally alter, or transform, a recollection').

18. E. Loftus, note 16, at 21.

19. Landsman, Reforming adversary procedure: a proposal concerning the psychology of memory and the testimony of disinterested witnesses, 45 *University of Pittsburg Law Review* 547, 550–1 n.15 (1984). 'This three stage analysis is so central to the concept of the human memory that it is virtually universally accepted among psychologists.' E. Loftus, note 16, at 21.

20. These three elements roughly correspond to those generally required for testimonial competency. See 2 J. Wigmore, *Evidence* ss. 478, 506 (Chadbourn rev. edn 1979). Wigmore states in s. 478 that the witness must: (1) know something of the matter to which she will testify and have received an impression (this element parallels the 'acquisition' stage); (2) have a recollection of these impressions (she must have 'retention' of these impressions); and (3) be able to communicate the recollection (she must be able to 'retrieve' the information and verbalize it). Section 506 of Wigmore's treatise specifically applies the same qualifications to children.

21. Expertise in an area may control the encoding process. Those who are less expert encode different features of an experience. Children, lacking expertise in sexual matters, may encode only broad features of the experience, while encoding nothing of the specifics. Loftus and Davies, note 17, at 54. This deficiency may be problematic when certain types of action (e.g. penetration) may be required for proving commission of the crime.

22. Ibid.; see also Goodman, note 3, at 160. ('Events that are . . . less central or less personally significant [or] events that never actually occurred (but might well have) may be especially subject to suggestion. In all of these situations the child's memory is likely to be weak or nonexistent, clearing the way for suggestive influences.')

23. Loftus and Davies, note 17, at 54 (citing for recent studies in support).

24. Goodman, note 3, at 160.

25. Loftus and Davies, note 17, at 54.

26. Ibid. The new information would simply be more accessible, especially if provided in suggestive questions asked during the interviewing process.

27. For a discussion of the problem as it relates to adults, see generally Landsman, note 19.

28. McIver, The case for a therapeutic interview in situations of alleged sexual molestation, *Oregon Defense Attorney*, June–July 1985, at 3. Examples of these types of questions include: 'Does daddy ever touch you when he comes in the room by himself?', when the child never mentioned daddy coming in by himself; and 'Does daddy say anything when he rubs your butt?', where there has been no mention of the father rubbing the child.

29. Ibid. at 4.

30. See E. Loftus, note 16, at 97–9; see also Goodman, note 3, at 161 (citing studies showing that adults tend to be more suggestible when an authoritative rather than a non-authoritative person asks leading questions).

31. Goodman, note 3, at 161.

32. Landsman, note 19, at 553 (citations omitted).

33. Loftus and Davies, note 17, at 64; Goodman, note 3, at 163 (noting, however, that further research is necessary before firm conclusions can be reached). See also H. Wakefield and R. Underwager, Excerpts from the Child Witness and Sexual Abuse 5 (unpublished manuscript) (no date) (available from the Institute of Psychological Therapies). 'The stronger and more certain the beliefs of the interrogator are about the event being investigated the stronger and more powerful the bias will be.' Ibid.

34. The parent would obviously be a person of high regard to the child. In divorce situations, the child may be feeling rejected or responsible and have an extra incentive to please the questioning parent. For a discussion of the effect of emotional reinforcing, see McIver, note 28, at 1.

35. See Landsman, note 19, at 555–6.

36. See H. Wakefield and R. Underwager, note 33, at 5.

37. Ibid. at 4–5.

38. Ibid.; see also McIver, note 28, at 4 (noting that with repeated conditioning interrogation, 'it is all too easy for the child to confuse objective and subjective reality').
39. A Hawaii judge, faced with this evidentiary problem, refused to permit two alleged victims of child sexual abuse to testify. *State* v. *McKellar*, Criminal No. 85–0553 (1st Cir. Haw., 15 Jan. 1986) (order granting defence's motion to disqualify Catherine Eaker and Catherine O'Bier). Basing his decision upon the expert testimony of Dr Ralph Underwager, Director of the Institute for Psychological Therapies, the judge concluded that the layered interviewing process used in the investigation of the alleged acts had rendered the girls 'unable to separate the facts from the learned experience and, consequently, their behavior is just the same as if they were abused. The abuse has become their reality.' Ibid, slip op. at 19.
40. The issue of whether children would consciously lie about abuse is here left unexplored. Older studies indicate that children would, but there is some strong authority to the contrary. Correlation between interviewing techniques and the probability of lying may be needed. See note 43 and accompanying text.
41. See Coleman, *False Allegations of Child Sexual Abuse; Have the Experts Been Caught With Their Pants Down?* 13–14 (1985) (unpublished manuscript).
42. See Loftus and Davies, note 17, at 51–2.
43. A recent study in Boston concluded that, out of 200 child sexual abuse cases studied, roughly 95 per cent of the children's accusations were accurate. Siles, Would a kid lie?, 71 *A.B.A.J.* 17 (1985).
44. Summit, The child abuse accommodation syndrome, 7 *Child Abuse and Neglect* 177 (1983).
45. Ibid. at 190–1.
46. Ibid. at 181–2.
47. Ibid. at 179.
48. Ibid.
49. Ibid. at 188.
50. Wakefield and Underwager suggest that the findings of psychologists and other mental health professionals are unreliable for use by the courts in determining the credibility of a child witness. The opinions of mental health professionals as to the credibility of a child accuser have often been shown to be determined by use of a few simple variables and a psychological evaluation rather than by a careful examination of the merits. Judges nonetheless commonly 'rubber stamp' the psychological conclusory report and base their decisions upon them. H. Wakefield and R. Underwager, note 33, at 17.
51. Coleman, note 41, at 2.
52. H. Wakefield and R. Underwager, note 33, at 17.
53. For the purposes of this article, we will use the most obvious situation: where the mother seeks to show that the father has abused the daughter. This analysis is also relevant, however, in cases where allegations are lodged against authority figures (e.g. pre-school teachers).
54. Summit, note 44, at 181.

55. Ibid. at 185.
56. Ibid. at 187.
57. Coleman, note 41, at 6.
58. Summit, note 44, at 190. Summit also states that 'the purpose of this paper then, is to provide a vehicle for . . . more effective clinical *advocacy* for the child within the family and within *the systems of child protection and criminal justice.*' Ibid. at 179–80 (emphasis added).
59. Coleman, note 41, at 13–14; see also Summit, note 44, at 190 ('It is contratherapeutic and unjust to expose legitimate victims to evaluations or treatment by therapists who cannot suspect or believe in unilateral sexual victimization of children by apparently normal adults.') Summit's statement by itself is true, but it has apparently not been taken at face value; rather, many followers take it as an urging to believe the allegations, not to believe in the possibility that they may be accurate.
60. Summit, note 44, at 188 ('The psychiatrist or other counseling specialist has a crucial role in early detection, treatment intervention, and *expert courtroom advocacy*. The specialist must help mobilize skeptical caretakers *into a position of belief*, acceptance, support and protection of the child') (emphasis added). Summit also notes that the children 'need an adult clinical advocate to *translate the child's world into adult-acceptable language.*' Ibid. at 183 (emphasis added). Does this not encourage the use of suggesting answers to the child? Further, if the child's own language is not 'adult-acceptable', should she be legally competent to testify in a court of law? The ability to communicate is a requisite to competency. See 2 J. Wigmore, note 20, s. 478, at 636–7.
61. *The Handbook of Clinical Intervention in Child Sexual Abuse* (S. Sgroi ed. 1984) [hereinafter *Handbook of Clinical Intervention*].
62. Blick, Porter and Sgroi, Validation of child sexual abuse, in *Handbook of Clinical Intervention*, note 61, at 39–41. Behavioural indicators are checklists of behaviour which indicate to the professional that abuse has occurred. The behavioural indicators listed in one representative checklist include: overly compliant behaviour, acting out aggressive behaviour, arriving at school early and leaving late with few if any absences, extraordinary fear of males, seductive behaviour with males, drop in school grades, and non-participation in school activities. *Intrafamily Sexual Abuse Project of Cuyahoga County, Training Manual: Identification, Reporting, Referral and Treatment of Child Sexual Abuse A–10* [hereinafter *Cuyahoga County Checklist*] (outlining behavioural indicators for use as 'Indicators or cues of sexual abuse in the victim').
63. See, e.g., Cuyahoga County Checklist, note 62.
64. Coleman, note 41, at 28.
65. Ibid. at 29.
66. Ibid. at 12.
67. The dolls are seldom anatomically 'correct'. The genitals are often oversized, suggesting to the child that, to please the interviewers, he should have something to say about genitals. H. Wakefield and R. Underwager, note 33, at 3; see also Schetky and Boverman, note 14, at 2–3 (detailing insistent use of anatomically correct doll by police investigator in the face of child's indifference and later, resistance to it); *State*

v. *McKellar*, Criminal No. 85–0553, slip op. at 18 (1st Cir. Haw., 15 Jan. 1986) (order granting defence's motion to disqualify Catherine Eaker and Catherine O'Bier) (relating the testimony of Dr Ralph Underwager suggesting that no evidence exists to suggest that abused children play any differently with these dolls than non-abused children).

68. Schetky and Boverman describe and comment on one instance in which this interview technique was used:

> At one point in the . . . interview, Michael said his father had 'shoved a stick' up his bottom. Officer Hammer, now elated at finally getting some incriminating evidence, promptly terminated the interview. Unanswered were such questions as What was the stick? A thermometer? An enema nozzle (history of constipation), a hand wiping him? The wooden spoon his mother used to paddle him? Or a penis? He also neglected to establish when or where this occurred and if anyone else was present, and what was said between them.

Schetky and Boverman, note 14, at 3.

69. Schetky and Boverman illustrate this interview technique with the following example:

> In case no. 3 an 8-year-old boy was told by his mother that he could never return home, never ride his bike, never see his father again and would have to go to the hospital where they would stick needles in him unless he admitted that his father had touched his bottom. The child's eventual admission resulted in father receiving a life sentence.

Ibid at 4.

70. 'Interviewers – verbally and non-verbally through facial expressions and the manner in which they respond to the child – pay more attention to [alleging sexual abuse] communications than to anything else a child might be trying to express.' McIver, note 28, at 1.

71. Ibid.

72. Schetky and Boverman, note 14, at 2.

73. 'I could tell what they wanted me to say by the way they asked the question,' said one boy in Minnesota who admitted that he had fabricated stories of sexual abuse. The youngest witnesses, note 1, at 74.

74. McIver, note 28, at 3.

75. H. Wakefield and R. Underwager, note 33, at 13, have noted that:

> While behaviors of anal and vaginal penetration with young children, monsters, killing of animals and so forth are so rare as to be highly improbable, they represent common fantasies of young children. When these fantasies are encouraged and reinforced by well-meaning therapists, they become real to the children telling them. When therapists do not keep in mind the actual patterns of sexual behavior of pedophiles, and when they believe that the child has, in fact, been abused, they will inadvertently encourage the child to develop this type of allegation.

76. 'The child may be interrogated repeatedly, however, by a wide variety of persons, including officers, social workers, prosecutors, therapists, parents and foster parents, siblings, and others.' Ibid. at 4.
77. 'The child, in his responses, tries to figure out and produce what he believes the adult wants to hear.' Ibid. at 6.
78. Ibid. at 5.
79. Protecting the child's interests may come in a variety of ways. Most interviewers assume that it is harmful to the child to have a court disbelieve her, and that it is desirable to remove [to jail] the abuser from the child's life. See Summit, note 4, at 186.
80. See notes 68–77 and accompanying text.
81. See E. Loftus, note 16.
82. 'The initial interrogation by officials may or may not be recorded with audio tape or video tape. There may or may not be notes or reports available from the officials later on in the process. Generally the amount of information available about the process of interrogation is minimal . . .' H. Wakefield and R. Underwager, note 33, at 4.
83. Ferraro and Herman, A middle american nightmare, *L.A.D.J.*, 7 Jan. 1985, at 4, col. 1; Minn. Att'y Gen., Report on Scott County Investigations 5 (12 Feb. 1985) (available from Minnesota Attorney General's Office).
84. Ferraro and Herman, note 83, at 4, col. 1.
85. Ibid.
86. Ibid.
87. Minn. Att'y Gen., note 83, at 1.
88. Ibid. After the two acquittals, Ms Morris was quoted as saying, 'This doesn't mean they are innocent. It means I didn't prove they were guilty. This means we live in a society that does not believe children.' Ferraro and Herman, note 83, at 4, col. 2. A few days later she said, 'I'm sick to death of things like the presumption of innocence.' Ibid. This kind of intense personal involvement by prosecuting authorities raises serious questions as to the validity of child sexual abuse prosecutions. A prosecutor who is 'sick' of the presumption of innocence may not fulfil his or her responsibilities in evaluating the evidence available for the prosecution.
89. Minn. Att'y Gen., note 83, at 17.
90. Ibid. at 16–17.
91. Ibid. at 17.
92. Ibid. at 12–16.
93. Ibid.
94. Ibid. at 9–11.
95. Ibid. at 9–10 ('The Scott County cases raise the issue of how long and how often one can continue to question children about abuse before running the risk of false accusation').
96. Ibid. at 9.
97. Ibid. at 9–10.
98. Ibid.
99. Ibid. at 9–10.
100. Ibid. The report did not address, however, the need to document the

type of questions used, so as to determine their suggestiveness.
101. Ibid. at 11–12.
102. Ibid.
103. This contention was one of the key objections in *State* v. *McKellar*, Criminal No. 85–0553, slip op. at 2 (1st Cir. Haw., 15 Jan. 1986).
104. 'The tragedy of Scott County goes beyond the inability to successfully prosecute individuals who may have committed child sexual abuse. Equally tragic is the possibility that some were unjustly accused and forced to endure long separations from their families.' Minn. Att'y Gen., note 83, at 17.
105. See, e.g., *McKellar*, slip op. at 19, in which the presiding judge had found that because of the interviewing process, the child lacked a present memory of the events from which he could testify. The judge disputed the finding by the prosecutor's expert that the child suffered from 'post-traumatic stress syndrome' that was caused by the alleged abuse. He held instead that it was impossible to attribute the condition to any particular incident. For an account of this trial, see Catterall, Children's testimony blocked, *National Law Journal*, 3 Feb. 1986, at 6, col. 1.
106. 7 J. Wigmore, *Treatise on Evidence* s. 2061 (Chadbourn rev. edn 1978).
107. The only exceptions to this rule are Nebraska and Washington, DC, which both 'still retain the blanket prohibitions against finding someone guilty of sexual abuse solely on the word of a child.' Galante, note 5, at 2, col. 2.
108. Note, The constitutionality of admitting the videotaped testimony at trial of sexually abused children, 7 *Whittier Law Review* 639, at 640 n.20 (1985). The absence of physical evidence is due to the general lack of force or sexual penetration in the usual occurrence of the act.
109. Federal Rule of Evidence 608(a) says: 'The credibility of a witness may be attacked or supported by evidence in the form of opinion or reputation, but subject to these limitations: (1) the evidence may refer only to character for truthfulness or untruthfulness . . .'
110. *United States* v. *Watson*, 669 F.2d 1374 (11th Cir. 1982). Consider this also in the context of expert testimony as it pertains to the victim's interviews. A court could theoretically block such testimony through Federal Rule of Evidence 608(a).
111. Federal Rule of Evidence 608(b) reads in pertinent part:

> Specific instances in the conduct of a witness, for the purpose of attacking or supporting his credibility, other than a conviction of crime as provided in rule 609, may not be proved by extrinsic evidence. They may, however, in the discretion of the court, if probative of truthfulness or untruthfulness, be required into on cross-examination of the witness (1) concerning his character for truthfulness or untruthfulness . . .

This rule has been accepted, at least as to its prohibition of extrinsic evidence, in at least 20 states. See generally State Correlation Tables, *Federal Rules of Evidence Service* (Callaghan); 3(A) J. Wigmore, *Evi-*

dence ss. 977–979 (Chadbourn rev. edn 1979) (certain evidence of prior acts not provable by extrinsic evidence to impeach a witness).
112. See E. Cleary, *McCormick on Evidence* s. 42 (3rd edn 1984) [hereinafter cited as *McCormick*].
113. See, e.g., *State* v. *Cantrall*, No. CR 196,821 (C.P. Ohio 1985) in which the child had, on three previous occasions, accused adults of abusive behaviour. The defence was allowed to question the child about whether he had made the accusations consistent with Federal Rule of Evidence 608(b)'s second sentence, and the child answered that he had. But the child also maintained that his allegations were true. The defence could not put on other witnesses to disprove his other allegations, so the jury heard only the child's answers, probably raising even more sympathy for him than before. It could, and should, be argued that such an application is unconstitutional. See note 118.
114. See *McCormick*, note 112, s. 42.
115. See 3(A) J. Wigmore, note 111, s. 979(1)(A), at 826.
116. Ibid.
117. See, e.g., *Davis* v. *Alaska*, 415 U.S. 308, 319 (1974) (state's interest in protecting a prosecution witness from the embarrassment of exposure of his juvenile record was outweighed by the defendant's 'paramount' constitutional right of confrontation).
118. One commentator has argued that, under a hybrid view of the rights to confrontation and compulsory process, the Constitution may guarantee the defendant's right to examine witnesses he produces which impact upon the veracity of prosecution witnesses. Weston, Confrontation and compulsory process: a unified theory of evidence for criminal cases, 91 *Harvard Law Review* 567, 590–93 (1978).
119. See generally Annotation, Necessity or permissibility of mental examination to determine competency or credibility of complainant in sexual offense prosecution, 45 *A.L.R.* 4th 310, 315 (1986) ('[The courts] have uniformly expressed or recognized the view that a judge lacks the power to actually make the complainant submit to a mental examination').
120. Ibid. at 317–24.
121. Ibid. at 324–8.
122. See H. Wakefield and R. Underwager, note 82 and accompanying text.
123. See Goodman, Golding and Haith, Jurors' reactions to child witnesses, 40 *J. Soc. Issues*, Summer 1984, at 140 (1984) (synthesizing then-existing studies with new findings of authors).
124. Ibid. at 142.
125. Ibid. at 144. The type of repetition which is connected with sexual abuse investigation might seriously reduce the consistency problem. See notes 39–40 and accompanying text.
126. Goodman, Golding and Haith, note 123, at 143.
127. Ibid.
128. Ibid.
129. Ibid at 143–4.
130. Ibid at 146.
131. '[O]ver time, information can become disassociated from its source and affect judgments regardless of its originally perceived credibility.' Ibid. at 141.

132. Ibid. at 148 (referring to conflicting studies on effect of discredited testimony).

133. Ibid. Note that only Connecticut requires such an instruction. See generally Annotation, Instructions to jury as to credibility of child's testimony in criminal case, 32 *A.L.R.* 4th 1196 (1984).

134. 'Although relevant, evidence may be excluded if its probative value is substantially outweighed by the danger of unfair prejudice . . . or misleading the jury' Federal Rule of Evidence 403.

135. Rules which correlate to Federal Rule of Evidence 403 may be found in Alaska, Arizona, Arkansas, California (California Evidence Code s. 352), Colorado, Delaware, Florida (Florida Evidence Code s. 90.403), Hawaii, Iowa, Maine, Michigan, Minnesota, Montana, Nebraska, Nevada (Stat. s. 48.035(1) (1979)), New Mexico, North Carolina, North Dakota, Ohio (Rule 403(A) makes exclusion mandatory where probative value is *substantially* outweighed), Oklahoma (Okla. Stat. Ann. ch. 12, s. 2403 (1980)), South Dakota (19–12–3 (1987)), Utah, Vermont, and Washington. Except as otherwise noted, these provisions may be found in the respective states' enacted Evidence Codes, under the number 403. See generally 1 J. Wigmore, *Evidence* s. 10(A), at 674–78 n.1 (Tiller rev. 1983).

136. See Dolan, Rule 403: the prejudice rule in evidence, 49 *S. Cal. Rev.* 220, 226. (1976).

137. Ibid. at 227–8. Dolan seems to say that jurors are not at fault for being prey to influence; the exclusion of prejudicial evidence with low probative value is not the result of a perception of jurors as 'low-grade morons', but rather is the result of a recognition that jurors have been raised in a society where trading in innuendo and hysteria has rarely proven to be wholly ineffective.

138. *Black's Law Dictionary* 1082 (5th edn 1979).

139. See pp. 261–4 on 'The nature of the child's psyche'; see also Comment, The probative value of testimony from the hypnotically refreshed recollection, 14 *Akron Law Review* 609, 622–9 (1981).

140. See pp. 260–4, 'Introduction' and 'The nature of the child's psyche'.

141. One should recognize, however, that merely hurting the defendant's case, no matter how badly, does not constitute unfair prejudice. See Dolan, note 136, at 238.

142. Ibid. at 241.

143. Ibid. at 284.

144. 2 J. Wigmore, note 20, s. 654, at 88 (Chadbourn rev. edn 1979). Federal Rule of Evidence 601 reads in relevant part: 'Every person is competent to be a witness except as otherwise provided in these rules.'

145. 2 J. Wigmore, note 20, s. 478.

146. Ariz. Rev. Stat. Ann. s. 12–2202 (1982); *Hendricks* v. *State*, 15 Ark. App. 378, 695 S.W.2d 843 (1985); Colo. Rev. Stat. s. 13–90–106 (1986) (statute amended to provide for child able to describe sexual offence in language appropriate for age); *State* v. *Rodriguez*, 180 Conn. 382, 429 A.2d 919 (1980); Idaho Code s. 9–202 (Supp. 1986); *People* v. *Sanchez*, 105 Ill. App. 3d 488, 434 N.E.2d 395 (1982); Ind. Code Ann. s. 34–1–14–4 (West 1983); *Payne* v. *Commonwealth*, 623 S.W.2d 867,

cert. denied, 456 U.S. 909 (1981); Minn. Stat. Ann. s. 595.02 subdivision 1(f) (West Supp. 1987) (although Minnesota has adopted the Federal Rules' 'all are competent' approach, the prohibition still exists against testimony of children incapable of receiving just impressions of the facts or relating them truly, but it is contained in the privilege section); Ohio Rule of Evidence 601(A); Or. Rev. Stat. s. 40.315 (1985); Wash. Rev. Code Ann. s. 5.60.050(2) (1963); *U.S.* v. *Lightly*, 677 F.2d 1027, 1028 (4th Cir. 1982) (notwithstanding Federal Rule of Evidence 601, which provides blanket competency to all witnesses, a witness in federal court will not be competent to testify where it can be shown that she does not have the capacity to recall); *U.S.* v. *Perez*, 526 F.2d 859 (5th Cir. 1975), cert. denied, 429 U.S. 846 (1976). Hawaii does not use these qualifications. Hawaii Rule of Evidence 601 (all persons are competent).

147. Federal Rule of Evidence 602 reads in relevant part:

> A witness *may not testify* to a matter unless evidence is introduced sufficient to support a finding that he has personal knowledge of the matter. Evidence to prove personal knowledge may, but need not, consist of the testimony of the witness himself. This rule is subject to the provisions of Rule 703, relating to opinion testimony by expert witnesses.

(Emphasis added.)

148. See Alaska Rule of Evidence 602; Arizona Rule of Evidence 602; Ark. Stat. s. 28–1001, Rule 602 (1976); California Evidence Code s. 702 (1966); Colorado Rule of Evidence 602; Delaware Uniform Rule of Evidence 602; Florida Stat. s. 90.604 (1977); Hawaii Rule of Evidence 602; Kansas Stat. Ann. 419 (1965); Maine Rule of Evidence 602; Michigan Rule of Evidence 602; Minnesota Rule of Evidence 602; Nebraska Rev. Stat. s. 27–602 (1975); Nevada Rev. Stat. s. 50.025 (1975); New Jersey Rule of Evidence 19; New Mexico Rule of Evidence 602; North Dakota Rule of Evidence 602; Ohio Evidence Rule 602; Oklahoma Stat. Ann. tit. 12 s. 2602 (1980); South Dakota Codified Laws Ann. s. 19–14–2 (1979); Texas Rule of Evidence 602; Utah Rule of Evidence 19; Vermont Rule of Evidence 602; Washington Rule of Evidence 602; Wisconsin Stat. s. 906.02 (1975); Wyoming Rule of Evidence 602.

149. McCormick, note 112, s. 10.

150. Ibid. at 25.

151. These might be in the nature of corroborating evidence.

152. See McCormick, note 112, at 23.

153. Ibid. at 24.

154. Criminal No. 85–0553 (1st Cir. Haw., 15 Jan. 1986).

155. Ibid., slip op. at 14–15.

156. Ibid., slip op. at 3.

157. Ibid. at 3. The state must lay a foundation from which the court may know that the witness is personally knowledgeable about the testimonial issue. 2 J. Wigmore, note 20, s. 650.

290   *Victim's Role in the Penal Process: Critical Views*

158. The manifest wisdom of the consideration of all the facts in determining the applicability of evidentiary rules appears to be at least tacitly approved by the Supreme Court under other circumstances. Note, for example, the Court's preference for consideration of the 'totality of the circumstances' in admissibility of line-up identification evidence questions. See *Neil* v. *Biggers*, 409 U.S. 188 (1972); *Simmons* v. *United States*, 390 U.S. 377 (1968).

159. The defendant's right to cross-examine under the Sixth and Fourteenth Amendments takes precedence over the evidentiary rules of the states. See, e.g., *Davis* v. *Alaska*, 415 U.S. 308, 320 (1974); Weston, note 140, at 579–80.

160. Since no significant decisions have been rendered dealing with this issue, the due process rights of the defendant will be analysed by analogy to two similar evidentiary areas. The first is eyewitness identification, which has long been recognized as a process subject to suggestive contamination. See, e.g., *Neil* v. *Biggers*, 409 U.S. 188 (1972); *United States* v. *Wade*, 388 U.S. 218 (1967). The second is hypnotically enhanced testimony. The similarities between hypnotic subjects and children who undergo suggestive interviewing are striking. The hypnotized person, like the alleged child victim, is hyperreceptive to suggestions by the hypnotist, whether express or implied, verbal or non-verbal, deliberate or unintended, or even unperceived by the hypnotist himself. The hypnotized person experiences a compelling desire to please the hypnotist by giving the responses he believes are expected. His critical judgment is accordingly impaired, causing him to credit vague recollections he would not have relied on before hypnosis. If the hypnotized person cannot actually recall an event, he will produce a 'pseudo memory' that may be compounded of irrelevant facts from an unrelated experience, 'confabulations' or fantasized material unconsciously invented to fill in the gaps, and conscious lies. *People* v. *Guerra*, 37 Cal. 3d 385, 412, 690 P.2d 635, 652, 208 Cal. Rptr. 162, 179 (1984) (citing review of numerous articles on hypnosis in scientific treatises and journals).

161. No state may 'deprive any person of life, liberty, or property, without due process of law . . .' US Constitution, Amendment XIV, s. 1.

162. See, e.g., *In re Winship*, 397 U.S. 358, 363 (1970).

163. Ibid.

164. 'In all criminal prosecutions, the accused shall enjoy the right to . . . be confronted with the witnesses against him . . .' US Constitution, Amendment VI; see also *Pointer* v. *Texas*, 380 U.S. 400 (1965) (applying Sixth Amendment to states through Fourteenth Amendment).

165. *Pointer*, 380 U.S. at 400.

166. See *Davis*, 415 U.S. at 318.

167. See Note, note 108, at 645–8.

168. *Guerra*, 37 Cal. 3d at 412, 690 P.2d at 652 (quoting *People* v. *Shirley*, 31 Cal. 3d 18, 66, 641 P.2d 775, 181 Cal. Rptr. 243 (1982)).

169. See *State* v. *Mena*, 128 Ariz. 226, 624 P.2d 1274 (1981) (excluding testimony of witnesses questioned under hypnosis). The exclusion of evidence which may be the product of suggestive practices was adopted

partially 'to determine whether the presence of his counsel is necessary to preserve defendant's basic right to a fair trial as affected by his right meaningfully to cross-examine the witnesses against him and to have effective assistance of counsel at the trial itself.' *Wade*, 388 U.S. at 227.
170. *Mena*, 128 Ariz. at 230, 624 P.2d at 1280. Also bear in mind that even testimony which is discredited can sway a jury. Goodman, Golding and Haith, note 123, at 148. In this light, the need for truly effective cross-examination becomes more pressing.
171. See Weston, note 118, at 598.
172. 388 U.S. 218 (1966).
173. Cf. *Simmons* v. *United States*, 390 U.S. 377, 384 (1968) (applying such a standard to pretrial identification by photograph).
174. See *Foster* v. *California*, 394 U.S. 440 (1969). But see *Neil* v. *Biggers*, 409 U.S. 188 (1972), which refused exclusion of testimony when there was sufficient indicia of its reliability. There, however, the indicia included corroborating evidence, which is often lacking in child sexual abuse cases. Further, that case involved only mildly suggestive techniques and an adult witness.
175. See *Neil*, 409 U.S. at 196–99.
176. See *State* v. *Mena*, 128 Ariz. 226, 624 P.2d 1274 (1981); see also *People* v. *Shirley*, 31 Cal. 3d 18, 641 P.2d 775, 181 Cal. Rptr. 243 (1982).
177. See *In re Winship*, 397 U.S. 358, 364 (1970).
178. Ibid.
179. See *Gregory* v. *City of Chicago*, 394 U.S. 111 (1969).
180. *Rochin* v. *California*, 342 U.S. 165, 173 (1952).
181. Ibid.
182. *Chambers* v. *Mississippi*, 410 U.S. 284, 302 (1973) (emphasis added).
183. Ibid. at 295.
184. *Ohio* v. *Roberts*, 448 U.S. 56, 64 (1980).
185. See Note, note 108, at 647–8.
186. See pp. 261–4 on 'The nature of the child's psyche'.
187. *In re Winship*, 397 U.S. 358, 372 (1970) (Harlan, J., concurring).
188. See *People* v. *Guerra*, 37 Cal. 3d 385, 690 P.2d 635, 208 Cal. Rptr. 162 (1984); *State* v. *Mena*, 128 Ariz. 226, 624 P.2d 1274 (1981).
189. See, e.g., *State* v. *Hurd*, 173 N.J. Super. 333, 414 A.2d 291 (1980).
190. *Wade*, 388 U.S. at 232.

Part Three
Initiatives to Help
Victims of Crime:
A Critical Appraisal

9 Placebo Justice:
Victim Recommendations and Offender Sentences in Sexual Assault Cases
Anthony Walsh

INTRODUCTION

After many years of neglect, crime victims have recently been redis-covered, and concern for them has become an important item on the agenda of the criminal justice system.[1] Feminist activists have exerted particular pressure on the criminal justice system to reform its atti-tudes and practices relating to the concerns of sexual assault victims.[2] One might reasonably expect that this upsurge of concern will result in sexual assault victims exerting greater influence on decision-making at all stages of the processing of offenders.

Victim characteristics have always had a measure of significance for the treatment of offenders. Throughout history, the probability of arrest and prosecution, as well as the severity of punishment, has varied according to the respective statuses of the victim and the offender.[3] Studies have shown that in contemporary America, police are less likely to bring charges against offenders who are related to their victims[4] and that police do respond to victims' wishes in making arrest decisions.[5] Victims' increased participation in the prosecution of offenders has been shown to increase the probability of conviction.[6] Victim concerns and activism do, therefore, appear to influence decisions in the early stages of offender processing.

It is unclear whether victims' involvement is limited to the early stages of processing, but Edward McCabe indicates that it is when he notes: '[i]f victims do become involved with the criminal justice system, they are more likely to participate and have influence during the initial stages of the process rather than the later stages.'[7] There are many stages in offender processing during which victim parti-cipation may influence the outcome. With the exception of parole decisions, however, the sentencing stage is the final opportunity that victims have to influence decisions regarding the offender's fate. But, as Hall points out: '[r]esearch data concerning the victim's role in the sentencing process is scant and unsatisfactory . . . [L]ittle attempt is made to clarify or measure the impact . . .'[8]

Studies that have addressed the issue of victim influence on sentencing have generally focused on various victim characteristics rather than on victim participation in processing. These studies have found minor effects on sentencing based on victim characteristics such as: judicial perceptions of the victim's character, any indication of victim cooperation (i.e. victim 'blameworthiness'),[9] the racial composition of the offender/victim dyad,[10] the victim's sex and alleged misconduct,[11] and the victim's race.[12] These studies, however, are based entirely on the passive role of the victim in the sentencing process. Victim characteristics, therefore, are said to have an impact on sentencing decisions independent of the victims' wishes and concerns. We located only one study where victims participated actively in sentencing decisions.[13] In this study, the victims directly expressed their wishes to the court.[14] This study, however, provided limited statistical analysis, failed to include dispositions of imprisonment and was primarily concerned with restitution for victims.

A major reason for this paucity of relevant studies is the rarity of jurisdictions in which victims are invited to express their sentencing wishes to the sentencing judge. This lack of victim input at the sentencing stage was a concern expressed by the President's Task Force on Victims of Crime when it recommended that '[j]udges should allow for, and give appropriate weight to, input at sentencing from victims of violent crime.'[15]

Under our judicial system, presently the only way that victims can influence sentencing decisions is through their expressed recommendations contained in a pre-sentence report. With reference to this point, McCabe states: '[w]hile little is known about these expressed [sentencing] preferences, these views probably have some, albeit minor, effects on sentencing decisions.'[16] In this study, we explore these effects on the sentencing of offenders convicted of sexual assault.

In our study we focused on the criminal code of Ohio. The criminal code of Ohio requires that a 'victim impact' statement be included in all pre-sentence reports and that a victim sentencing recommendation be included in cases involving personal assault.[17] On the surface, this requirement manifests an increased concern for victims and implies that victim recommendations are taken seriously and have a significant impact on sentencing. Eleanore Chelimsky, however, feels that such concern is spurious and that the pro-victim requirements reflect needs of the system such as good public relations, rather than the needs of victims.[18] If Chelimsky is correct, victim recommendations may have no effect at all on offender sentencing.

In addition to exploring the overall effect of victim recommendations on sentencing, this study attempts to determine if victim recommendations have a differential impact within various categories of victim/offender relationships. It is widely known that victims who are related to their assailants are less likely vigorously to seek the offenders' arrest and prosecution.[19] Therefore, it is reasonable to expect that the closer the relationship is between the offender and the victim, the less likely it is that the victim will recommend imprisonment. Actual sentences, however, do not necessarily reflect victim recommendations. In the case of sexual assault within the family, for instance, lenient victim recommendations may not translate into lenient sentencing given the general opprobrium attached to incestuous behaviour.[20] Conversely, assaults – sexual or otherwise – by strangers usually result in more severe sentences.[21]

Sexual activity which, although illegal, is apparently consensual, such as repeated encounters with under-age victims or the acceptance of money or other rewards by the victim, may result in lenient dispositions due to perceptions of victim 'blameworthiness'. Judicial perceptions of blameworthiness have been shown repeatedly to result in more lenient disposition for sex offenders.[22]

In this study we address five questions: (1) Do victim recommendations have any significant impact on sentencing independent of legally relevant considerations such as crime seriousness and prior record? (2) Do victims recommend leniency significantly more often as their relationship to the offender becomes closer? (3) Is there a differential impact of recommendations on sentencing according to victim/offender relationships? (4) Does the apparent victim's cooperation in his or her own victimization have a significant independent impact on victim recommendations and/or offender sentencing? and (5) Does the rendering of a victim recommendation, regardless of the type of recommendation, have any general independent impact on offenders for whom recommendations are made compared to offenders whose victims do not make a recommendation?

METHODS AND PROCEDURES

The data consisted of 417 sexual assault cases in a metropolitan Ohio county during the years 1980 through 1983. Of these cases, 248 victims (59.5 per cent) made a sentencing recommendation, and 169 victims (40.5 per cent) did not. The following crimes were represented in this study: rape, attempted rape, sexual battery, corruption of a minor and gross sexual imposition. All of these crimes were felonies and included incestuous and non-incestuous encounters. All of the offenders were male.

Sentences were rendered in terms of probation/prison dichotomies, the form in which victim recommendations were made known to the sentencing judge in the pre-sentence investigation reports (PSIs). These recommendations were made either by the victims themselves or by their parents or guardians if the victims were minors.[23]

Any study of sentencing must contain adequate controls for the effects of legally relevant variables such as crime seriousness and prior record. Our measures of crime seriousness and prior record were those measures actually in use by the Ohio courts and were based on non-binding sentencing guidelines.[24] Offender/victim relationships were coded as follows: father/stepfather ($n = 63$), other relative ($n = 33$), acquaintance ($n = 84$), and stranger ($n = 68$). Victim cooperation with the offender in the sexual encounter was coded 'Yes' ($n = 25$) and 'No' ($n = 223$). Victim cooperation was coded affirmatively only if the PSI contained unambiguous statements to this effect. Data analysis was based on chi-square and regression analysis and their associated statistics.[25]

RESULTS

We first examined findings relating to those cases for which some type of sentencing recommendation was made ($n = 248$). The preliminary chi-square analysis presented in Table 9.1 indicates that victim recommendations are significantly related to the sentence received ($X^2 = 4.98$, p < 0.05, tau b $= 0.14$). Seventy-one (28.6 per cent) offenders received a probation recommendation from their victims and 177 (71.4 per cent) received a recommendation of imprisonment. The computed odds ratio for these data is 1.9. This indicates that the odds in favour of a recommendation/sentence agreement are 1.9:1.[26] However, an analysis of the conditional odds – the odds that an

Table 9.1   Cross-tabulation of victim recommendation and sentence type

Sentence	Victim recommendation Probation	Prison	Totals
Probation	46 (64.8%)	87 (49.2%)	133 (53.6%)
Prison	25 (35.2%)	90 (50.8%)	115 (46.4%)
	71	177	248

$X^2 = 4.98$, $p < 0.05$, tau b $= 0.14$

Table 9.2   Numbers and percentages of judicial agreement with victim recommendations for probation, prison, and overall, broken down by offender/victim relationship

Offender/victim relationship	Total N	Probation N	%	Prison N	%	Overall N	%
Father/stepfather	63	47	55.3	16	12.5	28	44.4
Other relative	33	8	75.0	25	28.0	13	39.4
Acquaintance	84	14	85.7	70	48.6	46	54.8
Stranger	68	2	100.0	66	71.2	49	72.1
Totals	248	71	64.8	177	50.8	136	54.8

offender will receive a certain sentence given the type of victim recommendation he received – reveals that recommendation/sentence agreement is almost completely a function of probation recommendations. If an offender received a recommendation for probation from his victim, his odds of receiving probation are 1.84:1. On the other hand, if he received a recommendation of imprisonment, the odds that he will be incarcerated are almost even at 1.03:1.

An analysis of the various sub-categories of offender/victim relationship is presented in Table 9.2. This table reveals the divergent effects of recommendations on sentencing. In the father/stepfather category, 74.6 per cent of the victims ($n = 47$) recommended probation and 25.4 per cent ($n = 16$) recommended prison. The courts agreed with a probation recommendation in 55.3 per cent of the cases, however, the courts agreed with a prison recommendation in only 12.5 per cent of the cases. Victim recommendations were significantly related to sentences, but in a negative direction (X^2 (corrected) = 4.03, p < 0.05, tau b = –0.29).[27] The conditional odds of receiving probation given a probation recommendation were only 1.2:1 and the conditional odds of receiving a prison sentence given a prison recommendation were 7:1 against. The overall odds ratio was 5.6:1 against an offender receiving the recommended sentence in this category.

In the 'other relative' category, 8 offenders (24.2 per cent) received a probation recommendation and 25 offenders (75.8 per cent) received a recommendation of imprisonment. No recommendation/sentence relationship was observed for this category (X^2 (corrected) = 0.00).

In the 'acquaintance' category, 14 (16.7 per cent) of the offenders received a probation recommendation and 70 (83.3 per cent) received a recommendation for imprisonment. The recommendation/sentence relationship was significant for this category (X^2 (corrected) = 4.3, p < 0.05, tau b = 0.26). The odds ratio was 5.6:1 that an offender would receive the recommended sentence. Again, interpretive caution should be exercised because the conditional odds of receiving probation given a probation recommendation (6:1) primarily account for this agreement. The conditional odds of receiving a prison sentence given a prison recommendation were 1.1:1 against.

The statistics for 'stranger' category were uninterpretable because only 2 of the 68 offenders in this category received a probation recommendation. Both of these offenders received a recommended sentence. Of the 66 for whom prison was recommended, 71.2 per cent received a prison sentence and 28.5 per cent received probation.

Overall, Table 9.2 reveals a 'perfect' inverse relationship between the degree of closeness of the offender/victim relationship and judicial agreement with victims' recommendation in both the probation and prison categories. The percentage of probation agreements ranged from 55.3 per cent to 100 per cent and the percentage of prison agreements ranged from 12.5 per cent to 71.2 per cent.

The relationship between victim cooperation and sentence type (not shown in tabular form) was in the predicted direction, but it was not significant (X = 2.3 n.s., tau b = 0.10). The conditional odds for receiving probation if the victim cooperated in the assault were 2.1:1 and the conditional odds for receiving probation given non-cooperation were 1.1:1.

The relationship between victim cooperation and victim recommendation was significant (X = 7.4, p < 0.01, tau b = 0.17). In those cases where the victim cooperated in the offence, 52 per cent of the victims recommended probation; only 26 per cent of those victims who were not cooperative recommended probation. The conditional odds for a probation recommendation given victim cooperation were 1.1:1 and, given non-cooperation, the conditional odds were 2.8:1 against receiving a probation recommendation. These data suggest that the victim implicitly recognized his or her role in the offence by generally making a lenient sentencing recommendation.[28]

Regression analysis of the recommendation/sentence relationship

For our regression analysis of the recommendation/sentence relationship we dummy-coded the relationship variable and used the 'stranger' category as the reference category.[29] Table 9.3 reveals that victim recommendation has no effect on the sentence type received by sex offenders. Any agreement initially observed between recommendation and sentence is entirely mediated by the legally relevant variables of crime seriousness and prior record. The only other variable that even approaches significance is the dummy-coded acquaintance category. Victim cooperation has no independent impact on sentencing, indicating that judges do not ascribe great weight to

Table 9.3 Standardized betas and related statistics for variables regressed on sentence type

Variable	$\beta*$	t	sig.
Crime seriousness	0.556	9.2	0.0000
Prior record	0.255	4.9	0.0000
Acquaintance	0.102	1.5	0.1331
Father/stepfather	0.068	0.9	0.3906
Victim cooperation	0.053	1.0	0.3055
Other relative	0.025	0.4	0.6859
Victim recommendation	−0.024	−0.4	0.7087
(Constant)		−1.1	0.2597
Adjusted R^2 = 0.399, n = 248			

Coding: Sentence type: Probation = 0, Prison = 1.
       Victim cooperation: Yes = 0, No = 1.
       Victim recommendation: Probation = 0, Prison = 1.
       Relationship variables dummy coded.

302 *Initiatives to Help Victims of Crime*

Table 9.4   Standardized betas and associated statistics for the determinants of sentence type for father/stepfather and 'other' categories

Variable	Father/stepfather			Other		
	β*	t	sig.	β*	t	sig.
Prior record	0.621	6.1	0.0000	0.080	1.4	0.1558
Victim recommendation	−0.161	−1.5	0.1471	0.112	2.1	0.0394
Crime seriousness	0.041	0.4	0.6888	0.632	10.8	0.0000
Victim cooperation	0.023	0.2	0.8319	0.040	0.7	0.4754
(Constant)		0.7	0.4943		−1.7	0.0947
Adjusted	$R^2 = 0.410, n = 63$			$R^2 = 0.496, n = 185$		

Coding: Sentence type: Probation = 0, Prison = 1.
   Victim cooperation: Yes = 0, No = 1.
   Victim recommendation: Probation = 0, Prison = 1.
   Relationship variables dummy coded.

victim 'blameworthiness', after we statistically adjusted for the impact of legally relevant variables.

Due to the previously determined differential impact of victim recommendations on sentence type according to victim/offender relationship, we decided to run two separate regression analyses: one to assess the impact of victim recommendations on sentence type for close family members (father/stepfather) and one for all other victim/offender relationships combined. These results are presented in Table 9.4. In the father/stepfather category, we observed a weak, non-significant tendency for victim recommendations to be negatively related to sentence type. In the 'other' category, we observed, after adjusting for the effects of other variables, a weak but statistically significant positive relationship between recommendation and sentence.

The differential impact of the legally relevant variables in the two models is interesting. In the father/stepfather category, the most important variable is prior record, while in the 'other' category, prior record has no significant independent impact. Conversely, crime seriousness has no significant impact on sentencing in the father/stepfather category, but it is the most important determinant of sentencing in the 'other' category. Victim cooperation had no impact in either model. On the crime seriousness measure used in this jurisdiction, the 'other' category scored significantly higher than the father/stepfather category (means of 3.09 and 1.84, respectively, $t = 4.2$, p < 0.001). The relative lack of variance in crime seriousness for the father/stepfather category accounts for the inability of this variable to exert any independent effect on sentencing. The low crime seriousness mean also indicates that, legally speaking, incestuous encounters are considered less serious in relation to other sexual assaults. There was no significant difference on the measure of prior record (means of 3.94 and 3.62).

Determinants of victim recommendations

Consistent with our expectations, Table 9.5 shows that having father or stepfather status is the most powerful determinant of a probation recommendation. Victim cooperation remains a significant determinant of a probation recommendation after adjusting for the effects of the other variables in the model. Surprisingly, crime seriousness does not exert a significant independent effect on victim recommendations. It is important to recall, however, that two-thirds of the probation recommendations were made by victims whose assailants were fathers or stepfathers. Although the stranger category (represented by the constant) is reported as significant, it is meaningless since only two victims in this category recommended probation. These findings should be treated with caution since the mean of the dependent variable (0.714) approaches the upper range limit beyond which OLS regression can underestimate the effects of continuous variables (crime seriousness and prior record) relative to the effects of dummy variables.[30]

Table 9.5 Standardized betas and related statistics for the determinants of victim recommendation

Variable	β^*	t	sig.
Father/stepfather	−0.623	−9.1	0.0000
Victim cooperation	0.180	3.6	0.0004
Crime seriousness	0.111	1.8	0.0687
Other relative	−0.100	−1.6	0.1088
Acquaintance	−0.060	−0.9	0.3751
Prior record	−0.041	−0.8	0.4338
(Constant)		2.1	0.0334
Adjusted R^2 = 0.401, n = 248			

Coding: Sentence type: Probation = 0, Prison = 1.
Victim cooperation: Yes = 0, No = 1.
Victim recommendation: Probation = 0, Prison = 1.
Relationship variables dummy coded.

**Recommendation versus non-recommendation:
the effect on sentencing**

This section compares the sentencing of those offenders for whom a recommendation was made, regardless of the type of recommendation ($n = 248$), with the sentencing of those offenders for whom no victim recommendation was made ($n = 169$). A chi-square analysis (not shown in tabular form) revealed that, as a group, those offenders for whom a recommendation was made received significantly more lenient sentences ($X^2 = 12.4$, $p < 0.001$, tau b $= 0.17$) than did offenders receiving no recommendation. In the former group, 53.6 per cent received probation and 46.4 per cent were sent to prison. Of the 169 offenders who did not receive any recommendation from their victims, 36.1 per cent received probation and 63.9 per cent were sent to prison. The odds ratio (2.05:1) indicates that the latter group was just over twice as likely to be sent to prison as the former group.

The regression analysis presented in Table 9.6 indicates that this differential sentencing effect is independent of legally relevant variables and of victim cooperation. This effect is undoubtedly a function of the probation recommendations that were made. In other words, it appears likely that some of the sex offenders granted probation would have been imprisoned were it not for the probation recommendations they received from their victims. In general terms, then, the overall impact of victim recommendations in this jurisdiction appears to have been the mitigation of the offender's punishment.

Table 9.6 Standardized betas and related statistics assessing the impact on sentencing for offenders who received a recommendation and those who did not

Variable	β^*	t	sig.
Crime seriousness	0.466	11.7	0.0000
Prior record	0.293	7.3	0.0000
Recommendation made	0.133	3.5	0.0005
Victim cooperation	−0.005	−0.5	0.8874
(Constant)		0.5	0.6416
Adjusted $R^2 = 0.418$, $n = 417$			

Coding: Recommendation made: Yes = 0, no = 1.
       Other variables same as Table 9.3.

Characteristics of recommending and non-recommending victims

Because offenders were treated differently based simply on whether or not a sentencing recommendation was made, it would appear necessary to determine what differences, if any, exist between the characteristics of those cases. To make this determination, we examined the following variables: the offender/victim relationship, victim cooperation, crime seriousness as determined by the measure used by the Ohio courts, victim harm, the victim's sex, age and race, and the racial composition of the victim/offender dyad.

The offender/victim relationship had a significant effect on whether or not a recommendation was made ($X^2 = 9.0$, df = 3, p < 0.03, V = 0.15). Those victims in the acquaintance category, the category containing the greatest percentage of cooperating victims, were the least likely to make a recommendation (51.5 per cent). The percentages in the other categories were: stranger (60.2 per cent), father/stepfather (66.3 per cent), and other relative (71.7 per cent).

Consistent with these findings, we found that victims who cooperated with their assailants were significantly more likely to decline to make a sentencing recommendation ($X^2 = 6.7$, p < 0.01, tau b = −0.13). It is perhaps not surprising that these individuals would be reluctant to speak with a probation officer about sentencing for an illegal encounter in which they freely participated.

We found no differences in crime seriousness and victim harm between the recommending and non-recommending groups. The mean scores of the sentencing guidelines on crime seriousness for both groups were essentially similar ($t = -0.31$, n.s.). Victim harm was categorized as: (1) no harm; (2) minor harm; (3) hospitalized; (4) psychological; and (5) pregnancy.[31] The chi-square value for victim harm and whether or not a recommendation was made was not significant ($X^2 = 7.7$, df = 4, p > 0.10). To explore this further, we dichotomized the victim harm variable into 'some harm' and 'no harm' categories. This categorization also failed to provide a statistically significant difference ($X^2 = 1.6$).

The victim's sex ($X^2 = 0.9$), race ($X^2 = 1.7$) and age ($t = -0.54$), did not significantly differentiate between the recommending and non-recommending groups. There were 354 female victims and 63 male victims; 276 were white and 141 were black.

Among the 276 white victims of sexual assault, the race of the offender (224 whites and 52 blacks) had no significant impact on whether or not a recommendation was made ($X^2 = 0.7$). Among the black victims, the race of the offender (15 whites and 126 blacks) also made no significant difference ($X^2 = 0.1$). We then divided the sample into whites who were assaulted by whites ($n = 224$) and blacks who were assaulted by blacks ($n = 126$), disregarding the interracial assaults. This procedure also failed to differentiate significantly between the two groups in their propensity to make a sentencing recommendation ($X^2 = 1.1$). Thus, only victim/offender relationship and victim cooperation had any statistically significant effect on whether or not a sentencing recommendation was made.

DISCUSSION

Our findings suggest that requiring a victim impact statement and recommendation as part of the pre-sentence report is a mere genuflection to ritualistic legalism. Nonetheless, this requirement may have a placebo value in that it creates the impression that 'something is being done'. Based on our observation that there was greater overall agreement than disagreement between victim recommendations and imposed sentences (64.8 per cent for probation, 50.8 per cent for prison), the majority of victims in this jurisdiction may indeed feel that their wishes and concerns were taken into account. They do not know, of course, that this agreement is *almost entirely* mediated by legally relevant variables.

This study raises the question of whether or not victims should have a significant influence on the sentencing process. Certainly, a distinction must be made between the wishes of victims and the rights of defendants and the needs and requirements of the system. The fact that 89.5 per cent of the victims in this study who were sexually assaulted by non-relatives recommended imprisonment reveals a high level of vindictiveness. While this vindictiveness may be understandable, one of the primary functions of the law is to mitigate the natural urge for vengeance by subjecting personal grievances to evaluation by disinterested third parties and formalized rules. Victims certainly deserve more consideration by the law and its agents, but the law cannot simply become the instrument of their revenge.

It is an entirely different matter, however, when the courts ignore victim recommendations that their assailants be granted probation. While such a recommendation does not necessarily signify forgiveness, it is clearly inconsistent with a desire for revenge. The father/

stepfather category was the only category in which probation was recommended more often than imprisonment. To ignore the wishes of the victim for probation in these cases may amount to a double victimization, a victimization which may result in more detrimental effects than the sexual assault itself. This victimization may take the form of guilt, of the victim feeling responsible for the father's or stepfather's punishment, animosity from other family members toward the victim, and economic deprivation resulting from the offender's incarceration.

Of course, judges must consider issues that are broader than the possible implications of the sentence for the victim. In our criminal justice system, the offended party is society as a whole, rather than the individual. Criminal justice decision-makers perhaps feel that their primary responsibility is to protect the rest of society by ordering incarceration when it is warranted by legally relevant variables. By taking such action, they also send a symbolic message to potential offenders. This argument, however, has greater force in cases of acquaintance and stranger sexual assaults.

One might speculate that a recommendation of probation for fathers and stepfathers may, in some cases, result from threats of retribution, either from the offender or other family members, or from factors other than the victim's genuine concern for the fate of the offender. Our study does not answer this question. The only data available to us was the stated preference of the victims; we did not have access to their motivations.

There is a marked disregard for the preferences of victims of incestuous sexual assault. This tendency was true not only when the recommended disposition was for probation, but also when the stated preference was for incarceration. We suggest that the lack of agreement with probation recommendations for fathers and stepfathers convicted of sexual assault may reflect society's general distaste for incestuous sexual encounters. The greater lack of agreement with imprisonment recommendations in this category can only be explained in terms of legal and systemic considerations.

Our analysis of the groups for whom recommendations were and were not made revealed that those offenders who received a recommendation were significantly less likely, as a group, to be imprisoned. Since these two groups differed only in terms of whether or not they received a recommendation and since most of those receiving a recommendation received a prison recommendation, the observed sentencing differential appears to be almost entirely a function of

308   *Initiatives to Help Victims of Crime*

probation recommendations. If an offender, therefore, received a recommendation of probation from his victim, and if probation seemed warranted according to legal criteria, such as crime serious-ness and prior record, the recommendation tipped the scale in favour of probation and away from prison. If, however, prison appeared to be the legally warranted disposition, it was highly unlikely that an offender would receive probation even if the victim recommended it.

A comparison of the characteristics of those victims who made a sentencing recommendation with those victims who did not showed that of the nine variables tested only the victim/offender relationship and victim cooperation had any significant impact on the decision to recommend a probation sentence. We conclude that the requirement of a victim recommendation has some symbolic and possibly some substantive value. In cases where judges were uncertainly poised be-tween probation versus a prison decision, undoubtably more than one offender was granted probation because of a victim recommendation.

NOTES AND REFERENCES

1. See A. Karmen, *Crime Victims: An Introduction to Victimology* 3–23 (1984); Scherer, An overview of victimology, in Victimization of the Weak (1982).
2. See Rafter and Natalizi, Marxist feminism: implications for criminal justice, 27 *Crime and Delinquency* 81 (1981); Robin, Forcible rape: institutionalized sexism in the criminal justice system, 23 *Crime and Delinquency* 137 (1977).
3. See, e.g., H. Barnes, *The Story of Punishment* (1972).
4. See Truninger, Marital violence: the legal solutions, 23 *Hastings Law Journal* 259, 271 (1971).
5. See Smith and Visher, Street level justice: Situational determinants of police arrest decisions, 29 *Social Problems* 167, 173 (1981).
6. See Hall, The role of the victim in the prosecution disposition of a criminal case, in *Perspectives on Crime Victims* 318, 323 (1981).
7. McCabe, The quality of justice: victims of the criminal justice system, in *Victimization of the Weak* 128 (1982).
8. Hall, note 6, at 333.
9. Williams, The effects of victim characteristics on the disposition of violent crimes, in *Criminal Justice and the Victim* 177, 191 (1976).
10. See LaFree, The effects of sexual stratification by race on official reac-tions to rape, 45 *American Sociological Review* 842 (1980).
11. See Myers, Offended parties and official reactions: victims and the sen-tencing of criminal defendants, 46 *Sociological Quarterly* 529, 537–38 (1979).

12. See J. Foraker-Thomson, *Explaining Judicial Decisions to Order Restitution in the Second Judicial District of New Mexico* (1984) (paper presented at the annual meeting of the ACS).

13. See Davis, Kunreuther and Connick, Expanding the victim's role in the criminal court dispositional process: the results of an experiment, 75 *Journal of Criminal Law and Criminology* 491 (1984).

14. Ibid. at 498.

15. See President's Task Force on Victims of Crime: *Final Report* 76 (1982).

16. McCabe, note 7, at 132.

17. See Ohio Revised Code Ann. s. 2947.051 (Baldwin 1983). Davis, Kunreuther, and Connick feel that given what they term 'the strong disincentives' for court officials to consider victims' interests, victims' concerns will never be adequately addressed until we see 'legislative action mandating that victims be given the chance to express their opinions orally or in writing.' Davis, Kunreuther and Connick, note 13, at 505. The Ohio Revised Code provides victims with this opportunity. Ohio Revised Code Ann. s. 2947.051.

18. See Chelimsky, Serving victims: agency incentives and individuals, in *Evaluating Victim Services* (1981).

19. See Smith and Visher, note 5, *passim*.

20. See J. McCary, *Sexual Myths and Fallacies* (1971).

21. See Kleck, Racial discrimination in criminal sentencing: a critical evaluation of the evidence with additional evidence on the death penalty, 46 *American Sociological Review* 783 (1981).

22. See Williams, note 9, *passim*.

23. The validity of substituting the recommendation of a parent or guardian for that of the victim might be questioned. It is, however, the general practice of this probation department not to interview child victims of sexual assault, but rather to interview his or her parents or legal guardian and request a recommendation from them. The rationale for this is based on published statements of the chief court psychiatrist of this particular jurisdiction, Dr Henry Hartman: 'Intense emotional reactions on the part of parents, repeated questioning by police, unpleasant appearances and cross-examination in courtrooms may all be as traumatic or even more traumatic than the offense itself.' *Basic Psychiatry for Corrections Workers* 217 (1978). Thus, where the victim is a minor, obtaining parent or guardian recommendations is consistent with departmental procedure.

24. For a complete explanation of the measurement of these variables and of the sentencing guidelines, see Walsh, Differential sentencing patterns among felony sex offenders and non-sex offenders, 75 *Journal of Criminal Law and Criminology* 443, 445–7 (1984).

25. While there is debate regarding the appropriateness of using OLS regression techniques with dichotomous dependent variables, this technique is more readily interpretable and yields similar results to logistic regression when the mean on the dependent variable is close to 0.50; this is the case with the sentence variable in the present study. See Aldrich and Cnudde, Probing the bounds of conventional wisdom: a comparison of regression, probit, and discriminant analysis, 19 *American Journal of Political*

Science 571 (1975). Other authors go further in asserting the similarity of these techniques when the mean of the dependent variable ranges from 0.25 to 0.75. See, e.g., Bose, Household resources and U.S. women's work: factors affecting gainful employment at the turn of the century, 49 *American Sociological Review* 474, 480 (1984); Goodman, The relationship between modified and usual multiple-regression approaches to the analysis of dichotomous variables, in *Sociological Methodology* 86 (1976).

26. The odds ratio is the familiar crossproduct ratio for a 2×2 table: odds ratio = (f11)(f22)/(f21)(f12). The conditional odds are obtained by (f11)/(f21). See, e.g., D. Knoke and P. Burke, *Log Linear Models* 9–10 (1980).

27. The corrected chi-square is used when any cell of a 2×2 table contains less than five cases. The correction factor is applied by reducing the value of the term (F obs. − F exp.) by 0.5 before squaring the difference and dividing by the expected frequency for that cell.

28. As we noted in the methods section, victim cooperation was coded affirmatively only if the PSI contained unambiguous statements to this effect (i.e. the victim's own admission). Some may find it difficult to conceptualize the voluntary submission of a child to sexual encounters, and it may be especially difficult to conceptualize this submission if his or her father or stepfather was the offender. Nevertheless, such voluntary submission does occur, usually in return for money or other rewards such as being favoured over other siblings. Victim cooperation, however, is less frequent in the father/stepfather category than in the other relative or acquaintance categories. The numbers and percentages of cases in which victim cooperation occurred are as follows: father/stepfather = 5 (7.9 per cent); other relative = 4 (12.1 per cent); acquaintance = 14 (16.7 per cent); stranger = 2 (2.9 per cent). The chi-square for these data (not shown in tabular form) was significant ($X^2 = 8.3$ df = 3, p < 0.04, Cramer's V = 0.18).

29. Dummy variable analysis is a technique whereby a categorical independent variable is transformed into a set of $k − 1$ unordered variables so that separate effects of each category of the independent variable on the dependent variable can be estimated. The constant (the y intercept) and its associated statistics represent the independent effect and significance level for the reference category. See, e.g., D. Klienbaum and L. Kupper, *Applied Regression Analysis and Other Multivariable Methods* 188–9 (1978).

30. See, e.g., Bose, note 25; Vanneman and Pampel, The American perception of class and status, 42 *American Sociological Review* 422 (1977).

31. For a complete explanation of the victim harm variables, see Walsh, note 24.

10 The Victim/Offender Reconciliation Programme:

A Message to the Correctional Reformers*
Tony Dittenhoffer and
Richard V. Ericson

INTRODUCTION

In recent years there has been growing scepticism over the ability of
incarceration to meet the traditional goals of rehabilitation, deterrence and incapacitation. The prison system has also been criticized
for inhumane treatment, and the substantial cost of imprisonment has
been emphasized. Calls for restraint have been based also on the
over-use of prisons because many inmates are found to have committed offences that are regarded as non-serious.

Countless sources simultaneously echo the failures of imprisonment
and advocate a variety of new programmes. One consequence of this
is án expansion of community-based sentencing alternatives.[1] In programmes that range from probation and parole through to newer
alternatives such as community work orders, there is recent evidence
that three to four times as many offenders are now serving their sentence
in the community rather than in jail.[2] In addition, under increasing
pressure to reduce correctional costs, indications are that government
interest and support for such programmes will continue.[3]

The focus of the present research study is on one community
programme, the Victim/Offender Reconciliation Programme (VORP).
This is a relatively new sentencing alternative whereby the offender

* The research on which this paper is based was conducted at the Centre of Criminology, University of Toronto. This is a revised version of a paper presented to the
American Society of Criminology, Toronto, in November 1982.

convicted of a crime agrees to meet his victim in order to negotiate over the amount of harm done and further decide on mutually acceptable terms of compensation. Since it was first conceived in 1975, it has rapidly grown in popularity. In Ontario alone there are 24 VORP centres operating, and other centres across Canada have similar programmes.

In this paper we consider whether VORP is attaining its original goals. In particular we assess whether it is successfully serving as an alternative to incarceration. A common theme in corrections is that, while reformers and innovators justify and provide impetus to new correctional alternatives, the actual implementation of programmes often results in a contradiction of their ideas.[4] Various community sanctions purported to be alternatives to imprisonment frequently result in an extension of the social control of the state. Likewise, it is postulated that, owing to a myriad of operational realities and conflicting interests that surround VORP, it will fail to fulfil its goal as an alternative to prison.

THE VICTIM/OFFENDER RECONCILIATION PROGRAMME[5]

A criminal trial in a Southern Ontario city involved two offenders who were found to have gone on a drunken rampage, vandalizing the property of 22 victims and causing about $2,200 worth of damage. At the suggestion of a probation officer who had conducted a pre-sentence investigation, the trial judge remanded the case for three months so that the offenders could meet each victim and arrange to make restitution. It was the completion of this case which is cited as leading ultimately to an organized and well-defined Victim/Offender Reconciliation Programme.

Impetus for the programme was given by the probation officer, at present the coordinator for the programme, and a volunteer assistant associated with a local church group. Close liaison with several members of the legal system and people from the general community enabled them to enlist strong local support for the programme, and wide consultation permitted the input of many persons as the programme was set up. Funding was eventually obtained from the volunteer's church organization as well as provincial and federal government grants.

In the design of the programme, it was decided to limit VORP to the post-conviction level. Referral to the programme would be made through a stipulated condition of probation, yet voluntary participation in the project by both the victim and offender was considered requisite. Unwillingness on either side to meet and negotiate would result in the offender making restitution without a meeting. It was further decided that the programme would be most suitable to offences that involved identifiable victims, including wilful damage, common assault, theft and break-and-enter.

VORP is at present based in a house where intentions are to provide a comfortable residential setting for victim/offender meetings. It is administratively run by the coordinator and a full-time volunteer affiliated with the sponsoring church group, but great emphasis in the functioning of the programme has been placed on volunteers from the community. Under supervision, and following initial training, volunteers have the task of contacting the victim and offender, gaining their willingness to cooperate, and mediating their reconciliation and an agreement on restitution.

It was stated in an original project proposal that, consistent with recommendations of the Law Reform Commission of Canada, VORP is to serve as an alternative to the traditional criminal justice process: 'It is our feeling that in the criminal justice system there is a need to explore various alternatives in order to deal responsibly with victims and offenders as individuals . . . You are aware of the Law Reform Commission's work on "Restitution and Compensation" and on "Diversion". We agree with them that it should be the responsibility of the offender to the victim to make good the harm done.'[6]

Regarding the offender, the presumption was clear that the programme would be used as an alternative to jail. Such a goal was rooted in the belief that traditional ways of dealing with offenders are highly suspect. The goal was to 'rely on neither the punishment, nor the "rehabilitation" provided through the criminal justice system', and to avoid focus on 'change in individuals *per se*'.

Amongst other programme ideals, restitution itself is rarely emphasized. Payment without a victim/offender meeting is disfavoured, for restitution is important in so far as it assists in the attainment of other goals. What is considered important is reconciliation, returning the conflict to the victim and offender[7] so that they will 'accept each other as individuals with equal rights and responsibilities' and ultimately so that 'an imbalance in their relationship can be cured'.

Positive features of VORP are frequently conveyed to both the criminal justice community and the general public. These include the following: (1) VORP provides restitution to the victim; (2) it encourages the resolution of conflict and reconciliation; (3) it reduces trauma and anger in the victim by disclosing the real nature of the offender; (4) conversely it demonstrates to the offender the actual amount of harm; and (5) it provides a sanction which avoids the futility and expense of jail. It is this last advantage which is most often considered the hallmark of the programme.

THE 'WIDENING NET'

Past experience alone has become a compelling reason to doubt the propensity of the Victim/Offender Reconciliation Programme to serve as an alternative to imprisonment. A wide variety of attempts at criminal justice reform have resulted in failure.[8]

In the context of pre-trial diversion, Morris warned of the 'widening net' whereby diversion would ultimately result in more pervasive but less severe control over a substantially larger number of citizens.[9] While there is little evidence of less severity, greater pervasiveness would seem accurate. One author concluded that juveniles judged delinquent were under longer and closer surveillance than they would have been on regular probation, and, moreover, that it became the court's function to include whole families.[10] In his extensive study of a lower court system in Connecticut, Feeley found that pre-trial diversion programmes were an alternative to a fine at worst, and that one-fifth to one-third of the participants would have had their case dismissed had they chosen to go through the regular trial system.[11] In a critical evaluation of juvenile alternatives, similar findings led Rutherford and Benger to identify the 'shallow end principle'.[12] Instead of the programmes being directed towards offenders at the 'deep end' who would have gone to institutions, they are geared more towards minor and first offenders unlikely to have been incarcerated.

There is ample evidence that most post-trial community alternatives have also attached themselves to the widening net. Researchers have found both parole and mandatory supervision to be extensions of the surveillance of prisoners, and these options may actually increase the total time spent in prison.[13] Official statistics reveal that, since the emergence of probation in Canada, the number of suspended sentences has steadily declined and the use of probation has correspondingly increased at an even higher rate, indicating that it is an alternative among non-prison options.[14] In investigating whether the suspended sentence in England was relieving the strained capacity of prisons as intended, it was revealed that more non-violent offenders were receiving custodial sentences than before, and for longer periods of time.[15] It was concluded that the introduction of the suspended sentence may have had the ultimate effect of increasing the prison population by 25 to 30 per cent. In a study into the effect of community service orders in England, it was estimated that only one half of offenders in the programme would have otherwise been incarcerated.[16] In a wider study of the impact of community-based corrections in Saskatchewan it was found that the use of institutions has persistently increased rather than decreased, and that the total number of persons under supervision had tripled since the introduction of alternative programmes.[17]

It would seem that most community programmes risk becoming supplementary sanctions instead of alternative ones. Efforts in correctional reform seem invariably to result in greater punitiveness and more expansive social control. Critics have argued that, in addition to widening the net where a new set of offenders is drawn into correctional programmes, many community programmes are quite punitive and sometimes no more humane than prison.[18] In the case of VORP, the likelihood of fitting into this pattern is increased if one considers the observation of Cohen that the more benign and attractive a programme is, the more it is used and the wider it casts its net.[19]

It is difficult to be precise in explaining exact causes of the widening net phenomenon. The most widely used account stems from conflict theory. Within this orientation Boyd stated that, rather than provide offenders with special care, proponents of probation originally wanted to eradicate the 'undesirable life-style of the lowest classes'. Austin and Krisberg explained the widening net generally by pointing out contradictions in the political economy and ultimately recommended the reconstruction of society. Similarly, in Hylton's critical review of community corrections it is concluded that, to understand expanding control, 'the larger structural exigencies in advanced capitalist countries must be examined'. In developing his complex theory of punishment, Foucault also gave credence to the conflict perspective. He held that surveillance is the central function of correctional reform and that reform is part of the very programme of the penal apparatus.[20]

Despite the intuitive appeal to a conflict approach when dealing with the expansion of state control, certain assumptions have been challenged. Rather than dismiss the role of reformers and their humanitarian concerns, Rothman found their influence to be an important element in the evolution of corrections.[21] Ignatieff has argued against the assumed unity of a ruling class because his historical research suggests that rulers rarely thought and acted as a collective.[22] Further, Ignatieff contended that the state does not have a monopoly and that, more typically, social relations involving both conflict and compromise will define social change.

Ignatieff's recognition of conflict and interaction is fundamental to a different approach in explaining the widening net. From an organizational perspective, beyond the simple dictates of either humanitarian reformers or ruling elites, decisions in the criminal justice system are affected by its complex internal organization and by its relationship to the larger environment.

Feeley has found that lower courts are an aggregate of people pursuing different ends, and that the multiple individual interests work so that they counterbalance one another.[23] Discrediting the bureaucratic model posited by Blumberg,[24] Feeley argued that the courts are a decentralized, self-regulating system. Through his efforts to acquire a better understanding of how courts function, Feeley developed the 'pre-trial process model'. While it is true that the courts rarely achieve formal justice through a true adversarial setting, neither do they wholly neglect the need for justice. By plea bargaining and other methods of speedy adjudication, there can still be a thoughtful probing of facts and a satisfactory resolution to the interests of the several individuals involved. Though the system may seem chaotic and unreasonable to an outside observer, closer examination reveals a sense of logic to what occurs.

By focusing on competing interests, several researchers have provided a better understanding of the limited changes attained by different reform efforts. The transformation of new rules to fit within individual interests and the inertia of old practices has become a common motif.[25]

The research record suggests that profound changes are difficult to implement in the court system when they are not considered apposite by its members. Yet it has been demonstrated by the widening net phenomenon that change certainly can occur, even though it may not be in the direction originally intended by reformers. Rothman has documented a variety of instances in the Progressive Era where reform was made only to coincide with the interests of criminal control system administrators.[26]

POSSIBLE IMPEDIMENTS TO VORP

One external factor that may exert strong influence over the implementation of VORP is public attitudes. A recent nation-wide poll revealed that 63 per cent of Canadians believe that their local courts do not deal harshly enough with criminals and that the majority of Canadians rank crime as a major social issue.[27] This 'law-and-order syndrome' has been linked to the perception that the rate of violent crime is higher than is officially recognized[28] and also to economic uncertainty.[29]

This does not indicate that a programme such as VORP would be unpalatable to the public. Involvement of victims as a main component of the programme is undoubtedly a highly regarded feature, reflecting a current social trend to improve services to crime victims.[30] While strongly objecting to the use of alternatives to prison, the Canadian public (or agents of the court) might be content with the practice of placing minor offenders in VORP who would otherwise not have received a prison sentence or might be equally pleased with the practice of assigning VORP as an additional sentence for those offenders sent to jail.

Public attitudes in the present context, however, are only important in so far as they affect decision-making in the courts. Determination of whether public opinion could affect the implementation of VORP leads to consideration of the disposition and attitudes of the court members themselves. The sentencing outlook and practices of Canadian judges have been thoroughly studied by Hogarth.[31] He found that sentencing behaviour is mostly determined by a judge's own values on punishment, but that social constraints do exist. Public attitudes are important in the way that judges define them, and this is usually done in concordance with their own views. Thus, while the punitive expectations of the public will not independently determine the behaviour of the judge, Hogarth concluded that 'certain reality aspects of the social environment of a magistrate do penetrate his consciousness, resulting in a modification of his behaviour on the bench.'

There are indications that the views of judges are in concordance with public attitudes. It is expected that the 'crime control model' described by Packer is a salient ideal for most members of the court.[32] Moreover, Hogarth found that judges scored very high on his 'punishment corrects' scale. In his words: 'This factor was associated with the notion that offenders deserve and need punishment, in order to prevent them from committing further crime.' He added that costs to the offender are considered much less important than stopping crime, even if it means capital punishment. Therefore, because a strong belief in punishment prevails with most judges, and in view of substantial public support for harsher punishment, it can reasonably be expected that the use of community-based corrections will be restricted.

There are also a number of legal and practical issues surrounding VORP, further determining the manner in which members of the court will use the programme. Despite the strong appeal of having offenders provide restitution to their victims,[33] proposals generally fail to articulate with the traditional philosophy and procedures of the criminal court. It has been argued that there are legitimate reasons why the law has evolved to the point of ignoring the victim inasmuch as criminal offences are regarded as crimes against the state. Perhaps there are certain crimes that actually do threaten the social fabric and in which private interests are relatively unimportant. Klein has noted that this development of law was important to prevent conflicts from escalating into feuds, and that it afforded necessary protection to the offender where even a demand for restitution would spell disaster for himself and his family.[34] In contradistinction to the civil courts, the criminal court primarily developed to ensure that the offender received his just punishment.

This historic role of the law and criminal process suggests obstacles for VORP. As reported by Chasse in his review of legal problems in restitution, there is no established link between the purpose of criminal law and recompensing victims.[35] The absence of guiding principles and philosophical foundation, as witnessed through the limited number of clear statute laws and case decisions, is the essential barrier to admitting restitution into the criminal courts. While Chasse argues that it can still be in the interests of the state to see that the offender makes reparation to his victim, this can only be done by justification through traditional sentencing goals, ensuring that restitution has punishment and rehabilitative value for the offender. Such had been the concern in one important court decision where it was emphasized that restitution on a condition of probation was for the purpose of 'securing the good conduct of the offender.'[36]

There is fear that regular concessions to the victim will lead to partiality: 'So strongly is the public prosecutor's position as an impartial presenter of evidence insisted upon that many prosecutors argue that adopting a practice of regularly seeking restitution for the victim would raise a conflict of interest in the victim as a Crown witness, it would contradict the Crown prosecutor's position before the court, and it would derogate the appearance of justice.'[37] Where a victim's redress depends on a conviction, witnesses and the jury may become biased, and Crown counsel may be motivated to adduce evidence related to the loss but irrelevant to the offender's guilt. If a victim stands to gain from a conviction, he may be prompted to bring cases to court that he otherwise would not have and which bear little relation to criminal matters,[38] and he or trial witnesses may even be encouraged to alter their testimony.

Within the tradition of keeping the offender as the primary focus of attention, there is another concern that has been voiced by the courts. It was held in England and enacted in the Criminal Justice Act in 1972 that the court must be convinced of the ability of the offender to pay the amount ordered. It was felt that creating a debt far beyond what the offender could afford would tempt him into further crime. While similar requirements have not been legislated in Canada, it would appear that the courts share this concern. It has been stated that before an order of restitution can be placed on a probation order, the offender's means should be assessed, for a breach of probation is a serious matter in itself.[39] It has also been noted that failure to complete restitution might result in a jail term, and that this is equivalent to imprisonment for debt – a practice frowned upon in Canada and deemed unconstitutional in the United States.[40] Considering that many criminal offenders are either unemployed or working in low level occupations,[41] it could reasonably be anticipated that restitution will only be ordered in small amounts or not at all.

As stated previously, the criminal courts lack an adequate means for ascertaining the extent and worth of damages caused by offences. Serious questions of law and fact can arise, requiring careful and rule-guided investigation. Complex issues can arise out of the assignment of value to intangible losses; unclear legal title to goods; assignment of liability to cases involving multiple offenders and/or victims; and consideration of blameworthiness mitigated by victim culpability. Further, criminal court judges may be less aware than members of the civil court of the laws and procedures that pertain to these complexities. Nor, it is claimed, do the criminal courts have time to deal with sentencing sanctions that are less than expeditious, and it has been suggested that handling restitution in criminal courts will be more costly in the long run.[42]

These diverse issues will constrain court agents in using orders of restitution. This is suggested in Chasse's efforts to outline model legislation that would guide the courts in their decision-making.[43] Among four basic rules, he recommended that consideration for restitution be based only on the evidence already presented at trial, that the resolution of difficult issues be left to the civil courts, and that restitution be limited to small and tangible losses. The 1972 Criminal Justice Act in England had incorporated similar recommendations of an advisory council. Awards are limited to a maximum of £400 and subject to the following qualifications: the offender must have the means to pay; there must be no problems in assessing liability; and there can be no other sentencing considerations which are overriding.

These criteria are undoubtedly intended to give restitution a place without interfering with the criminal justice process. By keeping to small and straightforward amounts, the court is more able to maintain its central focus on the offender and give minimal attention to the losses of the victim. Ideally, this ensures that no one's interest in the outcome of the trial will change. Neither will the court place too great a burden on the offender, so that problems in enforcement can be minimized. Finally, considering only those losses that are easily ascertained obviates the apparent lack of expertise and other resources in the criminal court. Restitution sentences can then be issued as easily as other sentencing options.

At the same time, whether or not these guidelines for making restitution workable are made explicit, the potential use of restitution becomes clearer. First, the total number of cases eligible for restitution is more limited, potentially avoiding incarceration for fewer offenders than proponents of restitution may have expected. Secondly, it would seem that those offenders most ideally suited to receive a restitution order are also those less likely to be incarcerated. That is, the harm will be of relatively little value, directly attributable to one or two discrete events, and relatively unclouded by multiple unrelated incidents and victims, legal finery and problematic facts. The offender will also be perceived to have the means to pay back the damages. All of this suggests that those most likely to receive a restitution order would otherwise have been candidates for a suspended sentence or discharge, not a jail term.

In contrast to most restitution programmes, one benefit offered by VORP is that less concern needs to go to the offender's ability to pay. According to the ideals of the programme, restitution is more important in what it can achieve than in the actual amount. Thus, restitution can consist of partial payment, personal service to the community, or a mere apology, as long as reconciliation has occurred. Also, where monetary restitution is made, negotiation with the victim and supervision by the mediator should produce an amount and terms of payment that are realistically suited to the offender's financial situation.

For the same reason, there is a better environment for forwarding cases that are less clear in the amount of damages that should be paid. With both parties there to represent their own side in the presence of an impartial mediator, combined with the de-emphasis on restitution *per se*, VORP may be very suitable for complex cases involving intangible losses, multiple offenders or victim culpability.

Conversely, this flexibility may also be viewed as an undesirable aspect of the programme. By leaving the amount of restitution to be determined by VORP, the judge may actually be abdicating his sentencing responsibility. To this effect, it has been held by the British Columbia Court of Appeal that where restitution is left to the complete discretion of a probation officer the judge is improperly delegating his powers. While VORP clearly would not be operating if this ruling were strictly followed, it does suggest that the court might wish to reduce the freedom of the VORP parties in choosing an amount. Judges may curb discretion by ordering, for example, that all medical bills be paid, or that restitution not go over or under certain amounts. This would again restrict the type of cases forwarded to VORP because a judge would have greater difficulty in finding ways to limit discretion in cases that are complex and give no immediate indication of the approximate damage.

It is possible that an actual confrontation between the offender and victim will be construed as being highly conducive to rehabilitation. It may also be seen as a punitive measure, for restitution costs are supplemented by the offender having to face his angered victim. However, this victim/offender meeting may also deter the referral of several types of cases. According to the circumstances of a case, the court may decide that too much animosity exists on the part of either or both sides. Perhaps the parties will not be expected to agree to meet, or it could be predicted that further conflict will ensue out of a face-to-face meeting, perhaps leading to another offence. This might be based on the type of offence, the previous relationship between the parties, or the actual worth of the harm committed. In addition, certain 'undesirable' characteristics of the offender may dissuade the court from asking him to meet his victim. For example, the VORP workers themselves have requested that only offenders who have 'some limited verbal skills' be referred. Again, this increases the likelihood that cases selectively chosen as workable will not involve offenders bound for prison.

In sum, there are a variety of possible constraints that will prevent the Victim/Offender Reconciliation Programme from becoming an alternative to prison. The intentions of correctional reformers and the availability of a new sentencing alternative are two of the operational realities that bear on courtroom decision-making. In recognition of the courtroom as a complex organization, the implementation of VORP will most likely be determined by public expectations, the personality and attitudes of members of the court, administrative convenience, traditional practice and legal requirements. While many of these influences are expected to become impediments because of previous experience with simple restitution, additional impediments in VORP have been considered.

SOME RESEARCH FINDINGS

Over a five-month period, approximately twenty days were intermittently spent in a VORP office, learning of the programme through extensive discussion with the coordinator and full-time volunteer assistant, collecting data from all cases that went through the programme from April to November 1980, and observing activity in the office. Outside the office, structured interviews were conducted with judges, probation officers and prosecutors.

April 1980 was chosen as the beginning of the period for study because a new VORP filing system had begun at that time, making relevant case information more accessible. The VORP staff could not specify any changes in policy or practice that would make the resultant sample of forty-seven cases unrepresentative of the programme. Some rudimentary information was further collected from a Victim/Offender Reconciliation Programme in another Ontario city; this programme was less than a year old and could not profitably be studied to the same extent as the original programme.

Of the 47 cases which had entered the VORP office within the study period, two were deleted from the study because no activity had ever begun and information was inaccessible. The offender in one case had been jailed on a new offence before contact with VORP was made, and another offender had been charged with breach of probation because he refused to cooperate in making contact with a VORP worker. In the remainder of the cases, items of information were sometimes unavailable because either offender payments were still being made, no negotiated settlement had been obtained yet, or a victim/offender meeting was yet to be arranged. Altogether 51 offenders were involved in the programme; six cases involved two offenders. The majority (44) were male, and the average age was 22 years, ranging from 16 to 50. Information on the employment status of offenders at the time of trial was not always available, but in cases where it was available, 21 were employed and 16 were not, indicating that employment was not considered essential for admittance to the programme.

Almost one third of the offenders had been convicted of at least one criminal offence before the conviction that led to VORP. Six offenders had one prior offence, two had two, and eight had more than two. While information on the specific type of offences could not be ascertained, all but one of the offences were indictable. Hence, though it is clear that two-thirds of the offenders in VORP had no past convictions and that this is one indicator that offenders would not have been likely to receive a jail sentence, it is also clear that repeat offenders with serious convictions were being admitted to the programme. Most of the cases involved property crime, namely break-and-enter and/or theft. The average number of offences per offender was 4.5.

One hundred and fifty-nine victims were tallied across all cases, but three cases accounted for over half (54 per cent) of the victimizations and two-thirds of the cases involved one victim. Eighteen of the victims had received at least partial recovery from insurance (13 per cent), and 121 (76 per cent) had no insurance pertinent to their losses. Two-thirds of the victims were business establishments, not individuals.[44] Most were small commercial businesses with one or two proprietors, and in only 5 per cent of the total number could the victims be appropriately identified as corporate (e.g. telephone company, City Works Department, and the Unemployment Insurance Commission). Considering the nature of the victim and the offence, in 85 per cent of the cases offenders had no relationship with their victims prior to the offence.

Investigation of the terms of the sentences, with the exception of two cases which were referred to VORP at a pre-sentence stage, revealed that all referrals were ultimately made through a probation order. Of the 49 probation orders, 57 per cent stated that restitution was to be made specifically through VORP and 39 per cent stipulated that restitution was to be made in an amount determined with the victim and the probation officer. In one case that went through VORP the order included a specific amount of restitution, and in another the order made no mention of restitution. In the 47 cases that either directed the offender to VORP or simply required unspecified restitution through a probation officer, negotiations were sometimes restricted by the imposition of a maximum amount. In 15 probation orders (31 per cent) the judge ordered restitution 'not to exceed the amount of x dollars.'

The average length of probation was 16 months, either through a suspended sentence or through conditional discharge. In 20 cases (43 per cent) offenders received an additional sentence on one of their convictions: 11 received a community service order averaging 100 hours; six received an average fine of $188; and five received jail terms, which averaged 72 days. Two offenders received combinations of these sentences.

Most of the management of cases was shared by the VORP coordinator and a full-time assistant. Volunteers were given charge in only 31 per cent of the cases, but in another 15 per cent volunteers worked with the VORP staff and handled certain aspects of the cases. Regarding actual victim/offender contact, 11 cases were still in the early stage and it was not known whether contact would be made. There was victim/offender contact in 18 cases. In 16 there was no meeting: in two the victim could not be located; in five the offender would not agree to meet; in six the victim refused to meet; in one neither agreed to meet; and in two there was no attempt to set up a meeting. Of the 12 cases in which one or both of the parties refused to meet, a restitution amount was nevertheless determined in seven, and in three the matter was still in progress. Only one case was referred back to court because of failure to reach an agreement.

In 29 cases where a restitution amount was settled upon, at the point of study, total payment to be made was $12,958. Amounts ranged from nothing to $4,000, and the average payment per offender was $462. Owing to the complexity of determining losses and because of a major tenet of VORP that full monetary restitution is not always necessary, these figures cannot be used to reflect actual loss. One case was settled with an apology and two by a small donation to a charity. Insurance companies were also to be reimbursed in nine cases (20 per cent). In three cases this was stipulated by the judge in the probation order. A meeting between the offender and a representative of an insurance company had been arranged in four cases.

A number of issues can be raised and inferences drawn in respect to attaining the original VORP goals. Considering first the ideal of reconciliation and the resolution of conflict, it would seem that a narrow definition of conflict has been used. Crimes involving a pre-existing relationship were rare, and the offence was typically an impersonal violation against the property of a small business. However, it must be stressed that reconciliation as earlier defined by the programme innovators was never studied, and it is not known whether something was achieved in this direction.

Restitution was only important in so far as it is a tool conducive to reconciliation. However, a significant amount of money was usually to be paid by the offender (only three offenders escaped payment to victims), and the alternative of personal service was never once realized. Frequently, there was no victim/offender meeting throughout the process. Most significantly, one in five cases studied required the reimbursement of insurance companies. It is clear that insurance companies can only be described as indirect victims, and that a financial settlement is the main cause for negotiations in these instances. Taken together, these findings suggest that restitution is a basic feature of VORP, and that actual reconciliation has been given a lesser role.

Lastly, there is the important question of whether VORP is serving as an alternative to jail. The typical offender is a young male who committed crime in a single instance against the property of a commercial establishment, suggesting the conclusion that most VORP participants would not have gone to jail. However, there were some serious crimes, including assault, and, most important, one third of all the offenders had a past criminal record. Even though there were cases where more serious penalties were given in conjunction with VORP (including five sentences of imprisonment!), inability to correlate these important variables prevents discovery of their relationship. Without more information, it was impossible to determine whether the programme was properly serving as an alternative to incarceration. Hence, interviewing the central members involved in administering VORP became essential.

VORP staff

Through discussion with the coordinator and the assistant in the office of VORP, more detail was obtained on the actual procedure of the programme and some of the operational contingencies. In studying the management practices of the VORP staff, it must be understood that the programme is essentially reactive, for control over the intake of cases is often limited to the ability to persuade the court members who make referrals. However, the staff are not totally confined, for once a case has been assigned to them there are various manipulative techniques for conforming case management to their own interests. Despite some of the barriers that may have been encountered in the programme, the same basic ideals were held for VORP since its inception. The coordinator maintained that the ultimate purpose of the programme was still maintained to be reconciliation between the victim and offender, not simply restitution: 'Reconciliation is something which you can't engineer the same way as a writing of a contract, but I think philosophically it is a very important concept to have in mind that what we're doing is not just being bill collectors.'

As opposed to traditional methods of dealing with the offender and victim, the idea is to return the conflict to its rightful owners and allow the restoration of balance in the relationship. The assistant equally stressed that it was the 'concept' of the programme that was important and strongly resented judgments of the programme based on dollar amounts placed in the hands of the victims.

When a case is initially received in the VORP office, the first step is to enlist the willing participation of the offender. It had been stated in the programme design to be a prerequisite of the programme, yet second reflection would question the amount of real freedom that an offender might have in refusing a sentence proposed by the court. This became evident when reading some of the probation orders. For example, one order read: 'Report to a Probation Officer as required and through that Probation Officer and VORP you will make contact with the victim and you will arrive at some arrangement as to what has been stolen and what has been returned or what amount of money or restitution is needed and that will be done immediately.' Yet, despite such signs of coercion, it was seen in the data that six out of 51 offenders actually did opt out of a meeting with their victim. When queried on this point, the coordinator and the assistant independently replied that as long as a case was referred to VORP, the policy and guidelines of VORP would be followed. It was explained that there was no intention of countermanding the wishes of a judge, but that this was a basic tenet of the programme. Hence, there is opportunity for the offender to decline actual contact with the victim.

On the other hand, the VORP staff do have an interest in seeing that some victim/offender contact is made. Accompanying a programme brochure, an introductory letter sent to the offender is often likely to contain the specific order of the judge and convey the message that his participation in a meeting is a legal requirement. When asked whether he felt this was not coercive, the coordinator replied: 'I think there's certainly some coercion there. I don't doubt that at all, and yet at what point does that become a negative? . . . I know one guy where the thought of meeting the victim is scary and if he thought he would avoid that he would, but he doesn't feel that it's unfair . . . If that's what's behind it, then I'm not as concerned as if he's really resisting. If he's saying "look, I don't owe this bastard a penny," and then to meet him, somehow that's different for me.' In other words, the coordinator perceives degrees of voluntariness, and a lack of full voluntariness does not necessarily affect the end result to be achieved by a meeting.

A second step is to gain the participation of the victim. It has been found elsewhere that victims typically do not want to meet offenders,[45] and in the early formation of the VORP programme this is exactly what the staff reported to have found. This initial poor response rate was eventually eliminated by a polishing of technique. Before the victim is approached verbally, he is given an introductory letter with a brochure which describes the programme. The letter is generally assertive, paraphrasing the order of the judge that restitution is to be made to the victim, and saying that a staff member will soon be contacting him to arrange a meeting. There is no indication that victims may freely choose not to participate. One can surmise that victims often feel strongly committed by this approach.

A second aspect is also informative in the light of personal interests. The VORP workers' interest in seeing the victim participate in their programme is accomplished by emphasizing the main interest of the victim, restitution. Hence, in the training manual for VORP volunteers it is explicitly stated that the word 'reconciliation' is never to be used in gaining the support of the victim and that a discussion and payment of losses are given as the essential reasons for a meeting. While again this practice relates to the successful functioning of the programme, conflicting goals become apparent. On one side the primary goal is reconciliation, and on the other the need to meet the victim's expectation that his losses will be repaid. By their own admission, the coordinator and the assistant claim that the victim is often led to expect too much, more than the offender can afford and should be expected to pay. Because of their unclear vision of the purpose of VORP, victims naturally expect and push for full reimbursement for their losses. This competing interest may account for the observation that cases rarely resulted in token restitution through verbal apologies or personal service and instead resulted in average payment agreements over $450.

In cases where a meeting cannot be arranged because of objections on the part of either the victim or the offender, the VORP staff maintain their interest in reconciliation and reject the image of 'bill collectors'. Even though a meeting cannot be arranged, a restitution settlement is still sought and the liaison work through letters, telephone calls and individual meetings is still believed to be a step towards reconciliation. The coordinator described this as 'shuttle diplomacy'.

As argued earlier, VORP may present an advantage over ordinary restitution in that it presents a forum for assessing losses that are often unclear and complex. However, observation of cases and discussion with staff suggested that this benefit was not being fully realized. The staff did not investigate the facts themselves and relied heavily on the damages reported at trial and contained in the police report. In one observed case, an offender was driving around the countryside with a volunteer, agreeably repaying a long list of farmers for the damage he had done to their mail boxes. At one point in the list, the location of a farm was clearly unknown to the offender, and when they found it he stated that he had never damaged that particular mail box. Although they apparently believed the offender's story, the VORP staff insisted that he pay. They expressed regret and awkwardness about making this requirement, but they work under the presumption that the conviction of the offender is proof of both the crime and the damages disclosed during the trial.

A similar practice is found in the way the programme deals with multiple offenders. Cases were noted in which damages were caused by more than one offender, but they were handled as though the offender within the programme was solely responsible for all damages. At times this was a specific order of the judge, and often the VORP staff would make efforts to involve other convicted offenders before arranging settlement. However, they stated that they frequently decide to push towards full payment by a single offender. They readily justified this by referring to the legal practice of holding offenders 'jointly and severally' liable for all damage resulting from the commission of a crime.

These practices were not entrenched in previous policy decisions, nor in most cases were they overtly demanded by members of the court. Further, placing full and unquestioned liability on offenders in the programme would seem to detract from the goal of reconciliation and increase emphasis on compensation of the victim. One possible explanation for this is that it relieves the burden of investigation and expedites the processing of cases, reflecting the push towards administrative convenience. Secondly, as in studies cited previously which demonstrate the inertia of old practices and conservative boundaries to change, there is perhaps a desire to remain close to the old system of justice. As exemplified in the workers' reiteration of the law on joint and several liability, there is an unquestioned acceptance of the process that originally brought the case to the VORP office, and to delve heavily into facts is perceived as an implicit challenge to that traditional system.

There are other routine functions of the programme that appear to clash with original goals, but they more clearly reflect pressures from the surrounding environment. It was seen that several cases involved payment to insurance companies, sometimes under the order of judges. Reasons why the VORP staff are reluctant to deal with them are fairly evident, and in fact the staff claim they do not go out of their way to do so: 'If you have a multi-million dollar insurance company sitting down to negotiate with a 16-year-old unemployed offender, it's not negotiation. They are very unequal . . . It's also less personal and becomes a bureaucratic thing . . . Reconciliation becomes academic and it's strictly business.' There is also the personal feeling of the coordinator that insurance companies 'are professional victims and make their livelihood from the public's concern for becoming victims.'

The VORP staff nevertheless include insurance companies in the programme, and not only because of orders from the courtroom. It seems that VORP has become popular with insurance agents and they often make contact with the office once they learn that an offender has been referred who is responsible for the policy claims of their client. It was noted by the coordinator that this puts them into quick contact with the offender – whereas offenders are sometimes not easily located – and that it spares the companies the costs of civil litigation when they can arrange a restitution settlement through VORP. However, this pressuring interest is not totally foreign to the interests of others in the programme. The coordinator explained that where most companies would sue for costs anyway, VORP can save the offender court costs and is also more likely to strike a compromise on the actual losses to be reimbursed.

It was felt that VORP is often not used as an alternative to jail. However, this problem was not viewed as too significant because the coordinator felt that, with time and a much greater range of community sentence options, jails will simply become unnecessary. As compensation for the fact that VORP may not always be an alternative, and also as a reward for completing the assigned task, the coordinator claims that he often lays the offender's probation file dormant and encourages him to apply for an early termination.

Another problem in the nature of referred cases raised more concern among VORP staff members. A virtue of the programme was to be the fact that it allowed a new way of dealing with the offender by treating him as responsible and assigning him a constructive task. While a moderate fine or community service order are not incompatible with this, substantial penalties are sometimes added to the VORP order, including many days' imprisonment. The staff believe that this directly contradicts the philosophy of their programme. Further, it is reported to be operationally difficult for them because the offender often feels that he has already paid his debt, and this usually affects the level of his participation.

Judges

It is well understood that Canadian judges practise a wide degree of sentencing discretion.[46] As a decentralized system, the court lacks an administrative structure for institutional direction in sentencing, leaving judicial authority only roughly curbed by parliamentary acts and appeal decisions. Compounding the situation with VORP, the programme has not been given any direction by either of these sources. Hence the manner in which VORP is used will potentially be determined by a wide scope of variable interests on the part of judges.

When the judges were asked what they considered to be the major purpose and merits of VORP, most offered the same concepts. Notable was the fact that reconciliation *per se* was rarely brought into the conversation. Undoubtedly this is partly because reconciliation is a nebulous concept, and 'mutual exposure' seemed to be a preferred concept which addressed the actual relationship between the victim and offender. That is, a victim/offender meeting discloses to the offender the actual extent of harm caused to the victim, and conversely it shows the victim that the offender is not as he may have been imagined. Four of the six judges reiterated variations of this basic theme. For example, 'The meeting takes place, and all of a sudden the householder sees not a big, slavering psychotic, but some skinny 17-year-old kid who is probably a neighbour's kid down the block. All of a sudden all the feelings of fear and trauma are gone.'

These ideas were used to express the main benefit that is to be obtained from a face-to-face meeting. However, there was never mention of resolving conflict, and a strong implication throughout most of the interviews was that a victim/offender meeting would do little to affect the actual relationship. Considering that the programme usually involves impersonal property offences, it is more realistic to downplay interpersonal conflict and its resolution. At the same time, it is reasonable to expect that lack of interest in VORP's ability to solve conflict has significantly affected the types of cases that are referred.

Whether because it increased the involvement of the victim in the justice system, saved costs to society, or gave the victim what was owed to him, every one of the judges gave strong endorsement to VORP because of what it did for the victim. While concern for the victim may be part of a developing trend, there was some suggestion that VORP allows expression to an interest that has existed for some time.

> *Question*: How do you reconcile earlier court decisions that restitution to the victim is to be restricted?
> *Response*: 'I don't reconcile that. I just think that it's an attitude that has prevailed for many, many years and is certainly subject to change – it's not written in the tablets. In fact, I would like our society to become a victim-oriented society, looking more to the effects on the victim than concern for the rights, comfort and welfare of the accused . . .'

Concern for the victim did not mean that judges were not cognizant of certain limitations. One of them noted the possibility that restitution might prejudice the accused if overused, and another emphasized that the criminal justice system was not well-suited to assessing losses. While none of the judges objected to assigning VORP through a probation order, four expressed the need for better justification of restitution through new legislation. In response to an open question on legal issues, five of the six expressed concern over the ability of the offender to pay, and two were able to cite case-law in this regard. There were a number of unemployed offenders in VORP; three judges gave offender unemployment as the reason for imposing a maximum amount of restitution to be negotiated, thereby limiting what the offender would be required to pay. Confirming that VORP is not to be used for assessing unclear losses, two judges claimed to use a police estimate as the maximum amount when the victim's loss was vague and unsubstantiated:

> Unless the damage has been repaired and there's a bill in the Crown's file and he tells me, then I'll assess it at that amount, but if he tells me it's an estimate, then I say 'not to exceed'.

> Usually when we make restitution orders, we make them with rather specific figures in mind . . . I think what you're saying is that no damages have been proved here . . . and I'm expecting that if the offender takes the position that there was not that much loss, then the role of the Victim/Offender Reconciliation Programme is going to be to resolve that difference.

One judge stated that maximum figures were used to avoid improper delegation of sentencing authority.

Most of the judges maintained that traditional sentencing functions were being met by VORP. Two were sceptical about rehabilitation and deterrence generally, but five stressed its punitive aspect. Judges often noted the hardship that restitution can cause offenders, and they sometimes spoke of the humiliation resulting from a confrontation with the victim. Two judges felt that jails are not punitive enough, and that sentencing alternatives would be unnecessary if they were. This indicates that VORP may still be used as an alternative to jail, though for different reasons than reformers may have originally intended. It also suggests, as found in the data, that other sentencing dispositions will simultaneously be used, sometimes including jail.

This concern for punishment appeared to be only indirectly connected to the opinion of the public. One judge candidly explained that the public need for punishment and incapacitation were the only real justifications for punishment, and that judges who believe otherwise 'are only fooling themselves'. The extent to which public attitudes influenced his or other judges' use of VORP is not known. However, three judges perceived negative public attitudes towards the programme and believe that people fail to appreciate how onerous restitution can be to an offender.

In their focus on the ideal sort of offender for VORP, ability to pay was again said to be a concern, as well as the fact that he not be a committed offender. Reference was frequently made to young offenders without a record or with only a minor record. Sometimes more abstract qualities were looked for in the offender, such as an attitude of remorse, or 'proper motivation and intention', though the judges claimed to depend largely on other members of the court for this information.

> You've got to choose your people; this doesn't apply to every person. First of all, basically your dyed-in-the-wool, long-term, long-record criminal isn't an ideal situation unless you're absolutely satisfied that he's done an about-face and is rehabilitated. Really it's for your first offenders, primarily your young offenders because we're getting more young offenders in the system than we used to get. It has to be a person you assessed and feel they'll benefit from it . . . I suppose I might get ten per cent reported back that don't pay the fine. If you're only getting that then 90 per cent or 85 per cent success rate is pretty good, so you certainly have to have a feel for it.

In conjunction with the profile of typical VORP cases as outlined earlier, the judges' selection criteria for VORP strongly decrease the likelihood of the programme being directed towards offenders who would have otherwise gone to jail. This was confirmed by the explicit question, 'Do you think that VORP is a viable alternative to jail?' In three interviews, the judge replied that it was not:

> I have never thought of restitution as an alternative.

> It's not an alternative to jail . . . less than two per cent of the people I send to jail haven't had three, four or five convictions. I don't think whether VORP is there or not that it's going to change that pattern.

> The CSO [Community Service Order] is supposed to be more so than the restitution aspect . . . VORP is usually for a young offender that you're not going to send to jail and you think there is a possibility of rehabilitation. He's probably going to be alright and will work it and will make enough money to pay it.

The remaining three judges felt that VORP was an alternative to jail, at least at certain times. For example, one judge who sometimes used VORP as an alternative to jail was asked why it was not always an alternative. He replied:

> Not any program that has been brought out as an alternative to jail has lowered the jail population . . . [for example] the suspended sentence; sometimes we went so far as to dismiss a case because we didn't want to impose the penalty of a fine or jail, or there was a technical guilt and it seemed just not to merit that kind of punishment. So we never dismissed a case after that because it wasn't really a basic, honest dismissal of a case; it was just the practical thing to do . . . Then we were off the hook and used suspended sentences and we used them more and more in the community when we might have just given a nominal fine. But it didn't lower the jail population . . . Then we get discharges, and we give discharges to people where we might have suspended sentence without any terms.

An interest which separates judges from the VORP innovators is a greater desire to punish the offender than to reconcile him with his victim, and this may account for some of the problems in the programme that seem to impede conditions for reconciliation: lack of concern for voluntariness, repayment to insurance companies, the assignment of single offenders from multiple offender cases and the frequent use of additional punishments. Emphasizing the punitive aspect of the programme hinders reconciliation, and, as in the argument against setting rehabilitative goals within prison, it may be conceptually wrong to expect both constructive change and punishment to be achieved in the same setting. Moreover, motives to punish can be used to explain the fact that VORP is generally not perceived as an alternative to jail.

The judges were also interested in practicality and hoped to ensure that cases referred were smoothly operable. They were often unwilling to entrust to the programme cases involving complex and unclear losses and wished to avoid cases where offenders might need to perform personal service. Assault cases and cases involving prior relationships were avoided because of the potential for conflict in the meeting, and offenders who were 'young, responsible, and non-committed to crime' were often chosen as ideal candidates. As suggested earlier, selection criteria for workable cases go against the use of VORP as an alternative to prison and further explain the fact that judges generally claim not to use it as such.

Crown attorneys

While judges have final sentencing authority, prosecutors' suggestions for sentencing are taken into consideration. Two judges stated that in deciding whether to use VORP they relied heavily on the Crown attorney because prosecutors inevitably have information on all aspects of the case.

Many of the answers given to the interview questions by Crown attorneys were generally similar to those of the judges, though different emphasis was given to varying attributes of the programme. Again, 'mutual exposure' between victim and offender leading to a breaking down of fears and stereotypes was seen as a purpose of the programme. Actual reconciliation between victim and offender was a purpose acknowledged by only one of the six Crown attorneys. While judges considered VORP's benefits to victims to be important, Crown attorneys were more likely to see them as the primary advantage of the programme and focused their attention on this aspect repeatedly. They commonly stressed the need for greater involvement of the victim in the trial process and emphasized the victim's need to be compensated. One Crown attorney informed the interviewer that this was the essential function intended by the VORP innovators and that any positive results for the offender have always been secondary achievements. Another explained that the victim's interests are a central concern in the criminal process: 'A lot of times I'll say to a victim "Look, what are you looking for in this case? Do you want to see this guy go to jail?" A husband and wife normally say, "No, I don't want to see him go to jail, I want him to get assistance for a drinking problem . . ." So, you're getting input from the victim all the time.'

It is understandable that prosecutors should have considerable interest in victims because of their organizational function. Though police are heavily depended upon in criminal investigations,[47] Crown attorneys learn of the harm done to victims, whom they may often need to contact in the course of their own enquiries, perhaps for the purpose of testimony. It is not formally the prosecutor's role to represent victims, but, as one prosecutor noted, there is no one else to speak on their behalf. Along with the police, Crown attorneys are likely to be sympathetic to victims, having studied the losses and witnessed the aftermath of trauma and anger. In addition, through their contact with victims Crown attorneys, perhaps more than other court members, will become sensitized to relevant deficiencies in the court system. They are more likely to see the neglect of victims through their inability to participate in the trial and through the extent of losses which they must bear alone.[48] As contact persons representing the court, Crown attorneys may sometimes be called upon by victims to justify this neglect. It would thus be germane to the interest of Crown attorneys to support VORP because of what it can do for victims.

Crown attorneys asserted even more strongly than judges that VORP is not a viable alternative to jail. Only one out of six answered that it was an alternative in certain cases. The reluctance of the others to accept the programme as suitable alternative did not appear to relate to public demands; views on the status and importance of public attitudes towards VORP were varied. Four Crown attorneys maintained that rehabilitation was being achieved by the programme, thereby satisfying a traditional sentencing concern. However, in contradistinction to the viewpoint of judges, no Crown attorney attributed any punitive aspects to the programme. Rather, a strong and consistent outlook prevailing within the group was that VORP serves some good purposes but that it is necessary to look towards other sentences to satisfy the need for punishment.

> No, I don't think you can simply take a view that I paid a person off, therefore I bought my way out of jail . . . Secondly, the offence is one which is not simply committed against another individual, it is against the whole grain of society.

> No. I think VORP really is somebody putting the victim back where he should have been, which is what the accused should have to do legally, morally and everything else. If he did something to the victim, he should put the victim back in the same position he was in beforehand. I think in addition to that, if it's something that is serious, I don't see that getting involved in compensating the victim is a penalty.

Crown attorneys have readily accepted the notion that offenders have a debt to their victim, but this does not exclude the traditional 'debt to society'. Consistent with an earlier hypothesis, the programme can be favoured for certain features while others are rejected. With the availability of VORP, the offender can now be made to pay two debts, each requiring a different sentence. This fulfils the interest of Crown attorneys in better tending the needs of victims, and it further answers their apparent interest in seeing that the offender is sufficiently penalized for his crime, VORP alone being insufficient.

Crown attorneys believed that the ability of the offender to pay was unimportant, recognizing the programme's purported flexibility in allowing personal service and also believing that offenders can be encouraged to find jobs. Three of the six felt that VORP was good for unclear, though tangible, losses. Unlike those judges who imposed an exact maximum amount when the police estimate was unclear, they felt that open negotiations would allow settlement on the actual amount of damage. The basis for these beliefs in the wide applicability of VORP is not clear, but perhaps serious concern for the welfare of victims leads to greater tolerance of cases that may be less convenient administratively.

Probation officers

Interviews with probation officers were conducted in less detail under the presumption that they have less involvement than the other groups in the operation of VORP. All probation orders that require VORP or an unspecified amount of restitution are automatically transferred to the VORP office, and probation officers rarely forward cases that do not contain an order of restitution or specify an exact amount. The main discretion of the probation officer that can affect the programme is practised through the pre-sentence report. Though it is not known how frequently judges request a report when considering VORP, all the probation officers claimed that they do recommend the programme.[49]

A pivotal factor in understanding the views of the area probation officers is the realization that most of them had been in central contact with the programme in the past. Up to one year before the study, VORP had been administered out of the area probation office. Before it became segregated and delegated into the hands of a few staff, many probation officers would initiate and mediate victim/offender meetings of their own, and they often contributed in various ways to the overall development of the programme. Hence probation officers are much more aware of the original tenets and objectives of VORP.

The perceived purpose of reconciliation, as originally defined by the programme innovators, was one element which separated probation officers from judges and prosecutors. The theme of 'mutual exposure' was mentioned, but the officers frequently spoke in greater detail about what the victim/offender meeting could achieve. For instance, it was said that the programme was to compensate for the adversary system which pulls people apart, and to 'settle their minds at ease'. Like the VORP literature, three of the nine officers explicitly downplayed the importance of money, claiming that restitution was only to lead to other objectives. While they also endorsed the programme for its treatment of victims, they stressed its rehabilitative effect on the offender through the opportunity to 'purge his guilt' and the 'cathartic experience' gained from confrontation and compensation.

The probation officers were also more likely to see wider possibilities for the programme beyond straightforward property offences. With reconciliation and not restitution as the central ingredient, the problem of unclear losses was considered less important. Five officers felt that minor assault cases could be handled in meaningful ways. However, great emphasis was usually placed on the suitability of the offender for the programme. Confidence in its ability to distinguish the types of offenders who will prevent the programme from operating successfully could reasonably be expected of a profession that is ostensibly directed towards individual treatment and control.

The last factor which distinguished the probation officers from the other groups was their belief that VORP is a viable alternative to jail. Eight of the nine officers were confident that it was often a good sentence for the offender who normally receives a term of imprisonment:

> I do think that it's a viable alternative and this is one area where we ought to do a little more education because people still have the idea that probation is not a sentence, that he's gotten off easy, and sometimes probation is a lot harder than a short time in jail. I think the same thing goes for VORP.

> I like to see it used when the judge is considering jail . . . I definitely have had cases where the judge gave them the VORP programme, and had the programme not been running, they would have gone to jail.

The officer last quoted estimated that 60 to 75 per cent of the VORP offenders would have been imprisoned had the programme not existed.

A possible explanation for this difference in attitudes is that the probation officers' relative distance from most court activity prevents them from drawing an accurate picture of the types of cases that normally result in a jail sentence and those in which other sentence dispositions are used. Thus, concluding that VORP is an alternative to imprisonment may be based more on their own interests and also on the original objectives of the programme. Relating to their strong interests in rehabilitation and reconciliation as opposed to punishment, Hogarth found that probation officers scored significantly lower than judges in tests measuring beliefs that offenders need and deserve punishment.[50] Because of their differing objectives for the treatment of offenders, it is plausible that probation officers would have more of an interest in implementing successful alternatives to incarceration.

VORP in a second city

VORP had only been in progress in the second city of study for about a year, and fewer than twenty cases had been processed through it. The coordinator is a probation officer who conducts all VORP activity alone, in addition to his regular duties. He had assumed responsibility for setting up and administering the programme after the Ontario Ministry of Correctional Services had directed his area office to be one of many to implement a VORP programme. He volunteered to take charge because he had heard of the programme previously and he particularly favoured the idea of victim compensation, which he viewed as the major purpose of VORP.

When asked about other benefits of the programme, he expressed the view that it made probation more purposeful in that it provided the offender with a concrete and constructive task, and for this reason he attempts to terminate the probation order when restitution is complete. However, he is very doubtful that it leads to any positive change in the offender, nor does he feel that a victim/offender meeting will result in the resolution of conflict or affect their relationship in other ways: 'I'm hesitant to say that. I think that just superficially if the victim and offender meet and an agreement has been reached, and the offender fulfils the agreement, there has to be some reconciliation. If you just view the offence as a problem created financially for the victim, in that way I think it's safe to say that the problem has been reconciled, but I'm hesitant to get into the relationship business.' When asked whether the programme has any advantages over standard restitution made through a court clerk, he replied that a meeting between the victim and the offender leads to a more accurate estimate of damages. He also added that when cases are chosen carefully, there is sometimes a breakdown of mutual stereotypes.

In answer to what he considers to be the ideal case to go through the programme, he did not conceal his preference for cases which were administratively convenient. He prefers '16 to 20-year-old middle-class kids who maybe did something minor'. He further added that the victim should be 20 to 25 years old because he has found that older and more established people tend to be more set in their views against offenders. He claimed that when designing the programme he was also insistent that the offender have no history of violence, but this was originally done to gain the acceptability of the programme and he stated that he may alter that precondition. In an earlier memorandum circulated to all area probation officers, his programme criteria closely approximated his perceptions of an ideal case:

(a) *Type of Offences*: Theft, break and enter, property damage and fraud.

(b) *Type of Victim*: Victim must be clearly identifiable and will generally be an individual person or persons. Small family type businesses might also be considered.

(c) *Type of Offender*: Criteria here are primarily that there be no violence in the current offence and no past history of violence by the offender. Offenders with prior record may be considered, but not *confirmed criminals*. Offender should be employed or have a satisfactory work record. In the case of a student, the potential for satisfactorily carrying out the agreement (i.e. ability to secure part-time employment or perform certain tasks). (Italics in original.)

As implied by these criteria, the coordinator does not intend that VORP serve as an alternative to incarceration, and he conjectured that none of the offenders going through his programme would have otherwise gone to jail: 'I don't view it as an alternative to jail. I think that the community service order programme is an alternative to jail but the programme here has certainly not been designed as an alternative to incarceration.

In view of the amount of outside influence found in the original VORP programme, it is doubtful that the orientation of the coordinator wholly determines the way the programme operates. However, it would be reasonable to assume that the courtroom using this programme is an organizational environment similar to that of the first programme and would lead to broadly similar interests. Without endorsement of the original programme ideals by the only VORP administrator, it is unlikely that anyone else would attempt to preserve them. It is safe to conclude from this brief investigation that extending a reformative programme outside the reach of its innovators creates an even smaller likelihood that the programme's objectives will be met.

SUMMARY AND CONCLUSION

According to the original programme ideals, VORP was to provide a new sentencing alternative which would allow the offender to pay for his crime by a method more constructive than imprisonment. The victim would also gain, becoming more involved in the criminal justive process and further obtaining compensation for losses. A main benefit was to be reconciliation: resolving the conflict between the victim and offender and restoring balance to their relationship.

This investigation has revealed the manner in which the programme actually does operate, only partially obtaining its goals and departing substantially from the picture painted by most descriptions of the programme. The limited scope of the study has not permitted a full analysis of all the issues and hypotheses generated by earlier reasoning, but it is clear that the *modus operandi* of VORP is attributable to a multitude of interests. A few of these interests were common to all the groups interviewed and explain why the programme has successfully been accepted into the court system. The majority of respondents favoured the programme because of what it can do for the victim, and, for different reasons, most saw definite benefits to a victim/offender meeting. Beyond this, several competing interests surface, accounting for the types of cases usually referred and the way in which they are handled. Interests distinct from those of correctional reformers have particularly given credence to the theme that VORP is destined to become part of the widening net of social control, similar to many previous reforms which have enhanced the discretion of various officials in different ways.

It was postulated that the external environment would influence the operation of VORP, and that the punitive attitudes of the public might possibly affect courtroom decision-making. The interviews failed to demonstrate a visible impact because many respondents denied concern with public opinion, but if social constraints are mediated through individual attitudes and dispositions, as Hogarth found,[51] this would make public influence less apparent to those affected by it. However, more tangible influence from outside the courtroom became evident through the involvement of insurance companies. They often came into contact with the VORP office and were able to join negotiations, rendering reconciliatory goals meaningless.

The significance of individual attitudes was confirmed throughout the interviews, and these were found to be strongly rooted in organizational roles. The lack of interest in reconciliation and the negative attitude towards VORP as an alternative to prison that were common to both judges and prosecutors are a reflection of attitudes associated with their function in the courtroom. Punishment received particular emphasis in these groups, perhaps relating to a crime control model, and it was found to interfere directly with the reconciliation objective desired by the probation officers and VORP administrators.

Similarly, administrative interests were often seen to influence decision-making, as judges claimed to be very selective in choosing potential cases for VORP, assessing both the offender and the nature of his crime. As developed earlier, criteria for workability add to the likelihood that 'shallow end' offenders will be drawn into the programme. Description of these criteria in the interviews, in addition to many of the cases studied, would seem to confirm this hypothesis.

Further, administrative concerns led the coordinator of the second programme to consider the age of the victim before recommending VORP. The VORP workers' desire in the original programme to avoid a fact-finding function was also attributed to expediency.

Legal doctrine seemed to play a more limited role in determining interests in the courtroom. Improper delegation of sentencing authority did not materialize as an important issue, and while the ability of offenders to pay restitution was claimed by judges to be requisite to the programme, at least one-third of offenders whose cases were studied were unemployed. Strong and unanimous support for the programme was based on its services to victims. Because of their organizational function, prosecutors were especially favourable to the programme's ability to tend the needs of victims, regardless of whether it meant increasing the punishment of offenders.

Inherent in a broad study of interests in the complex setting of the courtroom is the fact that more questions are raised than answered. Further research is required to explore the potency of certain interests, thereby revealing the most important attributes of a sentencing programme. For example, interest in the welfare of victims seems to legitimize VORP as a sentencing option. If this aspect greatly overshadows all other interests in the programme, it is feasible that a different sort of compensation programme for victims would more completely satisfy this interest and simultaneously avoid the problems found to be associated with VORP.

Of further importance is the means by which interests both oppose and accommodate one another. In a study confined to the examination of past cases and interviews with individual members, it is easier to identify discrete interests than it is to determine their dynamic interrelationships. Some of the interplay between interests has been revealed, such as the VORP workers' attempts to maintain voluntary participation over judges' orders to participate, but much remains unexplored. Detailed observational accounts should further clarify the nature of the interactions between members and more accurately explain final outcomes.

Consistent with findings on other sentencing alternatives, the conclusion to this investigation is that VORP is probably not answering the need for alternatives to incarceration and that it too has become part of the 'widening net'. There were indications in some of the cases and also in the statements of a few judges that the programme may sometimes be used as an alternative to jail. Also, in consideration of those court members who place VORP in conjunction with other community-based sanctions, it is possible that VORP has made other sentencing options more attractive as alternatives. However, the nature of the majority of the cases studied combined with the results of the interviews indicates that on the whole VORP has contributed little to sparing offenders imprisonment. Instead of avoiding problems created by use of the prison system, another sentencing option has been implemented which pulls a different set of offenders deeper into the system of social control and inevitably increases cost.[52]

It is possible that, despite such evidence, VORP may yet be defended as a worthwhile programme. The appeal of the programme for what it can do for the victim, as one main benefit, may far outweigh questions of alternative sanctions for offenders and social control. What is important, however, is that the programme be recognized for how it actually operates rather than how it should operate. Then correctional planners and the public can make more informed decisions on whether or not to support such a programme.

Although leading proponents of VORP believe that it will become

a major viable alternative within time, the results of this study indicate that this is quite unlikely. The inertia of past practices and the
difficulty of attaining significant change in the legal system, as reported in the present study and many others, is reason enough to
doubt that the programme will yield significant change. Add to this
the wide array of conflicting interests that surround VORP and it is
difficult even to imagine circumstances that might lead to substantial
change.

It is important for correctional reformers to be more cautious in
their proposals. After acknowledging the many gains that a programme can offer, equal consideration must be given to all the
possible negative consequences that might develop. This must be
done in cognizance of the complexity of the legal system and also past
experience with reform efforts. Reformers who sincerely wish to
reduce depths of control by the criminal justice system must be
sensitive to the issues discussed herein. The recipe of appreciating
complexity and realizing the limits to our knowledge, along with a
dash of scepticism and a pinch of cynicism, might at least ensure that
overheated reform debates do not yield further digestive problems
for the social body.

NOTES AND REFERENCES

1. Carney *Corrections and the Community* (1977); Newton, Sentencing to
   community service and restitution (1979) 11 *Criminal Justice Abstracts*
   435; Solicitor General of Canada *International Conference on Alternatives to Imprisonment Report* (1982).
2. Hylton, Community corrections and social control: The case of Saskatchewan, Canada (1981) 5 *Contemporary Crises* 193; Hylton, *Rhetoric and
   reality: a critical appraisal of community correction programs* (1981)
   Department of Human Justice, University of Regina (unpublished).
3. Correctional Services Canada *The First Report of the Strategic Planning
   Committee* (1981).
4. For example Gaylin *et al. Doing Good: The Limits of Benevolence*
   (1978); Rothman *Conscience and Convenience* (1980).
5. This section is based on four sources of written information distributed
   by a VORP office under study: (1) a leaflet entitled 'Victim/Offender
   Reconciliation Project'; (2) a short document entitled 'The development
   of the Victim/Offender Reconciliation Project'; (3) a packaged collection
   of original letters and memoranda entitled 'The developmental stages of
   the Victim/Offender Reconciliation Project'; and (4) a volunteer's training manual.

6. Law Reform Commission of Canada *Restitution and Compensation and Fines* (1974); *Studies on Diversion* (1975).
7. Cf. Christie, Conflicts as property (1977) 17 *British Journal of Criminology* 1.
8. See Cohen, The punitive city: notes on the dispersal of social control (1979) 3 *Contemporary Crises* 339; Blomberg, Widening the net: an anomaly in the evaluation of diversion programs, in Klein and Teilmann (eds) *Handbook of Criminal Justice Evaluation* (1980); Austin and Krisberg, Wider, stronger and different nets: The dialectics of criminal justice reform (1981) 18 *Journal of Research in Crime and Delinquency* 164; Doleschal, The dangers of criminal justice reform (1982) 14 *Criminal Justice Abstracts*, 133.
9. Morris *The Future of Imprisonment* (1974).
10. Blomberg, Diversion and accelerated social control (1977) 68 *Journal of Criminal Law and Criminology* 274.
11. Feeley *The Process is the Punishment* (1979).
12. Rutherford and Bengar *Community Based Alternatives to Incarceration* (1976).
13. Goldsmith-Kasinsky, Critique of community corrections in Canada (1976) 4 *Crime and/et Justice* 115; Reasons, Toward community based corrections (1976) 4 *Crime and/et Justice* 108; and Rothman, note 4.
14. Boyd, An examination of probation (1977–8) 20 *Criminal Law Quarterly* 355. In Ontario between 1975 and 1980 the proportion of the population under probation orders increased threefold.
15. Sparks, The use of suspended sentences (1971) *Criminal Law Quarterly* 384
16. Pease *Community Service Assessed in 1976* (1977)
17. Hylton, note 2
18. Greenberg, Problems in community corrections (1975) 10 *Issues in Criminology* 1; Scull *Decarceration: Community Treatment and the Deviant – A Radical View* (1977)
19. Cohen, note 8
20. Boyd, note 14; Austin and Krisberg, note 8; Hylton, note 2; Foucault *Discipline and Punish: The Birth of the Prison* (1977).
21. Rothman, note 4.
22. Ignatieff, State, civil society, and total institutions: a critique of recent social histories of punishment, in Tonry and Morris (eds) *Crime and Justice: An Annual Review of Research*, vol. 3 (1981).
23. See note 11.
24. Blumberg *Criminal Justice* (1967)
25. For a review see Ericson and Baranek *The Ordering of Justice* (1982), ch. 7; Ericson and Baranek, Criminal law reform and two realities of the criminal process, in Doob and Greenspan (eds) *The Future of the Criminal Law* (1983).
26. See note 4.
27. Canadian Institute of Public Opinion *The Gallup Report* (15 November 1980); Solicitor General of Canada *Selected Trends in Criminal Justice* (1981).
28. Rankin, Changing attitudes toward capital punishment (1979) 58 *Social*

Forces 194; Doob and Roberts *Crime: Some Views of the Canadian Public* 1982.

29. Fattah, Moving to the right: a return to punishment? (1978) 6 *Crime and/et Justice* 79.
30. Norquay and Weiler *Services to Victims and Witnesses of Crime in Canada* (1981).
31. Hogarth *Sentencing as a Human Process* (1971).
32. Packer *The Limits of the Criminal Sanction* (1968); Feeley, Two models of the criminal justice system: an organizational perspective (1973) 7 *Law and Social Review*, 407.
33. For example, Law Reform Commission of Canada (1974), note 6
34. Klein, Revitalizing restitution: flogging a horse that may have been killed for just cause (1977–8) 20 *Criminal Law Quarterly* 383; Stenning and Ciano, Restitution and compensation and fines (1975) 7 *Ottawa Law Reports* 316.
35. Chasse, Restitution in Canadian criminal law (1977) 36 *Criminal Reports, New Series* 201.
36. Comment on *R* v *Zelensky* (1978) 41 C.C.C. (2d) 97, 86 D.L.R. (3d) 179, [1978] 2. S.C.R. 940, 2 C.R. (3d) 107, [1978] 3 W.W.R. 693, 21 N.R. 372, varg 33 C.C.C. (2d) 147, 73 D.L.R. (3d) 596, 36 C.R.N.S. 169, [1977] 1 W.W.R. 155.
37. See note 35.
38. Criminal courts are sensitive to the risk of being viewed as a 'collection agency'. See *R* v *Leclau* 23 C.R. 216 [1956] O.W.M. 336, 115 C.C.C. 297.
39. *R* v *Dashner* (1973) 15 C.C.C. (2d) 139 (B.C.A.A.).
40. See note 34.
41. Renner *The Adult Probationer in Ontario* (1978).
42. See note 34; McClean, Compensation and restitution orders (1973) 3 *Criminal Law Reports* 319.
43. See note 35.
44. Cf. Hagan *Victims Before the Law: The Organizational Domination of Criminal Law* (1983).
45. Smale and Spickenheuer, Feelings of guilt and need for retaliation in victims of serious crimes against property and persons (1979) 4 *Victimology* 75.
46. See note 31; Vining, Reforming Canadian sentencing practices: problems, prospects and lessons (1979) 17 *Osgoode Hall Law Journal* 355.
47. Ericson *Making Crime: A Study of Detective Work* (1981); Ericson *Reproducing Order: A Study of Police Patrol Work* (1982).
48. See note 30 for a review of problems and issues relating to crime victims
49. The relationship between recommendations in pre-sentencing reports and final sentence dispositions has been demonstrated in other studies, e.g. Hagan, The social and legal construction of criminal justice: a study of the pre-sentencing process (1975) 22 *Social Problems* 620.
50. See note 31.
51. Ibid.
52. See note 2; Chan and Ericson *Decarceration and the Economy of Penal Reform* (1981).

11 Restitution as Innovation or Unfilled Promise?*

Burt Galaway

INTRODUCTION

Sixteen years have elapsed since the establishment of the Minnesota Restitution Center in 1972. During this time requiring juvenile and adult offenders to make financial restitution to their victims has become an accepted practice in American criminal and juvenile justice. This article reviews what we have learned about restitution since 1972 and will consider restitution practices in light of early theory and work of Stephen Schafer.

In the twentieth century, restitution literature was very scant prior to 1970. In 1944, Irving Cohen, chief probation officer for Manhattan, published what is still a sound conceptual piece, in which he argued that restitution '. . . should be a part of a casework program, not a hit-and-miss method of collection unrelated to the broader possibilities.' Cohen perceived that restitution could be the basis for a relationship between the probationer and probation officer, could provide a greater awareness of the meaning of probation to the probationer, could provide a vehicle for resolution of inner conflicts arising from the forces within the offender rejecting restitution, could contribute to the satisfaction that the probationer would ultimately derive from a job well done, and could contribute to a decrease in tension and anxiety. In the late 1950s, Albert Eglash, a psychologist, wrote a series of brief articles, in which he also argued for the therapeutic benefits of what he called creative restitution (1958a;

* This article is based on a paper presented at the National Juvenile Restitution Conference held in June 1987. The conference was supported by the Office of Juvenile Justice and Delinquency Prevention (OJJDP) through the Restitution Education, Specialized Training and Technical Assistance (RESTTA) Project. The research involved was partially supported by technical assistance funds made available by the National Institute of Corrections (NIC). Information and points of view expressed in this paper are the responsibility of the author and do not necessarily reflect points of view or policy of RESTTA, OJJDP, NIC or the Department of Justice.

1958b; 1959c; Eglash and Papanek, 1959; Keve and Eglash, 1957).

The most prolific writer and scholar on the subject was Stephen Schafer, who, beginning in 1960 and until his death in 1976, published a series of articles and books in which he argued for reintroduction of restitution into the justice system (1960, 1965, 1968, 1970, 1972, 1975). His arguments remained remarkably consistent over the 16 years of publication. He decried the loss of victim interests in the administration of criminal law, which he traced to the centralization of state responsibility resulting in a focus on state interest to the exclusion of victim interest, and the failure to recognize that victims, as well as the state, are harmed by offences. He criticized the shift from victim harm to offender personality as the determinant of the gravity of the offence. Schafer argued that offenders should be made to understand that they have directly injured a victim, as well as the state, and that the noble way for offenders to make restitution is through the fruits of their own work. Restitution is a mechanism for reintegrating victim interest into the justice system, for contributing to the state interest in reforming offenders, and for providing a punishment for the offender. Schafer used terms like functional responsibility, restitutive concept of punishment, and punitive concept of restitution; restitution was described as a synthetic punishment which could unite all the objectives of corrections in a single method. Schafer developed an integrated concept of restitution; restitution provides a mechanism for integrating victim and offender interests and, second, provides a mechanism for integrating the purposes of punishment.

These two ideas provide criteria against which to compare current restitution programming. Does current restitution programming provide for integration of both offender and victim interest in the administration of juvenile and criminal justice? Schafer did not extend his argument as far as victim–offender meetings, a practice which was a part of the early Minnesota Restitution Center (Hudson and Galaway, 1974) and which is a key component of the victim–offender reconciliation projects (McKnight, 1981; Peachey, 1988) which were just emerging at the time of his death. This practice is consistent with Schafer's central position that the victim should be empowered to regain his or her historic role in the administration of justice.

The second criterion against which to weigh current restitution programmes is the extent to which these programmes explicitly fulfil a penal function–reformation, retribution, deterrence or some combination thereof. Schafer was clear in regard to his concept of punitive restitution, as well as a restitutive concept of punishment. However, he also argued that restitution should not become the only penalty for any class of offences because he was concerned that, within the class, there would be incidents for which restitution might not be a sufficient penalty to meet the state's need for punishment to symbolize the seriousness of the offence and, second, because of the possibility for wealthy offenders to buy their way out of punishment.

Restitution and community service

When Stephen Schafer used the term restitution, he had in mind money repayment by the offender to the victim. He did not push his analysis to the point of victim–offender contacts and, thus, did not consider the possibility of offender repayment in the form of service to the victim. And he certainly did not have in mind the possibility of offender repayment in service to the community. Albert Eglash, however, defined his concept of creative restitution broadly enough to include repayment through service to the community. Hudson and Galaway also accepted this broad concept in their early work and used the term symbolic restitution to refer to community service penalties (Galaway and Hudson, 1972). The National Juvenile Restitution Initiative continued the unfortunate practice of merging these two very distinct and different ideas, repayment to the victim and repayment to the community, under the rubric of restitution. But it is time to correct past conceptual errors and to make a clear and sharp distinction between sanctions which are directed towards restoring victim losses (monetary restitution and personal service restitution) and sanctions which are directed towards restoring community losses (fines and community service). These sanctions can all be classified into a general category of reparative or restorative sanctions because they have in common the idea that the penalty imposed upon the offender should result in repairing the damage or restoring losses. Repairing community losses, however, is quite different than repairing victim losses. Figure 11.1 presents a typology of restorative sanctions. I will be limiting the term restitution to mean repayment by the offender to the victim as a part of the criminal justice process; the concept of criminal justice process is broad enough to include diversion agreements entered into by prosecutors. Restitution is of two possible types: monetary restitution, in which the repayment is made

	Recipient	
	Victim	*Community*
	Monetary restitution	Fine or contribution to charity
Monetary		
Service	Personal service restitution	Community service

Form

Figure 11.1   Typology of restorative sanctions

in cash, and personal service restitution, in which the repayment is made in service provided to the victim. Restitution of either type can be linked in a package of penalties to community service, just as restitution can be linked to a fine or to probation. Linking penalties together is quite different than using the same term to describe very different penalties. The linking of restitution to community service may be a useful mechanism to address Schafer's concern about restitution as the sole penalty for any given class of offenses.

There is one area in which the conceptual distinction between restitution and community service becomes murky. Restitution programmes involving victim–offender mediation commonly find victims requesting the offender to complete service for the community rather than pay restitution directly to the victim. This is illustrated by the following agreement:

Tom and one of his co-defendants met on February 26 with Mr Jones from Riverview Construction Company. Repair costs for damages to the fence and window were waived because of the minimal cost of repairs. The value of two stolen walkie–talkies was $2,306.72. One was returned, so the total loss was $1,153.36. Tom is responsible for one-third, or $384.45, due to the presence of two co-defendants. Tom will perform 75 hours of community service. His time is valued at approximately $5.00 per hour. He will work at the Jonesville Neighborhood Improvement Association on Monday through Friday, starting May 13. He will work from 12.00 noon to 6.00 p.m. on Mondays, and 9.00 a.m. to 5.00 p.m. Tuesday through Friday. The work is to be completed by May 31.

Type service

	Individual placement	Supervised group
CJS imposed	**Type A** CJS requires offender to complete an individually designed community service sentence	**Type B** CJS requires offender to complete a community service sentence working alongside other offenders as part of a supervised work group
Victim donation	**Type C** Victim donates Service restitution to a community agency; plan individually designed for offender	**Type D** Victim donates service restitution to a community agency where offender works alongside other offenders as part of a supervised work group

Figure 11.2   Typology of community service

In this case, the victim and offender were in agreement on the amount of damages; the victim was entitled to restitution in either money or service but chose to donate the service to a community agency. Does this constitute community service? Under these circumstances, the restitution has been converted to community service by decision of the victim; this possibility suggests the need for further conceptual work regarding community service. Figure 11.2 suggests four polar types of community service based on two dimensions. The first dimension is who assigns the community service – the victim through assignment of restitution due him to a community organization or an official of the criminal justice system. The second dimension is the nature of the community service which is conceptualized as two polar types. Community service may be individually designed and the offender placed at a site as an individual; this type of community service will often make use of the current network of volunteer services in a community. The second type is community service

performed by offenders under group supervision, often supervised by
criminal justice officials; examples include conservation, reclamation,
and parks and road clean-up work. An extensive discussion of community service is not necessary for this article, although this conceptual framework may be helpful as we later consider possible links
between community service and restitution penalties.

WHAT HAVE WE LEARNED?

Stephen Schafer argued for restitution based on his historical analysis
and his belief that crime victims should be restored to a meaningful
role in the criminal law. At that time, there were no reported experiences of contemporary restitution programmes from which he could
draw conclusions. In 1972, the Minnesota Restitution Center received its first offenders, who were paroled from the Minnesota State
Prison after serving four months of their sentences. The ensuing years
have been marked by study development of restitution programming
within both the juvenile and adult justice systems and the emergence
of an extensive literature on the topic, including a reasonable number
of research studies (Galaway, Hudson and Novack, 1983). Three
conclusions can be drawn from the past 15 years of programme
development and research regarding restitution: (1) implementation
of restitution in both juvenile and adult systems is feasible; (2) there
is strong public and victim support for restitution; and (3) restitution
may accomplish utilitarian goals of punishment as well as being
defensible from a just deserts philosophy.

Restitution can be implemented

Restitution programming can be implemented without undue difficulty in both the juvenile and adult justice systems. The Minnesota
Restitution Center staff members were able successfully to implement restitution with serious adult property offenders within the
context of a community corrections centre; no difficulties were reported in negotiating restitution amounts, nor in securing compliance
with the negotiated agreements (Galaway and Hudson, 1975; Minnesota Department of Corrections, 1976). Restitution programmes
have now been successfully implemented by dozens of juvenile and
adult projects. The Office of Juvenile Justice and Delinquency Prevention National Juvenile Restitution Initiative funded 85 juvenile

restitution sites which reported 15,829 admissions and 14,012 closures during the first two years of operation; 86 per cent of the closures were successful, meaning that full compliance had been secured with the terms of the restitution requirements and that, while in the programme, the young person had not reoffended in ways that became known to the police (Schneider, Schneider, Griffith and Wilson, 1982). In 1979, the National Assessment of Adult Restitution Projects discovered 67 formal monetary restitution projects for adult offenders and conducted detailed studies of 11 of these projects (Hudson, Galaway and Novack, 1980:68, 139–79); project staff members did not report difficulty implementing restitution activities, although several reported implementation difficulties securing support of criminal justice system officials and funding. The 11 projects reported successful offender project completion rates ranging from 52 per cent to 91 per cent with a mean of 74 per cent. Early restitution programme developers often encountered skepticism; beliefs were advanced that restitution amounts could not be fairly determined, victims would cheat offenders, offenders would refuse to participate, or restitution requirements were not enforceable. The experience of the past 16 years indicates unequivocally that the skepticism of the early 1970s was unfounded. Restitution amounts have not been unduly difficult to determine, although, of course, there will be isolated cases where difficulties are encountered. Victims are not any more likely to inflate claims than offenders are likely to minimize damages; the hanging victim is relatively rare, although not entirely extinct, and, of course, the offender who will misrepresent is also not unknown.

Compliance with restitution orders is relatively high when efforts to secure compliance are systematically followed and the expectation that the offender will be responsible becomes a focus of work with the offender. Success at implementing a restitution programme and securing compliance with restitution requirements relates more to the willingness of staff to focus on restitution activities, as contrasted with other activities, than any intrinsic difficulties implementing restitution. The Dane County, Wisconsin, Juvenile Restitution Program randomly assigned youth with restitution orders to an experimental condition in which a group of staff focused exclusively on the restitution activities and to a control group in which compliance with restitution obligations was monitored by probation officers, along with the many other activities in which probation officers engage. Eighty-eight per cent of the youth in the programme (experimental) group completed all restitution orders, compared to 40 per cent of the youths in the ad hoc (control) group. Only 2 per cent of the youth in the programme group made no restitution at all, compared to 37 per cent in the *ad hoc* group (Schneider and Schneider, 1985:539). The 86 per cent compliance reported by the Juvenile Restitution Initiative may be higher than juvenile offenders' compliance with other requirements commonly associated with community sanctions, such as fines, curfews, driving restrictions and even completion of probation orders. The issue of whether restitution can be implemented no longer needs to be debated. Skeptics may still be encountered, but they are either ignorant of the experiences of the past 16 years or are using the argument that it can't be done to disguise an opinion that restitution should not be required. Arguing that a practice is feasible is quite different of course, from arguing that it is desirable.

The conclusion that implementing restitution programming is feasible extends also to programmes which bring victims and offenders together to negotiate restitution amounts. The best developed examples of this programming thrust are the victim–offender reconciliation projects (VORP) which began in 1973 in Kitchner, Ontario (Peachey, 1988) and have now been replicated at over 100 locations in Canada and the United States (Gehm and Umbreit, 1985), as well as West Germany (Dünkel and Rössner, 1988) and Great Britain (Ruddick, 1988; Watson, Boucherat and Davis, 1988). These are small projects, frequently operated outside criminal and juvenile justice systems, and are not as well known as some of the larger, more system-based restitution programmes. They are consistently reporting, however, that victims are willing to meet with offenders, that when meetings occur agreements are normally secured, and that high agreement compliance rates are being secured. The VORP project in Minneapolis and St Paul, Minnesota, has had two years' experience serving juvenile offenders, primarily burglars, and their victims including 168 offenders and 173 victims. Fifty-five per cent of the victims have agreed to participate, 95 per cent of the meetings have resulted in agreements, and, at this time, 93 per cent of the agreements have been successfully completed (Galaway, in press). Similar results are being reported by a national VORP information system, which, for the first year of operation ending in June 1986, reported that 60 per cent of the cases resulted in a victim–offender meeting, 27 per cent did not result in a meeting because of the victim declining to participate, and 13 per cent did not result in a meeting for other reasons (Gehm, 1986). Victim–offender negotiation of the restitution amount and the terms and conditions of payment was a part of the programme of the original Minnesota Restitution Center; during the first year of operation, 31 of 44 victims travelled to the Minnesota State Prison to meet their offenders and to negotiate restitution amounts, knowing that such activity would result in the offenders' serving shorter than usual sentences (Galaway and Hudson, 1975:359). Galaway and Hudson argued in 1972 that we should not make a priori assumptions about the willingness of victims to participate or the desirability of victim–offender meetings (Galaway and Hudson, 1972:409) but should be open to trying these ideas and learning from the experiences. Subsequent experiences suggest that assumptions should be made: more than 50 per cent of the victims will be willing to participate, and victim–offender negotiation is a viable method for arriving at restitution amounts and will be a constructive experience for both victims and offenders.

Restitution and penal purposes

Schafer decried the historical shift from victim loss to offender personality traits as indicators of offence gravity and perceived restitution as a means for rebalancing the scales of justice. He believed restitution was a tangible method by which society could symbolize indignation about the offence; more recent scholars have noted the potential for restitution to operationalize retributive or just deserts penal philosophy (McAnany, 1978; Watson, Boucherat and Davis, 1988). Central to the retributive position is the concept of proportionality between the severity of the penalty imposed and the seriousness of the offense; proportionality can be thought to have occurred when key actors – victims, offenders and the general public – perceive that the penalty imposed is fair. Fair means that the penalty is perceived as neither too harsh nor too lenient, given the seriousness of the offence.

Very limited research has been done regarding perceived fairness of a sentence. We are more likely to see research reports of victim or public satisfaction with a particular sentence rather than the perception of whether or not the sentence was fair. We do not know if satisfaction and fairness correlate highly with each other. The lack of attention to this concept is puzzling. Perhaps researchers and criminal justice system staff do not believe it is important to secure indications of victim, offender and general public perceptions of the fairness of the sentences. Perhaps the concept is considered to be too global and inadequately operationalized, or perhaps measurement difficulties detract from its use. Measurement difficulties stem from asking people to report perceived fairness in abstract situations without grounding the question in a specific victimization incident. Mcguire (1982) and Doob and Roberts (1983) found that the general public markedly shifts its perception of fairness (becoming substantially less harsh) as the public is presented with detailed information regarding the victimization incident. Mcguire's research found that victims of burglary were harsher in their sentencing recommendations for burglars generally than they were for the specific person who burglarized their home. Both Thomson and Ragona (1984) and Galaway (1984) point to the need to present specific victimization incidents rather than global concepts in dealing with public perceptions.

There have been a few reported studies of the extent to which victims, offenders and the general public perceive that restitution is a fair requirement. Kigin and Novack (1980) asked both victims and offenders in a juvenile restitution programme in which negotiated restitution was the only requirement imposed on first-offence juvenile offenders if it were fair for the offender to pay restitution. Questionnaires were completed after the restitution amount had been determined and six months after the offender completed the programme. Ninety-three per cent of the 373 offenders reported pre-programme that the requirement was fair, and 90 per cent òf 184 reported this post-programme; victim measures were not reported for the pre-programme group, but 78 per cent of 124 victims post-programme reported that they considered it fair for the offender to pay restitution (14 per cent said they didn't know and 7 per cent said no). Seventy-three per cent of the offenders pre-programme said that restitution was preferable to other penalties (16 per cent said they didn't know), and 78 per cent post-programme reported that restitution was preferable to other punishments (15 per cent said they didn't know). Forty-eight per cent of the victims reported that restitution was preferable to other punishments pre-programme (21 per cent said they didn't know), and 37 per cent post-programme reported that restitution was preferable to other punishments (25 per cent said they didn't know). The victims in the St Cloud project were asked, 'Given only one choice, which punishment would be fairest for your offender?' Sixty-nine per cent selected reparative sanctions (29 per cent monetary restitution, 3 per cent personal service restitution, and 37 per cent community service), 28 per cent probation, and 3 per cent selected jail or prison. Structured interviews were conducted with the youth, parents, victims, probation officers and police for youth ($n = 16$) with restitution dispositions from the St Louis County (Minnesota) Juvenile Court during four weeks in spring 1976. The majority of each group considered the restitution obligation fair for the youth, although youth, as a group, were less likely to report the obligation fair than were the other respondents (Galaway and Marsella, 1976). A sample of 101 offenders and 92 victims from 19 adult restitution programmes found that 61 per cent of the offenders and 60 per cent of the victims thought the financial restitution requirements were fair; 37 per cent of the offenders considered the requirements too harsh, compared to 3 per cent of the victims (Novack, Galaway and Hudson, 1980:66–7).

Restitution appears to be logically consistent with the notion of just deserts, and the limited available evidence suggests that restitution will generally be perceived as fair by victims, offenders and the general public. But, as Anne Schneider has pointed out (1986), arguments that restitution balances the scales of justice may not win the necessary support for the practice from key political leaders and criminal justice officials who are likely to demand that a sanction be effective in accomplishing utilitarian goals. While restitution has been defended from deterrence theory (Tittle, 1978:15–31), I am unaware of any efforts to test the general deterrent impact of restitution.

A body of evidence is beginning to emerge to suggest that restitution has as much or more impact on recidivism rates than other sanctions to which it has been compared. Whether this impact is being secured through the operation of specific deterrence or rehabilitation mechanisms is not presently possible to distinguish; often these two sets of mechanisms are difficult to separate. The Minnesota Restitution Center admitted a group of inmates randomly selected from a defined population pool of inmates admitted to the Minnesota State Prison. A follow-up study of this group, compared to a randomly selected control group from the same population, found no difference in the likelihood of return to prison between the two groups (Minnesota Department of Corrections, 1976). The restitution group, however, was somewhat more likely to have been returned to prison for technical parole violations, whereas the control group was more likely to have been returned to prison for a new offence. Another study, involving the same experimental group, compared the first 18 men released from the Minnesota State Prison to the Minnesota Restitution Center with a group of offenders released on conventional parole during the same time period, individually matched on age of first offence, number of previous felony convictions, age at release, type of release and race. Each offender was followed for 16 months. The restitution group had fewer convictions and was employed for a higher percentage of the 16-month follow-up than the comparison group (Heinz, Galaway and Hudson, 1976). A Canadian study (Bonta, Boyle, Motiuk and Sonnichsen, 1983:277–93) of adult offenders sentenced to a community corrections centre to participate in a restitution programme compared to a group of adult offenders sentenced to the same centre to participate in a work release programme found a higher rate of in-programme failures for the restitution when compared to the work release offenders. The two groups, however, were not comparable, inasmuch as the restitution programme offenders were younger and had a more serious criminal history than the work release offenders. Both groups were followed for two years after release from the community corrections centre; the restitution group had a slightly higher rate of reconviction than the work release group, although the differences were not statistically reliable. Guedalia (1979) studied 200 male juvenile offenders who had participated in a restitution programme in the Tulsa Juvenile Court and concluded '. . . offenders who are living with the natural parents, are not failing in school, and make contact with their victim are the most likely not to commit additional offenses.' Hofford (1981) reported an 18 per cent recidivism rate for youth in a juvenile restitution programme, compared with 30 per cent for youth on regular probation.

The best evidence of the impact of restitution on recidivism compared with other sanctions is the research generated by the National Juvenile Restitution Initiative. Anne Schneider (1986) reports recidivism studies for four juvenile restitution projects in which offenders were randomly assigned to restitution, compared to other correctional programming, permitting several tests of restitution *vis-à-vis* other programmes. One project compared restitution with weekend detention; another compared restitution with mental health counselling and with a group of offenders receiving a normal disposition in juvenile court; one compared restitution negotiated through a victim-offender mediation process with probation for a group of serious offenders; and one compared restitution as a sole sanction, with restitution plus probation, and with probation alone. In all of these studies, the youth in the restitution group did as well or better on recidivism measures than youth in the comparison groups. Another study in Dane County, Wisconsin (Schneider and Schneider 1985) found that a programmatic approach placing emphasis on the restitution requirement was more likely to result in the completion of restitution and that youth who completed ordered restitution were less likely to recidivate than those who did not.

One should be cautious in arguing that any correctional programme will have a long-term impact on recidivism rates; recidivism rates are more likely to be influenced by the overall response of the society and culture, including opportunities made available to offenders, than anything which happens during a time-limited correctional programme. But the extent to which a correctional requirement may affect the nature of the relationship between the offender and his or her society may influence employment and other opportunities made available to the offender. The emerging evidence indicates that one does not have to be reluctant to defend restitution as having an impact on recidivism; the evidence suggests that it will have as great or greater impact than other penalties. Such a conclusion might shift the basis for selecting penalties to issues such as cost to the taxpayer and humaneness to both victim and offender.

The experience and evidence since 1972 suggest that restitution may be the synthetic punishment conceptualized by Schafer. The practice appears to be broadly perceived as fair, and the evidence to date suggests that it may have a positive impact on the offender as reflected in a reduction of recidivism. While the evidence points in this direction, these conclusions should be reached with more tentativeness than the conclusions regarding feasibility.

Public and victim acceptance of restitution

There have been a series of studies over the past 15 years which tend to confirm the commonsense notion that the public generally, and victims as a subset of the public, will support the use of restitution as a penalty for offenders. Some of the studies go further than simply securing indication of support and provide evidence of public and victim support for the use of restitution as a substitute for other penalties, including jail or imprisonment.

A Minnesota poll (Metro Poll:1972) of adults in the Minneapolis-St Paul metropolitan area found 87 per cent of respondents favoured '. . . letting the criminal work to repay the victim directly while living in a halfway house.' John Gandy (1975) found strong support for the concept of creative restitution in his survey of Denver police, social work students, members of a women's service club, and probation and parole officers; Gandy made use of Eglash's concept of creative restitution, which includes monetary restitution, community service and personal service restitution. Hudson, Chesney and McLagan (1977a, 1977b) found strong support for restitution among state corrections administrators, legislators, and probation and parole officers. Eighty-nine per cent of the judges, prosecutors and defence counsel in the Bluestein *et al.* (1977) South Carolina study saw potential value for the use of monetary restitution and community service. Gandy and Galaway (1980) reported on a telephone survey of 500 randomly selected Columbia, South Carolina residents and found that these respondents saw restitution as a viable sanction for burglary, drunk driving, embezzlement, destruction of property and shoplifting, and found little evidence that the public wanted restitution used in conjunction with any other sanctions. Cannady (1980) reports that victims from both a juvenile restitution project and victims of regular probation offenders say that restitution is an appropriate penalty for juvenile offenders. Kigin and Novack (1980) asked their central Minnesota victims if a punishment other than restitution was preferable for their offender; 48 per cent responded no (31 per cent said yes and 21 per cent did not know).

Galaway (1984) conducted a national survey in New Zealand to test the proposition that citizens would support reduction in the use of incarceration for property offenders if there were a concurrent increase in use of restitution. Two independent random samples were drawn from the electoral rolls; respondents were presented with six brief offence/victimization incidents, were asked if they thought the offenders should be sentenced to prison and, if not, were asked to recommend non-custodial penalties from a supplied list. The list of non-custodial penalties for the experimental group included restitution to the victim; this item was not included for the control group. For five of the six incidents, the experimental group was less likely to recommend imprisonment, with the difference reaching the 0.05 level of significance; the experimental group was also less likely than the control group to recommend imprisonment for the sixth incident, but the difference did not reach the 0.05 level of significance. These results support the conclusion that the public would accept the use of restitution as a mechanism for reducing imprisonment.

Shaw's (1982) survey of the British public found that 66 per cent selected restitution as a preferred method for reducing the over-crowded prison populations; community service orders were selected by 85 per cent. Similar results have subsequently been reported by

Mayhew and Hough (1983, 1985) from their analysis of data in the British crime surveys.

Doob and Roberts (1983) asked a convenience sample of Toronto citizens what sentence they would favour for a 'first offender convicted of breaking and entering into a private home and stealing things worth $250'. Thirty-nine per cent favoured probation, 26 per cent a fine, 3 per cent a fine plus probation, 29 per cent prison, and 3 per cent said they didn't know. Doob and Roberts followed up with the question, 'now instead of (the selected sentence) would you be in favour of having the offender being ordered by the court to do a certain number of hours of work beneficial to community or the victim or in some way pay back the victim for the harm done?' Eighty-eight per cent responded affirmatively to this question, although those who had initially selected prison were less likely to tolerate a reparative sanction than were those who had selected other non-custodial sanctions.

Thomson and Ragona (1987) conducted a telephone survey of 816 randomly sampled Illinois citizens aged 18 and over. Respondents were presented with two hypothetical residential burglary cases involving an unarmed offender, first offence, entering an unoccupied house and taking $400; for one case, all property was recovered and returned to the victim; for a second case, no property was recovered, and the victim spent $300 on home security. Respondents were given four possible sentences from which to select – probation, probation and 80 hours of community service, one year of prison, two years of prison. After responding, the respondents were then given the information that probation would cost about $3,000, probation plus 80 hours of community service would cost about $5,000, one year of prison would cost about $15,000, and two years of prison would cost about $30,000, and were again asked to select a sentence. They report these results:

Only 15 per cent of the respondents selected imprisonment for the no victim loss burglary, and 30 per cent selected prison for the victim loss burglary without the cost information; the effect of cost information was to shift sentencing choices from incarceration to non-custodial sentences. The burglary scenarios presented to respondents represented factual situations which, under Illinois mandatory sentencing law, would have required a prison sentence. While this research does not explicitly relate to monetary restitution, it does suggest that Illinois citizens, in their response to burglary offenders,

	No victim loss		Victim loss of $700	
Preferred sentence	Before sanction cost	After sanction cost	Before sanction cost	After sanction cost
Probation	23%	39%	12%	23%
Probation and 80 hours CS	63%	54%	57%	58%
One year prison	10%	5%	23%	14%
Two years prison	5%	3%	7%	5%

are less harsh than the law of their state and, given the general acceptance of restitution, lends support to the notion that restitution and other reparative sanctions might well be used in place of imprisonment.

Seventy-two per cent of respondents in a recent North Carolina survey (Hickman-Maslin Research, 1986) selected strongly agree to the statement, 'non-violent offenders should be forced to work because they can earn money to pay restitution to their victims,' and an additional 21 per cent selected somewhat agree. Respondents were asked their views on community punishment, which was defined to include one or more of the following: community service work, victim restitution, following conditions of probation, receiving treatment for drug or alcohol addiction, and going to school. The question, 'are community punishments a good idea?' was asked twice. Between the first and second asking, respondents were told that imprisonment costs an average of $1,000 per month, community punishment costs less than half the cost of prison, and judges may design community punishments to fit a particular crime. The responses were:

	First asking	Second asking
Very good	19%	52%
Somewhat good	28%	33%
Depends/don't know	10%	6%
Somewhat bad	26%	4%
Very bad	17%	3%

The available evidence indicates favourable public opinion for reparative sanctions and, specifically, for restitution and further suggests that both victims and the general public will support moves toward using reparative sanctions instead of other types of penalties. While the evidence should not be considered definitive, there is sufficient indication of public and victim support to suggest the advisability of moving planfully in the direction of substituting restitution for other non-custodial penalties and substituting restitution, perhaps in combination with other non-custodial penalties, for penalties of incarceration.

In summary, the experience since 1972 has established that restitution is feasible and can be implemented, strongly suggests that restitution will be perceived as a fair penalty and will have as positive an impact on offender recidivism as other penalties, and indicates public and victim support for substituting restitution for other penalties, including incarceration. Restitution has moved beyond the innovation stage and is in the process of being institutionalized as a part of criminal and juvenile justice procedures. But will the promise which Schafer saw in restitution be fulfilled? Are restitution programmes being administered in ways which effectively integrate victim interest into the juvenile and adult justice system? Is restitution being used as a synthetic penalty?

TOWARDS FULFILLING THE PROMISE

Victim interest

The emerging evidence suggests that what victims most desire is information regarding their offenders and the criminal justice response to their offenders (Shapland, Willmore and Duff, 1985; Hinrichs, 1981; Forst and Hernon, 1985). Research confirms the experiences of victim–offender reconciliation projects; substantial numbers of victims – well over 50 per cent of the victims of property offenders – show an interest in an opportunity to participate in the justice system. Seventy per cent (31) of victims of the adult property offenders who participated in the Minnesota Restitution Center during the first year travelled to the Minnesota State Prison to meet their offenders and negotiate restitution agreements, fully aware that this would result in the offenders' early discharge from prison (Galaway and Hudson, 1975). Cannady reported that 15 of 17 victims of juvenile property offenders in Charleston, South Carolina, said they would be willing to meet with their offenders to negotiate a restitution (1980). Fifty per cent of the respondents of Gandy and

Galaway's survey of the adult population of Columbia, South Carolina, reported that, if malicious damage was done to their house, they would be willing to permit personal service restitution by the offenders; 39 per cent said they would not, and 19 per cent were undecided (Gandy and Galaway, 1980). Thirty-two per cent of the victims in the Miami, Florida, plea bargaining research appeared for conferences, despite the fact that their only contact was a letter of invitation; programme staff indicated that there were many difficulties notifying victims because of inaccurate addresses, and many victims probably never received the letter of invitation (Heinz and Kerstetter, 1979). In a survey of victims associated with 19 adult restitution projects, 46 per cent reported that they would prefer to meet with their offenders, if victimized again, to work out a restitution plan; 36 per cent said they would not want to meet, and 18 per cent did not respond (Novack, Galaway and Hudson, 1980). The Kigin and Novack study in central Minnesota found 74 per cent of the victims reported that they should be involved with their offenders in determining the restitution amount (1980). Seventy-one per cent of the victims of juvenile offenders referred to a restitution programme in the Tulsa, Oklahoma, juvenile court reported that they were willing to meet their offenders, 6 per cent indicated they did not want to meet their offenders, and the file material failed to report victims' decisions for the other 22 per cent of the victims (Galaway, Henzel, Ramsey and Wanyama, 1980).

Restitution programme managers need to assess carefully the extent to which their programme designs are providing opportunities to provide victims with regular information regarding each case and providing victims opportunities to participate in the justice process to further the potential for integrating victim interest in the juvenile and adult justice systems. The programmes which use victim–offender mediation provide models as to how opportunities can be extended to victims for participation and have documented that these procedures are feasible (PACT Institute of Justice, 1984; Peachey, Snyder and Teichroeb, 1983). John Haley, in his analysis of Japanese criminal procedure, suggests that the emphasis on confession, repentence and the seeking of forgiveness, through apology and restitution from the victim and victim's family, may contribute to the relatively low crime rates in Japan and are practices which may be transferable to western legal systems (Haley, 1988). Operating restitution programmes in a manner which would make these processes possible will be a step in this direction.

A recent survey of probation and parole officers and victim service workers, with samples drawn from the membership of the American Probation and Parole Association and the National Organization for Victim Assistance, offers some interesting comparisons of professional attitudes regarding victim–offender reconciliation (Shapiro, Omole and Schuman, 1986). Sixty-six per cent of the probation officers, compared to 43 per cent of the victim service providers, responded yes to the statement, 'there is need for victim–offender reconciliation programme'; 72 per cent of the probation officers, compared with 55 per cent of the victim service providers, responded yes to the statement of 'communication between victim and probationer should be encouraged if either desires it.' This survey suggests considerable probation officer support for providing victims with opportunities to participate in the justice system and the possibility of victim service providers' reservations about this. One potential barrier to providing victims with opportunities to participate may be the self-interest of victim service providers who may perceive the need to maintain position and responsibility by doing things for victims, rather than providing victims with information and opportunities for participation. Providing services to victims and providing opportunities for victims are not the same. Leslie Sebba offers a useful conceptual framework for making this distinction (1982). Sebba conceptualizes two models – an adversarial-retribution model and a social welfare-social defence model:

> The key to the dynamics of these two models is in the following: whereas under the adversary-retribution model the state would provide the machinery for the victim to achieve the desired objectives, whether prosecution or compensation-restitution; under the social defence-welfare model the state would not only stand in the shoes of the victim in prosecuting the offender, but would also stand in the shoes of the offender in compensating the victim. The victim would then have no direct claim against the offender in the matter of punishment, which would be left exclusively to the state.

The social defence-welfare model is likely to be preferred by professional and civil service classes because this model will concentrate power and resources with these groups, but will also result in a reduction in opportunities for direct victim participation.

The conceptual confusion between monetary restitution and community service will also detract from the potential for restitution to provide victims with participation opportunities. So long as community service operates under the rubric of restitution, there will be a substantial number of situations in which victim interest may be simply ignored as criminal justice officials substitute community service for restitution. While restitution and community service are quite distinct sanctions, the two can be linked together in at least three ways. Community service may be substituted for restitution. The victim may donate restitution to a community agency by asking the offender to do work for a community agency. Or, community service may be added to monetary restitution, if additional sanctions are necessary to meet the demands of proportionality. The only threat to victim interest is in the first possibility; we should generally discourage substituting community service sentencing for monetary restitution unless the victim consents to having his or her restitution donated to a community organization.

Restitution as a penalty

To Schafer, restitution was clearly a penalty and a synthetic penalty which could integrate the various purposes for criminal sanctions. An examination of sentencing and programme policy and programme operations is necessary to determine the extent to which restitution is administered as a penalty. Restitution as a penalty should replace other penalties; and, second, preference should be given to restitution, rather than penalties which do not hold open the possibility of opportunities for crime victims. Restitution as innovation may have required special projects to demonstrate feasibility. With feasibility established, it is time to integrate restitution with other criminal and juvenile justice practices. I have previously proposed that restitution become the focus for probation (Galaway, 1983; Galaway, 1985). Transforming probation so that restitution and other reparative sentences become the focus of probation work would move both probation and restitution into more central prominence as penalties.

With restitution defined as a penalty, a next step is to identify classes of offences for which it may be the sufficient and sole penalty. There have been some efforts to use restitution as a sole sanction; Anne Schneider's research (1986) suggests that this can be effective. An early study from the National Juvenile Restitution Initiative found that restitution as a sole sanction was more effective in securing successful programme completion than restitution and probation. The relationship between restitution and successful programme completion held when controls were imposed for offence seriousness and for prior delinquent histories of the juvenile offenders (Schneider, P. and Griffith, 1980).

Finally, for restitution to achieve its prominence as a penalty will require concentrated policy and programme development to use restitution, combined with other reparative sanctions, as a replacement for jail and prison for many, if not all, classes of property offences. The promise of restitution as a lower-cost penalty, as a synthetic penalty, and as a penalty which addresses victim interest will be achieved as restitution is used to reduce reliance on prisons and jails which do nothing for victims, burden taxpayers, and return offenders to society less competent to live law-abiding lives and probably more dangerous than when they were admitted.

Stephen Schafer was influenced by a series of debates on restitution and criminal justice which occurred at a series of international penitentiary congresses between 1870 and 1901. A group of Italian criminologists, primarily Henri Ferri and Raffaele Garofalo, were strong advocates for restitution. Garofalo (1914) delivered a paper at the 1901 conference in Brussels titled 'Enforced Reparation as a Substitute for Imprisonment'. He argued that prisons were being filled with relatively minor, short-term offenders, that overcrowding made it impossible to keep serious offenders who may be a real threat to society long enough to treat them effectively (Garofalo was a positivist who was enamoured with the potential of science, given sufficient time and resources, to change the behaviour of wayward individuals), and that offenders sentenced to short terms of imprisonment should not go to prison but, instead, be required to work and from their earnings make restitution to their victims.

REFERENCES

Bluestein, R., Hollinger, V., McCowan, L. and Moore, S. *Attitudes of the Legal Community Toward Creative Restitution, Victim Compensation, and Related Social Work Involvement.* Master Thesis, University of South Carolina College of Social Work, 1977.
Bonta, T., Boyle, T., Motiuk, L. and Sonnichsen, P. 'Restitution in correctional halfway houses: victim satisfaction, attitudes, and recidivism.' *Canadian Journal of Corrections*, 20, 1983, pp. 277–93.
Cannon, A. and Stanford, R. *Evaluation of the Juvenile Alternative Services*

368   *Initiatives to Help Victims of Crime*

Project. Tallahassee: Florida Department of Health and Rehabilitative Services, 1981.

Cohen, Irving. 'The integration of restitution in the probation services'. *Journal of Criminal Law, Criminology and Police Science, 34*, 1944, pp. 315–21.

Cannady, Lynn. *Evaluation of the Charleston Juvenile Restitution Project Final Report.* Washington: Metametrics. 1980.

Doob, Anthony and Roberts, Julian. *An Analysis of the Public's View of Sentencing.* University of Toronto Centre of Criminology, 1983.

Dunkel, Frieder and Rössner, Dieter. 'Victim/offender agreements in the Federal German Republic, Austria, and Switzerland'. In Martin Wright and Burt Galaway (eds), *Mediation and Criminal Justice: Victims, Offenders and Communities.* London: Sage, 1988.

Eglash, Albert. 'Creative restitution – a broader meaning for an old term'. *Journal of Criminal Law, Criminology, and Police Science, 48*, 1958a, pp. 612–22.

Eglash, Albert. 'Creative restitution: some suggestions for prison rehabilitation programs'. *American Journal of Corrections, 20* (6), 1958b, pp. 20–34.

Eglash, Albert. 'Creative restitution: its roots in psychiatry, religion, and law'. *British Journal of Delinquency, 10*, 1959, pp. 114–19.

Eglash, Albert and Papanek, E. 'Creative restitution: a correctional technique and a theory'. *Journal of Individual Psychology*, 1959, pp. 226–32.

Forst, Brian and Hennon, Jolene. *The Criminal Justice Response to Victim Harm* (National Institute of Justice Research in Brief). Washington, DC: US Department of Justice, 1985.

Galaway, Burt. 'Informal justice: mediation between offenders and victims'. *Legal and Ethical Problems of Crime Prevention and Intervention.* Berlin: Verlag de Gruyter, in press.

Galaway, Burt. 'Victim participation in the penal-corrective process'. *Victimology: An International Journal, 10* (1–4), 1985, pp. 617–30.

Galaway, Burt. *Public Acceptance of Restitution as an Alternative to Imprisonment for Property Offenders: A Survey.* Wellington, New Zealand: Department of Justice, 1984.

Galaway, Burt. 'Probation as a reparative sentence'. *Federal Probation, 46* (3), 1983, pp. 9–18.

Galaway, Burt, Henzel, Marjorie, Ramsey, Glenn and Wanyana, Bart. 'Victims and delinquents in the Tulsa juvenile court'. *Federal Probation, 44* (2), 1980, pp. 42–8.

Galaway, Burt and Hudson, Joe. 'Issues in the correctional implementation of restitution to victims of crime'. In B. Galaway and J. Hudson (eds), *Considering the Victim: Readings in Restitution and Victim Compensation.* Springfield, Illinois: Charles Thomas, 1975, pp. 351–60.

Galaway, Burt and Hudson, Joe. 'Restitution and rehabilitation: some central issues'. *Crime and Delinquency, 18*, 1972, pp. 403–10.

Galaway, Burt, Hudson, Joe and Novack, Steve. *Restitution and Community Service: An Annotated Bibliography.* Waltham, Massachusetts: National Institute for Sentencing Alternatives, Brandeis University, 1983.

Galaway, Burt and Marsella, William. 'An exploratory study of the perceived fairness of restitution as a sanction for juvenile offenders'. Paper presented at the Second International Symposium on Victimology, Boston, Massachusetts, September 1976.

Guedalia, Leonard. *Predicting Recidivism of Juvenile Delinquents on Restitutionary Probation from Selected Background Subject, and Program Variables*. PhD dissertation, The American University, Washington, DC, 1979.

Gandy, John. 'Attitudes toward the use of restitution.' In B. Galaway and J. Hudson (eds), *Offender Restitution in Theory and Action*. Lexington, Massachusetts: D.C. Heath/Lexington Books, 1975, pp. 119–29.

Gandy, John and Galaway, Burt. 'Restitution as a sanction for offenders: a publics' view'. In J. Hudson and B. Galaway (eds), *Victims, Offenders and Alternative Sanctions*. Lexington, Massachusetts: D.C. Heath/Lexington Books, 1980, pp. 89–100.

Garofalo, Raffaele. 'Enforced reparation as a substitute for imprisonment.' *Criminology*. Boston: Little, Brown, 1914. Also in J. Hudson and B. Galaway (eds), *Considering the Victim: Readings in Restitution and Victim Compensation*. Springfield, Illinois: Charles C. Thomas, 1975, pp. 43–53.

Gehm, John. *Reports from the National VORP Management Information System*: Valparaiso, Indiana: PACT Institute of Justice, 1986.

Gehm, John and Umbreit, Mark. *National VORP Directory*. Valparaiso, Indiana: PACT Institute of Justice, 1985.

Haley, John. 'Confession, repentence, and absolution: the leitmotif of criminal justice in Japan'. In Martin Wright and Burt Galaway (eds), *Mediation and Criminal Justice: Victims, Offenders and Communities*. London: Sage, 1988.

Heinz, Anne and Kerstetter, Wayne. 'Pretrial settlement conference: evaluation of a reform in plea bargaining'. *Law and Society Review*, *13*, 1979, pp. 349–66.

Heinz, J., Galaway, B. and Hudson, J. 'Restitution or parole: a follow-up study of adult offenders'. *Social Service Review*, *50* (1), 1976, pp. 148–56.

Hickman-Maslin Research. *Report Prepared for North Carolina Center on Crime and Punishment Based on a Survey of Registered Voters in the State of North Carolina*. Raleigh, NC: North Carolina Center on Crime and Punishment, 1986.

Hinrichs, Donald. *Report on the Juvenile Crime Victim Project: Attitudes and Needs of Victims of Juvenile Crime, Commonwealth of Pennsylvania*. Gettysburg: Gettysburg College, 1981.

Hoebel, E. Adamson. *The Law of Primitive Man*. Cambridge: Harvard University Press, 1954.

Hofford, Merry. *Juvenile Restitution Program Final Report*. Charleston, South Carolina: Trident United Way, 1981.

Hough, Mike and Mayhew, Pat. *Taking Account of Crime: Key Findings From the 1984 British Crime Survey* (Home Office Research Study No 85). London: Her Majesty's Stationery Office, 1985.

Hough, Mike and Mayhew, Pat. *Home Office Research Study No. 76*. London: Her Majesty's Stationery Office, 1983.

Hudson, Joe and Galaway, Burt. 'Undoing the wrong: the Minnesota Restitution Center.' *Social Work*, *19* (3), 1974, pp. 313–18.

Hudson, Joe, Galaway, Burt and Novack, Steve. *National Assessment of*

Adult Restitution Programs Final Report. Duluth, Minnesota: University of Minnesota School of Social Development, 1980.

Hudson, J., Chesney, S. and McLagen, J. *Parole and Probation Staff Perceptions of Restitution*. St Paul: Minnesota Department of Corrections, 1977a.

Hudson, J., Chesney, S. and McLagen, J. *Restitution as Perceived by State Legislators and Correctional Administrators*. St Paul: Minnesota Department of Corrections, 1977b.

Keve, Paul and Eglash, Albert. 'Payments on a debt to society'. *NPPA News*, *36* (4), 1957, pp. 1–2.

Korn, Richard and McCorkle, Lloyd. *Criminology and Penology*. New York: Holt, Rinehart & Winston, 1959.

Mcguire, Mike. *Burglary in a Dwelling*. London: Heinemann, 1982.

McAnany, Patrick. 'Restitution as idea and practice: the retributive prospect'. In B. Galaway and J. Hudson (eds), *Offender Restitution in Theory and Action*. Lexington, Massachusetts: D.C. Heath/Lexington Books, 1978, pp. 15–32.

McEwen, Craig and Maiman, Richard. 'Small claims mediations in Maine: an empirical assessment'. *Maine Law Review*, *33*, 1981, pp. 237–68.

McKnight (Edmonds), Dorothy. 'The Victim–Offender Reconciliation Project.' In B. Galaway and J. Hudson (eds), *Perspectives on Crime Victims*. St Louis: C.V. Mosby, 1981, pp. 292–8.

Metro poll (11 January 1982). *Minneapolis Star & Tribune*.

Minnesota Department of Corrections. *Interim Evaluation Results: Minnesota Restitution Center*. St Paul, Minnesota, 1976.

Novack, S., Galaway, B. and Hudson, J. 'Victim offender perceptions of the fairness of restitution and community service sanctions'. In J. Hudson and B. Galaway (eds), *Victims, Offenders and Alternative Sanctions*. Lexington, Massachusetts: D.C. Heath/Lexington Books, 1980, pp. 63–9.

PACT Institute of Justice. *The VORP Book*. Valparaiso, Indiana: PACT Institute of Justice, 1984.

Peachey, D., Snyder, B. and Teichroeb, A. *Mediation Primer: A Training Guide for Mediators in the Criminal Justice System*. Kitchner, Ontario: Community Justice Initiatives of Waterloo Region, 1983.

Peachey, Dean. 'Victim offender reconciliation: fruition and frustration in Kitchner.' In M. Wright and B. Galaway (eds), *Mediation and Criminal Justice: Victims, Offenders and Communities*. London: Sage, 1988.

Kigin, Robert and Novack, Steve. 'A rural restitution program for juvenile offenders and victims'. In J. Hudson and B. Galaway (eds), *Victims, Offenders, and Alternative Sanctions*. Lexington, Massachusetts: D.C. Heath/Lexington Books, 1980, pp. 131–6.

Ronsom, Robin. *Sentencing Criminal Offenders: Judicial Practice and Public Opinion*. Thesis for Master of Arts in Sociology, University of Auckland, New Zealand, 1984.

Ruddick, Rose. 'Mediation and reparation: the Coventry experience'. In M. Wright and B. Galaway (eds), *Mediation and Criminal Justice: Victims, Offenders and Communities*. London: Sage, 1988.

Schafer, Stephen. 'The proper role of a victim-compensation system'. *Crime and Delinquency*, *21* (1), 1975, pp. 45–49.

Schafer, Stephen. 'Corrective compensation'. *Trial Magazine*, May/June 1972, pp. 25–7.

Schafer, Stephen. 'Victim compensation and responsibility'. *Southern California Law Review*, *43* (1), 1970, pp. 55–67.

Schafer, Stephen. *The Victim and His Criminal*. New York: Random House, 1968.

Schafer, Stephen. 'Restitution to victims of crime – an old correctional aim modernized'. *Minnesota Law Review*, *50*, 1965, pp. 243–54.

Schafer, Stephen. *Restitution to Victims of Crime*. London: Stevens and Sons, 1960.

Schneider, Anne. 'Restitution and recidivism rates of juvenile offenders: four experimental studies'. *Criminology*, *24* (3), 1986, pp. 533–52.

Schneider, Anne and Schneider, Peter. 'A comparison of programmatic and ad hoc restitution in juvenile courts'. *Justice Quarterly*, *1* (4), 1985, pp. 529–47.

Schneider, Peter, Griffith, William, and Schneider, Anne C. 'Juvenile restitution as a sole sanction or condition of probation: an empirical analysis'. *Journal of Research in Crime and Delinquency*, *19* (1), 1982, pp. 47–65.

Schneider, Peter, Schneider, A., Griffith, W. and Wilson, M. *Two Year Report on the National Evaluation of the Juvenile Restitution Initiative: An Overview of Program Performance*. Eugene: Institute of Policy Analysis, 1982.

Sebba, Leslie. 'Victims' role in the penal process: a theoretical orientation'. *American Journal of Comparative Law*, *30*, 1982, pp. 217–40.

Shapiro, C., Omole, O. and Schuman, A. 'The role of victims and probation: building a collaborative relationship'. Unpublished manuscript, Rutgers University, School of Criminal Justice Program Resources Center, 1986.

Shaw, Stephen. *The People's Justice: A Major Poll of Public Attitudes on Crime and Punishment*. London: Prison Reform Trust, 1982.

Shapland, J., Willmore, J. and Duff, P. *Victims in the Criminal Justice System*. London: Gower, 1985.

Thomson, Douglas and Regona, Anthony. 'Popular moderation versus governmental authoritarianism: an interactionist view of public sentiments toward criminal sanctions'. *Crime and Delinquency*, *33* (2), 1987, pp. 337–57.

Tittle, Charles. 'Restitution and deterrence: an evaluation of compatibility'. In B. Galaway and J. Hudson (eds), *Offender Restitution in Theory and Action*. Lexington, Massachusetts: D.C. Heath/Lexington Books, 1977, pp. 33–58.

Umbreit, Mark. 'Victim/offender mediation: a national survey'. *Federal Probation*, *50* (4), 1986, pp. 53–6.

Watson, D., Boucherat, F. and Davis, G. 'Reparation for retributivists'. In M. Wright and B. Galaway (eds), *Mediation and Criminal Justice: Victims, Offenders and Communities*. London: Sage, 1988.

12 Community Control, Criminal Justice and Victim Services
Robert Elias

INTRODUCTION

Beginning in the mid-1960s, and especially since 1970, America has rediscovered the crime victim. Arguing that victims encounter a society that neglects their victimization, and a criminal justice system that imposes a second victimization, champions of crime victims have promoted policies designed to redress victim needs, and to restore victims to their full status in the criminal process.

Among the major victim initiatives has been a series of services provided nationwide. They address victim needs, both in and out of the criminal process. They try to lessen the burden of victimization, and launch victims back toward normal lives as quickly as possible. Most of these kinds of programmes have operated for at least ten years. Since in that time they should have matured into full efficiency, researchers have now been evaluating their results.

Although few detailed, empirical studies exist, much evidence has been amassed, nevertheless, to assess victim-service programmes. Much of the evaluation to date, however, has focused rather narrowly (although certainly important) on the programmes' immediate, practical outcomes. We have paid little attention to the plans' broader, political implications. That is, the plans' advantages and disadvantages have been analysed, but not the politics of their creation and operation, and more importantly, not the programmes' political role in the criminal justice system and broader society.

Evaluation should not simply assess whether we spend enough money for victim needs. Nor should we merely evaluate programme outcomes narrowly without considering victims' broader interests. Thus, this paper will discuss the 'micropolitics' and 'macropolitics' of victim services. The *micropolitical analysis* will examine the plans, their goals, operations and outcomes based on the narrowest, official or (in the case of independent programmes) private definition of programme objectives. The *macropolitical analysis* will examine the programmes' broader (and often unstated) roles and objectives *vis-à-vis* the overall criminal justice and political systems.

First, we will examine the various kinds of victim-service programmes, including their objectives, resources and relationships. Secondly, we will evaluate the programmes' political influences and outcomes. On the micro-level, the victim's perspective will be emphasized. On the macro-level, the perspectives of others, closely linked to victim services, will also be considered. For this bi-level evaluation, we will frequently use victim compensation as a representative victim programme. Thirdly, we will assess the implications of the micro- and macropolitical analysis for victims, victim services, criminal justice and the broader political system. And fourthly, we will suggest various criteria and strategies for evaluating victim services, for designing programmes that are effective yet sensitive to political goals and constraints, and for promoting greater community control of criminal justice generally.

VICTIM SERVICE PROGRAMMES

The definition of victim programmes varies, but the following eight types cover the range of services:

(1) *Victim compensation* exists in half the American states, and provides victims with government payments to restore the losses incurred from victimization. These are government programmes, funded primarily by state tax dollars, most of which exist as separate agencies, and which seek a close, working relationship with the rest of the criminal justice process (Elias, 1983c).

(2) *Offender restitution* exists theoretically in virtually every American jurisdiction, but its actual use has been limited largely to those judges who embrace restitution in their sentencing philosophy. A few, more formal programmes have been established in some states (Galaway, 1977). This approach makes offenders pay victims to reimburse them for lost property or physical damages. Restitution is a government programme, usually integral to the criminal justice process, and usually requires no additional spending. The more formal programmes are tied to corrections departments, and are usually funded by the national government (Elias, 1983c).

(3) *Victim-witness programmes* assist victims in the criminal process, providing information about the courts, alerts for court appearances, and conveniences. They help victims through the criminal process and try to enhance their participation and commitment. Most programmes are housed in police departments or prosecutor's offices, and are financed by the national government (Baluss, 1975).

(4) *Social-service referrals* direct victims to both public and private agencies for physical, psychological and living problems resulting from the victimization. The agencies include the welfare department, hospitals, mental-health clinics, and victim-compensation boards. Most programmes operate independently from the criminal process, and are located either separately or in hospitals. They are run by groups such as medical personnel, religious organizations or volunteer agencies. Their financing combines private and government sources (Friedman, 1976).

(5) *Crisis intervention* emphasizes emergency services for victims, particularly victims of violent crimes. These programmes specialize in satisfying victims' immediate physical and psychological needs. They exist in many forms, and frequently emphasize particular groups of victims (such as children, or women, or the elderly). Although these plans work very closely with medical facilities, they are independent of the criminal justice system and are often funded privately. Frequently, they are operated by special interest organizations such as women's groups (Dussich, 1981; Chesney and Schneider, 1981; Oberg and Pence, 1981).

(6) *Victim advocacy* is provided through relatively rare programmes that go beyond providing victim services narrowly in the criminal process, and beyond attending to victims' physical and psychological needs. Advocacy tries to give victims more control and input into criminal cases, and promote victim legislation. The host organizations for advocacy include offices both inside and outside the criminal justice system, but often they seek integration into law enforcement and the courts. These programmes are funded both privately and by government (Commission on Victim Witness Assistance, n.d.: Schneider and Schneider, 1981).

(7) *Mediation*, sometimes associated with neighbourhood justice, seeks to remove criminal disputes from the courts and relocate them in more informal settings. These programmes try to resolve cases by mutual agreement between the conflicting parties in a less threatening environment. By definition, this service is located outside the formal criminal process, and operated by some

private organization, such as a church or voluntary group. These plans are also funded both privately and by government (Davis, 1982).

(8) *Crime reduction* programmes try to reduce crime, particularly for victims thought to be susceptible to victimization. Victims participate in individual and group programmes emphasizing cooperation with law enforcement, the use of various protective devices, and the reformation of personal habits. These plans are frequently integral to the criminal process, particularly to police departments, although some programmes are created independently in the community. The police programmes are funded by the government, while community groups often support themselves (National Commission on Criminal Justice Standards and Goals, 1973).

Although the aforementioned services all attempt to address victim needs, they have many differences. The programmes' objectives vary between improving the victim's role in the criminal process, and improving the victim's well-being apart from law enforcement. Secondly, the plans vary between being inspired by government and being created spontaneously by private organizations. Thirdly, the programmes differ in their connection and relationship with the criminal justice process. And finally, since the programmes vary in their funding sources, differences exist in their financial independence from government. These provide important differences for evaluating the programmes' effectiveness.

EVALUATING VICTIM SERVICES

We can evaluate victim services in many ways, but we will stress three major approaches. First, 'process' evaluation assesses whether a particular programme is implemented according to its intended guidelines. Secondly, 'impact' evaluation assesses whether the programme's implementation produces a change in the desired direction (Nachmais, 1979). And thirdly, 'political' evaluation assesses the programme's role in the political system. We will emphasize the final approach, partly because it has been ignored, and partly because politics will ultimately define a programme's level of success, and for whose needs.

Since evaluating all victim programmes exceeds this paper's scope, we will focus upon victim compensation as a representative service. Its evaluation will help us identify some characteristics of victim services that should be avoided by those who are genuinely interested in pursuing victim needs.

Micro-level analysis

Initially, we must evaluate the practical effects of victim programmes, including the programmes' implementation, operation and outcomes. But, unlike most assessments of victim services, we must go beyond narrow (albeit important) goal-oriented evaluations, and examine the political influences that help shape the programmes. This will allow us to better understand and analyse each programme's outcomes.

Programme creation

Government creates many victim services, and thus we should expect the normal politics of formulating and legislating public policy. But, the politics of creating victim services go considerably beyond this commonsense notion. The establishment of victim-compensation programmes provides a good illustration.

In the late 1960s and early 1970s, creating compensation plans (and victim services, in general) was very popular with policy-makers. Providing for victims (like motherhood and apple pie) is a difficult issue to oppose. Consequently, the political manoeuvring associated with such programmes was atypical. In New York, for example, legislators strongly competed for the privilege of sponsoring the state's compensation programme. In fact, over fifty legislators co-sponsored the legislation, which may be a record. To be able to sponsor the programme and return to their constituency to publicize the plan as their inspiration was very valuable for building public opinion and electoral support.

But, does this imply a strong commitment to victims, and to the compensation programme? This can be measured in several ways, but programme funding levels may reveal the most. In fact, the flurry of sponsorship and support did not prevent many of the same legislators from voting against programme appropriations, or for funding so low as to preordain the plan's failure (Edelhertz and Geis, 1974). In fact, the programmes in Louisiana and Tennessee actually disbanded for lack of financial support. The political reality of victim services (such as victim compensation) indicates that official support might be only a half-hearted, opportunistic commitment to victims and their needs. We must recognize this if we ever hope to devise effective, alternative strategies.

Programme resources and visibility
The government's initial financial support for many victim services has often been minimal. But, has the funding improved once the programmes were firmly established?

Taking again the victim compensation example, financial records indicate that appropriations have not increased steadily. Where (in a few programmes) funding has continued to rise, the increases have been minimal, and nowhere near that needed for the programme to serve most victims. Again, in New York, the plan (one of the largest) serves less than 1 per cent of the state's *violent* crime victims (Crime Victims Compensation Board, 1978), and no victims of other crimes. Other victim services follow the same pattern: severely underfunded, short-term grants, declining support and eventual failure (Dussich, 1981).

Funding also helps determine the visibility of many victim services (Vaughn and Hofrichter, 1980). Although victim-compensation programmes, for example, received much publicity when first established, and periodic new doses of attention thereafter, the programmes were not necessarily accessible to victims. In fact, as the New Jersey and New York programmes illustrate, general visibility did not make specific application information available to victims (Elias, 1983c). Although some programmes have increased the application information conveyed to victims, most efforts have failed (Crime Victims Compensation Board, 1978; Elias, 1983c). A similar gap between creating services and making them accessible to victims also exists for other victim programmes.

Why would policy-makers create programmes, and then not actively encourage victims to participate? It could be because they lack a real commitment to victims and their problems, but it also could be because even minimally using the programmes would quickly deplete their funding, and perhaps force additional appropriations. Politics exist in virtually every funding decision made by government, as policy-makers try to juggle competing demands for resources. But, politics intervene in a special way when policy-makers do not strongly support the programmes in the first place. Victim services seem to be such programmes.

Programme operation
Long ago, we learned that politics and administration cannot be

divorced. What characterizes the management of organizations generally applies no less to victim programmes: political considerations significantly affect decision-making and outcomes. While some (Rich, 1981) have begun to recognize this for victim services, much more can be said.

A major political influence on administration occurs when agencies reflect official, instead of client, needs. This affects official behaviour internally, and its relationship to outside influences. For victim services, officials may be pursuing private needs over victim needs, and may be more concerned with their decision's effects on external political actors (such as legislators) than on victims.

For example, while some research has identified 'advocates' among compensation board officials in New York and New Jersey, most were better identified as 'neutrals'. That is, while a few administrators actively advocated victim rights and needs in their work, most worried more about themselves, their colleagues and the political officials to whom they answered (Elias, 1983c). Consequently, they tolerated working in victim programmes which only barely reach their intended recipients. We cannot totally blame administrative inaction, since political checks and funding limitations are restrictive. But, it illustrates how official needs dominate victim needs, nevertheless.

Victim-witness programmes, often reputed to 'use' victims for pursuing criminal cases the prosecutor deems important (Ash, 1972; Dubow and Becker, 1976), face a similar problem. Beyond recognizing how officials use victims, we must understand the political motivations behind these actions. Law enforcement rhetoric to the contrary, we have little evidence that uncooperative victims cause cases to be discontinued. In fact, in most jurisdictions, many victims want to participate, but never get the chance (Elias, 1983c; McDonald, 1976). Actually, the prosecution promotes more discontinued cases, and often intentionally. Prosecutors need not pursue against all suspects (Reiss, 1974; Ziegenhagen and Benyi, 1981). Instead, they pursue only cases they think they can win, since they are evaluated politically on their conviction record. A victim's value to the prosecution usually extends only to what he or she can add to that conviction rate.

Besides, victims and their representatives are clearly intruders or outsiders to the courtroom 'workgroups' (including prosecutors, defenders and judges) that often dominate the criminal process (Davis and Dill, 1978; Eisenstein and Jacob, 1977). That these characteristics might reflect structural problems and not the personal shortcomings of prosecutors and other official actors does little to reduce the victim's resulting exploitation and unmet needs (DuBow and Becker, 1976).

Programme outcomes
Perhaps the most important criteria by which to judge victim services lies in the programmes' impact. Most plans seek relatively narrow objectives. A truly effective programme, however, must satisfy victim needs. Some researchers and practitioners have evaluated the short-term outcomes of victim services (Dussich, 1981; Friedman, 1976; Rich, 1981; Schneider and Schneider, 1981; Ziegenhagen and Benyi, 1981), and thus we can analyse their findings and draw some of our own conclusions. From these conclusions, we can speculate about which programmes best serve victim needs, and about how to capture their characteristics in future programmes.

(1) *Victim compensation.* The most apparent goal of these plans, restoring victims through financial payments, is not being met for most victims. For many reasons, only very few victims receive assistance, and when given, it is often insufficient, and with much delay and inconvenience (Doerner, 1978; Elias, 1983c).
(2) *Offender restitution.* Although few programmes have had some success (Galaway, 1977), restitution has been mostly unused and ineffective. Many judges refuse to use it in sentencing, and when they do, the assailant is usually not apprehended or financially insolvent (Schneider and Schneider, 1981). For what it is worth to the victim, even programmes that successfully arrange restitution payments usually fail to provide the victim–offender interaction upon which this service is philosphically based (Gattuso Holman, 1976; McKnight, 1981).
(3) *Victim-Witness programmes.* These programmes seem to prefer official over victim needs. Most have not significantly enhanced victim involvement in cases, nor the satisfaction derived therefrom (Heinz and Kerstetter, 1981). Some have enhanced the victim's overall participation and control in criminal proceedings.
(4) *Social service referrals.* Although these programmes make numerous referrals, many providing victims with genuine assistance, the plans have numerous difficulties (Schneider and Schneider, 1981). First, many victims cannot be found since most do not pursue their cases, yet suffer from victimization's after-effects nevertheless. Victims avoid seeking assistance unless their

need is unbearable, because they feel the criminal process cannot meet their needs, or because they distrust law enforcers. For referral agencies outside the criminal process, many victims are similarly deterred, perceiving such programmes as yet additional examples of insensitive, aggravating and unresponsive bureaucracies. Secondly, these agencies often find their referrals ineffective because many social services do not address victim needs, or do not accept victim cases (Friedman, 1976).

(5) *Crisis intervention.* Organizations handling emergency needs of selected victims seem comparatively successful in their work. But, in an absolute sense, they still cannot serve the immediate needs of most victims. Many victims are unaware of these services, and if and when they find out, the emergency has often passed.

(6) *Victim advocacy.* Some successes for promoting victims' broader rights have occurred, especially when programmes exist independently from the criminal justice system (Dussich, 1976). But, the failures are many. First, relatively few programmes exist in the first place. Second, the status of victims' rights has changed little, and the criminal prosecution still emphasizes social interests, and not victim interests. Third, victims have not gained any clear control, or basis for consistent participation, in the criminal process (Schneider and Schneider, 1981). Victims and their advocates are still considered unwanted outsiders by many justice personnel (Ziegenhagen and Benyi, 1981).

(7) *Mediation.* Some of these programmes have been very successful (Danzig, 1974), yet theoretically their potential goes considerably beyond their current use (Christie, 1978). So few of these plans operate that they have not provided much relief for victims. Victims welcome such alternatives, however, even when they have not specifically experienced such programmes (Elias, 1983c).

(8) *Crime reduction.* While these programmes claim to build a sense of community and reduce crime (particularly for past victims), they may do neither (Schneider and Schneider, 1981). In theory, for example, these programmes should be contributing to crime reduction by promoting citizen assistance to police, increased reporting of criminal cases, and crime-prevention devices (Dussich, 1981). While some of these changes may have occurred, they have not affected the crime rate, except occasionally to displace it elsewhere (Elias, 1981).

These thumbnail evaluations of victim services may seem unduly harsh, and perhaps they overlook some important successes and favourable trends. Overall, however, while these services might be important to those few victims who use them, most victims' needs are not met, or even addressed. These programmes may not be completely incapable of meeting victims' problems. With more financing, for example, their efforts could be much more successful. Nevertheless, even some of the most ardent supporters of victim services have been discouraged by their overall ineffectiveness. With new cutbacks in government funding, the programmes' effect seems even more jeopardized.

From the victim's perspective, some programmes help much more than others. A few researchers have characterized the most effective programmes. One view, for example, suggests that victim services be run by private, quasi-public or non-profit groups which include broader programmes, beyond mere referrals, as well as education, prevention, advocacy and participation (Friedman, 1976). Another argues for independent programmes that emphasize outreach and advocacy, and which seek private support (Rich, 1981). Still another claims that the greater the state control of these services, the less the victim control (Ziegenhagen and Benyi, 1981). These views indicate that programmes should be independent of governmental control, such as service-referral groups, crisis-intervention centres, victim-advocacy organizations, mediation plans, and community-initiated, crime-control programmes.

While these programmes would reduce official control, they might also lack financial support. Nevertheless, their independence helps ensure that victim needs dominate. Such programmes should probably accept government financing when available, as long as it does not restrict the programme's operations. And, alternative resources might be available. For example, one study of rape crisis centres has listed at least twelve other sources besides government grants (O'Sullivan, 1978).

Summary
This micro-level analysis of victim services questions whether these programmes really satisfy their objectives, as narrowly defined, to any significant degree. While the programmes may satisfy official needs, they help few victims. Certain political factors contribute significantly to these plans' ineffectiveness. Officials do not seem very committed to assisting victims, since victim needs seem much less

important than their own. Moreover, administrative structures and incentives in criminal justice do not promote official sensitivity toward victims. Consequently, from a micro-political perspective, the meagre impact of these programmes is not surprising.

But, the political implications of victim services transcend merely the politics influencing their creation and operation. The plans have a broader role than usually imagined. What political functions do victim services perform that exceed merely our concern for victims?

Macro-level analysis

A macro-level analysis will assess the broader role victim-service programmes play in the overall political system. Can we identify additional purposes for victim programmes beyond the narrow objectives examined already? To do so, we must consider how we define victims when creating such programmes, and the philosophical basis for establishing victim services. We must consider more broadly whether victim programmes serve needs even higher than those of victims and programme administrators. We must examine whether such programmes seek crime control, or rather broader social control. Finally, we must evaluate whether victim programmes actually achieve these broader, political purposes. For this analysis, we must consider official perspectives much more than before.

Defining victims

It is no longer controversial to suggest that those who dominate the society impose their definitions of crime and criminals (Clinard and Quinney, 1967; Reiman, 1979). We conceptualize crime selectively and politically. Since what we regard as criminal also defines whom we consider crime victims, we conceptualize victimization selectively and politically, as well.

What determines whether we designate some harms as criminal victimizations, and not others? The concept 'victim' may symbolize the official definition of social harms or social problems (Quinney, 1972). Victims may include those people whose harm can be recognized without threatening the existing power structure. For example, officially identifying as victims people harmed by state violence, war, poverty, inequality or criminal 'corrections' would be threatening because it might trace the harm to the political system. Likewise, criminals are those officially identified as perpetrators of social harm, but that definition excludes many other kinds of threats and wrongdoers that we could define as crime and criminals (Reiman, 1979). Again, officially identifying as criminals people and institutions such as the police, the military, economic structures, business entities or the criminal justice process might also threaten the prevailing system. Consequently, defining victims and criminals must be done narrowly and selectively.

Victim compensation programmes again illustrate how such definitions affect victim services. Compensation plans define eligible victims very narrowly (Lamborn, 1976). One must meet all these requirements: state citizenship, violent crime victimization, rapid cooperation with board and law-enforcement officials, no past or present relationship with the offender, innocence of contributing to the crime and inability to collect payments elsewhere. In addition, almost all programmes require the claimant to satisfy a 'financial means test' that verifies, essentially, that the victim would qualify for public welfare. There is no rationale for most of these restrictions, yet if not satisfied, one does not qualify as a victim as far as compensation programmes are concerned. The same holds for other victim services, at least those dominated by government. In victim–witness programmes, for example, one usually does not qualify for the official status of victim unless he/she helps satisfy official needs, particularly by helping in selected prosecutions.

To begin with, these direct and indirect definitions of victims suggest that we might be ignoring wrongdoing that could be defined as crime, and thus ignoring people who suffer and who could be defined as victims (Reiman, 1979). Secondly, although already limited generally, the 'official' list of victims shrinks even further for victim-service programmes since they vastly reduce the categories of victims eligible for service. Thirdly, we might question the kinds of people eliminated, as compared to those who are served. We seem favourably biased towards those who cooperate with criminal justice, who do not know the offender, whose needs can be delayed, and who generate organized group support (Rich, 1981). Others are often eliminated by 'blaming victims' for their characteristics or circumstances. Should victims be penalized for not cooperating with a criminal process that consistently fails to meet their needs and which subjects them to a second victimization? Should the offender's family members be denied coverage for that accident of birth? Do many victims really 'provoke' the crime against them? Why do compensation programmes require such rapid applications when they often take more than two years to process?

The definitions of victims that characterize victim services reflect more than narrow administrative needs. The low visibility of such programmes, based on insufficient application information, derives not merely from inadequate resources, but also apparently from an official desire to limit the number of victims who apply, find themselves ineligible and then are alienated (if not angered) as a result.

Philosophy

In addition to how we define victims, we must examine the general philosophy we pursue toward potential recipients of various services. For example, the 'means test' used by compensation programmes replicates the criteria used by existing welfare agencies. Treating compensation as welfare reflects the programmes' broader role.

First, it prevents compensation from being a right, available to all victims. Instead, compensation becomes a narrowly circumscribed privilege. The victim remains a second-class citizen in criminal justice and government. Second, a welfare philosophy assigns victims to a marginal and stigmatized status in society, reflected in our disparaging national consciousness about public welfare and its recipients. Furthermore, it suggests that our approach to victimization mimics our approach to poverty: we will provide some remedial programmes, but we will not address the problem fundamentally.

Symbolic goals

We must distinguish between symbolic and tangible politics when assessing public policy. An important difference exists between programmes designed for some concrete impact or tangible change, and policies created more for their psychological or political appeal (Edelman, 1967). Are victim services, at least government plans, primarily symbolic in their intent or effect, and lacking in any significant, tangible impact?

Using our victim compensation example, it has been ten years since the first suggestion that such programmes might be no more than 'political placebos' (Chappell, 1972). Others have argued that the plans were created primarily for their psychological effects (Miers, 1980) or for their political advantages (Elias, 1983b). To assess these claims, we must examine the existing evaluations of compensation programmes. Since this requires us to consider the programmes' other objectives, we can also learn the additional functions that victim services seem to perform.

Beyond paying victims, compensation programmes also purport to help control crime, and to improve attitudes and cooperation among citizens (including victims) toward criminal justice, victim compensation and government. These goals intersect since improved attitudes would presumably produce more cooperation which would, in turn, help law enforcers prevent crime. But, since research indicates that most victims fail to qualify for compensation, that only about one in three eligible get compensation, and that when received, victims often consider it inadequate (Elias, 1983c), compensation cannot be achieving the aforementioned goals, if in fact they are being achieved at all. If the goals *are* met, could it be from the programme's symbolic effect, and not its substance (or lack thereof)?

Victim compensation has no apparent effect on the first objective: crime control. The programmes have neither reduced the crime rate, nor improved clearance and conviction rates (Doerner, 1976; Doerner, 1978b; Silverman and Doerner, 1979). But what about improving attitudes and cooperation?

To begin with, compensation has not produced a greater level of crime reporting nor willingness to prosecute nor more favourable attitudes – all important signs that people have not become more cooperative (Doerner, 1978a; Doerner, 1980). An analysis of New York and New Jersey crime victims shows that most victims encountering compensation programmes do not have better attitudes nor a greater willingness to cooperate than those not making a compensation claim. In fact, claimants have significantly *worse* attitudes than non-claimants, even when controlling for victim characteristics and previous victimization and post-victimization experiences. This occurs even though some claimants are compensated, and some of them are pleased with their award. Administrative obstacles, and not merely the lack of an award (or an insufficient one), also produce dissatisfaction (Elias, 1984a).

Compensation plans have not developed good attitudes and cooperation among victims, and have not overcome the negative experience most victims suffer from their victimization and their treatment in the criminal process. Disenchantment among claimants seems to come from their high expectations about getting an award, only to consistently find themselves either ineligible or unsuccessful. And, this does not even count those who may have discovered enough about the eligibility requirements before making a claim, and decided it was futile (Elias, 1984a).

The programmes seem to produce an unanticipated consequence: greater discontent with government and criminal justice than if the plans had never existed. But that negative consequence affects very few people. It alienates only dissatisfied (usually uncompensated or inadequately compensated) victim claimants. On the other hand, satisfied claimants support the programmes, government and criminal justice. And, most people – those not victimized in the first place – applaud the apparent concern for victims embodied in compensation programmes. This provides a good illustration of symbolic politics: the public appreciates the programme and hopes it will never need it, when in fact, should the programme ever be needed, for most people it will not effectively be there (Elias, 1984a)!

Social control

Shaping public opinion. The symbolism of victim compensation goes further. The now long-term call to address victim needs, and to reorient the criminal process away from the offender and toward the victim, has been closely associated with a 'law and order' approach to law enforcement (Dussich, 1981). Get-tough criminal policies have combined with an apparent concern for the victim (Curtis, 1976; Curtis, 1977). Adopting what many have viewed as repressive measures for handling crime will, however, meet some resistance in a self-proclaimed democratic system, unless these measures have considerable public support. Promoting victim-service programmes, such as compensation plans, shows policy-makers' apparent concern for the general public as potential victims, and apparently in return, the public supports high spending and tremendously strengthened police forces.

In this case, merely the 'symbol' of concern about victims ensured public support. Proving that such programmes actually provide substantial, or even minor, results has been unnecessary. The general public (except those actually experiencing the criminal process) has credited criminal justice officials with being concerned about victims. Yet most rank-and-file law enforcers still fail to provide victims with application information for compensation, and do not tell victims about the programmes, even in states that have had the programmes for over fifteen years (Elias, 1983c).

Why do we believe we must strengthen our police forces? Has our new preparedness reduced crime? If not, then what other functions do police forces perform? Some suggest that government cares less about reducing crime (and might even be content to maintain it at certain levels (Reiman, 1979)), and much more about social control

(Krisberg, 1975; Quinney, 1980; Wright, 1973). While this might be true, and while victim services might have helped enhance police forces, victim programmes may play an additional and more direct role in social control.

Controlling the poor? Crime affects some people and some communities more than others. Especially for our more serious (violent) crime, the poor and minorities suffer greater victimization, and in fact, commit more of these crimes themselves. These people often live in a degrading and desperate atmosphere (rarely of their own making), labelled some years ago as the 'subculture of violence' (Wolfgang and Ferracuti, 1967). In this setting, it seems almost a matter of chance as to who will strike first, and consequently, who will become the 'criminal' and who will become the 'victim' for any given criminal transaction. Many victims have previously committed crimes, and many criminals have previously been victimized (Buder, 1977; Elias, 1983c). The situation is dangerous, explosive and unpredictable (Elias, 1983b).

The poor and minorities, therefore, need victim services the most, and some means to control the rampant crime and violence in their communities. In the late 1960s, however, when the first signs of victim assistance arose, street crime was not the only disorder plaguing lower-class neighbourhoods. There was great turmoil over civil rights violations and the frustrations of dead-end poverty. Riots and massive disruptions occurred, and law enforcers were even less prepared for these outbreaks than for normal street crime.

We sought to soothe not only the discontent arising from criminal violence in the ghetto, but also the much more profound and threatening discontent against the state and the society, in general. Rather than addressing the sources of crime and poverty, however, the response (particularly if one examines Law Enforcement Assistance Administration spending from the late 1960s through the mid-1970s) seemed to mix toughness and pacification. 'Toughness' arose from court decisions giving freer reign to the police, and from vastly strengthened police departments, although the new hardware and technology (such as helicopters, mini-tanks, riot and surveillance equipment) seemed much more appropriate for controlling mass disturbances than individual crimes. 'Pacification' came through police-community programmes, but again, these programmes seemed more designed to calm tensions than to control crime (Center for Research on Criminal Justice, 1982; Elias, 1981). Victim assistance (including victim compensation) might be understood as a part of this appeasement, and not only as a criminal justice policy, but also as a social control policy (Elias, 1983b).

Compensation as welfare.   In this context, the role of compensation plans as welfare programmes acquires even greater significance. American welfare programmes may have served much more to appease a portion of the population psychologically than effectively to redistribute wealth, attack poverty or even serve as a security blanket for the poor. Our welfare rolls have risen (because more money has been provided and eligibility requirements lessened) in direct proportion to periodical outbreaks of massive discontent by the poor ever since the 1930s. When the disturbances have subsided, the welfare rolls consistently declined (because less money has been provided and eligibility requirements tightened). Thus, we seem to use public welfare as a social control mechanism (Piven and Cloward, 1971).

The criminal justice system may perform the same function. The same kind of ebb and flow in the prison population, corresponding to periods of social calm and discontent, has occurred, for example, even beyond any detectable changes in actual crime (Quinney, 1980). And, victim services such as victim compensation may provide an even better example of a social control policy.

Compensation plans are not merely criminal justice policies; they are also welfare policies. The plans potentially promote social control because poor people (who also live in the highest crime areas) comprise part of the general public that has most applauded this apparent show of concern for victims. It may not be coincidental that these programmes arose in the late 1960s precisely when welfare rolls expanded to cope (if we believe the previous argument) with urban discontent. It also may not be accidental that most arose within a few years of that crisis period or not at all, occurred predominantly in states whose cities were disrupted, and have been plagued by tentative and insufficient budgetary support ever since urban discontent declined in the early to mid-1970s (despite continuing violent crime victimization).

Other parallels between victim compensation and public welfare exist as well. Both programmes help some claimants, but many less than they should. Only about one-half of those eligible for public welfare receive it (Ryan, 1976), while victim compensation does even worse. Both programmes exclude people who arguably should qualify. Both provide inadequate awards to those they do pay. Both programmes fail to address the fundamental sources of the problem they claim to be combating. That is, welfare programmes do not genuinely seek to eliminate poverty, and compensation plans do not genuinely seek to eliminate crime or victim losses. Both programmes apply band-aids to the symptoms of poverty and crime, respectively, without addressing or counteracting their sources (Rich, 1981). Some suggest that we do not have the solutions to poverty and crime, but while we might not have all the answers, in fact, we are well aware of many causes and remedies. We refuse to act because to do so would challenge American mainstream institutions (Reiman, 1979).

Perhaps the interests and preferences of those who dominate public policy also limit us. But, we need not interpret this as purposeful intrigue. Instead, it might be the by-product of the 'mobilization of bias' in politics, or the set of predominant values, beliefs, rituals and institutional procedures that operate systematically and consistently to benefit certain persons and groups at the expense of others (Bachrach and Baratz, 1970; Schattschneider, 1960). Those favoured persons and groups perhaps have less incentives seriously to reduce (at least violent) crime and eliminate poverty (since they are rarely its victims), and may in fact, have very strong and material reasons for not doing so.

We may be socialized into either consciously or unconsciously accepting a status quo that favours bureaucratic convenience and privileged interests. We should not be surprised that we have no apparently genuine and substantive anti-crime and anti-poverty programmes in America. And victim services, such as victim compensation, do not appear to be very genuine and substantive victim and anti-crime programmes either.

Programme outcomes
Since earlier in our micro-analysis we examined the outcomes of victim services, we must now evaluate the programmes' wider effects, considering their other goals, and their broader political functions.

Like victim compensation, most other government-sponsored victim services seek more than merely restoring the victim in some way. They also seek some kind of control. In particular, victim-witness programmes seek to control victims in the criminal process. Victims often seem to be channelled into the process for official needs rather than victim needs (Elias, 1981).

Victim services also seem to ignore the value of serious crime control for preventing victims in the first place. While official rhetoric consistently emphasizes its concern for reducing crime, the policies actually promoted are ineffective. The programmes have little effect on reducing crime. Again, one might question the real commitment of public officials and law enforcers to eliminating crime, or even reducing it (Reiman, 1979). In fact, government-inspired victim services, as currently constituted, might actually increase crime by promoting discredited policies that only encourage crime, and do not effectively combat it. Furthermore, the victim orientation of these programmes may abdicate responsibility for addressing the sources of crime, since they emphasize a false contest (between offenders and victims) of rights (not needs) and promote complacency toward crime, now that some post-victimization relief appears available (Currie, 1978a; Curtis, 1976; Curtis, 1977). In sum, one wonders whether victim services seek social control, or crime control, or any kind of substantial assistance to victims at all.

Summary

A macro-level analysis of victim services allows us to view them from a broader, political perspective. Whether intentional or not, these programmes, particularly government-run ones, question the official commitment to victim needs, and suggest other, broader political functions. Government programmes define the kinds of victimization and victims eligible for services narrowly, and preserve the status quo, regardless of how it may promote crime. The philosophy of victim programmes comes from the welfare tradition (with all its negative connotations), and fails to enhance victim rights. The programmes largely lack substance, particularly for the many unserved victims, yet the public seems symbolically satisfied that something is being done for crime victims.

Victim services correspond to enhanced police forces (even though strengthened law enforcement has not reduced crime) and more to controlling social discontent than crime. We can add many victim services to our current public welfare agencies as organizations that 'manage' crime and poverty (through symbolic and tangible inducements), rather than eliminate their sources. Although some important differences among government-sponsored victim services exist, most either narrowly control victims or broadly control discontent rather than control crime or meet victim needs.

IMPLICATIONS AND STRATEGIES

Not all victim programmes are the same. Among the differences already compared, the most important seems to be whether or not they originate and operate within government, that is within the criminal justice system. Most evaluations of victim services suggest that they should be independent, non-profit organizations that promote victim interests without becoming institutionalized into the formal criminal justice process. This favours programmes such as service referral agencies, crisis intervention centres, victim advocacy groups, mediation plans and community controlled crime prevention. In the language of citizen participation theory, grass-roots citizen 'activism' works more effectively than government-mandated citizen 'involvement' (Boyte, 1980).

As for government programmes, should we continue to support them? They provide relatively few benefits, often manipulate the victim, and promote social control more than victim needs. Yet, some programmes may have redeeming value nevertheless. Despite their negative, or at least not very useful, characteristics, victim compensation and offender restitution probably should be continued, but vastly expanded. While they fall far short of their promise, these programmes do at least help a few victims, and could be structured and funded to help many more. But, we should harbour no illusions about the political functions of these programmes. Recognizing their broader political purposes and effects begins what might be efforts for genuine reform. That reform should never be merely raising funding to cover the current level of criminal losses, but must be directed more broadly and insistently towards significantly reducing crime in the first place.

On the other hand, government-based victim-witness programmes and crime prevention programmes should be avoided. Official victim-witness plans offer little hope of favouring victim needs over official needs. Court-oriented services can, however, be performed by independent organizations, preferably associated with victim advocacy centres. Such programmes can be effective if tied to neighbourhood cohesiveness and community involvement (Currie, 1982b; Shapiro and Gutierrez, 1982).

We should also reject government-sponsored crime prevention programmes. They do not reduce crime, they emphasize citizen involvement only after the crime, and their approach to crime prevention goes no further than promoting new gadgets, hardware, suspiciousness and restricted freedoms. They do not reduce our fear of crime, and in fact might increase it. They reflect police biases and middle- and upper-class interests, instead of lower-class needs. They consistently fail to examine the real and major sources of crime (such as poverty, unemployment, social dislocation, rampant competition, gun availability, overcriminalization, and so on), and fail to question how we define crime in the first place, with its tendency to exclude much middle- and upper-class wrongdoing (Reiman, 1979).

When occasionally police–community relations improve, it is only on police terms, and often both sides become disillusioned and distrustful. The plans fail to produce genuine citizen control of law enforcement, and only help police control the communities they serve. Police officers seem caught between those who genuinely care about victims and crime, and those who apparently do not. Unfortunately, the police and their programmes more often reflect the biases and interests of the latter than the former (Center for Research in Criminal Justice, 1982).

Community control

Promoting community-based and community controlled crime prevention groups can more positively meet victim needs, increase citizen activism and more clearly address the sources of crime and poverty in the first place. These kinds of programmes should be autonomous from the police. They should be organized community efforts that seek an independent and challenging, if not conflictual (Christie, 1978), relationship with law enforcement, recognizing that criminal justice efforts do not necessarily reduce crime or serve victims' best interests. Programmes should reject outworn, official criminal justice stereotypes about crime and criminals, and seek fundamental changes, not merely an adjustment or acceptance of official policies. The real and major sources of crime should be emphasized as well as how our present, distorted definitions of crime serve to 'weed out the wealthy' (Reiman, 1979).

We must seek greater citizen control at all criminal justice levels, not merely over the police. Citizens could become more involved in observing courts; influencing, monitoring and evaluating work, policies, appointments and budgets; and influencing criminal law definitions. Citizens might consider withholding their support and participation in an organized way until the criminal justice system and the broader political system become more responsive to citizen and victim needs.

Community programmes must take both a long-term and a short-term perspective. The 'burglar alarm mentality' which relies on short-sighted and individualistic protective measures must be rejected. Making a significant dent in the crime problem requires fundamental changes not only in criminal justice, but also in the broader society. Taking a longer-term perspective and challenging old solutions will require informed, committed leadership from experts in both citizen participation and criminal justice, as well as programmes of community education that counteract our current, fatalistic and misinformed criminal justice mentality (Bonfield, 1974; Wilson, 1975). We also need rational strategies that avoid subordination to law-enforcement officials and priorities, and a multi-issue approach that recognizes the interrelationship of crime and other social problems. In fact, crime could be a rallying issue for a much broader community organization. This would emphasize a more decentralized law enforcement, possibly creating alternative justice institutions (Brady, 1981).

In the meantime, we obviously need short-run protective measures. But, they should be placed in the context of broader community education and longer-term criminal justice and social change. We must avoid individualized responses such as guns, guard dogs, booby traps and mutual suspicion. Instead, we need a much more community-oriented strategy toward crime control, based on organizing community members and their environment. This approach would also avoid the vigilantism that has afflicted some citizen programmes in the past.

The community control approach to reducing crime also could be the broader foundation upon which other, more specific *victim* services and agencies would be based (Friedman, 1976). It could support independent victim witness and advocacy centres, crisis intervention and social service referral agencies, and community mediation, which might lead to a more decentralized, neighbourhood-based justice (Danzig and Lowy, 1975; Dussich, 1981; Merry, 1979; Nader, 1980; Spence, 1978).

In another sense, this strategy could unite the 'victim movement' with the 'citizens movement' (Boyte, 1980), and help us recognize that the crime problem, and the needs of victims, relate to broader social problems, all of which might be more subject to change through community-based organizations challenging the status quo.

This would give a new and much broader meaning to the concept of 'popular justice' (Elias, 1984b, 1985).

In sum, we must decide whether the political and criminal justice systems really work for the victims' and the public's best interests, and if not, what kinds of strategies we can design to counteract this tendency. The community approach would significantly transform our current reliance on official perspectives and solutions for coping with crime, for victim needs, and even other social ills. These needs will not be met until citizens, including victims, develop a base of control and power, and use it. While we must continue using some government services, we must also understand their political influences, and more importantly, their broader political functions. We must not promote the needs of victims by enhancing our police forces, cracking down on offenders, and limiting our freedom and control. Instead, our approach should be firmly rooted in progressive solutions to social ills, and in the democratic traditions of citizens participation and popular rule (Elias, 1982a).

REFERENCES

Ash, M. (1972), 'On witnesses: a radical critique of criminal court procedures', *Notre Dame Lawyer*, vol. 46, 382.
Bachrach, P. and Baratz, M. (1970), *Power and Poverty* (NY: Oxford University Press).
Baluss, M. (1975), *Integrated Services for Victims of Crime: A County Based Approach* (Washington: National Association of Counties Research Foundation).
Banfield, E. (1974), *The Unfriendly City Revisited* (Boston: Little, Brown).
Boyte, H. (1980), *The Backyard Revolution* (Philadelphia: Temple University Press).
Brady, J. (1981), 'Towards popular justice in the United States: the dialectics of community action', *Contemporary Crises*, 155.
Buder, L. (1977), 'Half of 1976 murder victims had police records', *New York Times*, 28 Aug., 9.
Center for Research on Criminal Justice (1982), *The Iron Fist and the Velvet Glove: An Analysis of U.S. Police* (Berkeley, Calif.: Center for Research on Criminal Justice).
Chappell, D. (1972), 'Providing for the victims of crime: political placebos or progressive programs?' *Adelaide Law Review*, vol. 4, 294.
Chesney, S. and Schneider, C. (1981), 'Crime victim centers: the Minnesota experiment', in B. Galaway and J. Husdon (eds). *Perspectives on Crime Victims* (St Louis: Mosby).

Christie, N. (1978), 'Conflicts as property', *British Journal of Criminology*, vol. 17, 1.

Clinard, M. and Quinney, R. (1967), *Criminal Behavior Systems* (NY: Holt, Rinehart & Winston).

Commission on Victim Witness Assistance (n.d.), *The Victim Advocate* (Washington, DC: National District Attorneys Association).

Crime Victims Compensation Board (1978), *1977–78 Annual Report* (Albany, NY: State of New York).

Currie, E. (1982a), 'Crime and ideology', *Working Papers* (May/June) 28.

Currie, E. (1982b), 'Fighting crime', *Working Papers* (July/Aug.) 17.

Curtis, L. (1977), 'The conservative new criminology', *Society*, vol. 14, 3.

Curtis, L. (1976), 'Victims, policy and the dangers of a conservative mentality', prepared for the 2nd International Symposium on Victimology.

Danzig, R. (1974), 'Towards the creation of a complementary decentralized system of criminal justice', *Stanford Law Review*, vol. 26, 1.

Danzig, R. and Lowy, M. (1975), 'Everyday disputes and mediation in the US', *Law and Society Review*, vol. 9, 675.

Davis, R. (1982), 'Mediation: the Brooklyn experiment', in R. Tomasic and M. Feeley (eds), *Neighborhood Justice* (New York: Longman).

Davis, R. and Dill, F. (1978), 'Comparative study of victim participation in Criminal court decision making', unpublished paper (NY: Vera Institute of Justice).

Doerner, W. *et al.* (1976), 'An analysis of victim compensation programs as a time-series experiment', *Victimology*, vol. 1, 295.

Doerner, W. *et al.* (1978a), 'An examination of the alleged latent effects of victim compensation programs upon crime reporting', *Lambda Alpha Epsilon Journal*, vol. 41, 71.

Doerner, W. *et al.* (1978b), 'A quasi-experimental analysis of selected victim compensation programs', *Canadian Journal of Criminology*, vol. 20, 239.

Doerner, W. *et al.* (1980), 'Impact of crime compensation upon victim attitudes toward the criminal justice system', *Victimology*, vol. 5, 61.

Dussich, J. (1976), 'Victim service models and their efficacy', In E. Viano (ed.), *Victims and Society* (Washington, DC: Visage Press).

Dussich, J. (1981), 'Evolving services for crime victims', in B. Galaway and J. Hudson (eds), *Perspectives on Crime Victims* (St Louis: Mosby).

Edelhertz, H. and Geis, G. (1974), *Public Compensation to Victims of Crime* (NY: Praeger).

Edelman, M. (1967), *The Symbolic Uses of Politics* (Urbana: University of Illinois Press).

Eisenstein, J., and Jacob, H. (1977), *Felony Justice* (Boston: Little, Brown).

Elias, R. (1981), 'Citizen participation in criminal justice: a critique', *Citizen Participation* (July/Aug. 1981) 6.

Elias, R. (1983a), 'Progressives and crime', *Social Policy*, vol. 13, 37.

Elias, R. (1983b), 'The symbolic politics of victim compensation', *Victimology* (Autumn) 18.

Elias, R. (1983c), *Victims of the System: Crime Victims and Compensation in American Politics and Criminal Justice* (New Brunswick, NJ: Transaction Books).

Elias, R. (1984), 'Alienating the victim: compensation and victim attitudes',

Journal of Social Issues, vol. 40, 103.

Elias, R. (1984b), 'Transcending our social reality of victimization', *Victimology*, vol. 9, 3.

Elias, R. (1985), *The Politics of Victimization: Victims, Victimology and Human Rights* (NY: Oxford University Press).

Friedman, D. (1976), 'A program to service crime victims', in E. Viano (ed.), *Victims and Society* (Washington, DC: Visage Press).

Galaway, B. (1977), 'The uses of restitution', *Crime and Delinquency*, vol. 23, 57.

Gattuso Holman, N. (1976), 'Criminal sentencing and victim compensation legislation: where is the victim?' in E. Viano (ed.), *Victims and Society* (Washington, DC: Visage Press).

Heinz, A. and Kerstetter, W. (1981), 'Pretrial settlement conference: evaluation of a reform in plea bargaining', in B. Galaway and J. Hudson (eds), *Perspectives on Crime Victims* (St Louis: Mosby).

Krisberg, B. (1975), *Crime and Privilege* (Englewood Cliffs, NJ: Prentice Hall).

Lamborn, L. (1976), 'Compensation for the child conceived in rape', in E. Viano (ed.), *Victims and Society* (Washington, DC: Visage Press).

McDonald, W. (1976), 'Criminal justice and the victim: an introduction', in W. McDonald (ed.), *Criminal Justice and the Victim* (Beverly Hills, Calif.: Sage).

McKnight, D. (1981), 'The Victim–Offender Reconciliation Project', in B. Galaway and J. Hudson (eds) *Perspectives on Crime Victims* (St Louis: Mosby).

Merry, S. (1979), 'Going to court: strategies of dispute management in an American neighborhood', *Law and Society Review*, vol. 13, 891.

Miers, D. (1980), 'Victim compensation as a labelling process', *Victimology*, vol. 5, 3.

Nachmais, D. (1979), *Public Policy Evaluation: Approaches and Methods* (New York: St. Martins Press).

Nader, L. (1980), *No Access to Law: Alternatives to the American Judicial System* (NY: Academic Press).

National Advisory Commission on Criminal Justice Standards and Goals (1973), *Community Crime Prevention* (Washington, DC: US Government Printing Office).

Oberg, S. and Pence, E. (1981), 'Responding to battered women', in B. Galaway and J. Hudson (eds), *Perspectives on Crime Victims* (St Louis: Mosby).

O'Sullivan, E. (1978), 'What has happened to rape crisis centers?' *Victimology*, vol. 3, 57.

Piven, F. and Cloward, R. (1971), *Regulating the Poor: the Functions of Public Welfare* (NY: Vintage).

Quinney, R. (1980), *Class, State and Crime* (NY: Longman).

Quinney, R. (1972), 'Who is the victim?' *Criminology*, 314.

Reiman, J. (1979), *The Rich Get Richer and the Poor Get Prison* (NY: John Wiley).

Reiss, A. (1974), 'Discretionary justice in the United States', *International Journal of Criminology and Penology*, vol. 2, 181.

Rich, R. (1981), 'Evaluating mental health services for victims: perspectives on politics and services in the United States', in S. Salasin (ed.), *Evaluating Victim Services* (Beverly Hills, Calif.: Sage).

Ryan, W. (1976), *Blaming the Victim* (NY: Vintage).

Schattschneider, E. (1960), *The Semi-Sovereign People* (NY: Holt, Rinehart & Winston).

Schneider, A. and Schneider, P. (1981), 'Victim assistance programs: an overview', in B. Galaway and J. Hudson (eds), *Perspectives on Crime Victims* (St Louis: Mosby).

Shapiro, C. and Gutierrez, L. (1982), 'Crime victim services', *Social Policy* (Summer) 50.

Silverman, S. and Doerner, W. (1979) 'The effect of victim compensation upon conviction rates', *Sociological Symposium*, vol. 25, 40.

Spence, J. (1978), 'Institutionalizing neighborhood courts: two Chilean experiences', *Law and Society Review*, vol. 13, 139.

Vaughn, J. and Hofrichter, R. (1980) 'Program visibility in state victim compensation programs', *Victimology*, 30.

Wilson, J. (1975), *Thinking About Crime* (NY: Basic Books).

Wolfgang, M. and Ferracuti, F. (1967), *The Subculture of Violence* (London: Social Science Paperbacks).

Wright, E. (1973), *The Politics of Punishment* (NY: Harper and Row).

Ziegenhagen, E. and Benyi, J. (1981), 'Victim interests, victim services, and social control', in B. Galaway and J. Hudson (eds), *Perspectives on Crime Victims* (St Louis: Mosby).

Epilogue

The United Nations Declaration of Basic Principles of Justice for Victims of Crime and Abuse of Power:
A Constructive Critique
Ezzat A. Fattah

> The victim's rights movement draws much of its energy from the horror story syndrome . . . Conservatives have seized the victim's rights issue and made it their own. In California, for example, the advocates of Proposition 8 were the traditional prosecution-oriented law-and-order leaders, while civil libertarians were the primary opponents. The President's Task Force on the Victims of Crime was also dominated by traditional conservative spokespersons.
>
> S. Walker (1985: 137)

> Many of the items on the Victim's Bill of Rights agenda are positively harmful and unconstitutional. The harm has a special, cruel irony to it: proposals designed to help crime victims turn out to hurt them.
>
> S. Walker (1985: 141)

THE UNITED NATIONS DECLARATION: A BRIEF HISTORY

The United Nations declaration owes its existence to a few dedicated individuals within and outside the UN. Miss Irene Mellup, who used to work in the Crime Prevention Section of the UN in New York, was mainly interested in a declaration on victims of abuse of power, while Professor Irvin Waller of the University of Ottawa was primarily preoccupied with victims of crime. The final declaration incorporating both categories of victims is the outcome of a lengthy process involving group discussions, lobbying and countless changes and compromises. At the outset there were actually two draft declarations. The first, on victims of crime, was drafted in 1983 by Waller. The second, on victims of crime, was drafted the same year by Professor LeRoy Lamborn from Wayne State University School of Law, at the request and with the blessing of Irene Mellup. At an *ad hoc* United Nations interregional meeting of experts held in Ottawa in July 1984 both drafts were discussed by a working group. As a result of the discussions, several changes were made and a single draft was prepared. This latter draft came under further debate during the Seventh UN Congress on the Prevention of Crime and the Treatment of Offenders, held in Milan, Italy, in 1985.[1]

Joutsen (1987) reports that what ultimately emerged from the discussion was a two-part draft. The main part, Part A, was entitled 'Relating to Victims of Crime', and it set out specific provisions on access to justice and fair treatment, restitution, compensation and social assistance. Part B, relating to 'Victims of Abuse of Power' was considerably more general and consisted of four brief paragraphs which called upon member states to grant civil and administrative relief to victims of abuse of power. After adoption by consensus by the Third Committee of the General Assembly on 11 November 1985, the declaration was formally approved by the General Assembly as a plenary body on 29 November 1985. In adopting it, the General Assembly noted that it was: '*Cognizant* that millions of people throughout the world suffer harm as a result of crime and the abuse of power and that the rights of these victims have not been adequately recognized' (see Joutsen, 1987, p. 68).

In the autumn of 1987, a lengthy document prepared by Professor Bassiouni, on the implementation of the General Assembly Resolution 40/43 (which contained in an annex the Declaration), was discussed at a meeting organized by the four major international associations: the International Society of Criminology, the International Association of Penal Law, the International Society of Social Defence, and the International Penal and Penitentiary Foundation. As a member of the Board of Directors of the International Society of Criminology, I was invited to attend the Milan meeting and to represent the Society. This paper is loosely based on the presentation I made on behalf of the International Society of Criminology. It should, however, be emphasized that the views expressed below are mine and mine alone and do not necessarily represent those of the

International Society. The present paper is not intended to be a detailed critique of the specific provisions contained in the UN declaration. Rather, it is a critical review of some of the new initiatives relative to victims of crime. Many of these initiatives pre-date the declaration, were incorporated in it and are still being introduced in various countries. The paper, like the one on the rhetoric in victimology (see Chapter 1), is an attempt to show that hollow slogans such as 'Justice for Victims', symbolic gestures such as 'victim impact statements', punitive measures such as 'fine victim surcharge', and political palliatives such as 'victim compensation schemes', aimed at placating the victim lobby and victim advocates, will do hardly anything to tangibly improve the lot of crime victims. What is necessary to achieve this goal is a new criminal justice paradigm, a new penal and sentencing philosophy that places the emphasis not on punishment and retaliation but on reparation, mediation and conciliation. In most instances these two sets of goals (retributive/restorative) are functionally incompatible. Parallel to this change, there needs to be another fundamental change in the traditional views on crime. The offence should cease to be regarded as an affront to the state and be viewed as an offence against the individual victim, not as a violation of an abstract law but a violation of the rights of the victim.

THE LEGAL STATUS OF CRIME VICTIMS

A declaration does not confer or bestow rights. It identifies, recognizes and affirms rights which already exist or should exist. Whatever basic rights victims of crime or victims of abuse of power may have did not stem from the United Nations declaration. They existed prior to the declaration and would have continued to exist had the declaration not been adopted. This is not to belittle the importance and significance of the declaration. It is simply to stress that protection of, and assistance to, victims will have to become part of the core values of society. Social commitment to victims will have to be deeply rooted in the general belief system. It is important, therefore, to establish the legal sources of the rights of victims. If action and policies are to be guided by more than just humanitarian concern for the victims and their plight, it is necessary to identify the legal as well as the social bases for both society's obligation and the offender's responsibility to the victim.

In the 1950s and the 1960s, when Margery Fry and others called for state compensation to victims of crime, there were serious attempts to determine the legal and philosophical foundations on which such compensation should be based. Among the theories advanced at the time were the legal tort theory, the social contract theory, the utilitarian theory, and the social solidarity theory, to mention but a few. Current concern for, and discussions of, victims' other rights have not been accompanied by any similar attempt. Probably the reason is that the emergence and enactment of Victims' Bills of Rights was the outcome of political and grass-roots initiatives rather than legal or juridical initiatives.

Since in law rights originate from and are closely linked to the person's status, to establish the rights to which victims of crime are entitled it is necessary to define their legal status. This is all the more important since in many jurisdictions, at present, victims seem to have no legal status. Prior to the amendments made to the Criminal Code of Canada in 1988,[2] this was made abundantly clear by court rulings in Ontario and British Columbia (see Rubel, Chapter 7, pp. 250–1). In November 1987, in a criminal case of dangerous driving resulting in the death of a 16-year-old youth, a Supreme Court judge in the province of British Columbia denied the prosecutor's request to submit a statement by the family of the victim. He quoted from a judgment of the High Court of Ontario in which the sentencing judge declared that 'the principles of sentencing establish guidelines for judges and do not include consideration of the effects of the tragic death upon the survivors' (*Vancouver Sun*, November 1987). This judicial statement suggests that the victim of crime (or his survivors in the case of death) does not enjoy any legal status and cannot, therefore, become legal party to the proceedings. It highlights the need to change fundamentally the way society looks upon crime and punishment if the victim is to become a full party in judicial proceedings and if he or she is to recover their lost status in the criminal process. In other words, what is urgently needed is a new paradigm of criminal justice. In this new paradigm – in reality a very old one – crime will no longer be viewed as a wrongful, sinful act that needs to be punished. It will be regarded as a harmful behaviour that needs to be redressed in the present and prevented in the future.

Victims were better off when there was no differentiation between civil and criminal law, when all harmful actions were civil torts. Victims were the principal protagonists when prosecutions were private, handled not by the Crown but by the person who suffered or his representative. The reduction of the victim to an inconsequential figure coincided with the emergence of the public prosecutor. (Galaway and Hudson, 1981).

But the real decline started with the emergence of a criminal law which viewed the criminal act not as an offence against the victim but as an offence against the sovereign and later the state. Gradually the victim, who used to be the central figure, in whose name and on whose behalf the proceedings were conducted, was reduced to the status of a witness used to buttress the Crown's case and abused if he refused to cooperate or to testify. Once the state monopolized the right to criminal prosecution and converted the 'wergeld' or the composition paid to the victim into a fine destined for the king's coffers, the victim became the forgotten man, a legal nonentity.

The historical decline of the victim is traced by the Law Reform Commission of Canada (1974) to the emergence of the criminal law. The Commission describes the process as follows:

> In Anglo-Saxon England there was no criminal law as we know it. Disputes were dealt with by a process greatly resembling our civil law. When an individual felt that he had suffered damage because of another's wrongful conduct he was permitted either to settle the matter by agreement or to proceed before a tribunal. Restitution was the order of the day and other sanctions, including imprisonment, were rarely used.
>
> As the common law developed, criminal law became a distinct branch of law. Numerous antisocial acts were seen to be 'offenses against the state' or 'crimes' rather than personal wrongs or torts. This tendency to characterize some wrongs as 'crimes' was encouraged by the practice under which the lands and property of convicted persons were forfeited to the king or feudal lord; fines, as well, became payable to feudal lords and not to the victim. The natural practice of compensating the victim or his relatives was discouraged by making it an offense to conceal the commission of a felony or convert the crime into a source of profit. In time, fines and property that would have gone in satisfaction of the victim's claims were diverted to the state. Compounding an offense (that is, accepting an economic benefit in satisfaction of the wrong done without the consent of the court or in a manner that is contrary to the public interest) still remains a crime under the Canadian Criminal Code and discourages private settlement or restitution.
>
> It would now seem that historical developments, however well intentioned, effectively removed the victim from sentencing policy and obscured the view that crime was social conflict.

(1974, p. 4–5)

This historical development leaves no doubt that it was by political ruse that the rulers usurped the legitimate rights of the victims, to the rulers' benefit. It is this usurpation that Christie (1977) refers to when he states that conflicts have been stolen from the parties directly involved and thereby have either disappeared or become other people's property. It is also a historical fact that with the passage of time the criminal law became a powerful tool of subjugation used by governments and rulers to consolidate their grip on the population and it is not a coincidence that many criminal codes begin with a section dealing with offences against the state.

At present, the administration of criminal justice emphasizes the roles played by professional, specialized third parties: judges, prosecutors, defence lawyers, experts, and others. While these third parties have assumed an increasingly important place in the criminal justice system, the victim's role has become largely peripheral and the victim has been treated by the system as largely irrelevant (see Galaway and Hudson, 1981, p. 229). Christie (1978) believes that the root problem of the administration of justice is that conflicts have become the property of professionals rather than people. He adds that by taking over the ownership of disputes between people, professionals have taken the community's opportunity to learn from individual disputes and develop structures for improving situations.

THE OLD AND NEW PARADIGMS OF CRIMINAL JUSTICE

Victims' current plight stems from the fact that crime is no longer regarded as a conflict between two individuals, two human beings, but between the offender and society. Viewed as such, crime generates not an obligation to the victim, but a debt to society, and once the criminal is punished the debt is paid. In this scenario, there is no place for the victim, no part for him to play. The recent report of the Canadian Sentencing Commission leads to the painful realization that despite all the current talk about victims of crime, their rights and their plight, this basic outlook has not changed. Instead of stating that the primary goal of sentencing is to repair the harm done to the victim by the offence and to prevent future harm, the Sentencing Commission (1987) regrettably declared that:

. . . the fundamental purpose of sentencing is to preserve the

authority of, and promote respect for, the law through the imposition of just sanctions.

(1987, p. 151)

Such abstract goals are responsible for the depersonalization and
dehumanization of the justice system, for the reification of both the
offender and the victim. In an era meant to become the golden age of
the victim, there seems to be a growing obsession with punishment,
euphemistically called 'just deserts'. And yet, having punishment as
the central focus of the criminal justice system is neither morally
legitimate nor practically effective. It can only act to the detriment of
the victim. Dispute settlement, mediation, reconciliation, arbitration, reparation are concepts foreign to a system centred on punishment, a system which regards the crime not as a human action but as
a legal infraction. Such a system acts to intensify the conflict rather
than settling it. And instead of bringing the feuding parties closer to
one another, it widens the gap that separates them. The obsession
with punishment leads to an unwarranted differentiation between
criminal and other types of victimization and results in grave injustices to those who offend and those who suffer.

In the new paradigm of criminal justice, the primary purpose of the
criminal law would be to heal the injury, repair the harm, compensate the loss and prevent further victimization. This requires among
other things a rethinking and a re-examination of the artificial boundaries which have been erected over the years between civil and
criminal law, between civil and criminal courts, as well as the artificial
distinction between crimes and torts. This artificial distinction, which
seemingly is taken for granted, is detrimental to the victims and their
interests. The greatest majority of criminal offences brought to trial
end in sentence to a fine. Civil cases end in the payment of damages.
Thus, the only actual difference in outcome between a civil and a
criminal case is that in the former the damages are paid to the person
who suffered the loss whereas in the latter it is the state that benefits
at the expense of the victim. And this is what has to change.

Unfortunately, the United Nations declaration on victims does
little, if anything at all, to bring about the needed transformation in
current views on crime and current attitudes and response to victims.
The band-aid remedies advocated by the declaration ignore the roots
of the present plight of crime victims. The philosophical, deontologic-
al and theological ideas and the political interests that led to the

emergence of the notions of crime and punishment are responsible for the decline of the victim. The constructive practices of reparation, composition, reconciliation gave way to punishments supposedly aimed at achieving retribution, expiation and atonement. Improving the victim's lot requires that the notion of crime be taken back to its sociological origins. Sociologically, crime is not a sin, it is not an immoral behaviour, it is a harmful, injurious act. Since crime is an inevitable feature of social life, it is only logical that it be considered in a secular, technological society as a social risk, as a hazard of modern life, not very different from other risks to which people are daily exposed (see Chapter 1). The way society responds to other social risks to minimize their occurrence and their effects should guide the action against crime. Crime is as much a fact of life as are natural disasters, traffic accidents, disease and death. But while other social risks are covered, in the welfare state, by some form of insurance, the risk of becoming a victim of crime is not adequately covered. Victim compensation schemes have done little to remedy or to improve this situation (see Elias, Chapter 12). Insufficient funding, inadequate information and stringent eligibility requirements have meant that the overwhelming majority of victims are excluded from the realm of compensation.[3] Because the funds allocated to these programmes are severely limited, more publicity and more applications can only result in lower awards and a higher rate of rejection. As to restitution by the offender, it remains, for obvious reasons, a seldom used and largely ineffective means of redress. The only potential of restitution is to be used instead of, and not in addition to, incarceration. In the present punitive climate, this is not a very attractive proposition.

The reluctance of governments to go beyond symbolic gestures, political palliatives and placebos to improve the plight of crime victims is quite evident in victim legislation introduced in several countries.

In 1987, for example, the Canadian government, following the steps of some American states, introduced in the federal Parliament a Bill (see note 2) aimed, among other things, at imposing a victim fine surcharge not exceeding 15 per cent of any fine that is imposed on the offender, or where no fine is imposed for the offence, ten thousand dollars. Instead of returning the fines to their original and legitimate owners by placing them in a fund earmarked for victim compensation, or using them to finance a comprehensive insurance scheme for crime victims, the new legislation is a clear attempt to finance the present compensation programmes by imposing an *additional* penalty on the offender. The fine surcharge concept is neither practical nor fair. Most offenders, particularly those charged with violent crimes, are unable to pay whatever fines they are sentenced to and have to spend additional time in prison for default. What the fine surcharge really does is to make an already bad situation much worse. The idea is also unfair because it penalizes all offenders and not only those who should be responsible for compensation. Most victimless crimes are punished by a fine. People convicted of these offences will be paying extra to make up for the stinginess of the government. Drug offenders and non-violent offenders will be charged what should have been paid by those who commit crimes of violence.

VICTIMS NEEDS AND VICTIMS SERVICES

The United Nations Declaration of Basic Principles of Justice for Victims of Crime and Abuse of Power contains provisions aimed at facilitating victims' access to justice and at ensuring that they are fairly treated by the justice system. Other provisions relate to the material, medical, psychological and social assistance that should be provided to victims. There are further provisions pertaining to restitution and compensation to victims. The implementation of the various provisions calls for changes at various levels: administrative, social and legislative.

The question of how crime victims are currently treated and how they *should* be treated by criminal justice personnel is an administrative issue. It has to do with the attitudes, policies and practices of the system and the interactions between those working in it and their clientele. As mentioned in Chapter 1, all users of the system have to be treated with courtesy, sensitivity, understanding and compassion, as well as respect for their dignity. This should be the case regardless of their role or characteristics, whether complainants or suspects, victims or offenders, young or old, male or female, rich or poor, white or black. Improving the general attitudes of those in the system to its users is both essential and beneficial. The training of criminal justice personnel should be designed to sensitize them to the needs and plight of their clients. Special training is necessary for those who will be called upon to deal with special categories or specific types of clients. Special training should also be mandatory for those whose activities dictate that they intervene in certain conflict situations such as family violence.

What are the needs of crime victims and how could these needs be met?[4] These are research issues. Some of the needs may be obvious, others are less evident. There are general needs and there are needs that are specific to certain categories or types of victims. Once the needs are properly identified the questions are: What existing services should cater to these needs? What services have to be created or strengthened to satisfy them adequately? This requires full assessment of existing services. Then political decisions will have to be made. Implementation of the declaration's provisions in this area is problematic because of the financial costs involved. As commitments by politicians do not usually match their rhetoric, it would be rather naive to expect, especially in times of economic restraint, that there will be massive infusion of funds into victim services. This, however, is the area where society can show the extent of its real commitment to victims.

Before embarking on the creation of large-scale victim services it is also necessary to assess some of the dangers involved.[5] Social services in the welfare state, whether run by professionals or volunteers, have a tendency to develop dependency among their clients and even to extract those clients from their social networks. In the long run, these networks, composed of relatives, neighbours, friends, peers and so on, are weakened as their members are freed from their social obligations. The professionalization of victim services presents yet another danger. The personalized care of the victim's social network is replaced by the depersonalized care of the state. The victim who, within his family, neighbourhood or small community, is treated as a person and who in such setting feels and acts as an individual is converted into a 'client' or a 'recipient of services'.[6] He or she has to suffer the dehumanization of being transformed from a person to a number. The psychological support and regeneration the victim feels when cared for by family or friends is replaced by the confusion and humiliation of having been placed in the hands of strangers who have to deal daily with dozens of other victims.

In addition to the dangers outlined above, there are the general dangers of intervention. In providing the care, help and support that victims need, caution has to be exercised to avoid causing greater harm to the victim. Intensive and/or excessive intervention can delay the natural healing process. It can prolong the agony and the trauma resulting from the offence, create undue anxieties about the crime situation and the risks of victimization, and nurture attitudes of mistrust or distrust among actual and potential victims. There are reasons to suspect that there might be a link between the new interventionist strategies and techniques with victims and the growing pains of victimization. This raises the question of whether the heightened fear of victimization, reported in recent years, is in any way related to the increasing attention and publicity being given to crime victims. Do policies of intervention prolong rather than shorten the traumatic effects of victimization? These are all questions worthy of serious exploration. The zeal to help and assist crime victims should not blind us to the potential dangers of our action (see Fattah, 1986).

The continual talk about victim services in recent years has already created or heightened expectations among crime victims. Such expectations, if not met, can only lead to various levels of dissatisfaction and frustration with the CJS and the greater society. The history of victim services, as brief as it may be, is one of unfulfilled promises and unmet expectations. There is ample empirical evidence of the inadequacy of the services and the frustrations that ensue. In England, Shapland (1986) detected a mismatch between victim expectations of the system and the system's assumptions about victim needs. Consequently, she warns that public statements about the worth of victims, which are later shown to be hollow, may rebound on any who set up such ineffective schemes. This is confirmed by her finding that by the end of police and court processes, there was a significant decline in victims' satisfaction with the police handling of the case and also a decline in attribution of positive qualities to the police generally. In the US, Elias (1983) found considerable disenchantment and even some evidence of greater discontent among applicants to victim compensation: delays, inconveniences, poor information, inability to participate, restrictive eligibility requirements, denial of awards in many cases, unrealistic ceilings and so on.

THE ROLE OF THE VICTIM IN THE CRIMINAL JUSTICE PROCESS

The United Nations declaration calls for 'allowing the views and concerns of victims to be presented and considered at appropriate stages of the proceedings where their personal interests are affected . . .' This provision raises fundamental questions about the victims' legal standing and their role in the criminal justice process, whether they should have a say in bail hearings, plea-bargaining, sentencing, parole hearings or parole decision-making and so on, and the form such input should take.[7]

A brief review of the initiatives taken in recent years to ensure victims' participation in the justice process suggests that the changes have been hastily introduced without a full assessment of their potential effects, or concern for whether or not they are compatible with existing policies and philosophies. The review also provides unmistakable clues to the real intentions behind victim legislation.

Thus a dispassionate analysis of the so-called victims' Bills of Rights inevitably leads to the conclusion that such a legislation is not meant to improve the lot of crime victims but to toughen an already harsh system of punishment. For example, Attorney General George Deukmejian's (who later became the state governor) comments on California's Proposition 8, 'The Victims' Bill of Rights', leave no doubt as to the real objectives underlying the legislation. Writing in a voters' brochure, Deukmejian said:

> There is absolutely no question that the passage of this proposition will result in more criminal convictions, more criminals being sentenced to state prison, and more protection of the law-abiding citizenry.
>
> (Quoted after Paltrow, 1982, p. 1)

The statement is very revealing of what seems to be the hidden agenda of those who are willing to exploit the noble cause of crime victims to bring about more punishment.

Though passed prior to the declaration, California's Proposition 8, the Victims' Bill of Rights, is certainly one of the strongest attempts to formalize the victim's role in the judicial process. The Bill gives the victims the right of allocution, that is the right to appear and be heard at felony sentencing hearings. A 1986 study by the McGeorge School of Law of the implementation of this right by state and local agencies revealed that less than three per cent of the eligible victims appeared at sentencing hearings. Another interesting finding is that the majority of judges and chief probation officers viewed allocution at sentencing as unnecessary while the majority of district attorneys viewed it favourably and were more confident than judges that it affected sentencing.

Obviously, the overwhelming majority of crime victims are unwilling, for one reason or another, to exercise whatever rights they may be given. Thus, one might question the practical value and returns of granting victims such rights despite strong objections from many quarters.[8]

VICTIM-IMPACT STATEMENTS

Do victim-impact statements and victim allocution have an impact on sentencing? If they do *not* influence the sentence, then they are bound, at least in the long run, to alienate the victims who in good faith exercise this right believing that it will have an impact on the court's decision. In case they *do* have an impact, one might question their effects on the principles of fairness and equality. The tiny minority of offenders in whose cases the right is exercised will receive harsher sanctions than others who had committed identical offences. In other words, if victim-impact statements have no impact on sentencing they can only heighten the victim's sense of irrelevance; if they do, they can only aggravate the problem of sentencing disparity.

Despite all these problems with victim-impact statements, at no time was there any serious challenge to the proposed Canadian legislation (Bill C-89) and only few voices were heard opposing the suggested procedural change.

In his testimony before the legislative Committee of the Canadian House of Commons on Bill C-89 (An Act to amend the Criminal Code – Victims of Crime), a distinguished Ontario lawyer, Paul Calarco (9 February 1988) criticized the Bill for being seriously flawed and for its failure to recognize the right of an accused person to a fair trial and the right of that accused person to test the Crown's case. He also predicted that once passed, the Bill will lead to longer trials, more appeals and greater legal costs, both to an accused person and to the public in terms of Crown attorneys and legal aid costs, as well as a greater court backlog. He added that the Bill may indeed lead to illegal sentences, depending of course on the constitutional challenges, and to an improper deprivation of the liberty of the subject (House of Commons, Issue no. 7, p. 5).

Addressing the specific issue of victim-impact statements, Calarco said:

> Finally, the victim impact statement is, in my respectful submission, completely inappropriate. The principles of sentencing do not look and should not look at how an individual offence has affected an individual complainant. If an individual complainant has

perhaps been emotionally shattered by an experience, instead of perhaps a six-month sentence, are we to say that the devastating effect on that victim would bring the sentence up to 12 or 18 months or more? Conversely, are we to say that if this complainant has forgiven the offender totally, or not had any adverse effect from the offence, that offender should then receive a suspended sentence rather than the six months society says should be imposed?

(1988–7, p. 9)

Calarco's statements before the House of Commons legislative Committee echoed those made by other lawyers. Earl Levy, president of the Criminal Lawyers Association of Ontario, was quoted in the *Globe and Mail* (11 April 1984) as saying '[Victim impact statement] injects an air of emotionalism in the sentencing procedure . . . I feel there are enough problems now with the disparity of sentencing.' Levy added that victim-impact statements will only compound that problem because with human nature being what it is, judges are bound to be affected by this air of emotionalism. Another lawyer, Richard Peck, who at the time was chairing the criminal justice section of the Canadian Bar Association, declared to *The Vancouver Sun* (21 September 1983, p. A3) that judges are expected to act dispassionately and that the justice system relies on impartial judges handing down sentences based on a well-tried set of criteria. He insisted that 'there is no place for vengeance in a dispassionate, logical sentencing process', and that victims 'should never directly influence the length of sentence'.

The same article (Still, 1983) quoted Vancouver lawyer Michael Bolton, who deplored the fact that the government appeared to be responding to pressure groups (the victim lobby) and expressed the opinion that organized groups, though serving a useful function in helping to alleviate the anguish felt by many crime victims, should not be involved in procedural reforms.

Political considerations overrode legal objections and the Bill was passed with an astounding majority and very little change. Victim-impact statements became, despite the reservations articulated by legal practitioners, part of the criminal code of Canada. It is still too early to assess the impact of this procedural change and to establish whether any of the predictions made by those who argued against the statements did in fact materialize. A recent development in the United States is worth noting, namely the fact that some courts have ruled that victim-impact statements are unconstitutional in capital cases (Sharman, 1988). There is also some evidence suggesting that at least some of the provisions contained in victim legislation under the guise of helping the victim may backfire. For example, one of the California Victims' Bill of Rights (Proposition 8) provisions is 'Truth in Evidence'. Originally this provision was intended as a way of eliminating the exclusionary rule, a rule that renders illegally obtained evidence inadmissible in court. This particular section of the California Bill stipulates that 'relevant evidence shall not be excluded in any criminal proceedings'. It turned out that such a provision is in fact a double-edged sword. Paltrow (1982) reports that under this new provision it became possible for lawyers in rape cases to have victims examined by psychiatrists or to question the victim about sexual activity she had engaged in shortly prior to the alleged rape.

There are several additional problems with victim-impact statements and the right of allocution. It has been pointed out (Neto, 1986, p. 7) that victims' interests are usually well enough represented by prosecutors and that victim intervention would add little that is useful to most cases and would impose upon an already overburdened system irrelevant information and requests.

It is also suggested that allowing the victim to play a direct role in the sentencing process injects an emotional element in what is meant to be a dispassionate and logical process (see above). Mention is also made that lengthy trials would become even longer because the accused will have to be given the right to challenge the victim's statement and to require the Crown to prove it.[9]

And with the overcrowding of prisons a wide use of this right may worsen an already intolerable situation since judges may mete out longer sentences or become reluctant to use alternatives to incarceration.

More important still is that if we allow the victim to play a direct role in sentencing and to ask for more punishment, then logically we will have to give the victim also the right to demand an acquittal or no punishment! Are we willing to substitute the victim's wish for what we currently believe is society's right? Or are we willing to follow the victim's desire only if the call is for more punishment? And what about the right to appeal? Should the victim be given the right to appeal if he or she is not satisfied with the sentence?

After reviewing the arguments for and against victim-impact statements, and after noting that many victims do not wish to be involved by giving evidence on the impact of offences on their lives, the

Victorian Sentencing Committee (Australia) concluded that the case against the introduction of victim-impact statements is more compelling than the case for them. Consequently, the Committee (1988) recommended that victim-impact statements not be adopted in Victoria (p. 545).

According to popular estimates (Ranish and Shichor, Chapter 6), about 90 per cent of the criminal cases in the US are disposed of through plea bargaining. This means that victims' involvement in the plea bargaining phase is even more important than at the sentencing stage. The growing trend of resorting to determinate sentences means that whatever input the victim may be allowed will have to be made at the stage of plea bargaining. The Canadian Sentencing Commission (1987) examined the issue and rejected the idea of victims becoming independent parties in plea negotiations. The Commission believed that this would be inconsistent with the ultimate responsibility of the Attorney General in each province for the prosecution of criminal code offences. The Commission added that such a concept could potentially precipitate an adversarial relationship between Crown counsel and victims and that such provision might render victims vulnerable to pressure from either the Crown prosecutor or defence counsel respecting a plea bargain.

VICTIMS' INVOLVEMENT IN THE PAROLE PROCESS

Where victims are given the right to appear before parole board panels, they seem to exercise this right even less frequently than before a judge conducting a sentencing hearing.

Victim participation at parole proceedings is now a reality in the US. McLeod (1987) identified 39 states where some form of active victim participation (that is the victim may do more than just attend the hearing) has been statutorily and/or administratively authorized. In 38 states, this is considered a victim's right and in the remaining one it is discretionary. The rapidity of legislation in this contentious area is all too surprising when one considers the apparent incompatibility of such policy with the stated goals of parole, together with the lack of empirical studies on the disparity in parole decisions which might result from a highly selective victim participation. Since the decision to grant or deny parole is based on an assessment of the prisoner's progress and his chances of success or failure, and since it has nothing or little to do with the punishment, it is difficult to see the relevance or the desirability of the victim's input. And since parole decision-making is often a subjective process it is easy to understand how it can be influenced by emotional pleas from the victim (see Ranish and Shichor, Chapter 6).

Since parole hearings can take place ten, twenty or thirty years after the crime has been committed, in practice the victim has to keep the authorities informed of every residential move he or she makes in order to receive the notification of the hearing. A growing number of jurisdictions are advising victims that receipt of advance notification is contingent upon the victim's maintenance of an updated address in parole board files (McLeod, 1987, p. 11). While in some states notification is automatic, in others, victim pre-registration is required. Automatic notification, needless to say, may act as an unwanted reminder of a crime committed a long time before. Mcleod reports that there were victims who resented the unsolicited board notice as an intrusion into their personal lives. In large part, these were victims who either did not want to be reminded of the traumatizing incident, or did not want their previously uninformed spouses or families to know that the victimization had occurred (McLeod, 1987, p. 11).

One danger to the principle of due process resulting from the new procedures is the one relating to disclosure. In at least 23 American states victim statements regarding parole are deemed to be confidential and, thus, are not subject to inmate review. In another eight states, disclosure decisions are made on a case-by-case basis at the discretion of victims or paroling officials (McLeod, 1987, p. 15). In other words, the inmate being considered for parole has no opportunity to challenge the veracity of the information provided by the victim or to offer a rebuttal to the victim's statements. The unchallenged information remains on file and can affect future parole decisions.

All this might be a small price to pay were it clear that the new procedures do have a beneficial effect on victims or that they do in practice have a desirable impact on the decisions. This, however, does not seem to be the case. Ranish and Shichor (Chapter 6) conclude that the evidence is clear: the two procedures they examined – victim's appearance at sentencing hearing and before parole board panels – have not had any dramatic impact on the way in which sentencing and parole decisions are rendered. After examining victim recommendations and offender sentences in sexual assault cases in a metropolitan Ohio county during the years 1980 to 1983, Walsh (Chapter 9) concluded that requiring a victim-impact statement and recommendation as part of the pre-sentence report is a mere genuflection to ritualistic legalism. Walsh further detected a marked disregard for the preferences of victims of incestuous sexual assault.

These are by no means the only criticisms made of the new victim initiatives. Another authority, Elias (Chapter 3), is critical of victim policy for its explicit or implicit assumption that defendants have too many rights and for emphasizing a contest between victim and offender rights as if the former have to be at the expense of the latter. Elias finds many of the resulting changes disturbing: mandatory and increased imprisonment, longer sentences and eliminating parole. These 'reforms', he suggests, seem to be a new dose of historically unsuccessful, get-tough policies that probably don't satisfy victim needs, including not being victimized in the first place. Elias passes a harsh judgment on the new victim initiatives. He writes:

> Yet for all the new initiatives, victims have gotten far less than promised. Rights have often been unenforced or unenforceable, participation sporadic or ill-advised, services precarious and underfunded, victim needs unsatisfied if not further jeopardized, and victimization increased, if not in court, then certainly in the streets.

CONCLUSION

A lot has been said and done about implementing the UN Declaration of Basic Principles of Justice for Victims of Crime and Abuse of Power. A successful implementation is a careful and enlightened implementation. It is an implementation based on a thorough assessment of the potential consequences and impact of the new policies, procedures and programmes. Unfortunately, many initiatives in the area of victims' rights seem to have been introduced without any such evaluation. *Post facto* evaluations, on the other hand, are available. The picture they paint of the impact such new initiatives have had is far from rosy and is clearly negative. This is neither a criticism nor an indictment of the principles underlying these new measures or some of the humanitarian intentions behind them. It is simply another reminder that within the current structure of our criminal justice system, band-aid measures are not likely to work or to have their desired effects. Some contribute to the further alienation of the victim while others heighten the victim's sense of irrelevance.

The reasons why many of these new initiatives do not work are not too difficult to comprehend. Some were conceived and set up for political and administrative purposes that had nothing to do with helping victims. This is particularly true of victim compensation schemes which have rightly been called political placebos (Chappell, 1973) or political palliatives (Burns, 1980). Many of these programmes, though propagated as a means of alleviating the suffering of the victim, were actually designed to increase victim reporting to the police and to improve victim cooperation with the criminal justice system. The primary benefits were seen as enhancing victim participation and collaboration, thus increasing the efficiency and effectiveness of the system.

The same can be said of victim assistance programmes. The major guiding influence is not compassionate or humanitarian consideration for victims, but the administrative goals of the agency. The Calgary Victim Services Programme, one of the first of its kind in Canada (started in 1977), is just one example of many. The programme is described in a document published by the Solicitor General Department in Ottawa. The document makes no secret of the fact that the objective of the programme 'is to develop a good working relationship with victims of crime in order to encourage their future cooperation with the police in crime prevention'. This statement tells a great deal about victim service programmes which were set up by various police departments in Canada as in other countries. It explains the distinct preference for having these programmes housed in police departments or public prosecutors' offices, rather than in the community. The hidden danger of many of these programmes is that they allow the police to have more control over the victim and for long periods of time.

Last but not least, some of the new rules on victim participation in criminal justice and parole processes do not meet the evidentiary standards required by the fundamental principle of due process. They risk heightening an already recognized disparity in sentencing and injecting an element of emotionality in what should be an impartial and unemotional process. Furthermore, as Ranish and Shichor (Chapter 6) point out, some of these initiatives are clearly designed to intimidate judges and parole board members and to influence these professionals in one specific policy direction – toward harsher punishment or denial of parole. The drastic results of such a policy on an already punitive justice system and an overcrowded prison system are not too difficult to figure out.

NOTES

1. The history of the UN declaration and the dynamics involved are outlined by Joutsen (1987), pp. 55–69.
2. To remedy the situation, Bill C-89 'An Act to amend the Criminal Code' (assented to on 21 July 1988) added to Section 662 of the Canadian Criminal Code the following subsection among others:

   For the purpose of determining the sentence to be imposed on an offender or whether the offender should be discharged pursuant to section 662.1 in respect of any offence, the court may consider a statement, prepared in accordance with subsection (1.2), of a victim of the offence describing the harm done to, or loss suffered by, the victim arising from the commission of the offence.

   Another subsection defines the victim as 'the person to whom harm is done or who suffers physical or emotional loss as a result of the commission of the offence' and adds that where the victim is dead, ill or otherwise incapable of making the statement, the definition would include 'the spouse or any relative of that person, anyone who has in law or in fact the custody of that person or is responsible for the care or support of that person or any dependent of that person'.
3. For a detailed analysis of victim compensation programmes in Canada see Fattah (1988).
4. The greatest and primary need of crime victims seems to be the need for information. The Canadian Federal-Provincial Task Force on Justice for Victims of Crime (1983) concluded that 'the most frequently expressed need by the great majority of victims interviewed is the need for information. To meet this need, it is not new services which are required, but a firm commitment on the part of the various criminal justice officials to let the victims know what is happening to "their" case' (p. 150); '. . . the key words are concern, consideration and communication' (p. 152). The South Australian Committee of Inquiry on Victims of Crimes concluded that the primary needs of crime victims were for social support and information.
5. For a discussion of some of the visible and hidden dangers of victim movements, see Fattah (1986).
6. In her critical analysis of the bureaucratization and professionalization of the shelter movement, Morgan (1981) shows how the victim, in this instance the battered wife, is transformed into a programme client. Morgan identifies other dangers as well. She explains, for example, how social control devices are masked under the cloak of modern professionalized services, how the requirements for evaluation and reporting can seriously compromise client confidentiality and how some clients get trapped as a result for welfare fraud, drug problems or parole violations. Morgan insists that the growth of the interventionist state has meant the growth of bureaucratic and professionalized forms penetrating into everyday life. She also quotes an early shelter organizer, Betsy Warrior, who warned against the 'exploitation by well – off professionals and bureaucrats who

fund themselves with the money obtained, rather than letting it benefit
the people whom it was secured for'.

7. Rossini (1987) points out that giving victims legal standing could allow
them to initiate criminal proceedings, contest a prosecutor's decision by
means of an appeal to the court, examine evidence in the course of a court
trial, and to make submissions regarding sentencing and parole. Referring
to the disparity which characterizes the existing system of sentencing and
parole, Grabosky (1985) suggests that to inject another element, particularly one so variable by virtue of its dependence upon the resiliency,
vindictiveness or other personality attributes of a victim, is to invite
further inconsistency, a situation which the criminal justice system could
ill afford.

8. Evidence from the US, Australia and the UK suggests that where the right
to appear is accorded to victims only a very small minority of victims take
up the opportunity. Walker (1985) notes that Arizona, Connecticut and
California already have laws giving the victim a voice in criminal proceedings. He suggests that the evidence indicates that in fact victims do not
want an active role. He refers to judge Lois Forer of Philadelphia who
routinely extends an invitation to victims but only few bother to appear.
And in Connecticut, where the victim's right to participate has become
law, victims appear at only about 3 per cent of all sentencings. The
percentage is strikingly similar to the one reported by Neto *et al.* (1986)
for California.

9. Rossini (1987) highlights some of the problems associated with greater
victim participation in the criminal justice process. She notes that there
are many reasons why victims may choose to participate only occasionally
which would make the criminal process arbitrary. The cost of separate
legal representation for a victim would be prohibitive for the majority.
Use of government funds for this purpose (e.g. through legal aid) would
add enormous financial costs to the state. The alternative of using Crown
prosecutors to act on a victim's behalf could lead to a conflict of interest,
particularly where the issue in question is the prosecution of a lesser
charge or a decision not to continue with the case. She also discusses the
problem of determining at what stage the victim should appear (p. 16).

REFERENCES

Australia (1981) *Report of the Committee of Inquiry on Victims of Crime.*
South Australia.
Australia (1986) *Victims Past, Victims Future: A South Australian Police
Perspective.* South Australia Police Department.
Australia (1988) Victorian Sentencing Committee. *Final Report.* Melbourne:
Government Printing Office.
Bassiouni, Ch. (1987) *Introduction to the United Nations Resolution and
Declaration of Basic Principles of Justice for Victims of Crime and Abuse of
Power.* Chicago: De Paul University.

Bassiouni, C. (1988) *International Protection of Victims*. Association Internationale de Droit Pénal. Toulouse: ERES.

Burns, P. (1980) *Criminal Injuries Compensation: Social Remedy or Political Palliative for Victims of Crime*. Toronto: Butterworths.

Canada (1988) House of Commons – Minutes of Proceedings and Evidence of the Legislative Committee on Bill C-89, An Act to Amend the Criminal Code (Victims of Crime). Ottawa: House of Commons.

Canada (1987) Canadian Sentencing Commission. *Final Report*. Ottawa: Ministry of Supply and Services.

Canada (1983) Canadian Federal-Provincial Task Force on Justice for Victims of Crime. *Report*. Ottawa: Ministry of Supply and Services.

Canada (1974) Law Reform Commission of Canada. *Restitution and Compensation – Fines*. Working Papers 5 and 6. Ottawa: Information Canada.

Chappell, D. (1972) *Providing for the victim of crime: political placebos or progressive programs? Adelaide Law Review*, Vol. 4, No. 2, pp. 294–306.

Christie, N. (1977) Conflicts as property. *British Journal of Criminology*, Vol. 17, No. 1, pp. 1–19.

Council of Europe (1985) *The Position of the Victim in the Framework of Criminal Law and Procedure*. Strasbourg.

Damaska, M. (1985) *Some Remarks on the Status of the Victim in Continental and Anglo-American Administration of Justice*. Paper presented at the 5th International Symposium on Victimology. Zagreb, Yugoslavia, August.

Dolliver, J.M. (1987) Victims' rights constitutional amendment: a bad idea whose time should not come. *The Wayne Law Review*, Vol. 34, No. 1, pp. 87–93.

Elias, R. (1983) *Victims of the System*. New Brunswick, NJ: Transaction Books.

Elias, R. (1986) Community control, criminal justice and victim services. In Ezzat A. Fattah (ed.), *From Crime Policy to Victim Policy*. London: Macmillan.

Elias, R. (1983) The symbolic politics of victim compensation. *Victimology*, Vol. 8, No. 1–2, pp. 213–24.

Elias, R. (1990) Which victim movement? The politics of victim policy. In A.J. Lurigio, W.G. Skogan and R.C. Davis (eds), *Victims of Crime: Problems, Policies and Programs*. Beverly Hills, Calif.: Sage.

Fattah, E.A. (1986) On some visible and hidden dangers of victim movements. In E.A. Fattah (ed.), *From Crime Policy to Victim Policy: Reorienting the Justice System*. London: Macmillan.

Fattah, E.A. (1988) *The Impact of Crime Prevention and Offender Rehabilitation Programs on the Costs of Victim Compensation – A Methodological Approach*. Unpublished report prepared under contract with the Ministry of Justice in Ottawa.

Forer, L.G. (1980) *Criminals and Victims: A Trial Judge Reflects on Crime and Punishment*. New York: W.W. Norton.

Galaway, B. and Hudson, J. (1981) *Perspectives on Crime Victims*. St. Louis: Mosby.

Galaway, B. (1988) Restitution as innovation or unfilled promise. *Federal Probation*, Vol. 51, pp. 3–14.

Gittler, J. (1984) Expanding the role of the victim in a criminal action: an overview of issues and problems. *Pepperdine Law Review*, Vol. 11, pp. 117–82.

Grabosky, P.N. (1985) *Crime Victims in Australia*. Canberra: Australian Institute of Criminology.

Henderson, L.N. (1985) The wrongs of victim's rights. *Stanford Law Review*, Vol. 37 (April), pp. 937–1021.

Joutsen, M. (1987) *The Role of the Victim of Crime in European Criminal Justice Systems*. Helsinki: Heuni.

MacDonald, W.F. (1978) Expanding the victim's role in the disposition decision: reform in search of a rationale. In Gallaway, B. and Hudson, J. (eds), *Offender Restitution in Theory and Action*. Boston, Mass.: Lexington, pp. 101–4.

Malarek, V. (1984) Voice-for-victim trend disturbs lawyers. *The Globe and Mail*, 11 April 1984.

Marshall, T.F. (1984) *Reparation, Conciliation and Mediation*. London: Home Office Research and Planning Unit, Paper No. 27.

McLeod, M. (1987) *Beyond the Law: An Examination of Policies and Procedures Governing the Nature of Victim Involvement at Parole*. Paper presented at the ASC meeting, Montreal, November.

Morgan, P. (1981) From battered wife to program client: the state's shaping of social problems. *Kapitalistate*, Vol. 9, pp. 17–39.

Neto, V. *et al.* (1986) *Victim Appearances at Sentencing Hearings Under the California Victims' Bill of Rights*. Sacramento: Center for Research, McGeorge School of Law.

Paltrow, S.J. (1982) Opposite effects: new anti-crime law in California is helping some accused felons. *The Wall Street Journal*, 26 November 1982.

Ranish, D.R. and Shichor, D. (1985) The victim's role in the penal process: recent developments in California. *Federal Probation*, Vol. 49, No. 1 (March), pp. 50–7.

Rossini, G. (1987) *Victims and the Criminal Justice System in South Australia*. Paper presented at the third annual conference of the Australian and New Zealand Society of Criminology.

Rubel, H.C. (1986) Victim participation in sentencing proceedings. *Criminal Law Quarterly*, Vol. 28, pp. 226–50.

Shapland, J., Willmore, J. and Duff, P. (1985) *Victims in the Criminal Justice system*. London: Gower.

Shapland, J. (1986) Victims and the criminal justice system. In E.A. Fattah (ed.), *From Crime Policy to Victim Policy*. London: Macmillan.

Shapland, J. (1986) Victim assistance and the criminal justice system: the victim's perspective. In E.A. Fattah (ed.), *From Crime Policy to Victim Policy*. London: Macmillan.

Sharman, J.R. (1988) Constitutional law: victim impact statements and the 8th Amendment. *Harvard Journal of Law and Public Policy*, Vol. 11 (Spring), pp. 583–93.

Talbert, P.A. (1988) The relevance of victim impact statements to the criminal sentencing decision. *UCLA Law Review*, Vol. 36, pp. 199–232.

Still, L. (1983) Victim say in sentencing just vengeance: lawyers. *The Vancouver Sun*, 21 September 1983, p. A3.

United Nations (1985) *Declaration of Basic Principles of Justice for Victims of*

Crime and Abuse of Power. New York: United Nations Department of Public Information.

United States (1982) President's Task Force on Victims of Crime. *Final Report.* Washington, DC: US Government Printing Office.

Walker, S. (1985) *Sense and Nonsense about Crime: A Policy Guide.* Monterey, Calif.: Brooks/Cole.

Walsh, A. (1986) Placebo justice: victim recommendations and offender sentences in sexual assault cases. *Journal of Criminal Law and Criminology*, Vol. 77, No. 4, pp. 1126–41.

Welling, S.N. (1987) Victim participation in plea bargains. *Washington University Law Quarterly*, Vol. 65, pp. 301–56.

Welling, S.N. (1988) Victims in the criminal process: a utilitarian analysis of victim participation in the charging decision. *Arizona Law Review*, Vol. 30, pp. 85–117.

Index

426 *Index*

Chesney, S. 374
Child Abuse Prevention and Treatment
Act (CAPTA–1974) 82
child abuse 14–23, 82–3
danger of legislation 17–23
see also child sexual abuse
child sexual abuse 3, 260–1
admissibility of child's
testimony 271–8
constitutional prohibition 274–6
evidentiary prohibition 271–4
danger of legislation 17–23
nature of the child's psyche 261–4,
268, 276
susceptibility to suggestion 262–4,
266, 275, 277–8
realities of sexual abuse trials
268–71, 278
realities of the interviewing
process 264–8, 277–8
children 35, 40, 58, 77, 84, 92, 93,
105, 124–5, 209
abuse of 14–23, 82–3
see also child sexual abuse
Children's Justice and Assistance
Act 82
Christie, N. 4, 380, 392, 406
Christie, Vigdis 67
citizen's arrest 196–7
City of Austin Hospital 39
civil actions 200, 202–5, 208–9, 318,
339
civil–criminal dichotomy 202–3
civil law systems 200
civil rights 78, 106
Clarke, R. 42–4
class 62–3, 92, 315–16, 392
clemency 201, 251
Clinard, M. 382
Code of Hamurabi 198
Cohen, I. 347
Commission on Law Enforcement and
Administration of Justice 65
community based sentencing 311–16,
320–1, 330, 343, 360–2, 366
and restitution 349–52
see also Victim/Offender Reconciliation Programme (VORP)
Community Crime Prevention Program
(1976) 83
compensation for victims 10–11, 44–
51, 64, 69–70, 75, 83, 84, 86–8, 103,
135–41, 208, 212–13, 241–2, 373
and Victim/Offender Reconciliation

Programme (VORP) 312–13,
328–9, 335, 338, 343
and victim service programs
(USA) 376–91
see also restitution
*Compensation and Restitution to Victims
of Crime* (Schafer) 206
Conciliation Model of the penal
process 210–11
conflict–theory 315–16
Congalton, A.A. 35–6, 38
Connecticut 314
continuances 116–18, 122
Convention on the Compensation of
Victims of Violent Crimes 84
corporal punishment 14–15
Cose, E. 7
Council of Europe 84
Cressey, R. 48–9, 51–2
Crime Control Model of the criminal
process 206–7, 317–18
crime prevention 83, 100, 103, 391–4
crime reduction 375, 380, 390
Crime Risk Index 66
Crime Victims Fund 81
Criminal and His Victim, The (von
Hentig) 29–31
Criminal Fines Improvement Act
(1987) 81
criminal justice 4, 406–9, 411–13
historical role of victim in 101–2,
224–9
models of 206–14
see also California; specific
countries
Criminal Justice Act (England
1972) 319–20
criminal law 195, 318
historical role of victim in 101–2
see also specific countries
Criminal Law Subcommittee of the
Senate Judiciary Committee 130
Criminal Procedure Law (Israel) 199
criminal proceedings 202–14
criminology 70–1, 107, 195, 206
crisis intervention 374
cross–examination of victims 22–3, 76,
113, 200–1, 247–8, 272, 274
Currie, E. 390, 391
Curtis, L. 390

damages 319–21, 340
Danielus, H. 85
Danzig, R. 380, 393

United Nations *continued*
    history of 401–3
    legal status of crime victims 403–6
    old and new paradigms of
        justice 406–9
    role of victim in criminal justice
        process 411–13
    victim-impact statements 413–16
    victims' involvement in parole
        process 416–18
    victims' needs 409–11
United States of America 11–14, 33–7,
    40–1, 49, 60–3
    Constitution 114, 120, 122, 260–1,
        274–6
    criminal law 64, 100, 205
        private prosecutions 199, 207–8
        role of victim in 102–7, 112–22,
          227–9, 243
    international legislation for
        victims 84–6
    National Crime Surveys 65–7, 226
    national legislation for victims 80–4
    restitution in criminal and juvenile
        justice 347–52, 373
        and penal purpose 355–9
        implementation 352–5
        public and victim acceptance
          of 359–63
        towards fulfilling the promise
          363–7
    state legislation for victims 75–80
    Supreme Court 90, 102–3, 114,
        120–1, 243, 276
    victim participation in parole
        process 416–18
    victim services 8–9, 47–9, 372–94
    see also Task Force on Victims of
        Crime
upper class 62–3
US Constitution 114, 120, 122, 260–1
    Due Process Clause 261, 274–6
US Dept of Justice 36–7
US National Commission on the Causes
    and Prevention of Violence 40–1
US Supreme Court 11, 90, 102–3, 114,
    120–1, 243, 276

Vaughn, J. 377
vehicle theft 36, 38, 43
vengeance 8–10, 126–9, 131, 202, 239,
    414
Viano, E. 91, 93
Victim and Witness Protection Act 90

Victim Bill of Rights 78–9, 83
    California 100, 118, 120, 135, 138,
        222, 224, 229–35, 401, 412–13,
        415
victim-impact statement 11, 76,
    413–16
victim movement 12–14, 45–51, 62,
    74–5, 401
    evaluating victim policy 86–95
    legislative policy and 75–86
    politics of 91–5
    see also specific organizations
Victim/Offender Reconciliation
    Programme (VORP) 311–16,
    322–5, 339–44, 354
    crown attorneys 335–7
    impediments to 317–22
    judges 330–5, 339, 342
    probation officers 337–9, 342
    staff 325–30, 342
    USA 348, 354–5, 363
victim participation in sentencing
    100, 113, 122–42
    California 222–4, 229–35
    Canada 238–55, 406–9, 413–16
    sexual offences (Ohio) 295–7, 308
victim policy, politics of 74–5
    evaluating 86–95
    international legislation 84–6
    legislative policy 75–86
    national legislation 80–4
    politics of 91–5
victim populations 33–42
victim precipitation 125–6
victim services 409–11
    Canada 47–8, 419
    USA 47–9, 75–6, 372–3
        evaluation 375–90
        implications and strategies 391–4
        programs 373–5
victim–witness legislation 249
victim–witness programmes 80–1,
    88–9, 195, 200, 227, 249, 374,
    378–9, 391
victimological literature 224–9
victimology
    brief history 29–31
    conflicting concepts 57–8
        anti-determinism 58, 69
        cruel and unusual punishment
          59–60, 68–9
        differential victimization 66–70
        direct victims of crime 64–5, 69
        enslavement of criminals 60, 68–9